Osip Mandelstam

Osip Mandelstam

A Biography

Ralph Dutli

Translated by Ben Fowkes

VERSO
London • New York

For Catherine, Boris and Olivier

swiss arts council

prohelvetia

With the support of the Swiss Arts Council Pro Helvetia

This English-language edition published by Verso 2023
First published in German by Ammann Verlag & Co., Zürich 2003
This edition licensed by Taschenbuch Verlag © S. Fischer Verlag, Frankfurt am Main 2005, 2016

1 3 5 7 9 10 8 6 4 2

Verso
UK: 6 Meard Street, London W1F 0EG
US: 388 Atlantic Avenue, Brooklyn, NY 11217
versobooks.com

Verso is the imprint of New Left Books

ISBN-13: 978-1-83976-158-4
ISBN-13: 978-1-83976-160-7 (UK EBK)
ISBN-13: 978-1-83976-161-4 (US EBK)

British Library Cataloguing in Publication Data
A catalogue record for this book is available from the British Library

Library of Congress Cataloging-in-Publication Data
A catalog record for this book is available from the Library of Congress

Typeset in Minion Pro by MJ&N Gavan, Truro, Cornwall
Printed and bound by CPI Group (UK) Ltd, Croydon CR0 4YY

Contents

My time, my beast, who will be able
To peer into your pupils
And with his own blood glue together
The vertebrae of two centuries?

[Translator's note: references to English-language publications have been added to the text. The author's explanatory interpolations are enclosed in double brackets.]

1

Of Myself I Will Not Speak

(The Pulverisation of Biography)

Osip Mandelstam is an iconic figure. In Russia, and all over the world, he is seen as a martyr for poetry, someone who paid with his life for his verses. He is known, above all, as a victim of political persecution and the author of a trenchant poem exposing Stalin as the 'corrupter of the human soul'.[1] His death in 1938 under appalling circumstances, in a forced labour camp, also contributed significantly to his worldwide fame. Mandelstam, victim of twentieth-century totalitarianism, imprisoned in a Kolyma Gulag: this is often the only way in which he is portrayed.

More than any other Russian poet, Mandelstam fills the bill of a legendary literary saint. All the elements of hagiography are ready to hand: his early vocation; his experience of poverty; his persecution; his martyrdom; and, finally, his triumph in the eyes of posterity. Mandelstam is seen as the embodiment of poesy, conforming to the cliché of the true poet's path of bitter suffering on earth. The proud and self-confident, sharp-tongued and

1 The anti-Stalin poem: O. Mandelstam, *Mitternacht in Moskau*, 165. (All subsequent references to texts by Mandelstam will be placed in brackets after the quotation, using the abbreviations indicated in the References for the title of the volume and the page number in the ten-volume collected edition of Mandelstam's works, edited by Ralph Dutli, published by the Ammann Verlag, Zürich. Thus, in this case: MM, 165.) Where an existing English translation has been used, references will similarly be placed in brackets after the quotation.

confrontational, witty and sensual Mandelstam, who loved life, and had absolutely no wish to become a martyr, is usually left out of the picture.

His posthumous fate also forms part of his legend. His widow, Nadezhda Mandelstam, played a leading role in this. Almost miraculously, she survived the Stalin epoch. She learned Mandelstam's poems by heart, so as to preserve them from suppression by the dictator's bloodhounds. She hid his papers in the attics and cellars of a few friends and accomplices. Finally, she had his work smuggled out of the country to the United States, and, in the first volume of her monumental memoirs, *Hope Against Hope* (1970), she revealed to an astonished world the extent of Mandelstam's isolation and persecution, but also the courageous way in which he stuck to his convictions through the darkest years of the Stalin terror.

Myths and legends create their own truth. They cover up the unsightly and the unheroic. They are cut-down versions of reality, but they are not entirely mendacious. People have withstood political repression and spiritual emptiness, harassment and interrogations in prison and even concentration camp life, not least because of the glow of their radiance. This applies both to the victims of an unjust regime who have remained anonymous and to those who have attained unofficial eminence, such as the popular singer Vladimir Vysotsky, he of the hoarse vodka-soaked voice, the idol of Soviet youth in the 1970s, who frankly recognised that Mandelstam's poems had saved him from madness and death.[2]

In her essay 'Poetry and Anthropology', the lyrical poet Olga Sedakova recalls the case of a dissident who was arrested in the 1970s and interrogated every day for several months. A certain moment arrived after which everything became a matter of indifference for him:

> I awoke with the feeling that today I would sign everything that was laid before me. Not because of fear, but because I didn't care. Nothing was important any more. Then Mandelstam's poem 'Theta and Iota of the Greek Flute' suddenly came into my mind. All of it, from beginning to end. And I experienced what religious people presumably feel during Communion … I sensed the whole world, literally the whole world, with myself as part of it. After this experience I was absolutely certain that I would not sign anything.[3]

---

2 Vysotsky and Mandelstam: O. S. Figurnova and M. V. Figurnova, *Osip i Nadezhda Mandel'shtamy v Rasskazakh Sovremennikov*, 388–9.

3 O. Sedakova, 'Poeziia i antropologiia', 12. The poem mentioned there: WH, 201. J. Brodsky, 'Less than One', 29; Brodsky, 'The Child of Civilization', 144.

Poems, of course, do not just bring comfort and allow people to hold out against oppression: they are complex aesthetic organisms. But we should not ignore the possibility that they may be magically effective in extreme situations. People who sleep safely in their beds and have not endured suffering should not be too quick to dismiss a captive's spiritual means of survival as an empty solace.

Here is another example: Joseph Brodsky, who won the Nobel Prize for Literature in 1987, was proud to associate himself in his 'Memories of Leningrad' with the generation of young Russian poets 'for whom Giotto and Mandelstam were more imperative than their own personal destinies'. In his essay 'The Child of Civilization' (1977) he emphasised Mandelstam's significance for the non-conformist artists and intellectuals of the Soviet Union in the 1960s and 1970s. Mandelstam's voice, he said, was a voice

> that stays behind when its owner is gone. He was … a modern Orpheus: sent to hell, he never returned, while his widow dodged across one sixth of the earth's surface, clutching the saucepan with his songs rolled up inside, memorizing them by night in the event that they were found by Furies with a search warrant. These are our metamorphoses, our myths.[4]

In this passage, Brodsky calls on the supreme myth about poetry, as it has come down to us from Ovid's *Metamorphoses* (Books 10 and 11) and Virgil's *Georgics* (Book 4). It is the myth of Orpheus, the 'flawless bard', the demigod, whose verses were heard with pleasure by wild animals, trees and even stones, who overcame the god of the underworld and even death itself with his singing, and who finally died a sacrificial death, decapitated by the Maenads. The epithet of the *modern* Orpheus encapsulates the terror of the twentieth century. Mandelstam, another flawless bard, also had to suffer political persecution, concentration camps and infernal torment.

But the persistent reduction of the poet's life to a tale of martyrdom has led to a failure to recognise Mandelstam's literary greatness, which was already evident long before Stalin came to power. In his obituary of Nadezhda Mandelstam (1981), Brodsky has this to say: 'It is an abominable fallacy that suffering makes for greater art. Suffering blinds, deafens, ruins, and often kills. Osip Mandelstam was a great poet *before* the revolution.'[5]

4 LG, 134–5; Brodsky, 'The Child of Civilization', 144.

5 The quotation from Brodsky's obituary of Nadezhda Mandelstam: Brodsky, 'The Child of Civilization', 153.

The Mandelstam myth was woven not just by Russian artists, dissidents and civil rights supporters. Western intellectuals who were strongly influenced by Nadezhda Mandelstam's memoirs also played a part. Pier Paolo Pasolini wrote in 1972 that Mandelstam lived 'like a dazzled creature on a completely unfamiliar meadow'. He therefore led a life of alienation, 'the model of which can perhaps be found in Kafka's novels or in his dreams'.[6] Mandelstam's life as Kafka's nightmare? Mandelstam as a Russian Josef K.? It is a tempting idea – after all, 'Osip' is a Russified form of the biblical name 'Joseph' … Or should we perhaps see Mandelstam as world poetry's 'Land Surveyor', struggling in vain against the obscure machinations of a hierarchy ensconced in an unfathomable *Castle* – or Kremlin? Does 'A Hunger Artist' come to mind? Or the tormented figure of K. in *The Trial*? Or the short story 'In the Penal Colony'? These are the twentieth century's visions of hell, which Pasolini thought he could perceive in Mandelstam's life. It should be added, however, that the Italian was one of the few writers who also paid attention to features of that life other than martyrdom. Hence his evaluation concludes with a fine paradox:

> Nimble, clever, witty, elegant, one might even say dandyish, joyful, sensual, always in love, honest, clear-sighted, and happy even in the darkness of nervous breakdown and political terror, youthful, indeed almost boyish, weird and sophisticated, loyal and imaginative, smiling and patient, Mandelstam has bestowed on us some of the most felicitous poetry of the century.[7]

The collapse of the Soviet Union in 1991 – the hundredth anniversary of Mandelstam's birth! – brought an end to the age of mythmaking. Mandelstam's elevation to cult-like status, which made him the patron saint of Russian poetry and the movement for citizens' rights, could not last forever. During 1990, the year before the end of the Soviet Union, it finally became possible to publish the whole of Mandelstam's works in Russia, but that date also marked the start of his de-mythologisation and of attempts to undermine his legacy. People started to produce anti-memoirs, which attempted to undermine the powerful hold exerted until then by Nadezhda Mandelstam's autobiographical writings. We shall

6 Pier Paolo Pasolini, in the newspaper *Il Tempo*, 3 December 1972, also included in the book *Descrizioni di descrizioni*, Turin, 1979, 8–12.

7 LG, 87.

examine this phase of the reception of Mandelstam in Russia in the final chapter of our book.

The above remarks underline the two big pitfalls that need to be avoided when writing a biography of Osip Mandelstam: on the one hand, a continued weaving of the legend of his sanctity, and, on the other, a modish attempt to destroy his personal reputation. Mandelstam does not need to be portrayed either as a saint or as a monster. For the whole of his life, he could not be anything other than what he was: a poet. If we adopt this approach, we can concentrate on what is essential: not the transfiguring myths of the past, or the scandalous revelations of the present, but the quality of his poetry. Mandelstam's position as one of the most significant poets of the twentieth century has never been seriously challenged, irrespective of fashionable swings in the reputational pendulum.

We therefore have to be careful to avoid both stumbling blocks, so that we neither surround him with the halo of legend, nor do a hatchet job on his personal life. Indeed, perhaps the whole genre of biography should be shunned. Mandelstam himself repeatedly expressed his disapproval of the biographical approach. He viewed it as a precursor of the novel, a genre he thought hopelessly outdated in the modern age. In his 1922 essay 'The End of the Novel' he writes:

> What happens to the novel after this is simply a story of the dispersion of biography as a form of personal existence; more than dispersion – the catastrophic collapse of biography ... Europeans are now cast out of their biographies, like balls from the pocket of the billiard table ... Besides, the interest in psychological motivation ... is radically undermined and discredited by the ... impotence of psychological motives before those real forces whose punitive verdict on psychological motivation becomes crueller from hour to hour.[8]

Dispersed biographies, human existences chucked around all over the place like billiard balls: the 'real forces' of the twentieth century and their cruel 'punitive verdict' seem to have brought an end to both the conventional novel and the traditional biography. Despite the way it summons up the location and atmosphere of his childhood, Mandelstam's essay in

8 GP, 162–3; S. Monas, *Osip Mandelstam's Selected Essays*, 103. This work will henceforth be referred to as SE. For a complete list of abbreviations of English-language works, see the Bibliography.

autobiography, *The Noise of Time* (1925), contains an abrupt denial of its autobiographical character:

> My desire is not to speak about myself but to track down the age, the noise and the germination of time. My memory is inimical to all that is personal … My memory is not loving but inimical, and it labours not to reproduce but to distance the past. The *raznochinets* needs no memory – it is enough for him to tell of the books he has read, and his biography is done.[9]

Let us calmly follow Mandelstam in reviling biography: biography is tyranny, and its enforced chronology – from birth to death – enslaves us. Voyeurism and fetishism are also inherent in the genre. To prise open the secrets of a person's life is an act of outrageous impudence.

The essential task is to understand the literary work of a poet, not to accumulate facts about his life. The vicissitudes of the poet's life experience pale into insignificance in the face of the eventfulness of his poetry, the miracles of his language. Poetry is a revolt against the rule of time, the tyranny of Chronos. A lifetime is nothing in comparison with the protracted and occult process of poetry's emergence. No one knew this better than Marina Tsvetaeva, who set down her memories of Mandelstam in 'History of a Dedication', written in 1931 during her Parisian exile: 'Humour aside, I think that whenever he was not writing (and he was always not-writing, namely, one poem in three months) he was pining. Without poems, Mandelstam didn't feel right sitting – or walking – or living – in this world.'[10] It was poetry that determined his life, not the rigid laws of chronology.

It would in any case be impossible to produce a voyeuristic chronicle of his day-to-day life, given the 'dispersal' of his biography by the 'real forces' of history. Even so, Mandelstam's creations did not emerge in an empty space, devoid of history. They were neither imaginary nor esoteric, nor were they capricious flights of fancy. The life behind and within the poems is a concrete life in a particular epoch, constantly contemporary.

---

9 RZ, 88; C. Brown, *Noise of Time*, 109–10. This work will henceforth be referred to as NT.

10 GW, 60–1; M. Tsvetaeva, *Art in the Light of Conscience*, 70. Henceforth the title of this work will be abbreviated as AL.

Mandelstam's poems are closely associated with the events and catastrophes of his life, particularly in the late 1930s. For this reason, and notwithstanding all the criticisms that can justifiably be levelled against biography as such, it is still possible to construct a biographical study of the poet's work including the statements of witnesses: to depict a life's work, placing this in the forefront, but also to treat this life as itself a piece of work, in order to peer into the eyes of the 'time-beast', the creature conjured up by Mandelstam in a poem written in October 1922 to encapsulate both his own epoch and other people's:

> My time, my beast, who will be able
> To peer into your pupils
> And with his own blood glue together
> The vertebrae of two centuries?[11]

11 TR, 139; I. Bernstein, *The Poems of Osip Mandelstam*, 14–15. References to this work will henceforth be placed in the text, abbreviated as PO.

2

Journey to Raspberry Town

(Warsaw 1891 and Pavlovsk 1892–1896)

Mandelstam's date and place of birth are mentioned just once in his poetry. It is as if, on that occasion, he gave his work a final stamp: that was the time, that was the place. It is in the eighth and final stanza of his late cycle 'Verses on the Unknown Soldier' (composed in February and March 1937), a requiem for the 'casually murdered millions', that he rehearses the date of his birth:

> And as I squeeze in my fist
> The faded year of my birth,
> My bloodless mouth whispers
> I was born on the night from the second
> To the third of January in one
> Unreliable year and the centuries
> Surround me with flames.
> (WH, 181; PO, 68)

In the night of 2 to 3 January 1891: that is the date according to the Julian calendar used in pre-revolutionary Russia. In the nineteenth century this differed from the Gregorian calendar by twelve days, hence the date in modern terms would be 14 to 15 January 1891. Mandelstam's birth is usually assumed to have taken place around midnight on 14–15 January 1891.[1]

It was an unhappy year, and an unfortunate location. Warsaw had been assigned to Russia at the Vienna Congress of 1815. Since the rising of 1830, bloodily suppressed by Field Marshal Paskevich, the fate of the city had been a festering sore for Polish nationalists. Warsaw lay at the western margin of a ruthlessly expansionist Russian Empire. Mandelstam's birthplace only turns up in his work as part of a nightmare. This is the journey to 'Raspberry Town' (in Russian: *Malinov*) described in the semi-fictional, semi-autobiographical prose text of 1928, *The Egyptian Stamp*. An atmosphere of flight, abduction and child substitution is conjured up in the dream, in which the Self is consumed by feelings of alienation, sorrow, shame and disgust:

> I was attached to someone else's family and carriage. A young Jew was counting some new hundred rouble notes that crackled with a wintry sound.
>
> 'Where are we going?' I asked an old woman in a gypsy shawl.
>
> 'To the city of Malinov', she replied, but with such aching melancholy that my heart contracted with an evil foreboding …
>
> But there was no city there. Instead, growing right in the snow, were some large, warty raspberries.
>
> 'But that's a raspberry patch' I gasped, beside myself with joy, and began to run with the others, filling my shoes with snow. My shoe came untied and because of that I was seized with a feeling of great guilt and disorder.
>
> And they led me into a hateful Warsaw room and made me drink water and eat onion. (RZ, 237–8; NT, 160)

This nightmarish journey into life is a symbolic representation of a difficult birth in a family felt to be alien. Instead of the traditional Russian welcome of bread and salt, he receives an insipid beverage and a bulb with a sharp taste. It is a dinner he is forced to consume.

The Mandelstam family had emigrated in the eighteenth century from Germany to Courland. Now part of present-day Latvia, the area lay

1 Birth certificate: E. Mandel'shtam, 'Vospominaniia', 175. There the date is given as 2 (14) January 1891. On M.'s Sorbonne enrolment form his date of birth is given as 2 January 1891 (Old Style).

between the Baltic Sea and the lower reaches of the River Düna (Russian: Dvina; Latvian: Daugava). Artisans had been invited into the country by its duke, Ernst Johann Biron (1690–1772). One of them was a Jewish watchmaker and jeweller who was descended from a rabbinical family, and still retained his ancient Hebrew name. The Mandelstams regarded this man as their ancestor. Osip only learned this fact of genealogy many years later, in the summer of 1928, in the Crimean resort of Yalta, when he brought Nadezhda's watch to be repaired. The watchmaker's wife was also a Mandelstam. As if by magic, she produced his family tree.[2]

The Mandelstams, therefore, did not belong to the branch of Polish Jewry that had experienced its 'Golden Age' under the Polish–Lithuanian kingdom, the period of economic prosperity and rich erudition which preceded the catastrophe of 1648, when the Cossack forces of Hetman Bohdan Khmelnytsky made an incursion into Ukraine, slaughtering over a hundred thousand Jews during their uprising against Polish rule. It was a frightful anticipation of all the later pogroms. At that time, though, Mandelstam's ancestors were still living in Germany, in a ghetto located in a town whose name we do not know.

Those ancestors may well have travelled to Germany along the Central European route. They were Ashkenazim (a name which derives from 'Ashkenaz', the word coined to describe Germany in medieval rabbinical literature). It is also possible that they did not start to move north until 1492, when the Jews were driven out of Spain ('Sefarad') by Queen Isabella of Castile. That is what Mandelstam himself preferred to believe.[3] When he was in exile in Voronezh in 1936, he read a book about the victims of the Inquisition, and he picked out the name of a Hispano-Jewish poet, insisting that 'at least a drop of his blood' ran in his veins. Nevertheless, Mandelstam's attitude towards his own Jewishness was not determined by 'the call of the blood'. As we shall show, it was complex and variable. He went through alternating phases of aloofness and rapprochement.

2 'The Family Tree': N. Mandelstam, *Hope Abandoned*, 576–7. This chapter is missing from the greatly shortened German edition *Generation ohne Tränen* (1975). There are no chapters missing from the English translation. However, the Russian publication of the second volume of memoirs, referred to as *Vtoraia Kniga*, includes commentaries not printed in the English edition. Nadezhda Mandelstam's untranslated third book was published in Paris as *Kniga Tret'ia*, in 1987. For the 'Golden Age', the 'Khmelnytsky Massacre' and the 'Ashkenazim', see H. Haumann, *A History of the East European Jews*, 30–1, 35 and 36.

3 M.'s 'imaginary' descent from a Hispano-Jewish poet: Mandelstam, *Hope Abandoned*, 563.

And the name Mandelstam? It is derived from the drupe of the almond tree, its seed kernel, and hidden within it there is a biblical association, a sign of election, because it refers back to the story of Aaron's rod. In the fourth book of Moses (Numbers 17:7) it is related that Aaron, of the house of Levi, was chosen as the first high priest, as his rod was the only one of the twelve that budded and produced almonds: 'And it came to pass, that on the morrow Moses went into the tabernacle of witness; and behold, the rod of Aaron was budded, and brought forth buds, and bloomed blossoms, and yielded almonds.' In a poem written in 1914 in memory of Vladislav Ozerov (1769–1816), the last playwright of the classical age of Russian literature, Mandelstam alludes to this scene, without naming either Aaron or his rod: 'Pain flowered for us in solemnity / As the prophet's holy staff flowered in the shrine.'[4]

The almond tree, with its fruit now sweet, now bitter, plays a significant part in the Old Testament. In the book of Kohelet, also known as The Preacher Solomon (Ecclesiastes 12:5), it is a symbol of evil days to come. Solomon warns the young to remember the Creator, and the inevitability of ageing and death: 'when … the almond tree shall flourish, and the grasshopper shall be a burden, and the caper-berry shall fail because man goeth to his long home, and the mourners go about the streets.'

Almond blossom is traditionally associated with the white hair of old age. The almond tree appears as nature's mourning representative in Mandelstam's political poem of May 1933, in which he condemns the famine inflicted on the Ukrainian peasantry by Stalin's policy of forced collectivisation:

> The views are hazy, it is as beautiful as ever
> The trees are in bud, swelling slightly,
> And are the real outsiders, and the almond,
> Blossoming with yesterday's stupidity, arouses pity.[5]

Mandelstam's father, Emil-Khazkel Benjaminovich Mandelstam (1856–1938), was born in Shagory, a *shtetl* in the Government of Kovno (Kaunas), which now lies within Lithuania. He was expected to become

---

4 ST, 137; O. Mandelstam, *Osip Mandelstam's Stone*, 173. References to this work will henceforth be placed in the text, abbreviated as OS.

5 MM, 143; O. Mandelstam, *The Moscow Notebooks*, 68. References to this work will henceforth be placed in the text, abbreviated as MN.

a rabbi, but he resisted his strictly Orthodox upbringing, lay in the attic at night learning German and read the prohibited literature of the West. The inhabitants of the Baltic Lands were very much drawn to German culture, owing to the connections forged by long years of history. Emil Mandelstam finally fled to Berlin from the narrowness of the *shtetl* environment.[6] Instead of regular attendance at the Yeshiva (the school for the study of the Talmud), he abandoned himself to the fascination of German literature and philosophy. He read Goethe, Schiller and Herder and studied Spinoza. But after six months, he ran out of money and was obliged to break off his studies. He returned to the Baltic Lands and started an apprenticeship as a glove-maker and dealer in leather. This had also been his father's profession.

Emil Mandelstam's Berlin adventure was a decisive step on the road to assimilation. His flight from the *shtetl* to Berlin and to German culture spiritually anticipated his son's flight to Russian culture. Mandelstam's father had fought his way out of the 'Talmudic wilds' into the German world as an autodidact; that is how his son described this formative act in *The Noise of Time* (1925), with ironic aloofness but also with a certain degree of admiration (RZ, 28; NT, 79).

> In essence, my father transferred me to a totally alien century and a distant, although completely un-Jewish, atmosphere. It was, if you will, the purest eighteenth, or even seventeenth, century of an enlightened ghetto somewhere in Hamburg. Religious interests had been eliminated completely. The philosophy of the Enlightenment was transformed into intricate Talmudist pantheism. Somewhere in the vicinity Spinoza is breeding his spiders in a jar. One has a presentiment of Rousseau and his natural man. (RZ, 41; NT, 85)

Round about 1820, the 'Haskala' (Enlightenment) movement had also reached the Jewish communities of Latvia and Lithuania. It had originated in Germany, and its goal was both intellectual emancipation and the achievement of citizens' rights for Jews. The *Jüdisches Lexikon* (Berlin 1929) and the *Encyclopaedia Judaica* (Jerusalem 1971) mention two members of the Mandelstam family who were important exponents of the Haskala movement. Benjamin ben Joseph Mandelstamm, who was

6 The flight of M.'s father to Berlin: E. Mandel'shtam, 'Vospominaniia', 121.

born in Shagory in 1805 and died in Simferopol in 1886, was a writer and a fighter for Jewish religious reform. His brother Leon (Arie Löb) Mandelstamm, who was born in 1819 in Shagory and died in 1889 in St Petersburg, championed the reform of the Jewish school system in Russia. The precise family relationship of these two brothers to Osip Mandelstam is uncertain. It is unlikely that Benjamin was his great-grandfather and Leon his great-granduncle, because Osip Mandelstam's grandparents on the father's side still lived according to the laws of traditional, Orthodox *shtetl* Judaism. But it is of some significance that the Mandelstam clan already had some members who were imbued with the ideas of the Haskala and favoured progressive reforms.

The family of Mandelstam's mother, Flora Osipovna Verblovskaia (1866–1916) had already travelled further along this path to assimilation. Her place of origin was the Lithuanian city of Vilna (Vilnius), the 'Jerusalem of the North', which was a stronghold of Jewish learning and a centre of the Haskala movement.[7] Flora Verblovskaia was born into a family of intellectuals, and as a schoolgirl she attended the Russian *gymnasium* in Vilna. The language of assimilation in Vilna was not Polish but Russian. A secular education was only possible in the state schools, where teaching was in Russian. An increasing number of young Jews passed through the Russian *gymnasia*, and they formed an intelligentsia in the Russian mould. These were the people called 'Litvaks'. As Mandelstam recalls in his autobiographical essay *The Noise of Time*, 'The word "intellectual" was pronounced by my mother, and especially by my grandmother, with pride' (RZ, 29; NT, 79).

Hence Mandelstam's parents both sprang from Latvian-Lithuanian Jewry and both lived under Russian Tsarist rule, but they came from families whose relationships with tradition diverged markedly: his father's background was Orthodox *shtetl* Judaism; his mother's was progressive urban Haskala Judaism. What both parents had in common, however, was their drive to assimilate. On 19 January 1889, in the city of Dünaburg (Dvinsk), thirty-three-year-old Emil Mandelstam, glove-maker and leather dealer with philosophical ambitions, married piano teacher Flora Verblovskaia, who was ten years his junior. The pair were at first obliged to reside in Warsaw because of Emil's profession, and their first son Osip came into the world there on 2–3 (14–15) January 1891.

7 The 'Jerusalem of the North': C. Miłosz, *Beginning with My Streets*, 23–6.

His given name, Osip, which Flora's father already bore, was a programme of assimilation in itself: it indicated their striving to become Russian. The firstborn would not be decorated with the biblical name of 'Iosif', but with a highly Russified, popular and almost peasant-like version: Osip, or 'Osia', as a term of endearment within the family. In a poem written in 1913, Mandelstam would recall the biblical Joseph, writing of Joseph the Dreamer, the favourite son of the Patriarch Jacob, who was sold into Egypt by his brothers and rose to become official dream interpreter at the Pharaoh's court (see Genesis, chapters 37 to 50):

The bread is poisoned and the air's drunk dry
How difficult to doctor wounds!
Joseph sold into Egypt
Could not have grieved so much for home![8]

The family's path to Russian culture was also reflected in their gradual movement towards the Russian capital. As early as the year after Osip's birth, they moved from Warsaw to Pavlovsk, where on 23 September 1892 the Mandelstams' second son, Alexander (Shura), was born.

Pavlovsk was a well-known town with splendid architecture, thirty-five kilometres south of Tsarskoye Selo ('the Tsar's village'), the Tsar's summer residence. It was dominated by the horseshoe-shaped palace built at the end of the eighteenth century by Charles Cameron and Vincenzo Brenna and intended for the use of Catherine II's son, the Grand Prince Pavel Petrovich, who later became Tsar Paul I (1796–1801). In addition to this elegant residence, there was a park with pavilions, bridges and water cascades, located in the valley of the River Slavianka. The little town of Pavlovsk, close to this elegant setting, offered a high-class environment for the Mandelstams, a Jewish family who wanted to rise in society and aspired to move to the country's capital. In *The Noise of Time*, Mandelstam calls Pavlovsk a 'Russian demi-Versailles', a town of 'court lackeys, State Councillors' widows, red-headed policemen, consumptive pedagogues' and corrupt officials (RZ, 10; NT, 69–70).

The young Osip was soon taken to a big occasion in the capital city:

8 ST, 117; B. Meares, *50 Poems. Osip Mandelstam*, 36. This book will henceforth be referred to as FP.

> My first conscious, sharp perceptions were of gloomy crowds of people in the streets. I was exactly three years old. It was 1894, and I had been brought from Pavlovsk to Petersburg because my parents wanted to see the ceremonies surrounding the funeral of Alexander III. (RZ, 21; NT, 75)

It was not easy for Jews to settle in the capital city. They did not have freedom of movement within the Tsarist Empire, and in principle they were limited to the western part of the country. In the context of the enlightened and pro-Jewish policy she pursued after the First Partition of Poland in 1772, Catherine II (1762–1796) initially allowed Jews to enter Russia. On 23 December 1791, however, in response to complaints from the merchants of Moscow, who feared that their businesses would suffer from Jewish competition, the Tsarina decreed that Jews could not settle in the Russian heartland. They had to remain within the 'Pale of Settlement', as it was called. This was formally established in 1804 via a 'Statute for the Jews', and remained in force until the First World War.[9]

Particularly strict rules applied to St Petersburg. Mandelstam's father had to fulfil certain rigorous conditions, and join the 'First Guild' of merchants, before he was permitted to live in the capital city and conduct business there. By 1897 he had achieved his aim: the Mandelstam family moved to St Petersburg. They settled first in the Kolomna district. This was only a temporary address; there were many others to follow. Even though the family had arrived, at least in appearance, it still wandered uneasily from one city district to another. Osip Mandelstam's brother Yevgeny remembered living at no fewer than seventeen addresses in the city during his childhood and youth![10]

It was Mandelstam's mother who repeatedly insisted on moving house. Perhaps she had hoped for more from their arrival in the imperial capital, or had she perhaps expected the place would be more conducive to the social ascent to which she aspired? The lack of stability, the atmosphere of nervous restlessness and the constant need to adjust to new surroundings – all these things inevitably left their mark on the Mandelstam children. In the whirlwind of images in Mandelstam's semi-fictional prose text *The*

---

9 The Jewish Pale of Settlement: Haumann, *A History of the East European Jews*, 80–91.

10 Places where the Mandelstam family lived in St Petersburg: E. Mandel'shtam, 'Vospominaniia', 125.

Egyptian Stamp (1928), one can still find memories of his family's restlessness and their 'unsuccessful domestic immortality' (RZ, 187; NT, 133).

The Mandelstams had long yearned to live in the Russian capital, and now they had arrived, but the final stage of their motion towards the centre did not produce a mood of tranquillity. The family's urban nomadism was inherited by its firstborn son, Osip. Mandelstam's work teems with Petersburg addresses. The capital city of the Russian Empire is deeply inscribed in his poetry and his prose. Despite his desire to be a Russian and European poet imbued with a 'nostalgia for world culture', Mandelstam would remain a Petersburg poet as well. As late as 1930, he would bewitchingly apostrophise the town, which had long since had a new name assigned to it, in a poem full of premonitions of the horrors to come, issuing a twofold appeal:

> I do not want to die yet, Petersburg! You still have
> All my friends' telephone numbers.
> Petersburg! I still have the addresses
> From which I can find the voices of the dead.
> (MM, 45; MN, 34)

3

Mother Tongue and Unfamiliar Sounds

(Petersburg Childhood 1897–1904)

For information on Mandelstam's pre-literary existence, we are dependent on the memoirs of his brother Yevgeny, but we also have his own autobiographical essay, *The Noise of Time*, which offers a wealth of precise, compact recollections of his early years. This is certainly a 'subjective', literary source, rather than a documentary one. It is also concerned with the poet's later path to mastery of the word. It is characteristic of Mandelstam's linguistic artistry that he exploits the different ways his father and his mother used language to indicate the contrast between the paternal and maternal elements in his cultural inheritance: 'The speech of the father and the speech of the mother – hasn't my own language been nourished my whole life by the confluence of these two languages, do they not compose its character?'

> My father had absolutely no language; his speech was tongue-tied and lacked the characteristics of a language. The Russian speech of a Polish Jew? No. The speech of a German Jew? No again. Perhaps a special Courland accent? I never heard such. A completely abstract, made-up language, the ornate and twisted speech of an autodidact, where normal words are intertwined with the ancient philosophical terms of Herder, Leibniz and Spinoza, the capricious syntax of a Talmudist, the artificial,

> not always finished, sentence. It was anything in the world, but not a language, neither Russian nor German. (RZ, 40–1; NT, 85)

Mandelstam's admiring portrait of his mother's handling of the Russian language stands out in vivid contrast against the background of his father's linguistic confusion:

> My mother's speech was clear and sonorous, without the least foreign admixture, with rather wide and too open vowels – the literary Great Russian language. Her vocabulary was poor and restricted, the locutions were trite, but it was a language, it had roots and confidence. Mother loved to speak and took joy in the roots and sounds of her Great Russian speech, impoverished by intellectual clichés. Was she not the first of her whole family to achieve pure and clear Russian sounds?[1]

For the Mandelstam family, which had already travelled a long way in the direction of assimilation, Yiddish was no longer a language of everyday communication.

The only family members who still spoke Yiddish were Emil Mandelstam's parents, the leather worker Benjamin Sundelovich Mandelstam and his wife Mere Abramovna, who had moved to Riga from Shagory, their *shtetl* in Courland. 'In my childhood I absolutely never heard Yiddish; only later did I hear an abundance of that melodious, always surprised and disappointed, interrogative language' (RZ, 40; NT, 84). Mandelstam's account of a visit to his grandparents in Riga in *The Noise of Time* demonstrates how far his parents had travelled towards assimilation and also the degree to which they had become alienated from traditional Judaism. Little Osip is left alone for a short while with his grandparents, who do not speak a word of Russian:

> Then my parents left to go to the city. My sombre grandfather and my sad, bustling grandmother made an effort to distract me with conversation and ruffled their feathers like offended old birds. I tried to explain to them that I wanted to go to Mama – they didn't understand. Then I represented my desire to leave by putting my index and middle fingers

1 RZ, 40; A. Spektor, 'Family Romances', 88–9.

> through the motions of walking on the table. Suddenly my grandfather drew from a drawer of a chest a black and yellow silk cloth, put it around my shoulders, and made me repeat after him words composed of unknown sounds; but, dissatisfied with my babble, he grew angry and shook his head in disapproval. I felt stifled and afraid. How my mother arrived just in time to save me I don't remember. (RZ, 43–4; NT, 86)

The 'black and yellow silk cloth' the grandfather draped around the little fellow's shoulders was a tallith (Yiddish: *talles*), the prayer shawl donned by Jewish men, but the 'unknown sounds', which exceeded even Yiddish in their strangeness, were Hebrew prayers. From then on, the colours black and yellow would be for Mandelstam the colours of strangeness, of alienation; they could even be vaguely threatening. The gesture made by moving two fingers across the tabletop symbolised flight: a flight which took him away from a Judaism incomprehensible to the child and no longer transmitted in a living form by his parents, and brought him closer and closer to Russia, to its language and culture.

In their breakneck struggle to assimilate, Mandelstam's parents had almost forgotten their roots. At one point, however, when they had already moved to St Petersburg, they had 'a fit of national contrition' (RZ, 27; NT, 78), and they hired a private tutor for their firstborn: the language of the Bible ought not to be forgotten entirely. But the children's story in Hebrew had a picture of a boy with the sad face of an adult, with whom little Osip found it impossible to identify himself. The lessons were a miserable failure.

Visits to the synagogue were also rare. Only on high holy days, when the Torah scroll was brought out of the Ark and put on display, did the Mandelstams make the journey. But this ritual too no longer had the power to influence the child's emerging intellect: 'All that I saw and heard there caused me to return home in a heavy stupor' (RZ, 38; NT, 84). The Jewish community in St Petersburg had long suffered under discriminatory legislation. Not until the reforms of Alexander II had taken effect did the community begin to prosper, so much so that in 1893 it was able to build a large synagogue and a cultural centre. The synagogue, built in a Moorish style, was located not far from the Marinsky Theatre, at the corner of Offitserskaia Street and Torgovaia Street (its present address: 2 Lermontov Prospekt).

> The synagogue, with its conical caps and onion domes, loses itself like some elegant exotic fig tree amongst the shabby buildings. Velveteen berets with pompoms, attendants and choristers on the point of physical exhaustion, clusters of seven-branched candelabra, tall velvet head-dresses. The Jewish ship, with its sonorous choirs and the astonishing voices of its children, lays in all sail, split as it is by some ancient storm into male and female halves. Having blundered into the women's balcony, I edged along as stealthily as a thief, hiding behind rafters. The Cantor, like Samson, collapsed the leonine building, he was answered by the velvet headdress, and the awesome equilibrium of vowels and consonants in the impeccably enunciated words imparted to the chant an invincible power. But how offensive was the crude speech of the rabbi: the ugly, even if correct, speech of the rabbi – though it was not ungrammatical; how vulgar when he uttered the words 'His Imperial Majesty', how utterly vulgar all that he said! (RZ, 39; NT, 84)

This is not the intimate observation of an insider. It is an outsider looking in. He is contemplating an alien, exotic ritual. Admittedly, the child finds the singing in the synagogue impressive (it has 'an invincible power'), but he hears it as an uninvolved listener, present accidentally. Apart from this, the obligatory visits had no impact; the feverish course of assimilation could no longer be stopped. The bookcase bore eloquent witness to this.

For the Mandelstams, the bookcase was a kind of family shrine in which the books stood before the sons as emblems of their origin and subsequent trajectory from Orthodox *shtetl* Judaism to the enlightened Haskalah Judaism of Vilna and then on to Russian culture. We need not be surprised that Mandelstam devoted a whole chapter of his autobiographical essay to this shrine to the family's history. 'The bookcase of early childhood is a man's companion for life. The arrangement of its shelves, the choice of books, the colours of the spines are for him the colour, height, and arrangement of world literature itself.'

Mandelstam describes the strata of this modest family library in the manner of a geologist, proceeding from the lowest and oldest level to the most recent, which for him was the most real. As he recalls it, the lowest level is 'the chaotic level': there the books do not stand next to one another side by side but lie 'like ruins'. That was where the Pentateuch (the five books of Moses), a history of the Jews and other paternal leftovers were to be found: 'This was the Judaic chaos thrown into the dust' (RZ, 26–7;

NT, 78). Osip's children's stories also quickly found their way there, when the boy rejected his Hebrew lessons.

Above the level of the 'Jewish ruins', continues Mandelstam in *The Noise of Time*, a certain kind of order starts to emerge in the bookcase. These books were 'the Germans', volumes which bore witness to his father's flight to Berlin and absorption in German culture: Schiller, Goethe, Kerner, Shakespeare in German (no doubt this was the famous translation by Schlegel and Tieck). 'All this was my father, fighting his way as an autodidact into the German world out of the Talmudic wilds.' But it is the Russian books that occupy the summit, among them, naturally, the great Alexander Pushkin (1799–1837):

> Still higher were my mother's Russian books – among them Pushkin, in Isakov's 1876 edition. I still think that was a splendid edition … My Isakov Pushkin was in a cassock of no colour at all, in a binding of schoolboy calico, in a brownish black, faded cassock with a tinge of earth and sand, he feared neither spots, nor fire, nor kerosene. For a quarter of a century, the black and sand cassock had lovingly absorbed everything into itself – so vividly do I sense the everyday spiritual beauty, the almost physical charm, of my mother's Pushkin. (RZ, 28–9; NT, 79)

'Splendid', 'lovingly', 'spiritual beauty', 'almost physical charm' – a love for Pushkin was strongly imprinted on the young Mandelstam. Throughout his life, as Nadezhda Mandelstam recalled in her memoirs, when Osip spoke about things and people particularly close to him, such as 'his mother for example, or Pushkin', it was only with a peculiar reticence, and even then he said very little. This remarkable timidity, this taciturn reverence, indicates the special character of his relationship with his great predecessor. Mandelstam's fellow poet and lifelong friend Anna Akhmatova writes in 'Pages from a Diary' that he had a 'strange, almost frightening, attitude' towards Pushkin.[2]

In the passage just quoted, the words 'my mother' are placed quite naturally alongside 'my Pushkin': the person who gave the child a language, a mother tongue in two senses, stands alongside the great poet. Mandelstam

2 M.'s peculiar reticence in speaking of his mother or Pushkin: N. Mandelstam, *Hope Against Hope*, 65. Mandelstam and Pushkin: A. Akhmatova, *My Half Century*, 96; R. Dutli, *Europas zarte Hände*, 27–59; I. Surat, '"Smert" poeta', 155–73.

also mentions other books in his mother's library: Lermontov, Turgenev, Dostoevsky, Nadson. None of these books has such an aura as 'my mother's Pushkin'. Flora Verblovskaia had received the book in the 1880s from the Russian *gymnasium* in Vilna as a prize for her diligence. It was a trophy, a testimony to her successful assimilation. Pushkin was a symbol of the world the young Mandelstam wanted to enter: the world of Russian poetry. His aim in life would be to become a poet in the mother tongue.

But, first, there came children's games and noisy extravaganzas. The imperial capital of St Petersburg was Mandelstam's magnificent playground as a child. This was the city of grandiose celebrations, funeral processions and military parades, pompous state ceremonies and sabre-rattling, which he amusedly portrays in the chapter entitled 'Childish Imperialism'. The streets of Petersburg aroused in the boy a 'thirst for big spectacles'. But the distance between the ostentatious, self-confidently boasting capital of Tsarism and the social aspirations and assimilation anxieties of Mandelstam's parents seemed unbridgeable:

> All of this elegant mirage of Petersburg was merely a dream, a brilliant covering thrown over the abyss, while round about there sprawled the chaos of Judaism – not a motherland, not a house, not a hearth, but precisely a chaos, the unknown womb world whence I had issued, which I feared, about which I made vague conjectures, and fled, always fled …
>
> The strong, ruddy, Russian year rolled through the calendar with decorated eggs, Christmas trees, steel skates from Finland, December, gaily bedecked Finnish cabdrivers, and the villa. But mixed up with all this was a phantom – the New Year in September – and the strange, cheerless holidays, grating upon the ear with their harsh names: Rosh Hashanah and Yom Kippur. (RZ, 23–4; NT, 76–7)

The Jewish New Year (Rosh Hashana) and the Day of Atonement (Yom Kippur) were nothing more than strange and unsettling sound combinations for the boy, who would rather throw himself head over heels into the festive occasions of the Russian church year. During his childhood and youth, Mandelstam's emotions constantly led him away from the 'black-yellow ritual' of a Judaism he felt was alien. He was wholeheartedly drawn towards Russian culture. His flight from Judaism was not just a rebellion against his parents; it was also a continuation of their own endeavours. But his rejection of his ancestral background would not be definitive. Decades later, a peculiar detour would lead to the 'return of the prodigal son'.

On 30 April 1898, Mandelstam's mother brought into the world a third son, Yevgeny. For the sake of all her sons, she tried to bring into their middle-class household a European atmosphere and a familiarity with spoken foreign languages. French and Swiss governesses were not only a middle-class status symbol in Petersburg; they were also an important source for the boys' first contact with foreign culture. 'So many French governesses were hired to look after me that all their features have become blurred and resolved into one general patch of portraiture.' These young Frenchwomen were contacted through the priest's office attached to the Roman Catholic Church of St Catherine on the Nevsky Prospekt. They gushed enthusiastically about Hugo, Lamartine, Napoleon and Molière, and little Osia asked them lots of questions about France. But the only information he gained from these interrogations was the notion 'that it is a beautiful country' (RZ, 22–3; NT, 76). His curiosity was awakened: this was the start of his lifelong 'dialogue with France', in particular with a line of French poets that stretched right from the Middle Ages into the twentieth century.[3]

His father's sullen separation from the family had already started by then. He became more and more silent, he was often unwell, and he lived almost entirely in his workroom, which was 'heavy with the odour of leathers, kidskin and calfskin' (RZ, 19; NT, 74). For his firstborn child, the smell of tanned leather would always signify 'the yoke of labour' (RZ, 26; NT, 77–8). The tannin-blackened hands of a dealer in leather goods no longer fitted in with the soaring heights of the father's earlier studies of literature and philosophy. His flight from the *shtetl* to Berlin now lay far in the past. Schiller, Herder and Spinoza were distant dreams. His morose silence was perhaps simply a reaction to the failure of his life to work out as he had planned.

The increasingly chilly relationship between Osip's parents was one reason why family life soon became cheerless. 'We laughed more and more rarely, and the sound of music was heard even less often,' his brother Yevgeny recalled. In one chapter of his semi-autobiographical essay, headed 'July Matveich', Mandelstam describes a family friend, Yuly Rosenthal, who was brought in to smooth over their numerous quarrels. The Mandelstam

3 M.'s 'dialogue with France': R. Dutli, *Ossip Mandelstam*, 56–311.

family, who according to Rosenthal were 'extraordinarily difficult and complex' (RZ, 65; NT, 99), evidently needed this generous peacemaker. Joseph Brodsky has conjectured that Mandelstam's persistent attempt to overcome 'Jewish chaos' had little to do with Judaism but was rather a way of fleeing from an oppressive and suffocating family atmosphere.[4]

His mother felt lonely and isolated while she was bringing up the children, but she saw it as her life's work. There was an element of stubbornness in her effort to offer the children as much as possible. Her firstborn, above all, owed her everything. Osip was her favourite son, and his wishes had preference. His brother Yevgeny recalls that Osip realised early on how gifted a child he was, and as a result developed a number of egoistic traits, such as the notion that everyone around him ought to serve him and his talent.

Flora Mandelstam wanted her three sons to become familiar with the theatre and classical music as well as foreign languages. *The Noise of Time* mentions a diversity of musical experiences in Mandelstam's childhood and youth, from the 'Tchaikovsky fever' experienced by the seashore at Riga in the summer holidays to the first performance of Scriabin's symphonic 'Fire Poem', *Prometheus*. The very first chapter of *The Noise of Time*, 'Music in Pavlovsk', evokes pilgrimages to the famous concerts which were held in the railway station of the town where the Mandelstam family lived when they first arrived in Russia:

> In the middle of the 1890s the whole of Petersburg rushed to Pavlovsk, as if to a kind of Elysium. The sound of the whistles of the steam locomotives and the bells rung before the departure of the trains mingled with the patriotic cacophony of the 1812 Overture, and this gigantic station, ruled by Tchaikovsky and Rubinstein, had its own peculiar aroma. The damp air of mouldy grass, the smell of rotten beetroot and hothouse roses competed with the powerful exhalations of the buffet, the acrid cigar smoke, the burnt smell of the air in the station and the cosmetics applied by a crowd of many thousands. (RZ, 10; NT, 69)

Two decades after these formative musical experiences, in his 1921 poem 'Concert at the Railway Station' – at a time when the music threatened

4 A suffocating family atmosphere: E. Mandel'shtam, 'Vospominaniia', 123. Speculations about M.'s rejection of 'Jewish chaos': J. Brodsky, *Bol'shaia Kniga Interv'iu*, 528. His egoistic traits: Mandel'shtam, 'Vospominaniia', 138.

to fall silent forever ('for the last time, we hear the sound of music') – Mandelstam returned in his poetry to the glass-domed station building of Pavlovsk and the musical rituals of his childhood:

> Immense park. The station a glass sphere
> A spell cast again on the iron world.
> The train carriage is borne away in state
> To the echoing feast in misty Elysium.
> Peacocks crying, a piano's bass notes –
> I'm late. I'm afraid. This is a dream.[5]

Flora Mandelstam may also have hoped that her firstborn son would enter the musical profession. One chapter of *The Noise of Time* hints at this. It is headed 'The Concerts of Hofmann and Kubelik'. The Petersburg triumphs of those two musicians took place in the winter season of 1903–1904. Twelve-year-old Osip was led into the Hotel Europa to be presented to Kubelik. 'Fearing that the boy might play the violin, Kubelik waved his little hand in alarm, but was immediately reassured and gave his autograph as he was requested to do.'

This passage appears to be an ironic reference to one of Isaac Babel's *Odessa Stories*, 'Awakening'. But it was not only in Odessa that music was regarded in Jewish families as an important route towards social recognition. More than one childhood was burdened by parental hopes that their loved one might turn out to be a musical virtuoso. What a stroke of luck for twentieth-century Russian literature that Isaac Babel cut his violin lessons! Escape from a prescribed destiny is also one of the themes of Marina Tsvetaeva's autobiographical text 'Mother and Music' (1935). As a child, she successfully maintained her literary vocation against her mother's wishes. Her mother was a gifted pianist, and she intended that her daughter would follow in her footsteps. But, instead, she writes: 'Silently and stubbornly I liquidated music.'

In Mandelstam's case, it was easier. His literary destiny gained the upper hand without a battle. He had his mother's aspirations to thank for many cultural stimuli, and, unlike Marina Tsvetaeva's mother, his was not tyrannical or selfish. He did not need to 'liquidate' music. The way he accommodated his mother's wishes was reflected in the whole of his

5 TR, 121; C. Brown and W. S. Merwin, 'Concert at the Railway Station', 51. This article will henceforth be referred to under the abbreviation CR.

work, from the early poems 'Bach' (1913) and 'Ode to Beethoven' (1914) to 'Concert at the Railway Station' (1921) and the 'Musical Score' fantasy in *The Egyptian Stamp* (1928), right up to 'The Violinist', the poem he wrote in 1935 when he was in exile in Voronezh. Mandelstam's work is shot through with music. It is as if his mother's wishes found fulfilment, but in a roundabout way, in the art of language.[6]

The most important decision taken by Mandelstam's parents, after the French governesses and the visits to concerts, was the choice of a school. They sent him to the progressive and liberal Tenishev School. In September 1899 Mandelstam started to attend the School for General Education on Zagorodny Prospekt, and the year after that he moved on to the Tenishev School at 33 Mokhovaia Street, which had just opened its doors. This school, founded by Prince Vyacheslav Tenishev for charitable reasons, modelled itself on the English system. It offered a practical programme, emphasising economic and scientific subjects, and it was one of the best Russian schools of the time. It was democratically organised, it paid no attention to distinctions of class, race or religion, and it encouraged a spirit of community and an attitude of mutual respect between students and teachers.

Mandelstam was lucky to go to this liberal and not particularly authoritarian school, even if it was not exactly likely to further his artistic inclinations. Prince Tenishev was a typical nineteenth-century positivist: mensuration, tabulation and statistics were the central aspects of his 'modern' educational programme. The school saw classical education, in the sense of the humanities as taught in *gymnasia*, involving fine literature and so on, as being of marginal significance. But at least the pupils had the freedom to discover the realm of fantasy and fable for themselves.

In later years, the school would produce other prominent alumni. For instance, the young Vladimir Nabokov became a pupil in January 1911. The very fact that the offspring of a liberal aristocratic family, who always arrived in a chauffeur-driven car, went to the same school as the oldest son of a Jewish leather merchant is some indication of the open-minded

6 References to music in M.'s poetry: 'Bach' (ST, 97; CP, 201); 'Ode to Beethoven' (ST, 153; CP, 203); 'Concert at the Railway Station' (TR, 121; CR, 51); the 'Musical Score' fantasy in *The Egyptian Stamp* (RZ, 214–15; NT, 198–9); 'The Violinist' (WH, 47; VN, 47). Apart from these examples, there is also the Schubert theme in TR, 53, as well as Mozart in MM, 175; WH, 43; RZ, 272 (NT, 189) and other places.

atmosphere of this institution, which was able to surmount social barriers. In his autobiography, *Speak, Memory*, Nabokov explains:

> Belonging as he did by choice to the great classless intelligentsia of Russia, my father thought it right to have me attend a school that was distinguished by its democratic principles, its policy of non-discrimination in matters of rank, race or creed, and its up-to-date educational methods.[7]

Mandelstam devotes a whole chapter of *The Noise of Time* to this school. The exuberant text contains pen portraits of his classmates, who were a variegated mixture, and of the crotchety headmaster, Ostrogorsky, along with other equally bizarre members of the teaching body. He describes the 'cruel and pointless' vivisection which was part of the biology lessons and he mentions all kinds of political meetings. The school's magnificent auditorium, with its glass ceiling, was among other things the meeting place of the 'Constitutional Democratic Party'. The steady advance of the school year was punctuated by free periods and rituals in memory of the literary fund founded in 1859. Football games – an English feature! – were particularly cherished, and they were an everyday occurrence. This stimulated Mandelstam into composing two jocular poems (BT, 107–9): 'Heavily and awkwardly / In this little choir of boys / He kicks the ball in all directions, / While the other guards his goal.' But he reserves any reference to the two decisive stimuli of his school years, one political and one literary, for two later sections of his autobiographical essay. For the first he was indebted to a politically active schoolmate; for the second, to a teacher who also wrote poetry.

7 The Tenishev School: Nabokov, *Speak, Memory*, 143.

4

Awakening the Beast of Literature

(Petersburg 1905–1906, Paris 1907–1908)

Mandelstam describes the most important meeting of his schooldays in the final chapter of *The Noise of Time*. Under the initially mystifying title 'In a Fur Coat above One's Station', he develops the notion of 'literary fury' and tells us whom he was indebted to for his impulsive, passionate attitude towards literature, which was destined to be the source of a great deal of personal misfortune. This was Vladimir Gippius (1876–1941), who taught literature to the higher classes of the Tenishev School. He was a pedagogue who wrote poetry in the Symbolist style, and he was the cousin of Zinaida Gippius, a Symbolist poet who was much better known. He also appears in Nabokov's autobiography, as 'a first rate, though somewhat esoteric, poet, whom I greatly admired', and as a teacher, a 'fierce man with red hair', who bedecked the boy's verses 'with fiery sarcasms.'[1]

His impact on Mandelstam was even greater than it was on Nabokov: 'The first literary encounter is irremediable.' This original figure was an out-and-out man of letters with a tendency towards lethargy. For Mandelstam, he was the model of a '*raznochinets*', of the 'propertyless intellectual' and 'angry *littérateur*' in a 'fur coat above his station in life' (RZ, 94–5;

1 On Vladimir Gippius: Nabokov, *Speak, Memory*, 185.

NT, 112–13), which in the eyes of the boy signified literature. He was a teacher of literature, but his ideas on the subject were not very settled:

> He had a kind of feral relationship to literature, as if it were the only source of animal warmth. He warmed himself on literature, he rubbed himself against it with his fur, the ruddy bristle of his hair, and his unshaven cheeks. He was a Romulus who hated his wolf mother, and, hating her, he taught others to love her ... I would come to him to wake up the beast of literature. To listen to him growl, to watch him toss and turn. I would come to my 'teacher of Russian' at home. The whole savour of the thing lay in that coming to him 'at home'. Even now it is difficult for me to free myself from the notion that I was then at literature's own house. Never again was literature to be a house, an apartment, a family, where red-haired little boys slept side by side in their netted cribs. (RZ, 96–7, 99; NT, 114, 115)

Under the guidance of this teacher of literature, Mandelstam formed 'personal relations with Russian writers, splenetic and loving liaisons filled with noble enviousness, jealousy, jocular disrespect, and grievous unfairness'. All the characteristics associated with Gippius can be found in the style of Mandelstam's essays.

The most important feature the incipient poet was able to take on from his teacher, though, was an inconvenient, impulsive temperament: 'literary fury'. He would continue to be imbued with this characteristic right up to the time of the political poems, including the fatal November 1933 epigram about the 'soul-corrupter and peasant-slayer' Stalin:

> Literary fury! If you didn't exist, what could I use to eat the salt of the earth? You are the seasoning in the unleavened bread of understanding, you are the joyful consciousness of injustice, you are the conspiratorial salt which is transmitted with a malicious bow from decade to decade, in a cut-glass salt cellar, with a serving cloth! That is why I so love to extinguish the heat of literature with frost and the barbed stars. Will it crunch like the crust of snow? Will it brighten up the frosty weather of the Nekrasovian streets? If it is genuine, the answer is yes. (RZ, 95; NT, 113)

Mandelstam would really pay a high price for his 'salt of conspiracy', and he would really have to extinguish the burning fever of literature with 'frost'. This is a rebellious manifesto and a visionary text! Moreover, his schooldays in the Tenishev *gymnasium* would be marked not only by literary rebellion but by political rebellion too.

Many Russian schoolchildren and students were radicalised around the time of the 1905 revolution. The Tsarist regime made one wrong decision after another. In foreign policy there was the fiasco of the Russo-Japanese War of 1904–1905, and at home it made serious errors in dealing with the forces that called for reform. 'Bloody Sunday', 22 January 1905, was the fateful day when a peaceful demonstration of almost 200,000 impoverished factory workers marched to the Tsar's Winter Palace bearing icons and crosses to call attention to their miserable situation. Tsar Nicholas II ordered his troops to fire at random into the crowd. Strikes and revolts broke out across the whole of Russia in response. 'Bloody Sunday' was the first step of the autocracy on the road to abdication. In London, meanwhile, the Bolsheviks reacted to the event by resolving on armed insurrection.

Mandelstam describes the approach of the 1905 revolution in the chapter of his autobiographical essay headed 'Sergey Ivanych'. This was the name of a strange student from whom he had received private lessons. He describes him as a veritable 'tutor of revolution' (RZ, 59; NT, 94). The fifteen-year-old Mandelstam came across pamphlets expressing socialist ideas. They may have come from his student tutor, or he may have sought them out himself. The most important of these short essays was Karl Kautsky's presentation of the 'Erfurt Programme', adopted by the German Social Democrats in October 1891. Gippius advised him to read Karl Marx's *Das Kapital* if he wanted to understand Marxism, but the boy returned quickly to the pamphlets. In those 'prehistoric years, when thought hungered after unity and harmoniousness, when the backbone of the age was becoming erect, when the heart needed more than anything the red blood of the aorta', Mandelstam was seeking a strong and harmonious attitude towards life (RZ, 69–71; NT, 99–100).

He spent the late summer of 1906 in Courland 'with the Erfurt Programme in his hands'. He was in the town of Segewold (now Sigulda), beside the River Aa (now Gauja), in the Baltic homeland of his forefathers. It was the last holiday he spent with his parents. The fifteen-year-old boy returned to the Tenishev School in the autumn 'as a completely prepared and finished Marxist'. A new schoolmate was waiting for him there, a 'serious opponent' and a future friend, Boris Sinani. A complete chapter of *The Noise of Time* is devoted to the Sinani family. The Sinanis were Karaites (Hebrew: *Karaim*), followers of a Jewish sect which recognised the Torah alone (the five books of Moses) and not the Talmud or rabbinical tradition. The Karaites had settled in Russia in the seventeenth and eighteenth centuries, mainly in the Crimean Peninsula.

But the Sinanis were also enthusiastic supporters of the Socialist Revolutionaries (SRs), the party founded by Victor Chernov in 1901, which had emerged from the radical section of the Russian Populist (*Narodnik*) movement. From the 1860s onwards, the *Narodniki* had proclaimed that a new social order would have to be based on the Russian peasantry. They advocated peasant socialism. Several more radical groupings had developed out of this movement, including the illegal revolutionary party *Narodnaia Volia* (The People's Will), founded in 1879, which carried out, among other actions, the assassination of Tsar Alexander II in 1881. The 'Combat Organisations' of the SR party also went over rapidly to the use of terror and assassination after 1901. Their political rivals in Russia were the Social Democrats, a party of Orthodox Marxists founded in 1898 by Plekhanov, which split into two groups in 1903, the Bolsheviks (under Lenin) and the Mensheviks (among them Plekhanov and Trotsky).

At first, the SR party was unequivocally the more dangerous grouping, more inclined towards terror. The teenage Mandelstam was caught up in their wake in 1906 during the final months of his school life at the Tenishev *gymnasium*, under the influence of his friend Boris Sinani. He was fascinated by Sinani and filled with enthusiasm by 'the clarity of his mind, his courage, and the presence of his spirit'. As late as 1923, Mandelstam could only utter his name 'with tenderness and respect' (RZ, 74; NT, 102).

Boris Sinani (1889–1911) was still a young man when he died. The chapter of *The Noise of Time* headed 'The Sinani Family' is Mandelstam's memorial to him. At a period of youthful restlessness, Boris had briefly given his schoolmate the opportunity to experience the political enthusiasm and 'genuine spirituality' he urgently needed:

> I was troubled and anxious. All the agitation of the times communicated itself to me. There were strange currents loosed about me – from the longing for suicide to the expectation of the end of the world. The literature of problems and idiotic universal questions had just taken its

> gloomy, malodorous leave, and the grimy, hairy hands of the traffickers in life and death were rendering the very words life and death repugnant. That was in very truth the night of ignorance! …
>
> That was all the vilest scum when compared to the world of the *Erfurt Programme*, the communist manifestoes and agrarian debates …
>
> These men did not traffic in the sense of life, but they had spirituality, and in their spare polemics there was more life and music than in all the writings of Leonid Andreyev. (RZ, 86–7; NT, 108–9)

The Sinani household, where the young Osip was often a guest, was frequented by revolutionaries and terrorists. The Tsarist secret service, the Okhrana, did not remain inactive. The years 1905–1907 were a period of heightened repression, and there were numerous arrests. Jews were increasingly under threat after the bloody suppression of the 1905 revolution, not only in the southern provinces of the Russian Empire where pogroms had traditionally occurred, but even in the capital, St Petersburg. The mystagogue Sergei Nilus published the *Protocols of the Elders of Zion*, which inspired a belief among contemporaries in a Jewish world conspiracy, although it has long since been exposed as a forgery produced by the Tsarist secret police. Tsar Nicholas II himself believed in the book's veracity. The Black Hundreds, an extremist organisation which was a reservoir for violent bands of anti-Semites, called on its supporters to 'smite the Jews', assigning them the traditional role of scapegoat. The Mandelstam family feared that they might fall victim to a pogrom. Osip's brother Yevgeny relates that his father acquired a small Browning pistol (for ladies), which was kept in a bedside cabinet.[2]

Mandelstam's parents had good reason to be uneasy about his new acquaintances. Their firstborn son even toyed with the idea of joining an SR 'Combat Organisation'. He wanted at least to become a propagandist for them; in March 1907, two months before he graduated from the Tenishev *gymnasium* with marks that were mediocre rather than good, he stood on a barrel in the street to make a fiery speech to the workers of the district where he lived. The occasion was the collapse of a ceiling in the Tauride Palace on 2 March 1907. That was the place where the State Duma held

2 The pogrom-like atmosphere in Russia after 1905, and the revolver bought by M.'s father: E. Mandel'shtam, 'Vospominaniia', 134. M. as an SR propagandist: the diary of S. Kablukov (entry for 18 August 1910) in O. Mandel'shtam, *Kamen'*, 241; P. Nerler, *Osip Mandel'shtam v Geidel'berge*, 257–8.

its sessions, and the parties of the left thought the accident was a Tsarist attack on a parliament the government detested.

Osip's involvement with the SRs was the gushing, ephemeral enthusiasm of a sixteen-year-old. But his 'socialist revolutionary past' was chalked up against him during the secret police investigations into the poet which led to his two arrests, in 1934 and 1938, because after the October Revolution and the civil war that followed, the Bolsheviks pursued both the SRs and the Menshevik Social Democrats, regarding them as their worst enemies (MR, 300–8).

In September 1907, Mandelstam even travelled with his schoolfriend Boris Sinani to the Finnish town of Raivola (now Roshchino in Russia) to be enrolled in a 'Combat Organisation' of the SR party, though he was not admitted because of his tender age. Too young to be a terrorist! Mandelstam's shocked parents decided to take action. They sent the sixteen-year-old abroad to study. The cosmopolitan city of Paris was chosen as his new home. Was this decision reckless or logical? Their offspring was exposed, they thought, to far greater dangers, in this case revolutionary ones, in Petersburg than in Paris. This was certainly the mildest and most fruitful period of deportation Mandelstam had to undergo in the whole of his life. He was being exiled to the capital city of poetry.

His sensible mother had once again made the correct choice. There is no longer any trace of revolutionary subversion in Osip's letters from Paris. But was Flora Mandelstam aware that the choice of Paris might possibly set back his education? After all, already in the nineteenth century, Paris, along with London and Geneva, was a favoured playground for Russian revolutionaries. This mild form of exile could well have led in the wrong direction. But, as it turned out, Flora had not made a mistake.

On 14 September 1907, Mandelstam took part in one more poetry evening in his former school, but by the beginning of October he was already on his way to foreign parts. First, he spent two weeks in Vilna, his mother's hometown; then he travelled on to Paris in the company of Yuly Rosenthal, the family friend and generous spirit 'with a head like Bismarck's' (RZ, 65; NT, 97).

A card sent from Vilna on 3 October 1907 already shows him carrying very little intellectual baggage, and there were no warning signs of political involvement: 'I am feeling very well on the journey … The weather has improved, and my head is almost free of thoughts' (MR, 7).

By the end of October, he had arrived in Paris. He enrolled at the

Sorbonne, in the 'Faculté des Lettres', as 'Joseph Mandelstamm', with the double M indicating the German origin of the name. The enrolment form he filled in is preserved in the French national archives.[3] His French is still clumsy. He gives as his address 14 Rue de la Sorbonne, which at that time was the Hotel Gerson, directly opposite the building that housed the famous university. All he needed to do to go to lectures was cross the street. Shortly afterwards, he moved into the house next door, 12 Rue de la Sorbonne, where visiting students attending the Collège de France located on the Rue des Écoles were accommodated in pleasant rooms. Here is a little hint for literary tourists visiting Paris: a plaque commemorating Mandelstam was affixed to the wall of this house on 1 February 1992.

Mandelstam went to the lectures given at the Collège de France by the medievalist Joseph Bédier and the philosopher Henri Bergson. Both men were to leave behind marked traces of their influence in his oeuvre. Throughout his life, Mandelstam was fascinated by French medieval literature, from the eleventh-century 'Song of Roland' to the verses of the late-medieval poet and vagabond François Villon (1431–1463?). He would dedicate one of his earliest essays to him (in 1913) and one of his last poems as well (in 1937) (WH, 203). In 1922, he translated lengthy extracts from a multitude of Old French texts for an anthology of medieval French epic poetry which was his own idea,[4] and in 1923 he wrote a review in which he praised Joseph Bédier's narrative synthesis *Le Roman de Tristan et Iseut* (1900) as a 'true miracle of reconstruction'.[5]

The other formative influence came from the Franco-Jewish philosopher Henri Bergson (1859–1941), who was one of the shining lights of French intellectual life at the turn of the century. Bergson's answer to the rationalism and faith in science that dominated the second half of the nineteenth century was to call for a return to intuition. His most important contribution to intellectual history was the development of new conceptions of consciousness as a flowing stream and of time as fluid. Time, he said, was 'durée pure' (pure duration), a process of becoming, immediate, incommensurable, continuous, only accessible to the intuition

3 M.'s Sorbonne enrolment form: Archives Nationales, Archival Reference AJ16/5002, reproduced in Struve, 'Mandel'shtam v Parizhe', 256.

4 M. and medieval French literature: R. Dutli, *Ossip Mandelstam*, 257–72 (the medieval French epic), 300–2 (Marie de France, Tristan-Sage).

5 GP, 211; O. Mandelstam, *The Collected Critical Prose and Letters*, 218. This work will henceforth be referred to as CC.

and inherently intense. The epoch offered no philosophy that was more poetic. This was a nourishing diet for a budding poet! Crowds of people clustered around outside the Collège de France listening to the lectures of this leading thinker; his voice could be heard through the windows that opened into the courtyard. One of Bergson's chief works, *L'Évolution créatrice* (Creative Evolution, 1907), was published while Mandelstam was in Paris. When he left the city, in May 1908, a copy was in his suitcase.[6]

This all sounds wonderfully scholarly, and it might lead us to conclude that he was a hardworking student. But he already felt that he was a poet. He wrote to his mother on 7 April 1908 telling her that this was 'a time of anticipation and poetic fever' and describing his lazy lifestyle as a Paris student.

> This is a proper spring for me now, in the fullest sense of the word …
> It is a time of anticipation and poetic fever …
> Here is how I pass my time:
> In the morning I go for a walk in the Jardin du Luxembourg. After breakfast I turn the daytime into evening – i.e. I cover up the window, make a fire and spend two or three hours like this …
> Then I have a burst of energy. I go for a walk, sometimes visit a café to write letters and then have my midday meal … We spend the afternoons in general chit-chat, which sometimes lasts into late in the evening.
> An endearing comedy.
> Recently, we have developed into a small international group of people, who are passionately keen to learn the language …
> And an unimaginable bacchanalia of words, gestures and intonations takes the stage, presided over by an unhappy landlady …
> A small anomaly: I feel 'homesick', not for Russia but for Finland.
> Here is another poem about Finland, and now, dearest Mama, goodbye.
> Your Osia. (MR, 8–9)

The 'small anomaly' he refers to is characteristic: by 'Finland' he means the family trips to Vyborg in winter and Teriöki in summer which punctuated his childhood and youth, along with the summer holidays by the

6 M. and Bergson: Dutli, *Ossip Mandelstam*, 42–7; A. Faivre Dupaigre, 'Bergsonovskoe chuvstvo vremeni'.

beach in Riga. A whole chapter of *The Noise of Time* is devoted to the way the Petersburgers soaked up Finland's aura (RZ, 34–7; NT, 81–3). The poem included with the letter to his mother is a dream-like summer memory in which he evokes Lake Saimaa and the *Kalevala*, the Finnish national epic. Nostalgia for a carefree holiday time … how far removed the young man is already from the Petersburg party quarrels between SRs and Social Democrats, from the 'Combat Organisations' and propagandists; how far, too, from his enthusiasm for Kautsky's Erfurt Programme!

In this letter, the dreamer and loafer refers to the 'endearing comedy' of his life. It is obvious that this phrase in his essay on François Villon, written between 1910 and 1913, reflects his own experience: 'Fifteenth-century Paris was already like a sea in which one could swim without ever experiencing boredom, oblivious of the rest of the universe' (GP, 26–7; CC, 55). Mandelstam's parents had indeed chosen the right medicine. The revolutionary temptation seemed to have been overcome, and a week later, on 14 April 1908, we see Mandelstam explaining to his esteemed former teacher of literature, Vladimir Gippius, how he has 'long been striving towards religion'. He speaks of Ibsen's 'cleansing fire', of Tolstoy and Gerhart Hauptmann, 'the two greatest apostles of love for people', and of Knut Hamsun's novel *Pan* (1894). Hamsun's natural mysticism, he says, has taught him, the young Mandelstam, 'to pray to an unacknowledged God' and it signifies a 'religion' which continues to be his own. Almost a checklist of the fashionable literary giants of the turn of the century!

Most important of all for Mandelstam, however, is the 'enthusiasm for the music of life' he finds in certain French poets, and, among the Russians, in Bryusov. And he adds: 'I am very alone here, and am occupied with practically nothing aside from poetry and music.'[7] He also mentions pieces he has written about Verlaine, Rodenbach and the Russian Symbolist Sologub, adding that he plans to write about Hamsun. These are the tender shoots of Mandelstam's later essays, although none of these youthful attempts has survived. The phrase 'enthusiasm for the music of life' also contains a hidden reference to Paul Verlaine (1844–1896) and his call for poetry to be musical, a programme set out in the first line of his 1874 poem 'Art poétique': 'Music above all else' (*De la musique avant toute chose*). The Symbolist Valery Bryusov (1873–1924) had made this poem famous in Russia in the 1890s.

7 MR, 10–11; C. Brown, *Mandelstam*, 35–6.

Verlaine and Bryusov were Mandelstam's literary favourites, as is confirmed by the memoirs of Mikhail Karpovich, who met the lonely Russian student on 24 December 1907 in a café on the Boulevard Saint-Michel. The young man, who was now almost seventeen years old, looked 'rather peculiar': like a young chicken. Either a chicken or a cockerel: contemporaries would always have recourse to inane avian comparisons when they wanted to characterise Mandelstam's youthful appearance. The young poet had ecstatically declaimed Bryusov's poem 'The Coming Huns' (1905), which was a hymn to the mounted hordes of the future, who would trample on the civilisation of an old, infirm world. He had recited poems by Paul Verlaine with equal enthusiasm, as well as his own Russian version of Verlaine's poem about Kaspar Hauser ('Je suis venu, calme orphelin'), which has not been preserved.[8] Mandelstam therefore favoured the Russian Symbolist's unrestrained dreams of an 'Asiatic' Russia, its arteries pulsating with fierce new blood, on the one hand, and Verlaine's self-questioning confession by a defeated and directionless human being, written in prison in 1873, on the other. For a seventeen-year-old, this was not a very surprising prospectus, combining world-weariness and reinvigoration.

His former revolutionism flared up again for a while in the spring of 1908, when the SR terrorist Grigory Gershuni, the organiser of the SR 'Combat Organisations', died in Paris. Gershuni appears briefly in the chapter of the autobiography headed 'The Sinani Family' (RZ, 85; NT, 108). The main speaker at a memorial ceremony organised by the SRs was Boris Savinkov. At the beginning of his speech Mandelstam suddenly gave a start, rose from his chair and remained on his feet throughout the speech, listening 'as if in a trance', with his mouth half open and his eyes half closed. What would his mother have thought if she had known about this! But his agitation was perhaps only a sign of melancholy nostalgia for Boris Sinani, the friend of his youth, and for the social revolutionary effervescence in which they had participated.[9]

Notwithstanding his lazy student life and his youthful reveries, Mandelstam's stay in Paris provided a whole range of important stimuli for his later work. Among these, in addition to his fascination for medieval

---

8 M. recites Verlaine and Bryusov: M. Karpovich, 'Moe znakomstvo s Mandel'shtamom' in V. Kreid and E. Necheporuk, *Osip Mandel'shtam i Ego Vremia*, 40–1. M. and Verlaine: Dutli, *Ossip Mandelstam*, 63–98.

9 M. at the memorial ceremony for Gershuni: Kreid and Necheporuk, *Osip Mandel'shtam i Ego Vremia*, 41; P. Nerler, 'Parizhskii semester Osipa Mandel'shtama', 260.

French literature and Bergson's new philosophy of duration, there was his encounter with a masterpiece of Gothic architecture: Notre Dame, the Parisian cathedral on the Île de la Cité. He would devote a programmatic poem to it in 1912 (ST, 85), and it also plays an important role in his manifesto 'The Morning of Acmeism' (1913), which revolves around the idea of building: 'Notre Dame is a celebration of physiology, its Dionysian debauch.'[10] A year after the end of his stay in Paris, the Notre Dame experience would still continue to echo powerfully. In a letter sent to Vyacheslav Ivanov from Montreux on 13 August 1909, he writes: 'When a person steps under the vaults of Notre Dame does he really ponder the truth of Catholicism, and does he not become a Catholic merely by virtue of being under those vaults?' (MR, 13; CC, 477). French images and themes would accompany Mandelstam for the whole of his life, right up to his period of exile in Voronezh.

He returned to Petersburg at the end of May 1908 without a diploma in his pocket, but with Bergson's new book *Creative Evolution* in his suitcase. The capital of poetry was henceforth an inalienable aspect of his experience. The 'beast of literature' had been awakened. His ears rang with the metrical music of Verlaine. And, like François Villon, the youthful Mandelstam had 'swum in the Parisian sea' and 'forgotten the rest of the universe'.

10 GP, 20; C. Brown, 'Mandelstam's Acmeist Manifesto', 50. Henceforth, this article will be referred to with the abbreviation AM.

5

The Fruit which Falls from the Tree

(Heidelberg 1909–1910 and Finland 1911)

In May 1908 the young student travelled back to Petersburg. After that, he spent July and August with his family as a tourist, visiting Switzerland for the first time. He was not particularly impressed by the country. Since Nikolai Karamzin's sentimental *Letters of a Russian Traveller* (1791), hymns in praise of Switzerland's astonishing displays of natural beauty had degenerated so far into cliché that, at the start of the twentieth century, a seventeen-year-old Russian could no longer join in as a matter of course with the chorus of adulation directed by tourists at Swiss scenery. Nevertheless, Mandelstam's ironic ice-cream poem of 1914 shows him flying away in his dreams to 'milky Alpine peaks' and a world of chocolate:

> 'Ice Cream!' Sun. Light airy cakes.
> A clear glass tumbler of water, icy cold.
> Our dreams take flight, into a chocolate world
> Of rosy dawns on milky Alpine peaks.[1]

Later, though, Mandelstam would have biting things to say about the 'well-ordered' country of the Swiss. In a review of Andrei Bely's *Diary*

1 M. and Switzerland: R. Dutli, *Europas zarte Hände*, 159–75; on the ice-cream poem: Dutli, *Ein Fest mit Mandelstam*, 93–7 ('divine ice'); ST, 135; OS, 171.

of an Eccentric written in 1923, he comments sarcastically on Symbolists and Anthroposophists, the Goetheanum in Dornach and a self-satisfied country run by hoteliers:

> What an absurd, tasteless idea to build a 'cathedral of universal wisdom' in such an inappropriate place! Surrounded by the Swiss, their hostels and hotels, the inhabitants live there cutting coupons and recuperating from illnesses. It is the most prosperous place in the world, a clean, neutral little piece of territory, and yet, at the same time, it is the most unclean corner of Europe because of its sated international prosperity. (GP, 205; CC, 213)

Mandelstam, whose life continued to be anything but shielded and safe, had little understanding for a country which was proud of its 'cleanliness' and 'neutrality'. Even during his first stay in Switzerland, in the summer of 1908, he undertook a hasty journey to Italy. He would later regret the shortness and pointlessness of the trip. He described it at the time in a letter to his brother Alexander ('Shura', 'Shurinka') written on 24 July 1908 on the train on the way to Genoa:

> Shurinka! I am on the way to Italy. It happened just like that. I have only 20 Francs – but that is of no importance. One day in Genoa, a couple of hours by the sea and then back to Berne. I am actually enjoying the rush. The train is winding through the narrow valley of the Rhône. The sides are steep – the rocks and the trees are shrouded in cloud. 'They' know nothing about this – for the moment of course.
>
> Addio!
>
> Osia. (MR, 12)

He says farewell in Italian, like a man of the world; this fits in well with the little excursion made by the seventeen-year-old Mandelstam, who has one or two silly ideas in his head. Meanwhile, his mother and younger brother Yevgeny are sitting obliviously in Berne. He spent no more than one day in Italy, a country he repeatedly dreamed of. There has been much speculation over whether Mandelstam visited the country again in later years, but there is no evidence for this. All the references to Italy in his work are the fantasies of a poet who was soon to be deprived of any possibility of travelling abroad. The Rome poems of 1913–1914 and 1937, the splendid Venice poem of 1920, the references to Verona, Ferrara, Florence and Tuscany associated with his enthusiasm for Petrarch, Ariosto and Tasso, and the great essay on Dante (1933) are all testimonies to journeys undertaken by the mind, not evidence that he actually stayed in those places.[2]

But the stay in Switzerland and the excursion to Genoa are of little moment in comparison with the really important event of 1908: Mandelstam's emergence as a poet. It is true that we know of two schoolboy poems from 1906, inspired by the suppression of the 1905 revolution. But they are allegorical and emotional invocations of fields of unmown wheat, weeping birch trees and Russian martyrdom which would have been well suited to Nikolai Nekrasov, the socially critical poet of the nineteenth century. In the last collection of Mandelstam's poetry published during his lifetime (1928), the year 1908, when he was seventeen years old, is represented by four poems. They start with a modest four-liner:

> A tentative hollow note
> As a pod falls from a tree
> In the constant melody
> Of the wood's deep quiet …
> (ST, 7; OS, 45)

In 1933, writing as an exile in Paris, Mandelstam's fellow poet Marina Tsvetaeva judged this first poem to be already outstanding. In the essay 'Poets with History and Poets without History' she describes the quatrain we have quoted as a proof of his early maturity and polish. Mandelstam, she wrote, is one of the poets who have 'no path' to follow: 'They are there from birth. Their childish babble is a sum, not a source.' The maturity of the young poet is symbolically expressed in the ripeness of the falling fruit. The stanza is itself the falling fruit which it depicts.[3]

---

2 M.'s Italy: the Rome poems of 1913–1914 and 1937 (ST, 123, 138, 141, 151; WH, 163); the Venice poem of 1920 (TR, 85); references to Verona, Ferrara, Florence and Tuscany as well as the poets Ariosto, Tasso, Petrarch and Dante and the sculptor Michelangelo: MM, 121–5, 145–55, 189–97; WH, 13, 113, 123, 163. See also the 1933 essay 'Conversation about Dante' (GD, 113–93; SE, 26–64). Schoolboy poems of 1906: Russian edition O. Mandel'shtam, *Sobranie Sochinenii v Chetyrekh Tomakh*, 1993, vol. 1, 31–2.

3 Marina Tsvetaeva's essay 'Poets with History and Poets without History', in AL, 147.

The separation of the fruit from the tree signifies the moment of letting go and of freedom, the beginning of Mandelstam's emancipation from his family and his ancestry, his release from control by other people. It represents a poetic voice which will quickly become unmistakably distinctive. And there is another poem from 1908 which shows an astonishingly early maturity. It speaks of 'toy wolves', which have nothing childish about them, of sorrow and of freedom. It is produced by someone who will later be renowned as the poet of the 'wolfhound century':

> In the wood there are Christmas trees
> With golden tinsel blazing,
> In the thickets toy wolves are gazing
> With terrifying eyes.
>
> O my prophetic sadness,
> O my silent freedom
> And the heavens' lifeless dome
> Of eternally laughing glass!
> (ST, 9; OS, 47)

The initial obstacles faced by the young man contributed to his early maturity. Heaven seemed to be sneering at him. When he returned to Petersburg in September 1908 to study at the university, he met with a setback. This was the law adopted by the Council of Ministers, and confirmed by the Tsar on 16 September, which discriminated against Jewish university entrants. Jews were allowed to make up only 3 per cent of the students at the capital's universities. And they had to have top marks. The 3 per cent quota was a forbidding obstacle for Mandelstam, who was only an average student.

He would overcome it formally in 1911 by getting baptised as a Christian. But, for the moment, the eighteen-year-old was discouraged. Instead, he passed the time by attending the lectures at the Petersburg Religious and Philosophical Society, and, from April 1909, the sessions of the 'Pro-Academy' held at the home of the Symbolist Vyacheslav Ivanov. Ivanov's house on Tavricheskaia Street beside the Tauride Gardens was a temple of scholarship and literature, frequented by many famous artists and intellectuals of the period, such as the philosopher Nikolai Berdyaev, the poets Alexander Blok, Andrei Bely and Fyodor Sologub and the writer

Mikhail Kuzmin … It was an honour to be admitted to Ivanov's 'Tower'. Mandelstam experienced his 'literary baptism' there on 16 May 1909. Ivanov praised his poems, although this was not unusual, as he tended to be generous with his compliments.

Frustrated as a student, but encouraged as a poet, Mandelstam spent the period from the end of July until September 1909 with his parents in Switzerland, in Beatenberg and Montreux. He sent a letter on the writing paper of the sanatorium 'L'Abri' on 13 August 1909 to Ivanov, commenting somewhat presumptuously on the latter's essays, and not forgetting to include a few words of advice to the already famous author. And this from a greenhorn whose first five poems would only be published a year later in a literary journal! After a few precocious utterances on literary matters, he reverts to the tone of a cosmopolitan traveller. He depicts the 'sacred quiet of the sanatorium' which is only interrupted by the gong that announces the midday meal and call to the evening game of roulette in the casino. He continues:

> I have a strange taste: I love the patches of electric light on Lac Léman, the deferential lackeys, the noiseless flight of the elevator, the marble vestibule of the hotel, and the Englishwomen who play Mozart in a half-darkened salon for an audience of two or three official listeners.
>
> I love bourgeois, European comfort and am attached to it not only physically but also emotionally.
>
> Perhaps my poor health is to blame for this? But I never ask myself whether it is good or bad. (MR, 14–15; CC, 478)

An irony of literary history: the youthful Mandelstam abandons himself to 'European luxury' not far from the 'Palace Hotel' in Montreux, which will later be the final resting place of his aristocratic younger contemporary, Vladimir Nabokov. When one thinks of Mandelstam's 'final resting place', the contrast could not be greater; it was Barrack 11 of the forced labour camp 'Vtoraya Rechka' near Vladivostok, where he expired on 27 December 1938, suffering from heart disease, half-starved and tortured by hallucinations. In general, Mandelstam's life would have very little in common with 'bourgeois, European luxury'. It makes the young dandy's confession look all the more curious.

Because it was temporarily impossible to secure a place at the University of St Petersburg, Mandelstam's parents had to look round for other options. Osip had already written to his mother in the letter he sent on 7 April 1908 from Paris: 'If they don't take me, I shall go to one of the German universities ... and combine the study of literature with the study of philosophy' (MR, 9). The German universities were in fact much more liberal than the Russian ones at that time, unless, like Bonn or Berlin, they were dominated by the Prussian spirit. There was no discriminatory 3 per cent quota for Jewish students in Germany. Boris Pasternak studied philosophy in Marburg in 1912 under the neo-Kantian Hermann Cohen. Osip Mandelstam went instead to Heidelberg.

In the second half of the nineteenth century, Heidelberg – like Göttingen previously – was 'a Mecca for Russian scholarship'.[4] The local Russian colony was, at times, so enormous that Heidelberg gave the impression of being a small Russian town. A particularly large group of student exiles came to Heidelberg after the disturbances of 1861, when the University of St Petersburg was closed temporarily by the Tsarist authorities. Mikhail Bakunin the anarchist and Alexander Herzen, the critic of Tsarism who lived in exile in London, regarded it as an important distribution centre for anti-Tsarist and revolutionary journals and pamphlets. In the 'Pirogov Reading Room' in Heidelberg, Russian students could read all the literature that was prohibited in their own country. Mandelstam, though, was no longer in danger of being converted to radicalism; by the end of September 1909, when he arrived in Heidelberg, his period of revolutionary temptation lay far in the past. It was purely as a young poet that he took up residence in the town on the Neckar.

He found a room in the 'Continental', a family boarding house run by a captain's widow, Frau Johnson. The address was 'Anlage 30'. It is now 'Friedrich-Ebert-Anlage 30', and since 1993 it has borne a plaque indicating that Mandelstam once lived there. The house was situated at a corner of the Old Town, at the foot of the Gaisberg. On 12 November 1909, Mandelstam registered for the winter semester 1909–1910 at the Philosophy Faculty of the University of Heidelberg, as 'Joseph Mandelstamm', using the same spelling as he had previously done at the Sorbonne. He continued and deepened the interests awakened at the Collège de France in 1907–1908: he attended the lectures of the Romance scholar Friedrich Neumann on 'The History of French Medieval Literature' and took part in his 'Practical Studies of Old French and Provençal Texts'. Mandelstam's essay on

4 Heidelberg as 'the Mecca of Russian scholarship': W. Birkenmaier, *Das russische Heidelberg*, 8–9. M. in Heidelberg: P. Nerler, *Osip Mandel'shtam v Geidel'berge*.

the late-medieval poet François Villon, printed in the Petersburg literary journal *Apollon* (no. 4, 1913), was presumably drafted in Heidelberg in 1910. At least, he himself would give 1910 as the date of composition in his 1928 collection of essays, *On Poetry*.

His fellow student Aaron Steinberg recalls that Mandelstam also heard lectures by Heidelberg philosophers Wilhelm Windelband (on Kant) and Emil Lask (on the history of modern philosophy).[5] He also attended the courses given by the art historian Henry Thode on 'The Elements of Art History' and 'The Great Venetian Painters of the Sixteenth Century'. Here too we can see the germs of a continuing interest. A complete section of his prose meditation *Journey to Armenia* (1931–1933), headed 'The French', idiosyncratically evokes the paintings of the Impressionists and the Post-Impressionists. And the sixteenth-century Venetians Titian and Tintoretto appear unexpectedly during the lonely exploration of Moscow portrayed in the 1931 poem 'Still Far from Patriarch or Sage':

> I enter puppet theatre museums
> Where opulent Rembrandts swell
> Glazed like Cordoban leather
> I marvel at Titian's horned mitres
> And Tintoretto's bright tints I admire
> For their myriad screaming parakeets.
> (MM, 105; FP, 76)

The stay in Heidelberg was an unusually fruitful and creative period for the young Mandelstam. Between fifteen and twenty-three poems are assigned to the 'Heidelberg cycle'.[6] He included most of them in his letters to the Symbolist poets Maximilian Voloshin and Vyacheslav Ivanov, emphatically requesting that they take notice of his work (MR, 16–19).

Ivanov was also the recipient of other letters from Mandelstam, in which the young poet displays a high degree of self-confidence. On 30 December 1909, he writes of his wish to emulate Paul Verlaine's *Romances sans paroles* (he includes one of his own poems with the letter) and to 'restrain' the intimate, personal nature of lyric 'with the bridle of rhythm' (MR, 19; CC, 480). This wish to place limits on the self is already a feature of the early Mandelstam. Moreover, the poet's attraction to Verlaine's work,

5 Recollections of Aaron Steinberg: Nerler, *Osip Mandel'shtam v Geidel'berge*, 31–34.

6 The Heidelberg cycle of poetry: Nerler, *Osip Mandel'shtam v Geidel'berge*, 63.

already evident in Paris, was confirmed during the Heidelberg period. But he did not include the youthful poems written in Heidelberg in the collections of his work he published in later years. The solitary exception is a poem written in December 1909, which he regarded as so important that he published it three times: in the expanded 1916 and 1923 editions of *Stone* and in his final collection *Poems* (1928):

> There is no need for speech
> And nothing to teach;
> How sad yet beautiful
> Is the dark brutal soul.
>
> It has nothing it wants to teach
> And lacks even the power of speech,
> But like a young dolphin swims
> Where the world's grey deeps are dim.
> (ST, 27; OS, 65)

This short poem gives a foretaste of the requirements laid down two years later by the Acmeist group of poets: doctrine must be rejected, and the poet should fall back on the dark and unrestrained soul.[7] These are the emphatic utterances of a poet, but they are dubious testimonials for a student, who ought surely to be struggling to gain an understanding of 'doctrine' and 'science'. The first version of the poem also included a revealing admission: 'In my heart I am still somewhat wild / Our comprehensible language is boring for me.' That is a good slogan for a poet who's just starting out … It already demonstrates that he has decided in favour of a different, supposedly 'dark', poetic language.

The young student was also timidly in love in Heidelberg. Traces of a first love affair – and of disappointment in love – can be found in several of these youthful poems.[8] The sculptural image of a sorrowful love is conjured up, in which an absent female 'you' is vainly awaited in a café. The lady addressed as a 'hermit' will always have to remain unknown to us.

7 Rejection of 'doctrine' and retreat to the 'soul of the beast' in the December 1909 Heidelberg poem: R. Dutli, 'Das bin ich. Das ist der Rhein', 64.

8 Three youthful poems written in Heidelberg ('The Moon Lights Up the Night-time Scene', 'Looking Down from the Wet Stone', 'The Place Grows Empty. The Evening Continues'): Dutli, 'Das bin ich. Das ist der Rhein', 69–72. For the early love poems, see R. Dutli, *Mandelstam, Heidelberg*, 47, 51, 59, 65 and 67.

Your place is empty. The wind
Keeps on, oppressed by your
Absence. The drink destined for you
Is steaming on the table.

So you will not approach with
The divining footsteps of a hermit;
And with sleepy lips you will not
Trace a design on the glass.[9]

The poems perhaps only express a youthful yearning for love, rather than an actual experience. In any case, they are notable for their repetition of the noun 'tenderness' and the adjective 'tender': 'Your joyful tenderness', and 'What does the music of my tender praises signify?' (these expressions come from poems written in 1909). The word 'tenderness' would possess a special aura in Mandelstam's later poems. 'Tenderness' is portrayed as the antipode of terrestrial 'heaviness' in a Crimea racked by civil war in a poem from March 1920: 'Heaviness and tenderness, you're sisters' (TR, 75; FP, 48). And the 'Lethe Poems' of October–November 1920 (TR, 87–9) evoke a descent into the underworld and its 'Stygian tenderness'. Tenderness and death will continue to be yoked together in mysterious proximity in Mandelstam's poetry.

The winter semester at Heidelberg finished at the end of February. Mandelstam had originally intended to attend the summer semester as well, but he did not appear. Perhaps this was because he was short of money, or perhaps he simply lacked perseverance. Mandelstam was by no means a hardworking student. At the beginning of March, he again attempted to travel to Italy, but whether he managed to get beyond the southern part of Switzerland remains doubtful. The only piece of evidence for the trip is one of his early religious poems, dated 'Lugano 1910'.[10] In it he conjures up the image of entering a church and contemplating the portraits of saints in fascination. The poem also brings out the young man's painfully ambiguous position: he is torn between his attraction to Christianity and the impossibility of cutting his ties to Judaism: 'In darkness, like a cunning snake / I drag myself to the foot of the Cross.'

9 O. Mandelstam, *Poems from Mandelstam*, 108. Henceforth: PM.
10 The poem 'Lugano 1910': Dutli, *Europas zarte Hände*, 162–4.

And I drink monastic tenderness
From rapt hearts,
Like the hopelessness of the cypress
At inexorable heights
I love the saints' bent eyebrows,
The colour in their faces,
The spots of gold and blood
On wax statue bodies.[11]

After his return to Petersburg, Mandelstam spent some time (until July 1910) in nearby Finland, the country for which he had been so homesick when he was in Paris. He stayed in Tallbacka, near Helsinki, and in Hangö (Finnish: Hanko). There he made the acquaintance of Sergei Kablukov, ten years his senior, who was the secretary of the Petersburg Philosophico-Religious Society. Kablukov's diary contains many entries recording his meetings with Mandelstam, which continued until 1917. Kablukov was interested in religious matters and in sacred music. The young poet seemed to him to be 'lackadaisical' and 'irresponsible', but he was impressed by his 'sensibility' and the 'fineness of his perceptions'. The very first entry in the diary tells us that Mandelstam is now ashamed of his youthful enthusiasm for revolution during the years 1906 and 1907.[12]

On 24 July 1910, he travelled by train to the Berlin suburb of Zehlendorf, where his mother was undergoing surgery. It would be his last trip to Western Europe. All his later journeys would be within the Tsarist Empire or its Soviet successor, or they would happen in his own head. In Berlin too, he worried about religious matters; he was struggling to attain a personal feeling for religion. The portraits of saints he saw at Lugano had fascinated and disturbed him; now he was concerned with the crucifixion of Christ, as in the poem 'Inexorable Words'. Christ on the Cross is compared with a water lily: 'The head hung like a calyx on a thin and alien stem.' He speaks of a 'petrified Judaea' and an 'exultant law'. The law of Moses is described as a stagnant, impenetrable pool and a dreary source. In contrast to that: the soaring Christ on the Cross. But the roots of the Christian plant lie in the nourishing water of Judaism.[13]

---

11 O. Mandelstam, *Complete Poetry*, 148–9. This work will henceforth be referred to as CP.

12 Kablukov's diary, in O. Mandel'shtam, *Kamen'*, 241–58.

13 The Crucifixion poem 'Inexorable Words': Mandel'shtam, *Kamen'*, 133; the

Mandelstam's early poems are not confessions of faith. They merely show the continuation of his painful struggle to achieve a sense of religion, which he had already referred to in his letter of 14 April 1908 from Paris to Vladimir Gippius (MR, 9–11). These poems should not lead us to conclude that he had been converted intellectually to Christianity. Another poem, written in November 1910, speaks of the dangerous and terrifying character of religious feeling: 'Terrible is for me the underwater stone of belief / Its fatal and ceaseless circling.' Later poems would display numerous Christian motifs.[14] Religious monuments, sacred spaces, the ceremony of the Eucharist and an Orthodox funeral service would all be invoked, and he would digress both to Rome and to Byzantium; in short, he would 'drink the cold mountain air of Christianity' (TR, 73). But Mandelstam would always be a poet, never a preacher. His work is an attempt to unify all the elements of Western and European culture and worship and synthesise them poetically. His confession of faith is his poetry. It adamantly rejects appropriation by any particular religion.

The crucified Christ in another poem represents not an aquatic plant but rather the Self, which is compared with a reed.[15] The 'thinking reed' was the image used by the French philosopher Blaise Pascal (1623–1662) to express humanity's misery and greatness, its fragility, but also its dignity as made possible by thought. The opening of the poem again evokes a 'dangerous swamp', the land of mud, the place of origin, the dismal birthplace. It is the 'Judaic chaos' of his family, which he would depict later in his autobiographical account. But the end of the poem reveals that the reed pursues a surprisingly independent life:

---

poems 'The Black Crucifix at the End of the Bed' (November 1910) and 'Stone of Belief': Mandel'shtam, *Kamen'*, 134.

14 Christian motifs in M.'s work: his invocation of religious monuments ('Notre-Dame': ST, 85; OS, 121); of sacred spaces ('Hagia Sophia': ST, 83; O. Mandelstam, *Selected Poems. Osip Mandelstam*, 186. This work will henceforth be referred to as SP); of Rome as a centre of faith ('The Pilgrim's Staff': ST, 151; OS, 183); of the Eucharist ('There the ciborium, like a golden sun': ST, 163; PM, 81); of the 'cold mountain air of Christianity' (TR, 73); and of the Orthodox funeral ceremony (TR, 117). The essay most powerfully imbued with Christian thought is 'Pushkin and Scriabin' (1916) (GP, 62–9; CC, 90–5).

15 M. and Pascal's 'thinking reed': Dutli, *Ossip Mandelstam*, 143–4. The Jewish theme in the 'Reed Poem': K. Taranovsky, *Essays on Mandel'shtam*, 51–64.

I grew out of a dangerous swamp,
Rustling like a reed,
And – with rapture, languor, caresses –
Inhale a prohibited life.
…
I enjoy this cruel injury;
And in a life like a dream
Secretly I envy everybody,
Secretly am in love with the world.[16]

This is a poem which speaks of being stuck in a swamp and suffering insults, and yet invokes the possibility of love and happiness. The young Mandelstam already knows how to handle poetic paradox. And in another poem, in which he compares himself with a blade of straw instead of a reed, he gives advice on his future path in life:

Feign tenderness, stand by the pillow,
Sing your life to sleep till its end,
As in legends, indulge your sorrow,
Treat proud ennui as your friend.
(ST, 41; OS, 79)

Between March and sometime in autumn 1911, Mandelstam lived mainly in Finnish sanatoria and boarding houses, in the towns of Hyvinkää, Konkkala and Mustamäki. He spent his time meditating on poems and waiting for the chance to pursue his university studies. His stay in Finland was interrupted by several trips to St Petersburg – mainly to concerts. Mandelstam loved the music of Alexander Scriabin, whose symphonic 'Poem of Fire', *Prometheus*, with its famous 'piano of light', created a furore when it was first performed on 9 March 1911.

In the same year, he became severely infected with typhus. He would long remember the journey to the hospital by ambulance carriage, the cold, the desire to sleep and the feverish dreams associated with this. A 1911 poem evokes this journey. It is a calm vision of the decrees of fate; it expresses his awareness that he is being conveyed by strangers (as in the carriage dream about 'Raspberry Town' in *The Egyptian Stamp*), which

16 ST, 39; Mandelstam, *Osip Mandelstam. The Eyesight of Wasps*, 40. Henceforth, the abbreviation EW will be used to identify this work.

is at the same time a sense of being wondrously lifted up in 'a stranger's hand'. Perhaps Durs Grünbein was thinking of this frame of mind when he insisted that Mandelstam had 'smuggled a basic feeling of confidence into modern literature'.[17]

> How slowly the horses go,
> Lanterns shining so dimly!
> These strangers probably know
> The place they are taking me.
>
> And I trust myself to their kindness,
> I am feeling cold, and I yearn
> To sleep; I was left at the turn
> To confront the starry brightness
>
> My feverish head sways
> And a strange hand's coolness is tender;
> The dark loom of fir trees
> Is not yet clear.
> (ST, 47; OS, 83)

When he was in Finland, he stayed for a short time in the Pension Linde near Mustamäki, which was frequented by Russian revolutionaries. He was well acquainted with Fyodor Linde, a mathematician and revolutionary who was ten years older than him. In August 1911, the police carried out a raid at the boarding house, making a number of arrests. When the raid took place, Mandelstam was not on the premises, but a year later, between June and December 1912, he was still under police observation during his visits to Finland, as he was suspected of anti-government agitation.[18]

In the spring of 1911, however, his mind was set on something far removed from this. He was looking round for a church where he could be baptised, because he wanted to begin his studies at the University of St Petersburg that autumn, and becoming a Christian would allow him to

17 M. 'smuggles a basic feeling of confidence into modern literature': D. Grünbein, *Gespräch mit Heinz-Norbert Jocks*, 14.

18 M. under police observation in 1912: P. Nerler and D. Zubarev, 'Nekii evrei Mandel'shtam'.

overcome the obstacle presented by the 3 per cent quota applied to Jews. On 14 May 1911, he underwent Christian baptism at the hands of a certain Pastor Rosen, according to the rites of the Episcopalian Methodists. His mother was not too worried that he had taken this step, but for his father, it was 'a serious trial', according to his younger brother Yevgeny.[19]

Why did Mandelstam not convert directly to Russian Orthodoxy? Why did he choose to join a group of outsiders, Finnish Methodists, who had absolutely no standing in the intolerant Tsarist Empire? Probably in order to underline the purely practical nature of his action. In that sense, it was an act of freedom and not a capitulation before the authorities' rigidity. His spiritual involvement in the Christian community – as shown in his essays and letters – would come later. All that was required for the present was a simple formal act of recognition. He would not lightly abandon the 'silent freedom' evoked by an early poem (1908). The fruit was sufficiently ripe to fall from the branch, away from the family, the call of the blood, and his literary predecessors. But the almond, like any other fruit, does not fall far from the tree.

19 The reaction of M.'s parents to his baptism: E. Mandel'shtam, 'Vospominaniia', 136.

6

No, Not the Moon, but the Bright Face of a Clock

(Petersburg 1912–1913)

On 18 August 1910, while Mandelstam was staying in Berlin, his first published poems appeared in print, in the Petersburg literary journal *Apollon* (no. 9, 1910). There were five of them in all, including the poem to which he later gave the title 'Silentium'.[1] That poem was a kind of dialogue with the views of two poets he admired: Paul Verlaine, who called for musical poetry in 'Art poétique' (1874), and Fyodor Tyutchev (1803–1873), who wrote in praise of silence, and of the unsaid, in his 1833 poem, also called 'Silentium'. Mandelstam echoes both aspirations in a single poem:

May my lips discover
What has always been mute,
Like a crystal note
That is newborn and pure.

1 M. included four of the five poems printed in *Apollon* (no. 9, 1910) in his first volume of poetry. They are 'A Body Was Given to Me', 'An Inexpressible Sorrow', 'A Snow Hive Cleaner than the Air', and 'Silentium': ST, 21, 23, 31, 33.

Aphrodite, remain foam!
Let the word become music again;
My heart, you must spurn hearts
Fused in that from which all things come.
(ST, 33; OS, 71)

Mandelstam's early poems were still clearly influenced by Russian Symbolism, the emergence of which in 1892 had introduced the 'Silver Age' of Russian poetry. The accolade of a 'Golden Age' was reserved for the generation of Alexander Pushkin (1799–1837). After the second half of the century, which was dominated by prose and largely concerned itself with social problems, the 'Silver Age' marked the rebirth of poetry and a new awareness of the importance of the word. It was accompanied by the discovery of Ibsen, Strindberg and Nietzsche and the reception of French Symbolism. The most important revelations were associated with the names of Edgar Allan Poe, Charles Baudelaire and Paul Verlaine. For the Symbolists, Baudelaire's sonnet 'Correspondances' was a key to understanding the nature of the world.

The Symbolists of the first generation (Constantin Balmont, Valery Bryusov, Zinaida Gippius and Fyodor Sologub) were oriented towards aestheticism. They were followed by a second generation (Alexander Blok, Andrei Bely and Vyacheslav Ivanov), which was increasingly inspired by mystical and religious ideas, and drew intellectual nourishment not only from French sources but from German and Russian thinkers (Schopenhauer, Nietzsche, Vladimir Solovyov). The sense of an approaching apocalypse after the national catastrophe of the Russo-Japanese War and the bloody suppression of the 1905 Revolution strengthened this tendency towards religious belief, theosophy and occultism. In any case, by 1910 Russian Symbolism was completely played out, and it offered little more than otherworldly speculations.

Mandelstam's first steps as a poet coincided with the end of the Symbolist movement. The world of his earliest poems was not yet that of the poet who has adopted the cult of building and is imbued with a belief in the power of human creativity. In the young Mandelstam, one can still perceive traces of the philosophical poems in which Tyutchev celebrated primeval chaos and darkness. The world he invokes is ruled by emptiness. It is a vaguely outlined, nocturnal world of shadows, of extreme fragility and disheartening impermanence. The grief that recurs in the poems is motiveless; it is the melancholy of a youthful Late Symbolist. Here is an example from 1910:

> I see the unbreathing moon
> And a sky deader than canvas;
> Your strange and morbid world
> I welcome, emptiness!
> (ST, 35; EW, 39)

Nevertheless, despite all this premature weariness with life, a very early poem by Mandelstam, 'Only Children's Books to Read' (1908), already shows a clear commitment to the earth and the material world:

> Life has made me mortally weary;
> I will take nothing it gives,
> But I love my land, poor as it is,
> For I've seen no other country.
> (ST, 13; OS, 51)

The young poet thus communes with 'naked', meagre nature; this is an important stage in his development. Mandelstam was later described by Joseph Brodsky as 'the modern Orpheus'. In 1911, he receives a visit from Orpheus himself, whom he apostrophises as the original poet and bard:

> Oh broad wind of Orpheus
> You will go away into the sea-worlds
> And cherishing an uncreated world,
> I forgot the unneeded 'I'.[2]

The 'I' soon became 'We'. On 14 March 1911, Mandelstam attended a literary evening in Vyacheslav Ivanov's 'Tower'. There he met the poet Anna Akhmatova, a taciturn, sphinx-like phenomenon in a black dress. She was two years older than him, lived in Tsarskoye Selo and had been married for a year to the poet Nikolai Gumilyov, whom Mandelstam had already met during his stay in Paris. It was only now that the meeting

2 ST, 57; M. Glazova, 'The Artist as Transgressor', 11–12. Referred to henceforth as AT.

with Gumilyov turned out to be fateful. The meeting with Akhmatova and Gumilyov would be one of the most important encounters of Mandelstam's life. Akhmatova was to be his intimate friend and his main interlocutor from that time onwards. And, according to Mandelstam, the dialogue with Gumilyov 'was never interrupted' (MR, 144–5), even by the latter's violent death (he was shot in 1921 as a 'counter-revolutionary').

When he made the acquaintance of the young pair, they were still just starting out on their poetic careers, although Gumilyov (1886–1921) had the advantage of being five years older. He had already published three books of poetry, made several trips to Africa, where he had gone big-game hunting, and experienced other adventures as well. Gumilyov advocated poetry of a neo-romantic, exotic kind, centred around heroic masculinity, and he was a great organiser and teacher of younger poets, whom he immediately impressed. Together with Sergei Gorodetsky, he founded the 'Poets' Guild', a discussion circle for young poets, which met for the first time on 20 October 1911 in Gorodetsky's house. These circles of people, who were not always like-minded, were typical of the literary life of Petersburg at that time. The meetings held by the Symbolist Vyacheslav Ivanov in the 'Tower', and the meetings of the 'Verse Academy' in the editorial offices of the journal *Apollon* from autumn 1909 onwards, were already a time-honoured tradition. The 'Poets' Guild' now rapidly became a new centre for the younger poets. Its meetings took place at the house occupied by Gumilyov and Akhmatova in Tsarskoye Selo. Mandelstam attended for the first time on 2 December 1911, and he was very soon 'the first violinist' at them, according to Akhmatova.

The time was ripe for a new grouping of young poets. But the Symbolists regarded them as ungrateful sons. On 13 April 1911, a fierce dispute arose in Ivanov's 'Tower' over Gumilyov's poem 'The Lost Son', because the host sharply rejected the 'unbiblical' associations of the text. A year later, on 18 February 1912, the matter came to a head. After hearing lectures by Vyacheslav Ivanov and Andrei Bely on the nature of Symbolism, Gumilyov and Gorodetsky came out in open opposition. The limit had been reached: their exit from the 'Tower' could no longer be prevented. On 1 March 1912, at a meeting of the Poets' Guild, Gumilyov proclaimed the founding of *Acmeism*. The name was derived from the Greek word *acme*, meaning the highest point, the flowering, the maturity. The goal was to overcome Russian Symbolism's preoccupation with the hereafter, its religious speculations (theosophy, occultism), its tendency to think in vague symbols and analogies.[3]

On 19 December 1912, in the Petersburg artists' tavern the 'Stray Dog', Gumilyov and Gorodetsky proclaimed their Acmeist manifestos. Both were published at the start of 1913 in the literary journal *Apollon* (no. 1). In his manifesto, entitled 'The Inheritance of Symbolism and Acmeism', Gumilyov wrote that Symbolism, with its 'dissolution of all images and things', could only have originated 'in the misty darkness of the Germanic forests'. But the Romance spirit of Acmeism loved 'the element of light, which separates objects off, and allows everything to be seen in clear outline'. Against the mystical and ecstatic attitude of the Symbolists he set the 'bright irony' of the Romance. Acmeism would say farewell to the Symbolist endeavour to know the hidden and the otherworldly. The Acmeists, he added, insist on the 'unknowability of the unknowable': 'What the unknown brings forth in us is an almost painfully sweet feeling, a childlike understanding, of our own lack of knowledge.' In his Heidelberg poem 'There Is No Need for Speech' (December 1909), Mandelstam had advocated a withdrawal into the 'dark' and 'beast-like' soul. This was now confirmed in Gumilyov's manifesto: 'As Adamists we are rather like forest beasts.'

Acmeism or Adamism? The poet Mikhail Kuzmin described his younger colleagues as 'Adamists'. He had prepared the way for them with his article 'On Beautiful Clarity' in the journal *Apollon* (no. 4, 1910). Gumilyov oscillated between the two designations, but he was happy to adopt the title 'Adamism', which he imbued with his own conception of 'manfulness' in ethics and poetry: for him, Adamism signified 'a manfully firm and clear vision of life'. He had in mind an artist who sees the world for the first time, like Adam, and gives objects new names. But the word 'Adamist' soon went out of use, whereas 'Acmeism' survived. In fact, the 'Adamist' notion of starting again from scratch did not correspond with the sense of tradition, '*maturity*' and 'flowering' incorporated in the name 'Acmeist'.

Gumilyov named four 'cornerstones of the Acmeist edifice', by which he meant the founding fathers or forerunners of the new poets, who explicitly locate themselves within a tradition. Shakespeare had shown them the inner world of human beings, Rabelais the physical body and its joys, Villon had revealed a life which 'has never doubted itself in the least, although it knows everything, God and depravity, death and immortality'.

3 The 'Poets' Guild' and 'Acmeism': O. Lekmanov, *Kniga ob Akmeizme*, 9–184.

Finally, Théophile Gautier had found 'the worthy garment of immaculate forms' for this life in his poetry.

The other manifesto, by Gorodetsky, referred to the 'catastrophe of Symbolism' and stressed the Acmeists' commitment to this earth, to the here and now: 'a struggle for *this* world, the resounding, colourful earth, which has forms, weight and time for our planet … The world is irrevocably accepted by Acmeism, in the totality of its beauty and ugliness.' Russian Symbolism was a profoundly pessimistic current, he added, which rejected the world as a diabolical nightmare in the manner of Schopenhauer. A typical Symbolist poem was Fyodor Sologub's 'Devil's Swing' of 1907. The Acmeists' new affirmation of the world signified that Russian poetry had regained its vitality.[4]

And what of Mandelstam? In the autumn of 1912, after initially hesitating, he joined the Acmeist group, which 'officially' consisted of only six people. Alongside the renowned troika of Gumilyov, Akhmatova and Mandelstam, it included Mikhail Zenkevich, Vladimir Narbut and Sergei Gorodetsky. Mandelstam also wrote a manifesto, 'The Morning of Acmeism', which was probably produced in May 1913 in association with the texts by Gumilyov and Gorodetsky but was not printed until 1919. He too called for the affirmation of life and the world, as an answer to the negative attitude of the Symbolists:

> The artist's greatest pride is to exist. He desires no other paradise than existence … Love the existence of the thing more than the thing itself and your own existence more than yourself: that is the highest commandment of Acmeism. (GP, 17, 21; AM, 47, 51)

Stimulated by Gumilyov's masonic metaphors (such as the 'cornerstones of the Acmeist edifice'), Mandelstam too stresses the 'spirit of building' and the 'fight against emptiness':

> The sharp edge of Acmeism is not the stiletto nor the sting of Decadence. Acmeism is for those who, seized with the spirit of building, do not cravenly refuse to bear its heavy weight, but joyously accept it, in order to awaken and use the forces architecturally sleeping in it … To build

4 The Acmeist manifestos of Gumilyov and Gorodetsky: T. Bek (ed.), *Antologiia Akmeizma*, 199–207.

> means to fight against emptiness, to hypnotize space. The fine arrow of the Gothic belltower is angry, because the whole sense of it is to stab heaven, to reproach it with its emptiness. (GP, 18, 20; AM, 49)

For Mandelstam, the exemplar of the triumph over space is the Gothic cathedral. In his 1912 poem 'Notre Dame' – note the audacity of a twenty-year-old – he literally combines his poetic programme with the masterpiece of Gothic architecture which had impressed him so much in Paris a few years earlier:

> Stronghold of Notre Dame, the more my attentive eyes
> Studied your gigantic ribs and frame
> Then the more often this reflection came:
> From cruel weight, I too will someday make beauty rise.
> (ST, 85; OS, 121)

Notre Dame (both building and poem) is the space already conquered, the awakened stone (awakened word), a testimony to shaping intelligence, sensuous abundance, the affirmation of life and the triumph of the human being, whether artisan, architect or poet. The fear of emptiness is overcome by the act of building.[5]

Mandelstam's first genuinely Acmeist poem, written in 1912, was seen by Nikolai Gumilyov as marking the actual 'turning point' in his poetic progress. It proclaims his rejection of the Symbolists' 'otherworldly' themes, their twinkling stars and hazy moonlight:

> No, not the moon, but the bright face of a clock
> Shines for me, and how can I be blamed
> If I sense the milkiness of faint stars?
> (ST, 69; AT, 12)

The poem is an affirmation of the here and now, of contemporaneity (the face of a clock!). A revolt against 'eternity' can be perceived in many of his early poems. It is already there in 'Do Not Talk to Me of Eternity', written in 1909 at Heidelberg (ST, 179) or 'A Snow Hive Cleaner than the Air', written in 1910:

5 The cult of architecture: R. Dutli, *Ossip Mandelstam*, 249–57.

And though ice diamonds glide
In the eternally frozen stream,
Here flickering dragonflies gleam,
Alive but an hour, blue-eyed.
(ST, 31; OS, 69)

Gumilyov had emphasised the inherent value of every manifestation ('All phenomena are brothers'). In his manifesto, Mandelstam proclaimed the 'law of identity', linking it with the 'ability to feel surprise' over the richness of existence:

> The ability to feel surprise is the poet's greatest virtue. But how then is one not to be surprised by that most fruitful of all laws, the law of identity? … Having thus acknowledged the sovereignty of the law of identity, poetry receives, without condition or limitation, life-long feudal possession of all existence. (GP, 21–2; AM, 50)

The 'law of identity' was a reproach to the Symbolists, who had wasted their time in looking for symbols and analogies. Ten years after the manifestos had been issued, Mandelstam continued his polemic against the Symbolists in the essay 'On the Nature of the Word' (1922):

> This is where professional Symbolism is headed. The power of perception has been demoralized. Nothing is real or authentic. The terrible contredanses of 'correspondences' [[author's note: Baudelaire's 'Correspondances']] all nodding to each other. Eternal winking. Not a single clear word, only hints and implications. The rose nods at the girl, the girl at the rose. Nobody wants to be himself … Acmeism arose out of repulsion: 'Away with Symbolism, long live the living rose!' (GP, 125, 128; SE, 92, 94)

The programme of Acmeism can be distilled from these three manifestos. It called for a return to the terrestrial, the organic and the concrete, a return to the spatially present three-dimensional object. It took its stand on artistic precision and craftsmanship, on the law of identity, on contemporaneity, on 'Apollonian clarity' and 'Romance irony'. And, not least, it advocated a positive attitude to the present world, as the only one accessible to humans and poets. Acmeism did not see itself as a world view but as a 'conspiracy' of a particular type. As Mandelstam wrote in his manifesto: 'There is no equality, no competition – there is the complicity of those united in a conspiracy against emptiness and non-existence.' The three leading Acmeists, Mandelstam, Akhmatova and Gumilyov, were the sworn conspirators referred to here. They were joined together in a lifelong 'three-way conversation' which was never broken off.

This complicity also gave rise to an attitude of wholesome modesty towards the calling of a poet, whom the Acmeists thought should have the ethos of a master craftsman. For the Symbolists the poet had been an ecstatic prophet, a high priest, a herald of extraterrestrial worlds. Mandelstam was strongly averse to the idea that the poet was an 'oracle', which was cultivated by the Symbolists, the 'great seducers' as Nadezhda Mandelstam called them, who met in the 'Tower', Vyacheslav Ivanov's Petersburg apartment.[6] He felt closer to Innokenty Annensky, the quiet Symbolist, classical philologist and translator of Euripides, who was also chosen as the posthumous teacher of Acmeism by Gumilyov and Akhmatova.

Mandelstam's abandonment of the bombast of 'symbols', and his expulsion from Ivanov's consecrated 'Tower', led him to confront reality face to face, in a sober manner. In 1912, the founding year of Acmeism, he observed a Protestant funeral in Petersburg. This inspired him to write the poem 'A Lutheran'. Its final stanza has the ring of a 'Protestant-Acmeist' manifesto:

> No need, I thought, for a flowery oration.
> We are not prophets nor do we prepare the way;
> We do not love heaven, do not fear damnation,
> And we burn without light, like candles at midday.
> (ST, 81)

Mandelstam's rejection of Symbolism's excessive concern with other worlds did not signify his abandonment of all metaphysics. He was only seeking the 'living equilibrium' (GP, 22) between rationality and mysticism, between 'the celebration of physiology' and 'metaphysical proof' (GP, 19–20; AM, 48, 50).

The Symbolists reacted with irritation to their rebellious offspring, who owed so much to them and failed to show any gratitude (even if Gumilyov

6 M. averse to the idea of the poet as an 'oracle': N. Mandelstam, *Hope Abandoned*, 44.

did invoke the 'inheritance' of Symbolism in his manifesto). As late as 1921, it was still possible to sense the disapproval and rancour in Alexander Blok's polemical essay 'Without Divinity, without Inspiration'.[7] The expressions used by Blok in condemning the Acmeists as ungrateful sons were one source of the attacks made upon them under the Soviet regime.

In their rejection of Symbolism, the Acmeists consciously relied on representatives of the world literary tradition as their predecessors and allies. But they were also faced with vociferous competitors who gave the impression of being far more radical. The Cubo-Futurists (David Burliuk, Velimir Khlebnikov, Alexei Kruchonykh and Vladimir Mayakovsky) cultivated a spirit of cultural revolution. They advocated starting again from the very beginning, and throwing the whole of traditional literature off the 'ship of modernity'. In their manifesto, issued in December 1912 under the title 'A Slap in the Face of Public Taste', they stated their claim to exclusive possession of literature: 'WE alone are the face of our time. Through us the horn of time blows in the art of the word … Throw Pushkin, Dostoevsky, Tolstoy etc. etc. off the "ship of modernity".'[8]

Mandelstam's manifesto 'The Morning of Acmeism' was directed against both opponents. In it, he attacked the Futurists as well as the Symbolists:

> For the Acmeists the conscious sense of the word, the Logos, is just as splendid a form as is music for the Symbolists.
>
> And if for the Futurists the word as such is still creeping on all fours, in Acmeism it has for the first time assumed a more adequate vertical position and has entered upon the stone age of its existence. (GP, 18; AM, 48)

'The Word as Such' was the title of the Futurist manifesto of April 1913, signed by Alexei Kruchonykh and Velimir Khlebnikov, which called for genuine word art. Their aim was to create what they called '*zaum*', a 'meta-logical' or 'trans-mental' language of sounds, liberated from the requirement to have meaning. Mandelstam countered this 'meta-logical' language, which 'crept on all fours', with the 'vertical' meaning represented by the *Logos*.

7 Blok's condemnation of the Acmeists in 1921 ('Without Divinity, without Inspiration'): Bek (ed.), *Antologiia Akmeizma*, 242–9.

8 The Futurist manifesto, 'A Slap in the Face of Public Taste' (1912). In German in V. Khlebnikov, *Werke 2 (Prosa)*, 107.

In March 1912 – exactly at the time when Acmeism was founded – Anna Akhmatova issued her first work, the book of poems entitled *Evening*. Mandelstam had so far published only a few poems in literary journals, but by the end of March 1913 he was able to follow suit: his first volume of poetry, *Stone*, was issued by the 'Acme' publishing house. It was a small green booklet, containing just twenty-three poems written between 1909 and 1913. The edition of 500 copies had to be financed and distributed by the author himself. Mandelstam's father provided the money. His brother Yevgeny remembers how he went with Osip to the printing works on Mokhovaia Street to collect all the copies. The two young men carried the freshly printed booklets to the Popov bookshop located at 66 Nevsky Prospekt, which had accepted them on commission. Osip sent his younger brother to the shop from time to time to find out how many copies had already been sold. When the figure reached forty-two, there were celebrations in the Mandelstam household.[9]

In 'Pages from a Diary', Anna Akhmatova recalls Mandelstam's first book:

> That was my first Mandelstam. The author of the green *Stone* (published by Acme) gave me a copy with the inscription: 'To Anna Akhmatova – flashes of consciousness in the forgetfulness of days. Respectfully, the Author.' With his peculiarly charming self-irony, Osip liked to tell the story of how an old Jew, the owner of the print shop where *Stone* was printed, congratulated him on the book's publication, shook his hand, and said 'Your writing will only get better and better, young man.'[10]

The title of this slender and self-confident initial offering was itself a programme of action. The Russian word *Kamen* (Stone) was an anagram of the group's name, *Akme*. According to Mandelstam's manifesto 'The Morning of Acmeism', 'the stone was the word', and the poet was the architect who builds with words, 'fights against emptiness' and 'hypnotises space' (GP, 20; AM, 49). The echoes of the first book reverberate in the architectural poems of 1912 – 'Hagia Sophia' and 'Notre Dame'. When

9 Yevgeny Mandelstam's memories of the way *Stone* was published: E. Mandel'shtam, 'Vospominaniia', 136.

10 Anna Akhmatova's memories of Mandelstam's first book: Akhmatova, *My Half Century*, 76–7.

he reviewed *Stone*, Gumilyov wrote: 'Mandelstam is as fond of buildings as other poets are of mountains or the sea.'

Although the small volume had an apparently unspectacular start in life, it did cause Mandelstam's fellow poets to sit up and take notice. The fact that the book was reviewed by the Acmeists Narbut, Gorodetsky and Gumilyov could be seen as a favour done by his colleagues; but the Futurist Vladimir Mayakovsky, who had also made his debut in 1913 with a book entitled simply *I*, paid close attention to the author of the little green book, and he soon knew many of its poems by heart. And, later still, when Mandelstam and Mayakovsky had gone in completely different directions, the 'drummer of the revolution' continued to treat the outsider Mandelstam with respect. On one occasion, as we know from Valentin Kataev's autobiographical novel *The Grass of Oblivion* (1963), Mandelstam's 1917 poem 'The Decembrist', which ends with the famous line 'Russia, Lethe, Lorelei' (TR, 37), was recited with great enthusiasm by Mayakovsky, who exclaimed afterwards: 'A work of genius!'

Notwithstanding his polemical attacks on the Futurists, Mandelstam was very attracted between 1912 and 1915 to the vehemence of their avant-garde.[11] The Futurist Benedict Livshits was one of his closest friends from the end of 1913. Several different critics commented on Mandelstam's closeness to Futurism, and his fellow poet Anna Akhmatova even feared that he might later come to be classified as a Futurist. A poet of any stature would in any case be bound to break out of the narrow framework of the words of a manifesto and the doctrines of a *school*. In *Stone*, Mandelstam created an original amalgam of Symbolism, Acmeism and Futurism. It was an early work which displayed a sovereign independence. Even so, he was by no means a lone wolf. For the whole of his life, he drew on the sense of being part of a 'We' which he shared with the Acmeists of 1912–1913.[12]

1913 was the year of the modernist explosion. It was a time of experiments and discoveries, a period of artistic fever. It was the year of the Russian avant-garde *par excellence*. As Roman Jakobson recalls: 'It was an unusual epoch with an extraordinarily large number of very talented

11 The early Mandelstam and Mayakovsky: A. Parnis, 'Shtrikhi k futuristicheskomu portretu', 186. M.'s closeness to the Futurists: Parnis, 'Shtrikhi'; J.-C. Lanne, 'Mandel'shtam I futurizm'.

12 The 'We' feeling of the Acmeists: the chapter 'We' in Mandelstam, *Hope Abandoned*, 39–40.

people. And it was a time when the young suddenly started to set the tone. We did not feel that we were beginners.'[13] Mandelstam too had a part in this transformation. He freely included the phenomena of modern life in his poetic universe: silent films (ST, 105), tennis and football (ST, 109, 187) and modern tourism (ST, 111). This was a modernity Mandelstam shared with Burliuk and Mayakovsky, along with the smell of petrol, the sound of motor horns and the sight of skyscrapers.

> It is May. Scraps of black cloud
> Cast a blight upon everything green,
> Motors everywhere, horns too loud,
> Lilacs reeking of gasoline.
> ('Tennis': ST, 109; OS, 147)

> In America factory whistles hoot
> And red skyscraper stacks
> Offer cold clouds a salute
> With lips that are smoked black.
> ('American Girl': ST, 111; OS, 149)

What was modern in Mandelstam was not so much the emergence of new subjects – the Futurists too had quickly included them in their repertoire – as the co-existence and 'living equilibrium' between solemnity and vulgarity, pathos and irony, cultural memory and sensory perception, the historically significant and the quaintly commonplace.

He had outgrown Symbolism, and the newly won freedom was immense and enticing. In Mandelstam, the last echoes of Symbolism accompany cheeky excursions into bars and taverns ('Golden Coin' and 'American Bar') and lofty sacred buildings ('Notre Dame' and 'Hagia Sophia'), and references to the divinities of musical history ('Bach' and 'Ode to Beethoven'), as well as the above-mentioned phenomena of modernity: the honking of motor horns, the smell of petrol, moving pictures and cocktails, tennis and tourism. A memory of Giorgione's painting *Judith and Holofernes*, which he had seen in the Hermitage Museum, Petersburg, suddenly flares up in Mandelstam's poem 'Football'. Modern mass sport and an exquisite biblically inspired Renaissance work – brought together in one place!

---

13 The year 1913 as the threshold of the modernist epoch: R. Jakobson, *Meine futuristischen Jahre*, 38; F. P. Ingold, *Der grosse Bruch*.

The daily life of the city, with its inconspicuous cast – doorkeepers, domestic servants, coachmen and people simply walking around – plays a part in a variety of poems, from the 'Petersburg Strophes' (1913) onwards. Ovid, having been exiled to the shores of the Black Sea, meets a yawning Petersburg doorkeeper, who reminds him of a Scythian. And, just as Ovid 'mixed Rome and snow in his song' (ST, 129), so Mandelstam unites the Eternal City with that endlessly non-eternal, light, transient and rapidly melting substance. There is a hymn to 'divine ice' almost next door to the 'Ode to Beethoven'. And by 'ice' he means ice for eating, ice cream.

Mandelstam was an urban poet, but in 1913 the big city was no more interesting to him than the *stele* on which an ancient Egyptian dignitary records his successes and depicts the joys of the next world in a very Acmeist fashion, relating them to the here and now ('An Egyptian'):

> And expecting the gleam of happiness
> I danced a refined and elegant
> Dance in the king's presence
> And not for nothing.
> (ST, 183; BT, 99/101; CP, 160)

Mandelstam's early pleasure in the world, an erotic feeling he transferred to individuals ('And I envy everybody discreetly / And discreetly love them all': ST, 39), fitted in well with Acmeist theories. He vigorously expressed the Acmeist respect for the 'inherent value of every manifestation'. For Mandelstam, Acmeism was also a way of life. It aimed to bring the whole of art into life, into the everyday, and to mould mere existence into a work of art.

The Symbolism of the 'Tower' now lay in the past. In this new era, the young poets held their poetry readings and disputations in artists' taverns, such as the 'Stray Dog' on 5 Mikhailovsky Square (these days called 'Artists' Square'), owned by Boris Pronin. A Bohemian culture grew up here, a culture in which the artists interacted, quarrelled and made friends again. Mandelstam's humorous verses and epigrams are intimately linked with the atmosphere that prevailed in the 'Stray Dog' just before the First World War.[14] This curious hothouse gave birth to an 'Anthology of Ancient Nonsense', lovingly produced by Mandelstam and others, along

14 Memories of the artists' tavern 'The Stray Dog': Akhmatova, *My Half Century*, 88; V. Shklovsky, *Kindheit und Jugend*, 106.

with sheer nonsense such as the four-liner referring to the ego-Futurist Igor Severyanin: 'A cow calmly eats its hay, / But the duchess eats gelée – / And almost at midday / The count goes mad in the chalet!' (BT, 93, 117).

This artists' pub had its own celebrations and burlesque rituals, and it stayed open until the early hours. It opened its doors around midnight, when the actors burst in after they had finished performing. The painter Sergei Sudeikin had decorated the ceiling of this Bohemian temple using themes taken from Baudelaire's *Fleurs du Mal*. The entrance was garnished with a 'Pig Book' bound in blue leather, in which the artists wrote their names and those of their guests, who were described as 'Pharmacists'. If they turned out to be generous, they were immediately promoted to 'Maecenases'.

Even a decade later, Mandelstam was still able to give a vivid picture of the 'Stray Dog' as part of his portrait of the 'Grotesque' Theatre at Rostov on Don (1922):

> What a place that was! What days they were! You climbed up from the coffin-sized cellar, with its feverishly hot, cramped atmosphere, electrified merely by the jokes, as noisy as a beehive, where people raged and bellowed but always remained orderly and self-controlled, to the hallway above, buried under fur coats and stoles, said your goodbyes, and then out onto Mikhail Square, and into the frosty night. You look up at the sky and the stars themselves seem dubious: they deliver quips, make biting remarks, and twinkle at you.
>
> And even the frosty air brings no refreshment, nor do the stars soothe. The snow crunches under the light runners of a hired sledge, the final flashes of Petersburg humour chase each other in the falling snow like 'demons invisible in moonlight', the nonsense of the last sketch dissolves into the rubbish of the snow, and the cold breath of the last joke, which has entered your blood 'like a cube of ice into champagne', will cool it down and turn it to ice, until it freezes hard.
>
> ... This public, once it was in the know, experienced the joke-culture, the university of ridicule, the academy of exquisite nonsense ... Genuine participants in this mysterious game of absolute nonsense could only be people who had 'gone to the edge', who had something to lose and who were driven towards this breath-taking 'nonsense-creation' by their inner desolation, by their premonition of the end. (GP, 106–8)

Mandelstam, who had already started to have his doubts about this way of life, reflected on the relaxed impudence and joyfulness of the atmosphere on the eve of tragic events in a poem written in 1913:

> We went insane from living indulgently.
> Wine before noon, by evening a heavy head.
> How can we sustain your feverish red,
> O drunken plague, and your vain revelry?
> (ST, 115; OS, 131)

The Futurists also frequented the 'Stray Dog'. Anna Akhmatova recalls that Mandelstam introduced Vladimir Mayakovsky to her there. Everyone was eating loudly, and the crockery was rattling, when Mayakovsky took it into his head to recite poetry. But Mandelstam went over to him and said: 'Mayakovsky, stop reciting poems. You're not a Roma orchestra.'

There was also jealousy in this beehive. As Viktor Shklovsky reports: 'People knew the value of a verse in that cellar. A successful line by Mandelstam aroused envy, admiration, and hatred.' It was normal for Acmeists and Futurists to needle one another – it fitted in with the culture of sharp-tongued polemic which was encouraged in this Bohemian milieu. On just one occasion, on 27 November 1913, an angry clash took place between Mandelstam and Velimir Khlebnikov, a brilliant 'eccentric of the purest water' (Roman Jakobson), the most important figure among the Cubo-Futurists. It is significant that the quarrel did not arise from a verbal dispute between Futurists and Acmeists but from a matter which was bound to affect Mandelstam deeply: the Beilis Affair, which according to chapter six of the memoirs of Benedict Livshits, *The One and a Half-Eyed Archer*, deeply stirred the emotions of contemporary poets as well as splitting Russian society into two camps.

The trial of Mendel Beilis, a Jew from Kyiv (formerly Kiev), who was accused in March 1911 of the ritual murder of a Christian boy, Andrei Yushchinsky, was instigated by anti-Semites. It was a painful revelation that the age-old, stereotypical myth about ritual murder by Jews had not been completely dispelled in modern Russia. The Beilis trial was a Russian Dreyfus case, and a range of prominent authors intervened in it. The eccentric conservative philosopher Vasily Rozanov exercised his journalistic talents between 1911 and 1913 in anti-Semitic agitation, while the short-story writer and journalist Vladimir Korolenko pleaded for Beilis's innocence and vigorously countered the slanderous clichés of the Russian anti-Semites. In the Beilis Affair, Korolenko showed himself to be an advocate of the calibre of Émile Zola, the French novelist who had intervened in the Dreyfus Affair in 1898 with his article 'J'accuse'.

Beilis was finally found not guilty in October 1913. On 27 November, in the 'Stray Dog', Khlebnikov recited a poem against Beilis, laced with anti-Jewish invective and curses. Mandelstam was very upset, and he challenged Khlebnikov to a duel. It was a hot-headed reaction. Duels had long been rejected and prohibited in Russia, but the challenge showed the extent of Mandelstam's fury: 'I feel insulted as a Jew and as a Russian and I challenge you to a duel. That was a vile thing to have said.' Reading this comment, it is impossible not to recognise that Mandelstam had a sense of attachment to Judaism, notwithstanding any temporary separation.

Viktor Shklovsky reports that both parties chose him as their second. It was suggested that the avant-garde artist Pavel Filonov should be the other second, but the voice of reason spoke in his reply: he refused, he said, to put the life of a poet at risk in an idiotic conflict. There is a deplorable tradition of death by duel in Russian literary history: Alexander Pushkin and Mikhail Lermontov both died far too soon in this manner. Mandelstam and Khlebnikov were reconciled by their seconds Shklovsky and Filonov.[15]

Mandelstam was not one to bear a grudge. His remarks in his 1922–1923 essays on the language experimenter and visionary Khlebnikov contain some of the most acute comments that could be made about the work of a man who was so different from him. This conflict with a poet he very much respected and admired was a painful test. His sorrow over what had taken place can be seen from a poem written in December 1913. In the first stanza he recalls the biblical figure of Joseph, the son of the patriarch Jacob, who was sold into Egypt by his brothers (Genesis, chapters 37 to 50). One must bear in mind that Osip is a Russified form of the biblical name Joseph.

15 The Beilis Affair: Livshits, *The One and a Half-Eyed Archer*, 437–9; Ingold, *Der grosse Bruch*, 41; R. Lauer, *Geschichte der russischen Literatur*, 438. M.'s quarrel with Khlebnikov: G. Amelin and V. Morderer, *Miry i Stolknoveniia*, 39–44; the two are reconciled by Filonov and Shklovsky: O. S. Figurnova and M. V. Figurnova, *Osip i Nadezhda Mandel'shtamy*, 47–8.

The bread is poisoned and the air's drunk dry
How difficult to doctor wounds!
Joseph sold into Egypt
Could not have grieved so much for home!
(ST, 117; FP, 36)

Osip, the brother who had been sold, had just experienced a moment of great loneliness in the bustling crowd of Petersburg Bohemians. A fellow poet had reminded him of his Jewishness with his contemptuous utterances. But the poem about incurable wounds and the bitterness of the present also evokes the poetry of the Bedouin, 'liberation through song', solace and self-healing through genuine poetry, and ultimate triumph:

And if a song's properly sung
With a full heart, then at last
All disappears; there remain
Just the singer, space and the stars!
(ST, 117; FP, 36)

7

Rome and Inner Freedom

(Petrograd and Koktebel 1914–1915)

In depicting the debates between Symbolists, Acmeists and Futurists and the activities of the Petersburg Bohemians, we have almost lost sight of Mandelstam's life as a student. After his Christian baptism in Finland in May 1911, there was no longer any obstacle to his entering the University of St Petersburg. On 10 September 1911, he enrolled in the Romance Language Department of the university's Faculty of History and Philology. As a student of Romance Languages, he was obliged to take an examination in Ancient Greek at the end of the first year, because the Tenishev School, with its concentration on natural science and business, had not offered a course in that language. During the summer of 1912, therefore, Mandelstam took Greek lessons from a fellow student. His name was Constantine Mochulsky, and he emigrated from Russia after the revolution. In 1945, having heard of Mandelstam's death in a labour camp, he published his memories about the poet in a Paris journal.[1] They throw a vivid light on both the rather unenthusiastic student Mandelstam and the inspired young poet of the same name:

1 M. takes Greek lessons and reads Homer: C. Mochulsky's 1945 article, reproduced in O. Lekmanov, *Mandel'shtam i Antichnost'*, 7–8.

> He would be monstrously late for our lessons and completely shaken by the secrets of Greek grammar that had been revealed to him. He would wave his hands, run about the room and declaim the declensions and conjugations in a sing-song voice. The reading of Homer was transformed into a fabulous event; adverbs, enclitics and pronouns hounded him in his sleep, and he entered into enigmatic personal relationships with them. When I informed him that the past participle of the verb *paideuo* 'to educate' was *pepaideukos*, he gasped with pleasure and was unable to study any more that day. He arrived at the next lesson with a guilty smile and said, 'I haven't prepared anything, but I've written a poem.' And without taking off his overcoat, he began to recite. I remember two stanzas:
>
> 'And the bell of the verbal desinences
> Shows me the way in the distance
> So that in the modest philologist's cell
> I might have respite from my griefs.
>
> Burdens and misfortunes are forgotten
> And the question that haunts me is:
> Does the aorist take the augment,
> And which voice is pepaideukos?'
> (BT, 91)
>
> He transformed grammar into poetry and declared that the more incomprehensible Homer was, the more beautiful. I was very afraid that he would flunk the exam, but fate saved him again, and by some miracle he withstood the test.[2]

Even so, he went on to fail an examination in Latin literature (including Catullus and Tibullus) held on 29 September 1915. This seems an exquisite irony of fate, when one bears in mind how skilfully he interwove the ancient authors, whether they were Romans like Catullus, Tibullus and Ovid or Greeks like Homer, Pindar, Alcaeus and Sappho, into the poems of his collections *Stone* (1916, 1923) and *Tristia* (1922). Mandelstam's reading of Homer is repeatedly echoed in his poetry.[3]

---

2 C. Brown, *Mandelstam*, 47.

3 Homer in M.'s poems: 'Orioles are in the woods, and vowels' length' (1914) and

Even the playful epigrams in the 'Anthology of Ancient Nonsense', which Mandelstam claimed in 1912 in the 'Stray Dog' were verses by a Roman poet called Ancus Stultitius (from the Latin *stultus* = stupid), demonstrate a familiarity with the classical epigram, in a parodied and distorted form: 'Delia, where have you been? Asleep in the arms of Morpheus / Woman, you're lying: I've been asleep there myself!' Or: 'Two lovers admire a gigantic star by night / But they realise in the morning: it was just the moon' (BT, 93, 119).

Only as a poet could Mandelstam come to terms with literature, both ancient and modern. He could not always do what was required of students. His approach to foreign literature was intuitive and transformative, never academic. His real 'university studies' were pursued in the Poets' Guild, where philology (the love of words) was much admired. But the two spheres did overlap occasionally. In his essay 'About the Nature of the Word' (1922), Mandelstam calls up the vision of an ideal university conducted 'in a small group', and later, in the angry *Fourth Prose* (1929–1930), he refers to a militant 'philology' emerging from such a group:

> Literature is a social phenomenon, philology is a domestic phenomenon, of the study. Literature is a public lecture, the street; philology is a university seminar, the family … Philology: it is a family because every family sustains itself by intonation and by citation, by quotation marks. In a family, the most lazily spoken word has its special standing. And an infinite, unique, purely philological literary nuancing forms the background of family life. (GP, 119; SE, 88)

> Think how beautiful Mother Philology once was, and how she looks today … How pure-blooded, how uncompromising she was then, but how mongrelized and tame she is today. (RZ, 261; MN, 318–19)

He was failing as a student, and he was soon to break off his studies entirely; but he was already a well-known poet. 1913 was also his first year as an essayist. The essay 'About the Interlocutor' appeared in number 2 of the journal *Apollon*. It already puts forward the conception of a

---

'Insomnia, Homer, the Sails – Stretched Out' (1915) – ST, 133 and 169; 'Out of the bottle the stream of golden honey poured so slowly' (1917) – TR, 39–41; EW, 53 – which concludes: 'And leaving his ship, canvas worn out on the seas, / Odysseus came back, filled with time and space.'

dialogue with the reader, so essential in Mandelstam's view. The reader is the 'providential interlocutor' of the future, the 'secret addressee' of a poetic 'message in a bottle' tossed into the sea: 'The letter in the bottle was addressed to its finder. I found it. That means, then, that I am its secret addressee' (GP, 9; SE, 77). Here speaks a poet who already seems to foresee that he will meet with little understanding from his contemporaries, and who therefore catapults his poetry into the future.

A sense of certainty, a conviction that he is 'in the right' as a poet, pervades even this first essay: 'For poetry is the consciousness of one's rightness' (GP, 10; SE, 78). This attitude of mind prefigures the 'moral strength' of Acmeism, claimed by Mandelstam in his 1922 essay 'On the Nature of the Word'. It was a distinctive feature of the attitude of the three most significant Acmeists – Mandelstam, Akhmatova and Gumilyov – towards totalitarian power. They would, of course, have to pay dearly for their radical 'consciousness of their own rightness'. For them, the pitiless cruelty of the future would have little in common with the fantasies of the Futurists.

'Inner freedom' was another core aspiration of the young Mandelstam. This was something he owed to a certain nineteenth-century Russian philosopher. In the boisterous and superficial environment of Petersburg bohemianism, his liberation from Symbolism, his recently achieved thematic, stylistic and philosophical freedom, was in danger of becoming flat and insipid. He sought to give this freedom a new meaning. In this new mood, he happened to come across the *Works and Letters* of the philosopher Piotr Chaadaev (1794–1856), which had just been edited by Mikhail Gershenzon (in 1913–1914).

Chaadaev was one of the most controversial Russian thinkers. He was Russia's first ardent 'Westerniser'; he was fascinated by Europe, Roman Catholicism and the papacy. His thesis that Byzantine Russian Orthodoxy offered a 'distorted idea' of Christianity, which was responsible for Russia's lack of history and culture, was viewed by many as treasonable, but it had a tremendously catalytic effect, as it set off the long dispute between 'Westernisers' and 'Slavophiles' over Russia's relationship with Europe. When in 1836 Chaadaev's 'First Philosophical Letter' came out, the author was battered by a wave of furious indignation. The Tsar declared him to be of unsound mind, and sentenced him to one and a half years' house arrest. On 19 October 1836, Alexander Pushkin wrote a famous letter replying to Chaadaev about Russia's historical role. In it, he argued that Europe had only been able to prosper because Russia had beaten off the Mongol invasion. Chaadaev's rejoinder, the *Apology of a Madman*, came out a year later. He continued to maintain that the West was culturally superior, but he softened his negative view of Orthodoxy, and he recognised that Russia too would have a special historical mission in the future. Mandelstam, now burning with enthusiasm for Chaadaev's ideas, wrote an essay on him in 1914–1915, which was printed in the journal *Apollon* (nos 6–7, 1915). It was a strongly positive appreciation of the prominent 'Westerniser'. Mandelstam emphasises Chaadaev's 'return to Russia' as a proof of his 'inner freedom' – but, in his love for Russia, he fails to mention the infamous repression suffered by that unconventional thinker. Chaadaev would be a formative influence on the young poet. Anyone seeking to find out why Mandelstam remained in Russia rather than emigrating after the Bolsheviks had carried out the October Revolution, even though he had 'lived in the West' intellectually, would do well to bear in mind the following early confession of faith:

> Chaadaev's thought is Russian in its sources, and Russian even where it flows towards Rome. Only a Russian could have discovered a West which is denser, more concrete, than the historical West itself …
>
> For Chaadaev, there was only one gift that Russia had: moral freedom, the freedom of choice …
>
> I think that a country and a people have already justified themselves if they have created even one completely free man who wanted and knew how to use his freedom …
>
> Chaadaev was the first Russian who in actual fact, in his ideas, had lived in the West and found the road back …
>
> And how many of us have spiritually emigrated to the West! And how many among us live in unconscious duplicity, whose bodies are here, but whose spirits have remained there! …
>
> Having allotted us inner freedom, Russia presents us with a choice, and those who have made this choice are genuine Russian people wherever they may attach themselves. But woe unto those who, after having circled about close to their home nest, faintheartedly return! (GP, 59–61; SE, 120–1)

Chaadaev is the hero of Mandelstam's 1914 poem 'The Pilgrim's Staff' (ST, 151), which reads almost like an affirmation of his beliefs. It presents a cheerful pilgrim who has travelled to Rome, cast aside his 'domestic gloom', discovered his freedom and brought it back to Russia.

My staff, my freedom,
My being's core –
Will the people's truth soon become
A truth I can share?
(ST, 151; OS, 183)

Under Chaadaev's influence, Mandelstam now passed through what was in truth a 'Catholic phase'. A whole series of poems written between 1913 and 1915 demonstrates his fascination for the Rome of the papacy:

Let's talk of Rome – the marvellous city!
The dome's triumph has made her complete.
Let us hear the Apostles' Creed.
Rainbows hover and dust swirls by.
(ST, 123; OS, 157)

Mandelstam even imagines he is a monk, in the poem 'O the Coolness of the Catholic Tonsure!' But his dream of Rome and the West would soon come up against a harsh reality. On 1 August 1914 the German Empire declared war on Russia. Mandelstam reacted with the poem 'Europe', which tenderly evokes the misty outlines of the continent (ST, 145).[4]

Like a crab or starfish from the Mediterranean,
The sea washed up this continent, last of them all.
Grown used to America, to vast Asia's sprawl,
Ocean licks at Europe and begins to weaken.

Her living coastlines have been carved away,
Peninsulas sculptured to fragility;
Outlines of bays are almost womanly,
The slackened bow of Genoa, Biscay.
(ST, 145; OS, 181)

4 On the poem 'Europe': R. Dutli, *Europas zarte Hände*, 118–19.

But it was not just the map of Europe that changed. Shortly after the war broke out, in September 1914, Reims Cathedral was destroyed by German forces. Mandelstam reacted by writing his first anti-war poem: 'Reims and Cologne'. He links the Gothic architecture he had celebrated in 'Notre Dame' (1912) with a pacifist, European message. Thanks to the Gothic style, German Cologne had become a 'brother' to French Reims. His poem ends with this lament: 'What you have done to my brother in Reims!' This would not be Mandelstam's only anti-war poem.

He never allowed himself to be drawn into producing hymns of hate or jingoism of the kind practised at that time by a wide range of poets (including the Acmeist Gorodetsky). His commitment to Russia was of a more intimate nature. His desire to share Russia's fate right up to the bitter end is already evident in a poem written in 1913 (which was prohibited by the censorship from appearing in the second [1916] edition of *Stone*):

> Bells chime, shadows of emperors and kings …
> Oh Russia, on rock, on blood,
> Bless me with the burden, at least, of
> Sharing your final punishment!
> (ST, 191; CP, 155)

As early as 1914, therefore, when the peoples of Europe were starting out on their fratricidal war, Mandelstam became a European. His condemnation of nationalism is already inscribed in the essay on his model of freedom, Chaadaev: 'What a striking contrast to nationalism, to that beggary of the spirit which appeals incessantly to the monstrous tribunal of the crowd!' (GP, 60; SE, 121) The nationalism that was rampant everywhere is resolutely excluded from the sphere of poetry in an essay which was written in 1914 but remained a fragment. Its subject was André Chénier (1762–1794), the poet and martyr of the French Revolution, who rebelled against the outrageous executions of the time and was himself sent to the guillotine on 25 July 1794, just two days before the fall of Robespierre and the end of the Reign of Terror. Mandelstam identified himself with this poet, as had Alexander Pushkin before him. The essay on Chénier presents poetry as a utopia of fraternal understanding, a vision which doubtless bore the imprint of the military events of 1914.[5]

5 M. and André Chénier: Dutli, *Europas zarte Hände*, 145–71.

> Thus in poetry the boundaries of the national are destroyed, and the elements of one language exchange greetings with those of another over the heads of space and time, for all languages are linked by a fraternal bond, which rests firmly on the freedom and domesticity of each one, and within this freedom they are fraternally akin, and, each from his own home, they call out to each other. (GP, 51–2; SE, 127)

Mandelstam did not want to limit himself to writing poems and essays. He was exempt from military service because of his heart trouble, but he travelled to Warsaw on 22 December 1914 to volunteer as a hospital orderly. The enterprise was destined to end in a fiasco. His friend Sergei Kablukov wrote reproachfully in his diary on 25 December: 'Anyone who knows him will understand what a ridiculous and stupid plan this is.' Even so, neither Kablukov nor anyone else was able to prevent him from trying. By 5 January he was already back in Petersburg, which was now Petrograd, because it had had to abandon its inappropriately German-sounding name owing to the war with Germany.

The ultra-sensitive Mandelstam was found to be unfit to enter medical service. Was it because he was simply unable to stand the sight of the groaning and mutilated victims of the war? Kablukov reported on 26 January that he had telephoned Mandelstam, who told him that he had not lasted for more than two weeks in the hospital, that he had returned home ingloriously and that he had hidden his failure from everyone. After that, he never again spoke of his journey to Warsaw, although Anna Akhmatova notes in her 'Pages from a Diary' that he had been shocked by seeing the city's ghetto. The journey to Warsaw, his birthplace, reacquainted him with his Jewish origin. And it was his last trip westwards.[6]

The Warsaw fiasco showed once again that Mandelstam could only be a poet and nothing else. He was not cut out to be either a war hero or an angel of mercy ministering to the wounded. But as a poet he sought out new masks to wear in the early years of the war. First he imagined that he had been sold into Egypt as Joseph the Dreamer by his brothers. Then he slipped into the mask of Chaadaev as a pilgrim travelling to Rome. Out of whose mouth is he speaking? This mutual interpenetration of forms of consciousness is an important characteristic of Mandelstam's classical

6 The Warsaw fiasco as recorded in Kablukov's diary: O. Mandel'shtam, *Kamen'*, 249; M.'s reaction to seeing the ghetto: A. Akhmatova, *My Half Century*, 90.

modernity. Even in his earliest poetic creations, Homer and Socrates play star roles, alongside Edgar Allan Poe, Paul Verlaine, Charles Dickens, Macpherson's Ossian, Ovid, Racine, Euripides and many more. With a light touch, Mandelstam abolishes all national boundaries, and conjures up different times and places, different worlds. In the poem 'I Have Not Heard the Tales of Ossian' (1914) he sings:

I have received a blessed legacy –
A foreign poet left me his wandering dreams,
And we can freely choose to think scornfully
How dull our kindred and surroundings seem.

And this may not be the only precious thing
That skips over grandsons, passing to their sons,
And a skald reshapes once more another's song
And sings it as his own.
(ST, 143; OS, 179)

Mandelstam's self-identification with the exiled poet Ovid, who was banished in 8 C.E. by the Emperor Augustus to the Black Sea, 'the end of the world', was particularly momentous, because he was associating himself with a victim of political repression, with a symbol of exile, and he would repeatedly return to Ovid in his later poems.[7] This was a visionary anticipation of what would happen to him in the 1930s.

His enthusiasm for Rome, however, had its limits, which had already been reached in August 1914, when the war broke out. It is outweighed by the need for a renewal of humanism:

Let the names of flowering cities
Caress the ear with their brief time of fame.
It's not Rome the city that lives through the centuries
But man's place in the universal scheme.

Kings try to capture that, and priests attempt
To use it when they justify a war;
Lacking that, houses and altars deserve contempt

7 M.'s Ovid poems: Dutli, *Europas zarte Hände*, 7–25.

Like a wretched heap of rubbish, nothing more.
(ST, 141; OS, 177)

The 'Catholic phase' Mandelstam passed through under the inspiration of Chaadaev reflected a personal need; it was an important stage in his spiritual development towards 'inner freedom'. But this is a poet who cannot be pinned down to a particular set of religious beliefs. He was not fitted to be either a war hero or a preacher. Nevertheless, the spring of 1915 saw the creation of his most 'Christian' poem, dedicated to the Eucharist: 'There the ciborium, like a golden sun'. It was invoked as a movable feast, a moment 'outside of time', the 'eternal noon' in a sacred space and an overwhelming manifestation of abundance: 'To take into your hands the whole world, like a plain apple' (ST, 163; PM, 81).

Mandelstam never dissociated himself from any of the spiritual stages he passed through. Instead, he let them permeate and enrich one another. His true talent was the *freedom* with which he treated them, a 'wondrous freedom' which he invokes in a poetic prayer, also written in the spring of 1915:

Freedom is a wondrous marvel
Sweet to crave in candlelight
'Stay with me before you travel'
Cried Devotion in the night.

You are crowned by me alone
Hold your freedom in regard
As a law that's carved in stone
Heed it with a loving heart.

As a law that's carved in stone,
Freedom I betroth to wed.
That light crown will then alone
Always stay upon my head.[8]

The 'silent freedom' in one of the earliest poems (1908), the 'inner freedom' of the Chaadaev essay of 1914, the 'wondrous freedom' in the 1915 poem,

8 ST, 167; E. Sarkisyants, online translation, *RuVerses: Osip Mandelshtam*.

all appear to show that even in his youth, Mandelstam intended to be freedom's advocate and champion.

Sergei Kablukov noted in his diary on 24 June 1915 that Mandelstam had come to see him, bringing three new poems. One poem was about the Eucharist. Another was about the wonders of freedom. His mind was evidently able to encompass both these ideas at once. The theme of the third was the Name of God sect which had emerged on Mount Athos around 1910, a group for whom the word 'God' was God himself. Since he was himself a kind of eccentric monk who worshipped the art of the word, Mandelstam was moved by the 'power of the name', and in this poem he firmly and irrevocably proclaims his commitment to the word:

Muzhiks rejoice in every cell,
The venerators of God's name:
The Word is total joy to them
And heals their pain.
(ST, 159; OS, 197)

Shortly after his visit to Kablukov, Mandelstam made his first trip to the Crimea. He arrived in Koktebel on 30 June 1915. The poet and painter Maximilian Voloshin was accustomed to holding an 'open house' there, and he provided accommodation to a number of artists throughout the summer. Marina Tsvetaeva was also a guest until mid-July, and their paths crossed for the first time. But the two of them 'did not connect'. Marina was not yet open to any interaction with Mandelstam. Her lesbian affair with the poetess Sofia Parnok, which began in October 1914, would take over the whole of 1915.[9] Tsvetaeva's concise description of her 1915 meeting with Mandelstam in 'History of a Dedication', written in 1931 during her Paris exile, depicts the occasion as a silent pantomime: 'I was walking to the sea, and he – from the sea. At the gate of the Voloshin garden, we passed each other by' (GW, 68; AL, 76). Not a word was exchanged; this was a meeting of two silent souls. The words – and what words they were! – would come later.

The Crimean Peninsula was settled early in classical times by the Greeks. The ancient name of the peninsula was *Tauris*. It was Iphigenia's mythical place of exile. Voloshin's Koktebel refuge lay on the south-eastern coast at

9 Marina Tsvetaeva and Sofia Parnok: see the seventeen-part cycle of poems 'The Friend' (1914–1915) in M. Tsvetaeva, *Liebesgedichte*, 5–30.

the foot of the mountain called *Kara-Dag* ('Black Mountain') in the Turkic language of the Crimean Tatars. It was close to the town of Feodosiia, Theodosia in ancient times, which was founded by Greek settlers in the sixth century B.C.E. Mandelstam was immediately enchanted by the spare beauty of this hilly landscape by the sea, which Marina Tsvetaeva describes so impressively in her memoirs:

> Bare rocks, the moraine of the shore, no bush or shoot, no greenery except high up in the mountains (huge peonies, child's-head-sized), and apart from that: feathergrass, wormwood, sea, desert ... Koktebel (the eastern Crimea, Cimmeria, land of the Amazons, a second Greece) ... Koktebel – no flowers. A sheer acute angle of rock. (There is a tradition that in one of its rocks, that could only be reached by swimming, is the entrance to Hades). (GW, 70; SE, 127)

The summer months at Voloshin's house were also the scene of social activities for the artists. There were joyful celebrations, masked balls, concerts and collective walks. In this free atmosphere, poets and painters could exchange ideas and declaim poems to one another throughout the night under the aegis of the 'genius of friendship', as Marina Tsvetaeva would describe Voloshin in her 1933 obituary essay 'A Living Word about a Living Man'. She also stresses the importance of Voloshin's artists' refuge in 'History of a Dedication': 'To all who have lived in it, Koktebel is a second homeland, for many it's the birthplace of the spirit' (GW, 77; AL, 83). It was one of the few places where Mandelstam could feel he was in good hands. Here is Tsvetaeva again:

> In Koktebel, Mandelstam was the general favourite, it may have been the one time, the once in a lifetime, that the poet had good luck, for he was surrounded by *ears* – for his poems – and by *hearts* – for his frailties. (GW, 73; AL, 80)

This is an affectionate description of Mandelstam's role as an amusing eccentric. Voloshin's mother teased him in a friendly fashion, but she also complained that he was 'untidy, slovenly and inconsiderate', that he covered the sofa with cigarette ends, rummaged around in the bookshelves and then left the books he had found all over the place. Voloshin himself found him 'inexpressibly peculiar' and 'foolish, like a genuine poet'. Vladislav Khodasevich is less benevolent, calling him 'the laughing-stock of all of Koktebel' in a letter of 18 July 1916.[10]

Whether as a spoiled child or a figure of fun, Mandelstam was a prominent visitor to the resort. But no one guessed how important his sojourns in the Crimea were for the eccentric poet himself. Throughout his life, the Crimea would remain the promised land. It was a kind of balcony overlooking the Mediterranean region, which was the cradle of European culture (the Black Sea acted as a connecting link). In Mandelstam's dreams, the peninsula would always signify the south, warmth and a piece of Europe. He would create some of his finest poems there.

The summer of 1915, the period of his first stay in Koktebel, was no exception. He wrote two more poems about Ovid, the exile on the shores of the Black Sea, whom he adapted to his own situation, moving him from his historical place of exile, Tomis (the Romanian Constanța), to the Crimea so as to bring him closer (ST, 173 and 199). And he also wrote his famous poem about sleeplessness, thereby inserting himself into the Russian tradition of insomniac poetry, which goes back to the example of Alexander Pushkin in 1830, and which reached its zenith with the modern 'sleepless generation' of Russian poets, which includes Mandelstam, Tsvetaeva, Akhmatova and others.[11]

The perusal of Homer's *Iliad* (the 'list of ships', the catalogue of the Achaeans' vessels in Book 2) and the roar of the Black Sea merge into one. Civilisation and nature permeate each other, different historical epochs become confused. The Trojan War is evoked, but the First World War cannot be forgotten, even in the Koktebel refuge. Warships lie at anchor in the harbours of the Crimea. That is perhaps why the poem requires the reader to reflect on the omnipotence of love as the great contrast to war:

Insomnia. Homer. Tautly swelling sails.
I've read the catalogue of ships half through:
This wedge of cranes, this outstretched brood
That once took wing across the Aegean isles.

10 M. in Koktebel: V. P. Kupchenko, 'Osip Mandel'shtam v Kimmerii', 189 and 191.
11 The poem 'Insomnia. Homer': N. Å. Nilsson, 'Insomnia. Homer', 35–46.

A train of cranes outstretched towards alien frontiers,
The foam of gods crowns the leaders' kingly hair.
Where sail you to? If Helen were not there,
What would Troy mean to you, O warriors of Greece?

Both Homer and the sea: all things are moved by love;
To whom shall I pay heed? Homer here is silent
And the dark sea thunders, eloquent,
And rumbling heavily, it breaks beneath my bed.
(ST, 169; FP, 37)

'Both Homer and the sea: all things are moved by love': this is a play on the final verse of Dante's *Divine Comedy*, the thirty-third stanza of the *Paradiso*: 'Love, which moves the sun and stars' (*L'amor che move il sole e l'altre stelle*). The sea (Russian: *more*, which has a similar sound to the Italian word for love, *amore*) is a hidden presence in the name of Homer. A Greek name, a Russian word and a Latin-Italian word are united in the name of poetry. Thus the 'fraternal bond of all languages' dreamed of in Mandelstam's essay about Chénier becomes a reality.

'All things are moved by love': until then love had hardly been mentioned in Mandelstam's poetry, apart from a couple of tender evocations in his early poems as a student in Heidelberg. But a poem written in 1912 has this to say:

My turn will come yet –
I feel the wings spreading.
So be it – but where is the target
Where living thought's arrow is heading?

Perhaps I will come back here
When my path and my time both fade:
I could not love there
And here I am afraid.
(ST, 65; OS, 101)

'I could not love' and 'I am afraid' to love: this conclusion manifestly dominated Mandelstam's work up to 1915. Anna Akhmatova relates that Mandelstam was in love with the beautiful artist Anna Zelmanova-

Chudovskaia, who painted a well-known picture of him in 1914. He sat sideways for the portrait, holding a cigarette, with his head thrown back in characteristic fashion. But this love affair left no traces in his work. He wrote no poems for her, because 'he didn't yet know how to write love poetry, as he complained bitterly to me' (Akhmatova). But he would soon overcome this problem, with the assistance of a lady who was an expert in both love and love poems.[12]

12 M.'s love for Anna Zelmanova-Chudovskaia: Akhmatova, *My Half Century*, 89.

8

Florence in Moscow

(Moscow, Koktebel, Petrograd 1916)

At the beginning of 1916 an expanded second edition of Mandelstam's book of poetry, *Stone*, was issued by the Petrograd publisher 'The Hyperborean', run by Mikhail Lozinsky, a poet who moved in Acmeist circles and later translated Dante into Russian. The book now contained sixty-nine poems, and it received highly favourable reviews. The literary historian Viktor Zhirmunsky, who was associated with the Formalists, wrote an essay in 1916 entitled 'The Surmounters of Symbolism', which is of fundamental importance in evaluating the Acmeist movement. Never again would these poets find such a competent and sympathetic contemporary critic: under the Soviet regime they would suffer decades of ostracism. Zhirmunsky described Mandelstam's poetry as 'the poetry of poetry', using Friedrich Schlegel's expression, and he bore witness to the 'gorgeously unexpected' nature of his metaphors. Mandelstam's second *Stone* was a combination of the poems he had written between the ages of seventeen and twenty-four. It was a splendid summation of his early years as a poet.[1]

Marina Tsvetaeva travelled to Petrograd at the end of 1915 to see her friend Sofia Parnok. These were the last days of a relationship whose

1 Reviews of the second edition of *Stone*: O. Mandel'shtam, *Kamen'*, 218–40; 'The Surmounters of Symbolism' (1916): V. Zhirmunskii, 'Preodolevshie simvolizm', 123 and 128.

break-up she described as 'the first catastrophe' of her life. On 7 January 1916, she took part in a poetry-reading evening among friends. This was an occasion she would still revert to in 1936 in her Paris exile, in her essay about her memories of the poet Mikhail Kuzmin, published under the title 'Otherworldly Evening'. She met Mandelstam there in a genuine sense for the first time, after their 'non-meeting' in the summer of 1915 in Koktebel. He was immediately impressed by her character and her poetry. Her poems proclaimed her passionate identification with Germany, a country whose poems and fairy tales had accompanied her throughout her childhood and whose language she was so familiar with that she was able to conduct a high-level correspondence with Rainer Maria Rilke in the summer of 1926. It needed someone with Tsvetaeva's audacity to proclaim, while the world war was raging: 'Germany – my infatuation! / Germany – my love!' That evening she also recited an anti-war poem she had written on 3 October 1915: 'I know a truth – away with former truths! Men should not fight each other on this earth.'

One of the poets present on this occasion was particularly impressed: Mandelstam himself. He too had been thinking of writing a poem against the war, taking up again the thread he had previously started to develop in 'Reims and Cologne'. Some days later he finished 'Menagerie', an 'ode to peace' which invokes European brotherhood and the common origin of the wartime opponents Germany and Russia:

> But I sing the wine of the times,
> The fount of the Italian language,
> The great Aryan cradle,
> And Slavonic and German flax.[2]

The two of them must surely have talked about their opposition to the war when they met. It was almost like a conspiracy: two of the best Russian poets of the twentieth century refused to write the warmongering patriotic verses which were both customary and required at that time. Later, in her obituary of Voloshin, 'A Living Word about a Living Man' (1933), Tsvetaeva would describe Mandelstam's reference to the flax of Slavs and Germans as an 'ingenious formula'. On 10 January 1916, Mandelstam dedicated his new volume of poetry to his colleague with the words 'For Marina Tsvetaeva – a sign in stone.'

2 TR, 13; O. Mandelstam, *Tristia*, 12. This work will henceforth be referred to as MT.

Ten days later, when the young Marina returned to Moscow (having broken up completely with Sofia Parnok), Mandelstam followed. On 5 February, he made the journey back to Petrograd, but he would travel to Moscow repeatedly during the next few months to see her. As she later recalled, his 'comings and goings (raids and *flights*)' would always take her by surprise (GW, 64; AL, 73). And he would soon surprise her with his poems. But it was, in fact, Marina who opened the poetic dialogue.

On 12 February 1916, just after he had left Moscow, she wrote a farewell poem to him. The beginning is an ending, the ending is a beginning: she loved this paradox. In the poem, she repeatedly emphasises the distance and strangeness that separates them, but she overcomes this distance twice, in the first and in the last stanzas, with a *kiss*. It is one of the most beautiful poems ever addressed by one poet to another.

> No one has taken anything away –
> There is even a sweetness for me in being apart.
> I kiss you now across the many
> Hundreds of miles that separate us.
> …
> No one has ever stared more
> Tenderly or more fixedly after you …
> I kiss you – across hundreds of
> Separating years.[3]

By the end of March 1916, Marina Tsvetaeva had written nine poems altogether for her Petersburg fellow poet. They were full of outlandish and tender confessions. On 18 February she wrote: 'Today in you I've come to venerate / Some heavenly child – *of ten years old*.'[4] The whole cycle is a complex portrait in which strong sensitivity is combined with severity: 'You proud fellow, always ready to deceive.' Sombre premonitions of Mandelstam's later fate keep emerging in the poems. The very first one speaks of a 'fearful flight'. And, on 17 March, Marina writes a poem envisaging a scenario in which his life is ended by violence and torture. It reads like a prophecy of his second and final arrest on 2 May 1938:

3 GW, 7; M. Tsvetaeva, *Selected Poems*, 11.

4 GW, 11; M. Tsvetaeva, *Milestones*, 13. Henceforth, this work will be referred to by the abbreviation MI.

Neither your songs, gift of heaven,
Will save you, nor the haughtiest purse of your lips,
…
With bare hands they'll take you – stubborn! Grim! –
The land will ring all night with your shrieking!
They'll scatter your wings unto all four winds,
Seraph! – Young eaglet! –
(GW, 17; MI, 27)

Those 'days from February to June 1916' were 'marvellous' recalls Tsvetaeva in 'History of a Dedication' (1931). It was, she says, a time illuminated by poetry, 'when I was giving Mandelstam Moscow' (GW, 78; AL, 83). They walked together through the city 'like distinguished foreigners' (GW, 11; MI, 13). In the penultimate poem of Tsvetaeva's cycle the gesture of giving, a transfer from hand to hand, becomes explicit: 'From these my hands – a town not formed with hands, / Receive, my strange, my handsome brother' (GW, 21; MI, 59). Until then, Moscow had hardly existed for the Petersburg poet Mandelstam. Now, he received a gift of the five Kremlin cathedrals from his friend and fellow poet, along with all the other churches in the city. When Marina initiated him into the treasures of Holy Russia, Mandelstam was an alien in three senses in this paradise of Orthodox religiosity: as a Jew, as a Petersburger and as a European whose face was turned to the West.

Tsvetaeva's final poem to Mandelstam, sent on 31 March 1916, is also the most erotic one. The protective and solicitous blessing on his departure has vanished, and she no longer addresses the poet as a divine ten-year-old. Passion bursts forth, the 'animal bellow' of the blood, desire, even if she immediately wants to take everything back again:

Bellow, big heart, roar loudly!
Kiss with brute passion, love!
Ah, but what bestial shouting!
Insolent – ah! – blood
…
Pack up that pert demeanour,
Best light a candle quick,
Just so that things between us

Don't turn out – as I wish.
(GW, 23; MI, 61)

How far did this erotic togetherness go? Did it go beyond 'frolics' and kisses? The question is of no interest. What is important, what survives, is what they gave each other: the poems.[5]

And how did Mandelstam reply? A poem written in February 1916 depicts the astonishment of a stranger stepping onto the cathedral square of the Kremlin. But Marina's physiognomy also finds its way into this poetic portrait of the Cathedral of the Dormition (*Uspensky Sobor*). Osip believes he can recognise her raised eyebrows in its stone vaults.

In the polyphony of young girls' choirs
All tender churches sing in their own true voice,
And from the stone arches of the Assumption's tiers
I conjure up round brows and rejoice.

And from the vaults that archangels support
At some fantastic height I saw the city.
In the Acropolis walls I was by sadness gnawed
For a Russian name and for Russian beauty.

Is it not a wonder that we imagine gardens
Where pigeons flutter in the hot blue air
When the black nun sings from Orthodox notes?
Sweet Assumption – Florence in Moscow!

And Moscow's penticupolar cathedrals,
With their Italianate yet Russian soul,
Call forth for me a vision of Aurora,
But with a Russian name and in a coat of fur.
(TR, 15; FP, 38)

Marina is also woven into the fabric of the poem more subtly, when the poet exclaims: 'Florence in Moscow!' This is certainly a reference to the fact that the Cathedral of the Dormition, the oldest of the Kremlin

5 M.'s poetic dialogue with Marina Tsvetaeva: R. Dutli, 'Uns bleibt als Einziges der Name', 117–37.

cathedrals, was built between 1475 and 1479 by the Florentine architect Aristotele Fioravanti. But 'Florentsia' ('the flowering') is also an etymologically precise rendering of the name 'Tsvetaeva' (from the Russian stem *tsvet*: colour, flower, blossom). Tsvetaeva is Florence in Moscow![6]

But the expression 'Florence in Moscow' is more than a poetic play on words: it symbolises the programme to which Mandelstam was dedicated throughout his life, which was to combine a genuinely Russian culture with the culture of Western Europe in a new synthesis. The poem shows us a Moscow permeated by elements from the three cities of Athens (the Acropolis), Rome (Aurora, the goddess of sunrise) and Florence (Fioravanti's architecture). Mandelstam appears to accept the Moscow presented to him by Marina, but he immediately imbues it with his own character, a European character made up of Athens, Rome and Florence. The archaic, Eastern, holy Moscow manifests itself in Mandelstam in an unprecedentedly European costume, brightly lit in a European manner.

But the second poem, dating from March 1916, has already begun to take on the darkest of all possible shadings. A sledge trip through snow-covered Moscow turns into a journey through Russian history, a history drenched in religious myths, political murders and violent seizures of power. It begins with the 'Time of Troubles' which set in after the death of Ivan the Terrible in 1584. The poet's Self travels through Moscow side by side with Marina, identifying itself momentarily with two murdered Tsareviches: Dmitry, the youngest son of Ivan the Terrible, and Alexei, executed in 1718 on the orders of his own father, Peter the Great:

> In a sledge packed deep in straw we lurched
> With the fateful matting scarcely covering us
> All around enormous Moscow's arc
> From the Sparrow Hills to a favourite church.
> …
> The raw distance was dark with flocks of birds;
> The thongs have cramped my knotted arms;
> The prince is carried out; my body goes fearfully numb
> As fire is set to the rust-red straw.
> (TR, 17; FP, 39)

6 Etymological link between 'Florence' and 'Tsvetaeva' according to V. Borisov in his commentary in the Russian edition of Mandelstam's works (Mandel'shtam, *Sochineniia v Dvukh Tomakh*, vol. 1, 475).

The poem is a curiously early premonition of Mandelstam's own violent death. His acceptance of Moscow's darkest side, after the Europe-inspired brightness of the first poem for Marina, carried him as far as to imagine a new 'Time of Troubles', and to foretell his own execution. This was in the year 1916, before a revolution had even broken out in Russia.

The Moscow 'raids and flights' had ended; but Mandelstam visited his fascinating fellow poet and Moscow muse again at the end of May 1916. She was living in Alexandrov, in the province of Vladimir, a hundred kilometres north-east of Moscow. This was the area from which her family originated. Tsvetaeva describes Mandelstam's impetuous visit in 'History of a Dedication': she tells of their trips to the cemetery and his superstitious fear of the dead, of wild bulls and a black-clothed nun. And she also describes his precipitate departure for the Crimea, which marked the break-up of their relationship. She presents her account of Mandelstam's visit, and his peculiarities and anxieties, with tenderly ironic humour and without a trace of malice. She had long been accustomed to the ritual of Mandelstam's departures: 'His departure was unexpected: not so much for me, with my four months' – February to June – experience of Mandelstam comings and goings (raids and flights) as for him, with his childish longing for home, which he always ran away from' (GW, 64; AL, 73).

No other memoirist was able to enter into Mandelstam's inner turmoil in those years as sympathetically as Marina Tsvetaeva:

> It must be said that Mandelstam, whether at the cemetery or on a walk, or at the fair, wherever he was, always wanted to go home. And always before the other person (I) did. And when home – invariably – he wanted to go out. I think – humour aside – that whenever he was not writing (and he was always not-writing, namely, one poem in three months), he was pining. Without poems Mandelstam didn't feel right sitting – or walking – or living – in this world (GW, 60–1; AL, 70).

The scene of his departure is both comical and moving: his cry, 'I do not want to go to the Crimea', echoed back to her along with the smoke from the locomotive. He did in fact go to the Crimea, to the house of Maximilian Voloshin, just as he had the previous year, arriving on 7 June 1916. He had hardly got there when he wrote his last poem to Marina: 'Disbelieving the Miracle of Resurrection' (EW, 52). Strangely, this final poem is also the most erotic one. He too overcomes distance and strangeness *with kisses*, just like Tsvetaeva in the very first poem of her love cycle. He speaks of the two different worlds they inhabit, and of the wideness of the gap between Marina's part of northern Russia around medieval Vladimir (which was the Russian capital before the rise of Moscow, and until 1328 the seat of the Metropolitan), and the southerly Crimea, the ancient *Tauris*, his beloved prospect of the Mediterranean.

After the apparently ritual kisses – on the elbow, the forehead and the wrist ('Under a strand of dark-complexioned gold, / I kiss your hand whose turquoise bracelet / Leaves a strip of white: / Here in Tauris the ardent summers / Work such wonders') – the end of the poem evokes what the two poets have in common: their belief in the power of the word, in the magic of the name, in poetry, which overcomes time and death.

> For us only a name remains
> A sound miraculous and lasting.
> Take from me these grains of sand:
> I'm pouring them from hand to hand.
> (TR, 27; EW, 52)

The sand he is holding in his hands (the present moment) suggests the sand in the clocks (time), and this, in turn, suggests the sand in the sea (eternity). Poems are what Mandelstam wants to give Marina, poems that pass through his hands, time that exists in his hands. Poetic immortality.

The significance of this meeting between two great twentieth-century Russian poets can hardly be overestimated. One of the prophecies uttered by Marina in the poetry she donated to Mandelstam was this: 'You will never regret that you loved me' (GW, 21). Mandelstam was fascinated by this female poet, who conducted her many love affairs with freedom and informality. She had been married since 1912 to Sergei Efron, she had a daughter, Ariadna, and had just ended her stormy relationship of 1914–1915 with Sofia Parnok. Tsvetaeva was a revelation to Mandelstam. Not only did she 'give Moscow' to him, she also revealed to him the all-embracing power of Eros. In a letter sent on 21 July 1916 to Piotr Yurkevich, after the break with Mandelstam had taken place when he left Alexandrov, she was already distancing herself ironically from the episode:

> I shall never forget how furious I was made this spring by a human being – a poet, a wonderful creature, I loved him very much – who walked

> with me through the Kremlin and had no eyes for the river Moskva or the cathedrals. He talked to me uninterruptedly – about myself. I said to him: 'Don't you understand that the sky – raise your head and look at it – is a thousand times greater than I, do you really believe that on such a day I can think about your love, or anyone else's?' (GW, 126–7)

And, seven years later, on 25 July 1923, in a letter to the literary critic Alexander Bakhrakh, she added: 'I was twenty years old, and I said the same thing to your favourite poet Mandelstam: "What does Marina signify, when there is Moscow?! When there is spring?! Oh, you don't *really* love me!" I have always found this narrowness suffocating. Love the *world* – in me, not *me* – in the world. So that "Marina" signifies "world", and not the world "Marina".'

So that Marina signifies the world … even Nadezhda Mandelstam, ridiculed as she was by Tsvetaeva as a jealous wife, would later estimate this relationship at its true value, and maintain that Marina had in a sense freed her Mandelstam from a spell, and indeed in two senses – by introducing him to Moscow and to Eros.[7]

> It was a magic gift, because with only Petersburg, without Moscow, it would have been impossible to breathe freely, to acquire the true feeling for Russia and the inner freedom of which M. speaks …
>
> I am sure my relationship with M. would not have been formed so easily and simply if he had not previously encountered Marina with her verve and her wild passions. She released his zest for life and his capacity for spontaneous and unstinting love which so much struck me at the very beginning.[8]

Once more, therefore, in summer 1916, Mandelstam plunges into the atmosphere of the Crimea, remembers the experience with Tsvetaeva, which was more than merely erotic, and kisses her retrospectively. This summer of 1916 is marked both by his separation from this embodiment of feminine poetry and by another, truly tragic, event: the loss of the first influential woman in his life – not Tsvetaeva, but his mother.[9]

---

7 M. is liberated by his relationship with Marina Tsvetaeva: N. Mandelstam, *Hope Abandoned*, 525 ('Old Friends').

8 Ibid.

9 The summer of 1916 in Koktebel: V. P. Kupchenko, 'Osip Mandel'shtam v Kimmerii', 191.

His brother Alexander had now joined him in Koktebel. For the first few weeks, he enjoyed the summer and the modest fame he had now achieved as a poet, as he explains to his mother on 20 July 1916 in an enthusiastic letter which presents a rather false picture of what really happened (his appearance on the Feodosiia stage on 18 July, at which Voloshin and Khodasevich also read their poems, was actually a disaster, as he was howled down by the public because his poems were 'incomprehensible'):

> The day before yesterday we were driven to Feodosiia with great pomp: automobiles, supper with the Governor. I read, beaming white in my tennis outfit, from the stage of the summer theatre. We returned in the morning and spent yesterday resting. This autumn I will definitely take my examinations. Please find out the dates. (MR, 24; CC, 483)

In fact, he was about to be faced with a different kind of test. The letter just quoted would be his last to his mother. A few days later, on 26 July 1916, she died in Petrograd of a stroke. It was a bitter death, as she was estranged from her husband, who had had a lover for some time. Her sons Osip and Alexander immediately travelled to Petrograd, but they only arrived in time to see her buried. Mandelstam's younger brother Yevgeny writes in his memoirs of the 'disintegration of the Mandelstam family' after her death. The three sons blamed themselves for their self-centredness and lack of consideration. Osip was oppressed by a feeling of guilt towards his mother, to whom he owed so much. After the funeral he wrote a guilt-ridden poem about the 'black sun', which also led him to look back at his Jewish heritage:

> The night is irredeemable
> But it is still daylight where you are.
> At the gates of Jerusalem
> A black sun has risen.
>
> A yellow sun is more terrible –
> Lulla, lulla, lullaby –
> In their temple, bright with daylight,
> Judaeans were burying my mother.

Not partaking of grace
And deprived of holy services,
Judaeans were chanting
A woman's burial service.

And over my mother rang out
The Israelite voices.
I woke up in my cradle,
Illuminated by a black sun.[10]

The poem interweaves a memorial to the dead with a lullaby: the mother dies, the son is born. A new birth arises from the spirit of mourning. It is Mandelstam's own highly individual 'Kaddish' prayer. Jewish funeral rites were already alien to him. The traditional refrain of Russian cradle songs, 'bayu – bayushki – bayu' (hushaby baby, hushaby), which Mikhail Lermontov introduced to Russian poetry in his 'Cossack Lullaby', appears in Mandelstam's poem.

Reflection on his Jewish antecedents, which passed from mother to son, leads him to reaffirm his dissociation: 'Not partaking of grace / And deprived of holy services, / Judaeans were chanting.' The Israelite fathers have lost their 'grace', they are no longer priests. This is an allusion to the expulsion of the priests, the 'Kohanim', after the destruction of the Second Temple by the Romans, in the year 70 C.E. But Mandelstam transfers his mother to the temple of a heavenly Jerusalem, a place where the dead woman will now live outside time. The poem is almost torn apart by the tension between two emotions: mourning for his Jewish mother and dissociation from Judaism, whose god is meant to be praised by the 'Kaddish' prayer for the dead.[11]

During this phase of his creative life, Mandelstam came closer to Christianity than he ever had before (and as we shall see, some time would still have to elapse before the return of the 'prodigal son'). However, this was no longer the Christianity of Roman Catholicism, which had fascinated him between 1913 and 1915 under the influence of Chaadaev. He was already viewing Rome from a distance in the poem he sent in March 1916 to Marina Tsvetaeva about the 'Time of Troubles':

10 TR, 29; V. Terras, 'The Black Sun', 50. This article will henceforth be referred to as BS.

11 'The Night Is Irredeemable': L. M. Olschner, *Der feste Buchstab*, 264.

'Rome's far away / And he never loved Rome anyway' (TR, 17; FP, 39). Marina had introduced him to the aura of the Kremlin cathedrals, of the old, holy, Orthodox Russia. Now he wanted to follow this path a little further.

Mandelstam's 'most Christian' text is the essay 'Scriabin and Christianity' (later renamed 'Pushkin and Scriabin'), only fragments of which have survived.[12] It was written in autumn 1916 and it culminates in a defence of Christian art. It was a response to the death on 27 April 1915 of the composer Alexander Scriabin, whom Mandelstam greatly admired. He included the first performance of Scriabin's *Prometheus Symphony* – a piece in which the orchestra, the choir and the composer's famous 'piano of light' combined to create a work of total art – as a significant event when he wrote his autobiographical essay *The Noise of Time* (RZ, 46–7, 198; NT, 88). The Russian theologian and universal scholar Pavel Florensky gave the graveside speech at Scriabin's funeral, and what he said set the tone for all later appreciations of the composer.

Mandelstam's fragmentary essay on Scriabin has contradictory elements: on the one hand, he associates Scriabin with 'Russia's guilt', which involved abandoning Christianity and turning to Buddhism and theosophy. Scriabin was at one time an enthusiastic disciple of the 'theosophist' Elena Blavatskaya, whose spiritualist secret teachings had a strong following in Russian intellectual circles at the turn of the century. But, on the other hand, Mandelstam praised the composer as a 'raving Hellene' who had 'conquered oblivion', because after overcoming the temptations of theosophy he had found his way back to the 'Christian mystery' under the influence of Vyacheslav Ivanov. Mandelstam's essay refers approvingly to various suggestions made by contemporary obituarists, such as the philosopher-theologians Nikolai Berdyaev and Sergei Bulgakov. Despite its fragmentary character, the essay is unmistakably an apologia, written in defence of the freedom of Christian art:

> Christian art is free. It is, in the full meaning of the phrase, 'art for art's sake'. No necessity of any kind, even the highest, clouds its bright inner freedom, for its prototype, that which it imitates, is the very redemption of the world by Christ … Art cannot be a sacrifice, for a sacrifice has already been made; it cannot be redemption, for the world along

12 The essay 'Scriabin and Christianity': A. Mets, 'O. Mandel'shtam', 66–9.

> with the artist has already been redeemed. What then is left? A joyful commerce with the divine, like the game played by the Father with his children, a hide-and-seek of the spirit! … Christian artists are as it were the freedmen of the idea of redemption, rather than slaves, and they are not preachers. Our whole two-thousand-year-old culture, thanks to the miraculous mercy of Christianity, is the world's release into freedom for the sake of play, for spiritual joy, for the free 'imitation of Christ'. (GP, 64; SE, 137)

Here, we see the first formulation of the 'spiritual joy' which Nadezhda Mandelstam would again and again observe in her husband with amazement. Reflection on the deaths of Pushkin and Scriabin finally leads Mandelstam to an insight inspired by the idea of the 'imitation of Christ', an insight with serious implications for his own existence:

> I wish to speak of Scriabin's death as of the highest act of his creativity. It seems to me that an artist's death ought not to be excluded from the chain of his creative achievements, but rather examined as the last conclusive link. (GP, 62; SE, 136)

His mother's death had made him reflect on his own death and the death of artists in general. But, in November and December 1916, he would also take up the lyrical theme of love and death, inspired by Marina Tsvetaeva. A meeting with two beautiful women provided the occasion for this. One was the Georgian princess and well-known Petersburg beauty Salomeia Andronikova, who ran a literary salon in the capital. The Petersburg artists were fascinated by her. As late as 1940, Anna Akhmatova recalled her in the poem 'The Shadow' as the radiant 'beauty of the year thirteen' whose 'mountain eyes' delivered 'tender light impartially on everyone through black eyelashes'.

While visiting Andronikova in November 1916, Mandelstam met her cousin Tinatina Dzhordzhadze. He would elevate this accidental meeting with another 'beautiful Georgian' into a poem which blended Petersburg with ancient Rome:

Timidly, you bent your neck
But no cameo – no Romans
I feel sorry for the tanned Tinatina
Roman girl on the banks of the Neva.[13]
(TR, 31; MT, 18)

But it was to the revered Salomeia Andronikova that he dedicated his mysterious poem of love, death and sleeplessness, 'Solominka' (Little Straw), written in December 1916. Several other women surface in this poem as well: Lenore and Ligeia, who die and come back to life in stories by Edgar Allan Poe, and Honoré Balzac's androgynous and angelic 'Séraphita'. In this poem, the enamoured poet also plays games with words, adding an affectionate form of the given name Salome (*soloma*, which means 'straw') to a magical invocation of the other three women:

Oh, resonant Salome, like a hollow, dried-out straw,
You've drunk the whole of death and become more tender still.
Snapped is that lovely lifeless straw,
Not Salomeia, no, but sweet Salome still.
...
No, it isn't that Straw in solemn satin hung,
Above the black Neva in that enormous room.
For twelve months long the hour of death's been sung
And pale blue ice streams into the gloom.
...
I've learned those blessed words by heart:
Eleonora, Salomeia, Ligeia, Seraphita;
The Neva is flowing through that enormous room
And blue blood is streaming from the granite.[14]
(TR, 33, 35; FP, 40)

This invocation of love, drowning and death showed that after the spell cast by Tsvetaeva, Mandelstam was now able to introduce eroticism into his poetry. This led his pious, right-thinking acquaintance Kablukov to confide the following outraged comments to his diary on 2 January 1917:

13 Poem for Tinatina, the 'beautiful Georgian': Dutli, *Europas zarte Hände*, 101–16.

14 The 'Solominka' poem: C. Brown, *Mandelstam*, 237–44; K. Taranovsky, *Essays on Mandel'shtam*, 147–9.

> Our last conversation revolved around his last, clearly erotic, poems, which reflected his experiences of the last few months. Some woman has evidently come into his life. In his mind there is a certain connection between religion and eroticism which seems to me to be blasphemous. He admitted this connection himself, and he said that the sphere of sex was particularly dangerous for him as he had freed himself from Judaism and he knew that he was on a dangerous path and that his situation was dreadful; but he did not have the strength to step away from this path and he couldn't even force himself to stop writing poetry in this period of erotic madness. He saw no other way out of this situation than to convert as soon as possible to Orthodoxy.[15]

It does not really matter whether Mandelstam was genuinely prepared to be converted or simply wanted to fit in with the views of his devout interlocutor. More important was the admission that he lacked the strength 'to step away from this path' and that he was unable to stop writing poems 'in this period of erotic madness'. Mandelstam's 'erotic poems' for Marina Tsvetaeva, Tinatina Dzhordzhadze and Salomeia Andronikova may have been 'blasphemous' in the eyes of the pious Kablukov, but they were a magnificent addition to the stock of Russian lyric poetry.

For Mandelstam, the year 1916 was more impregnated with love and death than any other he had experienced. First, his relationship with Marina soared to the heights and fell to the ground in pieces; then he had to mourn the death of his mother, while in his essay on Scriabin he describes the death of the artist as his 'final creative act'. That was a lot of death for a single year of life – 'For twelve months long the hour of death's been sung' – but it was not a bad preparation for the approaching year of revolution and the age of upheaval that followed.

15 O. Mandel'shtam, *Kamen'*, 256.

9

Nightingale Fever

(Petrograd, the Crimea, Moscow 1917–1918)

The Russian population was hungry and freezing in February 1917. Every day there were disturbances and strikes. Russia was a land consumed by war: both externally, where the world war continued to rage, and internally. The starving workers needed bread, and the exhausted soldiers demanded an end to the war. The women's demonstration of 23 February 1917 hastened the end of Tsarist rule. On 25 February, Nicholas II gave the order to suppress the disturbances by all means necessary, thereby making the same mistake as in 1905 on the occasion of 'Bloody Sunday'. The Petrograd garrison mutinied on the night of 27 February and made common cause with the demonstrating workers. In the next few days, the pressure from below increased by leaps and bounds. Finally, a Provisional Government was formed under Prince Lvov, and on 2 March the Tsar was forced to sign a statement of abdication. Russia was then a republic for a few months, but the situation was far from being either peaceful or orderly. The events of February and March were just the beginning of an all-embracing process of disintegration.

Mandelstam's story *The Egyptian Stamp* (1928) metamorphoses the atmosphere in Russia between the two revolutions into a cascade of disturbing images. Parnok, his anti-hero and alter ego, is living under a 'lemonade government' (RZ, 201; NT, 141) which looks on helplessly as the country sinks into chaos. In one of the episodes of the story, Parnok observes a furious mob of people lynching someone, and he is the only person who attempts to dissuade them. He then tries to call the police, and sound the alarm to the authorities, but in vain, because 'the state had vanished' and was 'sleeping like a carp' (RZ, 209; NT, 145). The Russian newspapers of the time are indeed full of reports of lynch mobs and cruel acts of revenge. In the story, Parnok is utterly disgusted by the violence, brutality and loss of moral restraint which accompany the overall atmosphere of dissolution:

> They stink of bloated bowels, thought Parnok, and was for some reason reminded of the terrible word 'entrails'. And he felt slightly sick … Petersburg had declared itself Nero, and was as loathsome as if it were eating a soup of crushed flies. (RZ, 205, 209; NT, 143, 145)

In June 1917, Mandelstam fled from the violence in Petrograd to the Crimea, where he had spent the two preceding summers. There was nothing left in the capital to hold him back. He had finally decided to withdraw from his course of studies at the university, and on 18 May 1917 he received a leaving certificate. In the Crimea, he hoped to recover his equilibrium, renew his strength and contemplate the course his life had taken so far. Over a decade later, in January 1931, he would recall his flight from Petrograd in these lines:

> And sensing future executions I escaped from the roar of revolution
> To the Nereids by the Black Sea.[1]

Shortly before his departure for the Crimea in June 1917 he wrote a political poem: 'The Decembrist'. It was a meditation on the Decembrist rising against the autocracy of Tsar Nicholas I, which was defeated on 14 December 1825 in the Senate Square of Petersburg. The five leading Decembrists were executed, and most of their followers were condemned to hard-labour exile in Siberia. The poem invokes the historic dream of 'sweet civic liberties'. It was printed in the Petrograd newspaper *Novaia Zhizn* (New Life) on 24 December 1917, hence after the Bolsheviks had taken power. In it, Mandelstam attempted to remind his contemporaries

1 MM, 47; O. Mandelstam, *The Moscow Notebooks*, 35.

and the new regime of the high ideals of the Decembrists. This was no coincidence; he was making a conscious connection. His poem was written exactly a hundred years after Alexander Pushkin's ode 'Freedom' (1817), but in Mandelstam's poem, 'civic liberties' are not allowed to triumph, and chaos will continue to reign for a long time. This is the message of the final stanza (which Mayakovsky used to recite with enthusiasm!):

> Everything is confused, and there's no one to say,
> As things grow colder,
> 'Everything is confused,' nor sweetly repeat:
> Russia, Lethe, Lorelei.
> (TR, 37; MT, 25)

The world war was still going on. The Lethe, the river of oblivion that runs through the underworld, lay between Russia and the German Lorelei. The Provisional Government wanted to continue the war in the name of 'a sense of revolutionary and national honour', but the Kerensky offensive of 18 June 1917 turned out to be a fiasco. In Petrograd, meanwhile, the Bolsheviks were organising mass demonstrations of workers and soldiers against the war.

While he was in the Crimea, Mandelstam found refuge under the protective wing of various Petersburg acquaintances. He had no money. He travelled first to Alushta, then on 22 June to Koktebel (again staying with Voloshin). At the end of July, he moved back to Alushta, then to Feodosiia, where he stayed until September. It was a miniature Odyssey, but, most importantly for him, he was in his beloved Crimea. At the beginning of August he stayed as a guest in the Alushta *dacha* of Salomeia Andronikova, the addressee of the 'Solominka' poem of December 1916.[2] On Salomeia's name day, 3 August, the summer guests performed a playful comedy they had jointly composed. It was entitled *Coffee House of the Broken Hearts, or Savonarola in Tauris*. Mandelstam appeared as the sweet-toothed poet Don José della Tige d'Amande. 'Tige d'Amande' (almond stem) was a distortion of his surname into pseudo-aristocratic French. But the summer was not occupied entirely with such frivolities.

On 11 and 16 August, Mandelstam wrote two of his finest Crimean poems. They were meditations on death and on life. Let us mention the

---

2 Russian word for a small country villa.

second one first: in it the asphodel, the lily of the underworld, which according to Greek mythology grows luxuriantly in Hades, is conjured up in this magical incantation:

> Transparent Spring's grey asphodels
> Are still far away.
> While sand rustles, waves boil.
> Here, like Persephone, my soul
> Fights to enter the circle of light.
> In the kingdom of the dead
> There are no such things
> As charming sunburned arms.
> (TR, 43; MT, 26)

The motif of the sunburned arms is connected with his memories of Marina Tsvetaeva and the temptations of erotic love. The January 1931 poem in which he recalls his flight from Petrograd does not just speak of 'future executions' and the journey to the Black Sea, but also commemorates beautiful women: 'I took so much embarrassment, stress and grief / From the tender Europeanised beauties of my past' (MM, 47; MN, 35).

One of these 'tender Europeanised beauties' was Vera Sudeikina, the lovely wife of the artist Sergei Sudeikin, who had painted the ceiling of the 'Stray Dog', the Petersburg temple of the Bohemians. Shortly before 11 August, while he was a guest in her dacha, Mandelstam wrote an imperishable, classic meditation on the nature of time. In it, he conjures up an instant of 'pure duration'. The long-drawn-out metre, the classical anapaest, indicates the calm flow, the stream, of time: 'Like heavy barrels the peaceful days roll on' (TR, 39; EW, 53).

Vera Sudeikina emigrated after the revolution, and later became Igor Stravinsky's second wife. She remembered how Mandelstam had visited her, and how they had walked together to the vineyard:

> We did not have much more to show him. Nor did we have anything to feed him, apart from tea and honey. Without bread. But the conversation was lively, and it was not about politics but about art, literature and painting … He came again on 11 August, bringing his poem with him.[3]

3 Vera Stravinsky's memoirs (published in New York in 1982), as quoted in

Out of the bottle the stream of golden honey poured so slowly
That she had time to murmur (she who'd invited us),
Here, in sad Tauris, where fate has led us,
We shan't be bored. She glanced over her shoulder.
…
After tea we came into the great brown garden,
Dark blinds lowered like eyelids on the windows,
Past white columns to see the grapes
Where sun-lit glass has sluiced the sleepy mountain.

The vine, I said, lives on like ancient battles –
Leafy-headed horsemen fight in flowery flourishes.
Knowledge of Hellas is here in stony Tauris –
And the golden acres, rusty furrows.
(TR, 39; EW, 53)

The honey the hostess pours from the bottle contains reminders of classical antiquity, which fascinate Mandelstam. Bees and honey have been allegories for poets and poetry ever since Plato's dialogue *Ion*. Honey was not only the universal curative in ancient medicine, it was also a symbol of the transition to another world, a burial object, an offering to goddesses of death. Honey, grapes, the vineyard (as the domain of the god Dionysus) – all these things reminded Mandelstam of the gifts of Greece in myth and literature. There is a glancing reference to Penelope, the wife of Odysseus, a symbol of loyalty and steadfastness. Jason, who along with the Argonauts brought the golden fleece back from Colchis, appears indirectly in the question 'Golden fleece, where are you, golden fleece?' And finally the cunning Odysseus, who returns 'filled with time and space'. The poem speaks not of his misadventures, but of the storms that matured him:

Well, in the white room silence stays like a spinning-wheel.
A smell of vinegar and paint, and wine fresh from the cellar.
Do you remember, in the Grecian house, the wife dear to all:
Not Helen – the other – how long she spent spinning?

O. Mandel'shtam, *Polnoe Sobranie Stikhotvorenii*, 547, note 83; T. Nikol'skaia, R. Timenchik and A. Mets, *Kofeinia razbitykh Serdets*, 19.

Golden fleece, where are you, golden fleece?
The whole journey a thundering of the sea's weighty waves.
And leaving his ship, canvas worn out on the seas,
Odysseus came back, filled with time and space.
(TR, 39; EW, 53)

With this poem of pure duration, Mandelstam produced a counterpoint to the upheavals of the epoch, which were in progress exactly at that point: it was a way of invoking Western cultural continuity. But death and the kingdom of the dead are not just present as an implied threat in the Asphodel poem; they are present in the Odysseus poem too.[4]

Very soon, Mandelstam started to comment on the political events in his own words. He returned to Petrograd on 11 October 1917. The agony of the government and the state was continuing, the army was in dissolution, and there was no longer a police force. The Provisional Government, led since 8 July by Prime Minister Alexander Kerensky, had not succeeded in seating itself firmly in power, ending the war, or gaining the support of the masses. On 10 October, on the eve of Mandelstam's return to the capital, the Bolsheviks decided at a secret meeting of their Central Committee to seize power in an armed insurrection. The rising was set to take place on 25 October (7 November New Style) and the planning was done by Leon Trotsky. It was later presented by the Bolsheviks as a great and heroic deed, and exaggeratedly depicted by the director Eisenstein as the 'storming of the Winter Palace' in his film *October*, made in 1927 to celebrate the tenth anniversary of the seizure of power. In reality, it was a simple, unspectacular putsch. Trotsky quickly organised the occupation of all the important points in the city, without meeting any resistance. Only the Winter Palace, where the Provisional Government had taken refuge, was defended, by cadets and the women's battalion, and it was not taken until one and a half days later.

The entry for 27 October in the diary of the poetess Zinaida Gippius contains a description of these 'revolutionary' occurrences which is far removed from the way they were presented later for propaganda purposes:

4 The Odysseus poem as the evocation of another world: H. Rothe, 'Mandel'shtam – Argonaute und Odysseus', 390–2.

> A few short remarks on the Winter Palace ... The cadets and the women defended themselves as well as they could against the gangs of soldiers advancing at the rear of the building, and they beat them back until the ministers decided to put an end to the senseless bloodshed. The insurgents had in any case already penetrated inside the palace with the help of traitors ... As soon as the revolutionary troops ... had overrun the palace they started plundering and destroying everything. They broke into the storerooms, they got hold of the silver. What they could not take away, they smashed ... They dragged the ladies of the Women's Battalion, many of them wounded, to the Pavlovsky barracks, and raped all of them.[5]

The next day, it was as if Russia's first bourgeois-socialist government had disappeared from the face of the earth. Some of the ministers were arrested, but Kerensky was able to escape from the city and go underground. The whole uproar passed by in the blink of an eye. This was a phantom revolution, rather than a mass rising. To quote Zinaida Gippius again: 'Petersburg's population maintains an angry and melancholy silence, as unfriendly as October itself. What disgusting, black, terrible, shameful days these are.' In Moscow, however, there were fierce battles: the city was not in Bolshevik hands until a week later, on 2 (15) November 1917. Before this, on 26 October (8 November New Style) the Soviet of People's Commissars was established as the organ of government, and the decrees on ending the war and dividing the land among the peasants were issued.

The Bolsheviks' triumph was followed by an ignominious setback. Lenin's party only received 25 per cent of the votes at the elections for a Constituent Assembly, held on 25 November (8 December), while the Mensheviks and SRs together received 62 per cent. Despite this, the Bolsheviks held on to power, and on 6 (19) January 1918 they abruptly dissolved the Constituent Assembly with the aid of Red troop detachments.

Mandelstam reacted to the October upheaval within a few days; he was one of the first poets to do so. He composed an angry and bitter poem

---

5 Diary entries on the October putsch: Z. Gippius, *Dnevniki*, vol. 1, 593 and 597. [Publisher's note: there is no evidence of the mass rape referred to by Gippius – even the arch–Cold War prosecutor of the Bolsheviks, Richard Pipes, fails to cite a source for this claim when he repeats it in his works, although it became a recurring trope in White denunciations of the Bolshevik Revolution.]

against the 'yoke of violence and malice' in which he also paid homage to Kerensky. In it, Lenin is flayed as a usurper and described as 'October's favourite'. The poem was printed on 15 November 1917 in the newspaper of the SRs, *Volia Naroda* (People's Will):

When October's favourite was making us
A brutal, angry yoke,
And armoured killer-cars sprang up,
And low-browed machine-gunners –

'Crucify Kerensky!' the soldier cried,
And a vicious rabble applauded:
Pilate said we could hang our hearts on bayonets,
And our hearts stopped beating.
(TR, 179; CP, 171)

Alexander Kerensky, the prime minister of the Provisional Government, belonged to the Socialist Revolutionary Party, whose ideals Mandelstam had shared in part in his earlier years. For many intellectuals, the party embodied the liberal principles of the nineteenth century. In his poem on October, Mandelstam describes the SRs as 'Peter's pups': in other words, heirs of the civilising endeavours of Peter the Great. After October Kerensky stayed underground, and then, having evaded the Bolsheviks' attempts to find him, he left Russia in March 1918 and settled in London as an exile.

This poem is Mandelstam's first and sharpest denunciation of the October Revolution, and it makes it impossible to doubt his attitude. One line of it reads: 'The state is racked by storms and frenzied masks are worn.' His early hostility to the Bolsheviks was still being brought up against him in the secret police investigation which led to his second (and final) arrest on 2 May 1938: 'He had a completely negative attitude towards the Great Proletarian Revolution, he described the Soviet government as a "government of usurpers" and he slandered Soviet power in his literary works of the time' (MR, 300).

Mandelstam refused to join the chorus of jubilation, unlike Alexander Blok, whose poem 'The Twelve' became the gospel of the revolution. It portrays a patrol of twelve Red Guards moving through Petrograd. The group is joined by Jesus Christ, who thereby makes them his 'apostles'.

Mayakovsky wrote the poem 'Our March' in November 1917 and recited it in the city's taverns. But the 'drummer of the revolution' also celebrated its jubilees: his 'Ode to the Revolution' appeared on 7 November 1918, its first anniversary, and his poem 'Very Good!', which he described as 'The October Revolution, cast in bronze', was written in 1927 for the tenth anniversary.

Anna Akhmatova writes in 'Pages from a Diary': 'Mandelstam responded to the revolution as a fully formed and well-known poet, albeit in a limited circle. He was one of the first to write on civic themes.'[6] The Kerensky poem is one of three that Mandelstam devoted to the 'losers of the revolution' in November 1917. In the second the Self appears as a 'late patriarch in the Moscow of destruction' (TR, 181), and is compared with Patriarch Tikhon, who proclaimed an anathema against the Bolsheviks on 6 January 1918. The third poem was dedicated to Anton Kartashov, the historian of the Russian Orthodox Church who had been appointed Minister for Religious Affairs in the Provisional Government on 1 September 1917. This was the poem 'A Young Levite among the Priests' (TR, 47; BS, 49).

In ancient Israel, a Levite was a servant of the temple. He was subordinated to the priests (Kohanim), and he originally came from the tribe of Levi. In Mandelstam's poem, the Levite seems to resemble the prophet Jeremiah, whose warning voice foretold the destruction of Jerusalem: 'He said: the yellow of the sky gives cause to worry / Over the Euphrates it is already night, run, priests.' It was from the direction of the Euphrates river that the Babylonians attacked Judaea, an attack which led in 587 B.C.E. to the destruction of the First Temple. According to Nadezhda Mandelstam's recollection, Mandelstam saw himself as the Levite, warning of the downfall of Jerusalem-Petersburg and the destruction of civilisation.[7] Here is the final stanza of the poem:

> He was with us when on the river bank
> We wrapped the Sabbath in precious linen
> And illuminated the night of Jerusalem
> And the fumes of non-being with a heavy menorah.
> (TR, 47; BS, 49)

---

6 Akhmatova on M.'s poems on political themes during the revolution: A. Akhmatova, *My Half Century*, 93.

7 M. as 'young Levite' and Jeremiah: N. Mandelstam, *Hope Abandoned*, 125 ('The Young Levite').

Of all Mandelstam's poems, this is the one with the strongest infusion of Jewish elements. He sings of the priests of the temple and of a Levite, of the night of Judaea and the destruction of the temple, of Shabbat and the menorah, the seven-branched ritual candelabrum of the Jewish liturgy. But, according to Nadezhda Mandelstam, it is also one of the poems with a Christian inspiration: the 'sabbath' wrapped in precious linen is the body of Christ taken down from the Cross. The downfall of Jerusalem-Petersburg fades into the burial of Christ. The fact that the text of Mandelstam that is most imbued with Jewish cultural elements also evokes the burial of Christ is only an apparent self-contradiction: it is, rather, a renewed manifestation of his poetic synthesis between Judaism and Christianity, between the Old Testament and the New.

Mandelstam thought that the poets were also among the 'losers of the revolution'. The 'yoke of violence and malice' would inevitably bear down on them as well. It is not surprising that in December 1917, he turned to his fellow poet and close friend Anna Akhmatova to bemoan what had been lost. The very title of the poem 'To Cassandra', which is dedicated to her, harks back to a soothsayer and bringer of bad tidings, the daughter of Priam, who foretold the downfall of Troy.

> Time blossomed and I did not reach for
> Your lips, Cassandra, your eyes, Cassandra,
> But in December – oh, what a solemn vigil
> – Memory torments us!
>
> In December of 1917
> We lost everything, and love too:
> This one robbed himself,
> That one was robbed by the people …
>
> But if life is a necessary madness,
> And a masted forest is tall homes – then
> Run, armless victory,
> Icy plague!
> (TR, 51; CP, 96)

This description of the revolution as an 'armless victory' makes 'To Cassandra' one of Mandelstam's most negative statements about the

October upheaval.[8] The Kerensky poem was another. Like the latter, this poem also appeared in the Socialist Revolutionary Party's newspaper, *Volia Naroda*, in this case in the 31 December 1917 issue.

It again shows how the isolated individual is threatened by wolves. In the Kerensky poem, he is a 'free citizen' walking among a masked and frenzied mob, while in the poem 'The Decembrist', published a week earlier, on 24 December, in *Novaia Zhizn'*, but written in June, he is the embodiment of the individual who revolts against arbitrary power and demands both freedom and citizens' rights. A fine thread can be traced from the individual threatened by wolves in 1917 to Mandelstam's famous March 1931 poem on the 'wolfhound century' (MM, 57), in which he will affirm twice that he is 'not a wolf by blood'.

> A square, and armoured cars, and
> I see a man, frightening
> Wolves with burning logs:
> Freedom, Equality, Order!
> (TR, 51; CP, 96)

This emphasis on freedom and the law also looks back to Alexander Pushkin's 1817 ode 'Freedom'. It is not surprising that the next stanza of the poem evokes the 'sun of Alexander', Mandelstam's great predecessor. Its visionary aspect also applies to the future of the person addressed as 'Cassandra': Akhmatova. The final stanza predicts all the blows of fate she had to suffer: bans on publication, the repeated imprisonment of Lev, the son of her first marriage, to Nikolai Gumilyov, and personal humiliations and degradations, culminating in the decree of 14 August 1946 by which the Politburo member Andrei Zhdanov publicly slandered her by calling her 'half a nun, half a whore'.[9] This stanza also alludes to the fate of the prophetess Cassandra, who was raped by Greek soldiers after the capture of Troy, dragged into slavery in Mycenae and finally murdered. The violation of Cassandra is the image Mandelstam uses to refer to the barbaric onslaught of the new Scythians on art and beauty:

---

8 The poem 'To Cassandra': N. Å. Nilsson, 'To Cassandra', 105–13; R. Dutli, *Europas zarte Hände*, 38–43.

9 Zhdanov's defamatory remarks about Akhmatova: T. Bek (ed.), *Antologiia Akmeizma*, 282–5.

> In that crazy capital on the Neva,
> Some Scythian holiday,
> Some sickening loud ball,
> They'll rip the kerchief off that lovely head.
> (CP, 96–7)

Anna Akhmatova was Mandelstam's most important conversation partner in the first winter of the revolution. The feeling of 'We' the Acmeists had possessed in 1912–1913 was now reborn and transmuted into a sense that they shared a community of fate. Their poetic solidarity and friendship were re-affirmed. It was in 1917 that Akhmatova published her third book of poetry, *The White Flock*. It was some years since she had lived with Gumilyov, and in 1918 she obtained a divorce and married the Assyriologist Vladimir Shileiko. She writes in 'Pages from a Diary' of the intensive discussions she had with Mandelstam during the winter of 1917–1918:

> Mandelstam would often come to take me out for rides in a horse-drawn cab past the incredible potholes of the revolutionary winter, amidst the celebrated bonfires that burned almost until May, and we would listen to the gunfire wafting from who knows where. That's how we would drive to readings at the Academy of Arts, where they held benefits for the wounded and where we both read several times. Osip was also with me at Butomo Nezvanova's concert at the Conservatory when she sang Schubert. All the poems Mandelstam addressed to me date from this period.[10]

A poem written in January 1918 reflects the strong impression made by the Schubert concert, as themes from the songs *Die schöne Müllerin* (Wilhelm Müller), 'Der Erlkönig' (Goethe) and 'Der Doppelgänger' (Heine) are woven into it. It is as if the two poets had sought in the 'intoxication of music' an antidote to the dominant 'rattle of gunfire' (TR, 53). On one occasion, Akhmatova had fallen ill and was feverish. Mandelstam visited her and helped her to light the oven. This led in February to the mysterious poem 'That Tick-tock of Grasshoppers', with its images of fire and fever. The final stanza invokes 'nightingale fever', the obsessive,

10 Akhmatova's memories of the 'winter of revolution' and her meetings with Mandelstam, 1917–1918: Akhmatova, *My Half Century*, 93–4.

feverish versifying during the disorders of the period of revolution which is also intended to ward off the death that surrounds them on all sides:

Because death is blameless,
And there isn't a cure,
In the nightingale's fever
A beating heart remains.
(TR, 57; MT, 48)

The two of them recited poems to one another: this was also an antidote to violence, plundering and anarchy. Throughout his life, Mandelstam was fascinated by Anna Akhmatova's grave and dignified manner of recitation. Whether she was reciting her own poems or other people's, he hung onto every word from this new embodiment of the prophetess Cassandra. He sought to explain this fascination in a poem written at the time:

Your wonderful pronunciation:
The dry call of a predatory bird
Or, rather, the living image of
Silken sheets of lightning.
(TR, 55; MT, 33)

It almost turns into a love poem. Perhaps, in those winter nights, Mandelstam was looking for something more than discussions with a fellow poet: 'And in your whisper, so much silk / And so much air, and so much light / That as if blinded we both drink / The sunless brew of windy night.' Their nocturnal meetings and feverish poetry readings gradually grew too much for Akhmatova, who was soon to marry Vladimir Shileiko: 'I had to explain to Osip that we shouldn't be meeting so often, because it could give people grounds for misconstruing the nature of our relationship, and he unexpectedly got very offended, and roughly in March he disappeared completely.'

Mandelstam was quick to recognise Akhmatova's qualities as a poet. He wrote a review of a selection of her poetry printed in *Almanac of the Muses*, a volume which appeared in Petrograd in 1916. In this review, not published during his lifetime, he wrote: 'The voice of renunciation grows ever stronger in Akhmatova's verse, and, at the present moment, her poetry is close to becoming a major symbol of Russia's grandeur' (GP, 73; CC, 107). It was Mandelstam's good fortune that there were periods in which he interacted intensively with the two most significant Russian poetesses of the twentieth century. First there was Marina Tsvetaeva, from January to June 1916; she was followed by 'Cassandra', Anna Akhmatova, from December 1917 to February 1918. Mandelstam and Akhmatova shared a mutual devotion to 'the nightingale's fever' during the gloomy nights of the first winter of revolution.

On 7 December 1917, the Soviet of People's Commissars, chaired by Lenin, decided to create the Cheka (Special Commission for the Fight against Counter-Revolution and Sabotage) and appointed 'Iron' Felix Dzerzhinsky to head it. On his appointment, he called on the People's Commissars to use 'organised violence against counter-revolutionary activists'. A little later, on 5 September 1918, in the context of the 'Red terror' officially unleashed by Lenin after the anarchist Fanny Kaplan had attempted to assassinate him on 30 August, the Cheka was declared an 'unerring' organ with unlimited powers, including the right to shoot suspects without court proceedings. In addition, the murder of Uritsky, the head of the Petrograd Cheka, by Leonid Kannegisser, which also took place on 30 August, was followed by the immediate execution of 500 hostages.

The Bolsheviks had already proclaimed in 1918 that they would 'force mankind into happiness with an iron hand'. On 19 January 1918 (New Style), they dispersed the Constituent Assembly. On 3 March, the Treaty of Brest-Litovsk was signed, and, for Russia, the world war was at an end. But the year 1918 also marked the beginning of a new and ferocious conflict, the Russian Civil War, between the 'White' Tsarist troops and the Red Army organised by Trotsky. The main theatres of war were at first Siberia and the Ural-Volga region. In Petrograd, the civil war resulted in severe food supply problems, made worse by exceptionally cold weather.

Mandelstam was under no illusion about the scale of the disaster. The agony of his beloved Petersburg had begun. Even a year before the revolution, in May 1916, he had described the place as a city of death, the realm of the underworld goddess Proserpina. Petropolis had turned into Necropolis, which is what Mandelstam's respected predecessor Chaadaev had called the city in his *Philosophical Letters* (1830).

We shall leave our bones in transparent Petropolis,
Where Proserpina rules over us.
We drink the deadly air with every breath,
And every hour is the anniversary of our death.
(TR, 23; EW, 51)

Dilapidation and neglect rapidly eroded the city's former magnificence. In March 1918, Mandelstam wrote a poem on the subject which was full of apocalyptic images. It was a necrology with the following refrain, repeated four times: 'Your brother, Petropolis, is dying' (TR, 59). The 'window onto Europe' raised from the Neva swamps by Peter the Great, at the cost of countless human lives, soon ceased to be the capital of the state. On the twelfth of the month, the Bolsheviks moved the seat of government to Moscow. At the end of March, the People's Commissar for Enlightenment, Lunacharsky, offered a compromise to the 'creative intelligentsia of the bourgeoisie'. Admittedly, the Proletkult poets received the most encouragement, but even so, Lunacharsky's signal did offer artists and intellectuals a ray of hope. In April 1918, Mandelstam received a temporary appointment to the press office of the Central Commission for the Evacuation of Petrograd. He travelled repeatedly to Moscow in this capacity.

In May 1918, he wrote the poem 'The Twilight of Freedom', with which, to use the conventional cliché, he 'greeted the revolution'. But it was hardly a celebration of the Bolshevik triumph. The ambiguous nature of this 'twilight' is clear from the outset:

Let us celebrate, my brothers, freedom's twilight,
The great twilight year.
Into the seething waters of night
A heavy wood of snares is lowered.
You are arising into dead years
O sun, my judges, people.[11]

In Russian, as well as in German, the word 'twilight' (*sumerki*) can signify both daybreak and sunset. It is not surprising, therefore, that Mandelstam was compelled by the censor to remove both the title of the poem and the

11 TR, 63; O. Mandelstam, *Osip Mandelstam. Selected Poems*, 53. This work will henceforth be referred to as OM.

first two verses ('twilight' appears three times!) when it was published in his last volume of poetry in 1928. The poem is full of ominous symbols. No one knows what the 'snares' will bring up from the 'seething waters'. It speaks of 'numb' years, of 'dull' years, not of sounding years. To the sensitive ears of Mandelstam, who placed the sense of hearing at the absolute summit of human faculties, this was an epithet with dangerous overtones!

In the second stanza the 'ship of the time' is sinking: this is manifestly a shipwreck. In the third, the 'swallows' – an image for souls, but also for poets (as in Hölderlin: 'Poets, like swallows, are free') – are 'fettered to warring legions'. At the same time the sun grows ever darker, and finally becomes invisible: 'The sun cannot be seen, the earth is sailing.' This poem, like the December 1917 poem 'To Cassandra', is largely about loss: loss of freedom, sound, time and light.[12]

Even so, and despite all the gloom, the last of the four stanzas encourages Mandelstam's contemporaries to risk the upheaval:

> Well then let us try. A huge clumsy
> Creaking, turning of the wheel,
> The earth is sailing. Be manful, men.
> As with a plough, dividing the ocean
> We will remember in Lethe's freezing cold
> That the earth cost us ten heavens.
> (AT, 24)

Mandelstam was far from sharing the blind enthusiasm of the Proletkult poets, even if he consciously borrowed some of their rhetoric, as when he invokes the rising 'sun' of the revolution or refers to 'brothers' or 'warring legions'. His poem is a warning against naïve revolutionary euphoria, and it also expresses a tragic awareness of the harsh and difficult times to come. At the end of the twenties, Mandelstam said to the poet Postupalsky: 'Decide for yourself whether these verses contain more hope or more hopelessness. But it is the spirit of willingness that is most important.'[13]

---

12 'The Twilight of Freedom': N. Å. Nilsson, 'Sumerki Svobody', 47–68; N. Å. Nilsson, 'Mandel'shtam's *Sumerki* Poems', 467–80. Hölderlin's analogy between the souls of poets and swallows is to be found in his poem 'Die Wanderung': 'But it's the Caucasus I desire / Because I heard the news today / Wafted on the breeze / That poets just like swallows must be free.'

13 M. on the 'spirit of willingness': commentary in the Russian edition of his works, O. Mandel'shtam, *Sochineniia v Dvukh Tomakh*, vol. 1, 483.

Mandelstam's ambiguous poem about the revolution had little in common with the high-spirited enthusiasm of Mayakovsky, the 'drummer of the revolution'. In any case, the latter's rapturous approval was not repaid in kind by the holders of power. Lenin's comments on Mayakovsky's poem in celebration of the revolution, '150,000,000' (1919–1920) are well known: 'Nonsensical, utterly foolish, and pretentious rubbish … Lunacharsky should be soundly thrashed for this Futurism. Lenin.'[14] Even contemporaries who were closely associated with the former Futurist have described Mayakovsky's relationship with reality as 'unbelievably naïve' (Roman Jakobson).[15]

Mandelstam's extremely complex poem appeared on 24 May 1918 in the Petrograd newspaper *The Banner of Labour*. This organ of the Left SRs also published verses on the revolution by several other notable poets. Alexander Blok's famous poem 'The Twelve' appeared there on 3 March. In addition, on 19 May, some days before Mandelstam's poem, Sergei Yesenin's utopian offering 'Inoniya' (Other Land) was printed. It relates the dream of the 'Prophet Yesenin Sergei' about a peasant paradise, inspired by the biblical prophet Jeremiah.

A month after Mandelstam's poem was printed in it, the newspaper was suppressed, as part of the repressive measures being taken at that time against the Left SRs. Who were the Left SRs? They were a group of revolutionaries who had been expelled from the main body of the SRs at their June 1917 congress and had replied by setting up their own party. They refused to cooperate with the Provisional Government and actively participated in the October Revolution. But in March 1918, they protested against the Treaty of Brest-Litovsk by resigning from the coalition government they had entered into with the Bolsheviks. Four months later, after a failed attempt at a putsch, they were forced into illegality by the holders of power.

Mandelstam's tragic and courageous call to risk revolution despite everything occupies an isolated position in his work. Most of the poems he produced in May 1918 were different: sombre and melancholy. While the capital was being moved from Petrograd to Moscow, government offices were temporarily housed in the Moscow hotel 'Metropol'. One of the poems portrays the view from the hotel balcony to the Bolshoi Theatre,

---

14 Lenin's comments on Mayakovsky's poem '150,000,000', in German in W. Majakowski, *Werke in zehn Bänden, Zweites Buch*, 449.

15 Mayakovsky's 'naivité': R. Jakobson, *Meine futuristischen Jahre*, 94.

which was directly opposite. Crowds of 'mourning revellers' stream out of the theatre like the participants in a 'midnight wake'. A 'mob excited by the games' buries the 'nocturnal sun' and Moscow arises like a 'new Herculaneum' (TR, 61), a reference to the town which was buried under a deluge of mud when Vesuvius erupted in the year 79 C.E. In his *Tristia* poems, Mandelstam merges Petersburg into an ancient 'Petropolis', like Rome, Venice, Jerusalem and Troy, but Moscow he equates with a Roman provincial town choked in mud. The cultivated Petersburg poet feels alienated in the new capital. It could even be said that he hates it:

> It's all alien, for us, in this obscene metropolis,
> With her dry, hard ground,
> And Sukharevka, her raving grain market,
> And the horrible look of her pirate Kremlin.
> (TR, 183; CP, 315)

He characterises the Bolshevik capital as vulgar, greedy and rapacious, as a 'dark wood' which wants to rule the world, 'as a broad peasant woman crushing half the universe'. He portrays the city as opportunistic, obsequious and submissive to those in power: 'In bargaining it's a clever fox, / But small and servile in face of a prince.' He was only prepared to exclude from this sharply satirical portrait the Moscow churches, the buildings Marina Tsvetaeva had commended so passionately in February 1916: 'Only your churches – sweet-smelling honeycombs / Like wild honey buried deep in the woods.'

On 1 June 1918, thanks to Lunacharsky's recommendation, Mandelstam received an official position in this alien town. His task was to lead the section for the 'artistic education of students' within the 'university reform' department of the People's Commissariat of Enlightenment. His poem 'The Twilight of Freedom' had perhaps helped him to get the job. But he was only able to last out a few months in this new situation. He was not one of those enlightened clerks who have created some of the twentieth century's best modern works of literature, such as Constantine Cavafy, Franz Kafka or Fernando Pessoa. Mandelstam was completely unsuited to doing orderly work in an office; in fact, he was quite simply a professional failure – if one leaves aside his vocation as a poet.

It was a grim omen for everything that happened later when, in the same month of June 1918, he had his first clash with a representative of the new state. The Cheka agent Blumkin had swaggered into the Moscow 'Poets' Café' publicly boasting about his power to make life or death decisions. He was waving a bundle of execution orders supposedly signed in advance by Dzerzhinsky. He only needed to add a name, he said, and any 'weak-kneed intellectual' could be liquidated within the hour. Thereupon, Mandelstam, 'who quivers at the sight of a dentist's drill as if it were a guillotine, suddenly jumps up, runs over to Blumkin, grabs the bundle of blank forms, and tears them to bits'. This account comes from *Petersburg Winters* (1928), the memoirs of Georgy Ivanov, an Acmeist poet who emigrated to Paris in 1923, although admittedly many of the incidents he recorded were somewhat embellished with fabulous stories.

Nadezhda Mandelstam devotes a certain amount of space to this episode in a chapter of her memoirs *Hope Against Hope* which is entitled 'Thou Shalt Not Kill'. She reports Osip's strong aversion to the death penalty and to shootings in general. Blumkin is said to have replied to the poet's protest against his murderous boasting by drawing his revolver and threatening to shoot him on the spot. A few days later, on 6 July 1918, Blumkin assassinated the German ambassador, Count von Mirbach. This was planned as the signal for an insurrection attempt by the Left SRs, though it turned into an act of 'political suicide' (Günther Stökl).

Blumkin would repeat his threat against Mandelstam on several occasions in subsequent years. After the June 1918 incident, the poet ran in agitation from the café to call on Larissa Reissner, who was married to the Bolshevik Fyodor Raskolnikov and had access to the people in power. She accompanied Mandelstam on 1 July when he went to see Dzerzhinsky, the head of the Cheka, to complain about Blumkin. But, despite a promise made by the 'iron' People's Commissar, the revolver-brandishing Cheka hero was not molested, and, indeed, in 1919 he was officially amnestied for the murder of Mirbach.[16]

The atmosphere continued to grow more and more violent, and Blumkin felt his brutality was justified by the spirit of the age. Nadezhda Mandelstam later commented laconically: 'The head-hunting mentality spread among us like an infection.' In his memoirs, entitled *Necropolis*, Vladislav Khodasevich tells of an evening at which the poet Sergei Yesenin and his friend Blumkin – the same Blumkin! – were present. Yesenin was flirting

---

16 Georgy Ivanov on M.'s clash with Blumkin: G. Ivanov, *Disintegration of the Atom*, 122. M. complains to Dzerzhinsky about Blumkin: commentary section of N. Mandelstam, *Hope Against Hope*, 481–2.

with a woman, and he asked her: 'Would you like to *see* some executions? I can arrange that immediately for you through Blumkin.'[17]

Nadezhda Mandelstam has depicted her husband's instinctive endeavour to keep his distance from the holders of power. Here is another episode from that period: as an employee of the press office of the Evacuation Commission, Mandelstam was once obliged to spend a night in the Kremlin, in the dwelling of a top official, Gorbunov. In the morning, he went to the dining hall. The rumour spread that Trotsky would soon emerge to have his breakfast. Mandelstam got up, quickly picked up his coat and fled from the scene. In starving Moscow, he preferred to leave behind a plate that was full for once, rather than stay.

Later on, he was as unable to explain this impulse to flee as he was to explain his instinctive opposition to Blumkin's homicidal boastfulness and his support for a person completely unknown to him, whom the man with the revolver wanted to shoot. Without a doubt, Mandelstam was traumatised by his clash with Blumkin. He feared the Chekist's vengeance. The contradiction between his over-sensitivity and anxiety, on the one hand, and his outbursts of fury, his attacks of well-nigh suicidal courage, on the other, would remain a leitmotif of his life. The Blumkin incident put him into a state of anxiety and depression. The mysterious 'Telephone' poem of June 1918 suggests that he was perhaps even toying with ideas of suicide: 'In this wild and dreadful world of terror / You, midnight burial's gruesome friend / In the strict and lofty studio / Of the suicide – the telephone!' (TR, 185).

In August 1918, Mandelstam was very late in returning from his summer break to his place of work in the People's Commissariat of Enlightenment. He received a reprimand for 'unacceptable absence' and neglect of duty. His tardiness was also probably a response to his traumatic experience. On 20 October 1918, the poet Alexander Blok noted in his diary that Mandelstam had visited him in Petrograd, and that he had told him 'interesting details' about the assassination of Mirbach. These 'details' are more likely to have concerned Blumkin, the man who carried out the assassination, and who haunted Mandelstam in his nightmares.

After his arrest in May 1934, Mandelstam would declare under interrogation that at the end of 1918, he had started to suffer a 'political depression, brought about by the harsh methods used to put into effect

---

17 The Yesenin–Blumkin episode: V. Khodasevich, *Necropolis*, 138.

'The speech of the father and the speech of the mother – hasn't my own language been nourished my whole life by the confluence of these two languages?': Photographs of Flora Verblovskaia and Emil-Khazkel Mandelstam taken at the time of their marriage in 1889.

'My first conscious, sharp perceptions were of gloomy crowds of people in the streets.' Photograph of Osip Mandelstam, in Pavlovsk, 1894.

'The strong, ruddy, Russian year rolled through the calendar.' The brothers Osia – standing – and Shura (Alexander) Mandelstam (Photograph, 1896).

'He had a kind of feral relationship to literature, as if it were the only source of animal warmth.' Vladimir Gippius, Mandelstam's literature teacher at the Tenishev School from 1904.

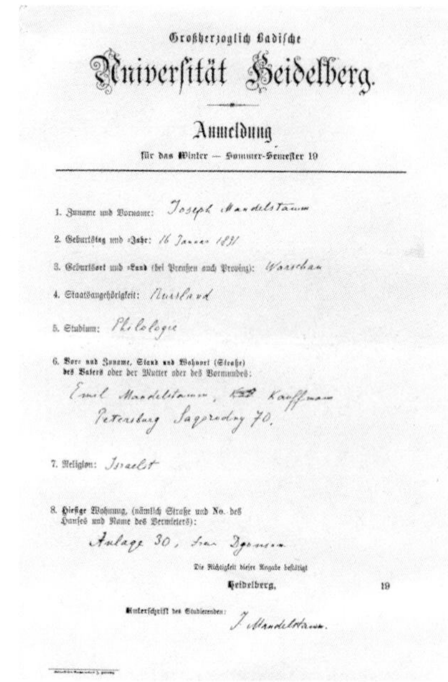

Großherzoglich Badische
Universität Heidelberg.

Anmeldung
für das Winter — Sommer-Semester 19

1. Zuname und Vorname: Joseph Mandelstamm
2. Geburtstag und -Jahr: 16 Januar 1891
3. Geburtsort und -Land (bei Preußen auch Provinz): Warschau
4. Staatsangehörigkeit: Russland
5. Studium: Philologie
6. Vor- und Zuname, Stand und Wohnort (Straße) des Vaters oder der Mutter oder des Vormundes:
Emil Mandelstamm, Kauffmann
Petersburg Sagorodny 70.
7. Religion: Israelit
8. Hiesige Wohnung, (nämlich Straße und No. des Hauses und Name des Vermieters):
Anlage 30, Frau Iggerson

Die Richtigkeit dieser Angabe bestätigt
Heidelberg, 19

Unterschrift des Studierenden: J. Mandelstamm.

Reproduction of Heidelberg University registration form in the name of 'Joseph Mandelstamm'.

'I feel "homesick", not for Russia but for Finland.' Mandelstam in Vyborg, 1911 (with two unidentified women).

'How can I be blamed / If I sense the milkiness of faint stars?' Osip Mandelstam, 1912.

'Joseph sold into Egypt / Could not have grieved so much for home!' Facsimile of the manuscript of Mandelstam's poem 'The Bread is Poisoned and Air's Drunk Dry', 1913.

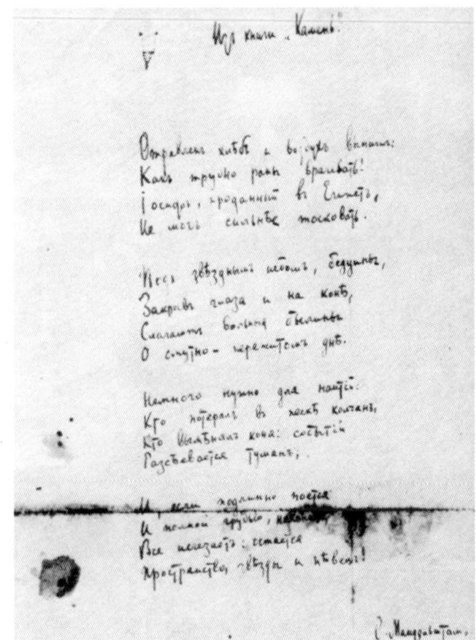

'The stone is the word.' Photograph of the title page of Mandelstam's first book of poetry, *Stone*, Akme Press, St Petersburg 1913.

О. МАНДЕЛЬШТАМЪ.

КАМЕНЬ

СТИХИ.

АКМЭ.

С.-ПЕТЕРБУРГЪ.

'A mole who burrowed enough passageways in the earth to last for a century.' The Cubo-Futurist Velimir Khlebnikov, 1912.

'A struggle for planet earth'. Two authors of Acmeist manifestos, Nikolai Gumilyov and Sergei Gorodetsky, 1913.

'Thus in poetry the boundaries of the national are destroyed.' Osip Mandelstam, Kornei Chukovsky, Benedict Livshits and Yury Annenkov (from left to right), August 1914.

'I have received a blessed legacy / A foreign poet left me his wandering dreams'. Drawing by Piotr Miturich, 'Osip Mandelstam 1915'.

'A selfless song is its own praise': Osip Mandelstam in 1914.

The poet and painter Maximilian Voloshin (1877–1932), whose house in Koktebel on the Crimean Peninsula was a place of refuge for many artists; Mandelstam spent the summer months of 1915, 1916 and 1917 there as a guest.

'I could not love there, / And here I am afraid.' Portrait of Osip Mandelstam by Anna Zelmanova-Chudovskaia, 1914.

'No one has ever stared more / Tenderly or more fixedly after you.' Marina Tsvetaeva in the 'marvellous days' of 1916, when she 'was giving Mandelstam Moscow', and writing many poems to him.

'I've learned those blessed words by heart.' Osip Mandelstam in 1916.

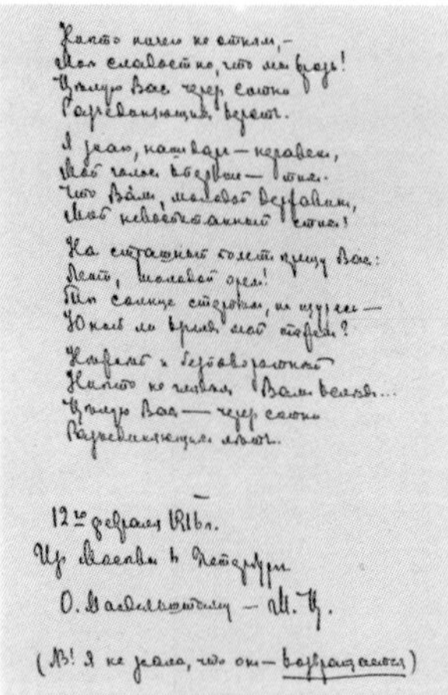

'I kiss you – across hundreds of / Separating years.' Autograph of Marina Tsvetaeva's first poem to Mandelstam (12 February 1916), written down in 1931 for Salomeia Andronikova-Galpern, the addressee of Mandelstam's 'Solominka' poem (December 1916).

'Time blossomed and I did not reach for / Your lips, Cassandra, your eyes, Cassandra.' Anna Akhmatova, 'one of the symbols of Russia's greatness' according to Mandelstam in 1916.

'I smile with your smile and I hear your voice in the silence.' Photograph of Nadezhda Khazina, who became acquainted with Mandelstam on 1 May 1919 in Kyiv.

'In memory of our future meeting.' Nadezhda Khazina as a young girl – this is the photograph she gave Mandelstam in August 1919 on the occasion of his departure from Kyiv.

'I wasn't made for prison.' Osip Mandelstam at the time of the civil war, 1919.

'All we have left to us is kisses.' Photograph of the actress Olga Arbenina, to whom Mandelstam dedicated love poems in autumn 1920.

'A real literary steamroller, with enough temperament for ten people.' Photograph of Viktor Shklovsky, the author of *Sentimental Journey* (1923).

'My time, my beast, who will be able / To peer into your pupils?' The Third Edition of *Stone* (1923), issued by the State Publishing House. Jacket design by Alexander Rodchenko.

A 'first-rate seculariser of poetry' beside the 'drummer of the revolution', who had become a didactic poet. Photograph of Boris Pasternak and Vladimir Mayakovsky.

'My conversation with Kolya never was and never will be broken off.' Photograph of Nikolai Gumilyov, leader of the Acmeists, fellow poet and friend of Mandelstam, shot in Petrograd in 1921 as a 'counter-revolutionary'.

the dictatorship of the proletariat'.[18] The clash with Blumkin certainly played a decisive part in this. Mandelstam's poem 'Tristia', which bears the date 1918, is evidence of his growing alienation at this time, and his feeling that he was beginning a period of 'inner exile'. He was inspired by Ovid and the poems he had written in exile, namely *Tristia* and *Epistulae ex Ponto* (Letters from the Black Sea). Mandelstam's interest in the Roman poet, who was exiled to Tomis, 'the end of the world', by the Emperor Augustus in the year 8 C.E., had already been aroused in 1914 and 1915. Now he put himself in Ovid's place during the last night he spent in Rome before he went into exile, as described in the third elegy of Book 1 of *Tristia* ('Cum subit illius tristissima noctis imago / quae mihi supremum tempus in urbe fuit') ['When the very sad image comes into my mind of that night / Which was the last time I ever spent in the city']:

> I've acquired the craft of separating
> In the unbraided laments of the night.
> With oxen chewing and tedious waiting,
> The city watch drags out the hour till light,
> I revere the ritual of that night when cockerels crow,
> When tear-stained eyes strained afar and long,
> Assuming the burden of the wayfarers' woe,
> And women's weeping mingled with the Muses' song.
> (TR, 65; FP, 47)

An important aspect of Mandelstam's poems around the time of the October Revolution and the Russian Civil War is the way classical motifs and mythical figures (Odysseus, Cassandra, Persephone, Proserpina and so on) are blended into the Russian present. This is only one of the indications that Mandelstam, in opposition to the society's blind faith in progress and the government's propaganda about a 'bright future', had developed a cyclical view of history and was convinced that similar combinations of events would recur again and again. As he says in 'Tristia': 'Everything has been before and again will come to pass / And sweet for us is only the instant of recognition.' The return of the past is reflected in the poem itself: it contains a multiplicity of literary reminiscences, which are the fragmentary voices of 'returning' predecessors – Homer,

18 M.'s 'political depression' in 1918 according to the minutes of his 1934 interrogation: V. Shentalinsky, *Arrested Voices*, 177.

Tibullus, Ovid, Batyushkov, Pushkin – and it represents Mandelstam's own panoramic synopsis of lyrical themes such as departure, exile, love, prophecy and death.

The two most important poems of 1918 – the poem about the revolution, 'Twilight of Freedom', which works with stock images from the Proletkult stable, and 'Tristia', the poem inspired by Ovid – are only apparently contradictory. Both speak of tragic loss and uncertainty about the future. The nature of the 'new life' proclaimed by the cockerel in the second poem remains uncertain, as do the kinds of 'separations' and 'partings' that are in prospect. Mandelstam would have to undergo further bitter lessons in the 'craft of separating' in his future life and in the poetry of the coming years.

Notwithstanding his 'political depression', Mandelstam did his work effectively in the People's Commissariat of Enlightenment during the last two months of 1918. Within the framework of university reform, he was intensively engaged in eurhythmics, and in drafting a proposal for an Institute for Eurhythmic Education. This was a somewhat fashionable idea at the time. The Swiss educationalist and composer Émile Jaques-Dalcroze (1865–1950) had worked out a system of eurhythmic education, which consisted in a harmonious combination of physical exercise, psychological stimuli and music. He opened his first School of Movement in 1910 in Hellerau, a suburb of Dresden. He had enthusiastic imitators everywhere, not least in revolutionary Russia. Eurhythmics studios were established in Petrograd and Moscow, and they were not disdained by interested poets such as Alexander Blok, Mikhail Kuzmin and Vladimir Pyast.

The desire for movement and rhythm was something the poet Mandelstam had in common with the newly forming society. As part of his lecturing activities, he wrote the essay 'Government and Rhythm'. A striking aspect of it is Mandelstam's stress on the individual personality, despite all his concern for the 'collective': 'While organizing society … we tend to forget that what must be organized first and foremost is the individual' (GP, 77; CC, 108). Mandelstam writes of two renaissances: the Italian Renaissance in the name of the individual, and the second renaissance, the Russian Revolution, in the name of the collective. A typical feature of his approach here is the assertion that in the second manifestation of rebirth, 'philology', or 'love of the word', has suffered, has clearly undergone a defeat. He succinctly draws attention to the 'anti-philological character of our age', which has 'betrayed philology' (GP, 79; CC, 109).

This is not far removed from the more radical division of mankind into 'friends' and 'foes' of the word in the next essay, 'The Word and Culture', written in 1921. After all, 'Government and Rhythm' itself contains the resonantly oracular utterance 'We live under a barbarian sky, yet we are still Hellenes' (CC, 109).

The theme of the approach of barbarism had long been a literary commonplace in Russia. The Symbolist poets, weary of civilisation, had seen the barbarians coming, and they welcomed them. Valery Bryusov ended his poem 'The Coming Huns' (1904–1905) with a salute to the invaders. And in one of his last poems (30 January 1918), Alexander Blok identified himself with the 'Scythians': 'We are Scythians, Asiatics.' Both men offered their services to the Bolsheviks. Bryusov quickly became a party member and the director of the literature department in the People's Commissariat of Enlightenment, but Blok, who was more sensitive, and had called on his contemporaries to hear the 'music of the revolution' in his January 1918 essay 'Intelligentsia and Revolution', would soon suffocate in the new 'Scythian' air. Nowhere in his work had Mandelstam greeted the coming of the Huns, the Scythians or the barbarians. He was a European who did not share this fashionable weariness with civilisation, and he would continue his effort to remain a Hellene under a barbarian sky.

In February 1919, the Bolsheviks put the Left SRs under further pressure by arresting many of them. Mandelstam had good reason to fear this wave of repression. His poems against the Bolsheviks – the Kerensky poem on the 'yoke of malice and violence' and the ominously prophetic verses 'To Cassandra' – had appeared in November and December 1917 in SR newspapers. It was perhaps this anxiety that led him abruptly to give up his position in Lunacharsky's People's Commissariat. Or was he sacked for blatant 'neglect of duty'? Or was his habit of leaving any regular job after a few weeks simply too ingrained to be resisted?

Whatever the reason, he again fled in the usual direction: southwards. In the middle of February, he travelled to Kharkov, in Ukraine. He would not see Moscow again for almost another two years. Shortly before his departure, on 30 January 1919, the manifesto 'The Morning of Acmeism', which he had already written in 1913, appeared in the Voronezh journal *Sirene*, which was edited by his Acmeist colleague Vladimir Narbut. It was a message from another age, an anachronistic siren song. It was a life-affirming call from a distant past whose echoes had not yet died away.

10

A Girl's Forehead in the Civil War

(Kyiv, Feodosiia, Tbilisi 1919–1920)

The civil war year of 1919 was one of the cruellest in the whole of Russia's history. Boris Pilnyak summed it up concisely in his semi-documentary novel *The Naked Year* (1922): 'There was no bread. There was no food. Everywhere hunger and death, lies, horror and dismay – it was the year nineteen.' Mandelstam's brother Yevgeny also recalls this terrible year: 'Epidemics, the collapse of ways of communication, hunger, bagmen.' The 'bagmen' were people who swarmed out of the town into the countryside in order to get hold of anything edible. Yevgeny also describes what he saw when he arrived at the Kursk station in Moscow: living victims of typhus lay on the station platform, jumbled together with those already dead.[1]

During the period of 'war communism', Moscow was ruled not by the new regime, but by hunger, an agonising hunger which left its mark on many of the literary works of the time. There were even cases of cannibalism. An entry in the diary of the Symbolist Zinaida Gippius for 22 November 1919 reads:

> Do you know what 'Chinese meat' is? It is known that the Cheka gives the corpses of those it has shot to the animals in the Zoological Garden. Here with us, and in Moscow as well. The executioners are Chinese. But

1 The year of civil war, 1919: E. Mandel'shtam, 'Vospominaniia', 148–9.

> they steal: they do not deliver all the corpses. They hold back the younger ones so as to sell them as veal. Doctor N. bought some veal 'with bone' and he recognised a human bone.

In his *Novel Without Lies* (1926) about his friendship with Sergei Yesenin, Anatoly Mariengof describes the numerous equestrian corpses which lined the roads of Moscow in 1919: 'Horses would fall on the streets, die, and clutter the roadways with their carcasses ... Opposite the main post office lay two bloated carcasses, one black, missing a tail, the other white with bared teeth. Atop the white one sat two ravens, pecking eye-jelly out of the hollow sockets.'[2]

In *A Sentimental Journey* (1923) Viktor Shklovsky recalls meals consisting of nothing more than frost-damaged potatoes ('And Petersburg had nothing to eat but frozen potatoes for two or three years') and horse meat, which was 'almost runny'. 'Horse meat was cooked in whale oil. At least it was called whale oil. Actually it was spermaceti [[a wax-like substance extracted from the head of the sperm whale, and used in the pharmaceutical industry (RD)]], which works fine in face creams, but sets your teeth on edge.'[3]

Mandelstam's departure from Moscow in the middle of February 1919 was also a flight from the hunger and ever-present violence that ravaged the city. But southern Russia was itself a civil war theatre, fiercely contested between the 'White' generals, Denikin and Wrangel, and Trotsky's Red Army. During the summer of 1919 Denikin conquered broad tracts of the area, although the Red Army was able to defeat his attempt to 'march on Moscow'.

Mandelstam found employment again in the Ukrainian city of Kharkov, though the job did not last longer than any of the other jobs he had held in the past or would hold in the future. He was appointed to lead the poetry section of the All-Ukrainian Literature Committee, under the Provisional Workers' and Peasants' Government of Ukraine. He wrote articles in newspapers and organised poetry readings. At the end of April, he moved again, this time to Kyiv, which had been in the hands of the Red Army since 5 February 1919. He repeatedly took part in collective poetry readings in the city.

---

2 A. Mariengof, *A Novel without Lies*, 49.

3 Human flesh and horse meat: Z. Gippius, *Dnevniki*, vol. 2, 260; V. Shklovsky, *A Sentimental Journey*, 180.

In Kyiv, he often visited the well-known artists' club 'KHLAM', which was located in the cellar of the Hotel Continental on Nikolaevskaia Street. The name of the club (which can be loosely translated as 'Junk Shop') referred ironically to its fluctuating clientele. It was an acronym composed of the initial letters of the words 'Painters – Writers – Actors – Musicians'. It was in 'KHLAM' on 1 May 1919 that Mandelstam met the young art student Nadezhda Khazina. This fateful meeting was one of the most important events of his life. Nadezhda came from an assimilated Kyivian-Jewish background. Her father, Iakov Khazin, was a lawyer, her mother a doctor. She was born on 31 October 1899 in Saratov, a town on the Volga, and as a child she had travelled with her parents to several Western European countries. Now she was studying painting under Alexandra Exter, one of the most important artists of the Russian avant-garde, who had played a decisive part in the emergence of both Cubo-Futurism and Constructivism, but would soon flee from the Bolsheviks to Odessa, whence she later emigrated to Paris.

Nadezhda was nineteen years old, almost nine years younger than Osip, and at that time she was reckless and provocative, behaviour which corresponded exactly with the prevailing atmosphere. She was a typical product of the era, clearly on the side of the revolution, hungry for life, thirsting for new experiences and eager for adventure. In a television interview of 1973, Nadezhda Mandelstam (as she would later be called) gave an account of this first meeting. On the very first night, she and Osip went to bed together. 'It simply happened so', she said in English, with her inimitable Russian accent. And she continued: 'We were the beginning of the sexual revolution. We had nothing to lose.' The revolution had also brought with it a new sexual morality, which only a few years later was suffocated by state-imposed prudery. Alexandra Kollontai, the revolutionary who was a strong advocate of women's rights, made the well-known statement that making love is no different from drinking a glass of water.

The two young artists 'had nothing to lose' when they spent this happy evening of the First of May in the crowded basement bar. The civil war was raging around the town of Kyiv, power was held alternately by Red and White forces, and the situation was marked by pogroms, executions and terror on all sides. Here death was in control. In the second volume of her memoirs, in the chapters 'Devastation' and 'We', Nadezhda explains in detail how important this first meeting was. They both regarded 1 May 1919 as 'their day', although they became separated shortly afterwards and did not meet again for one and a half years. When, during the winter of 1925–1926, Nadezhda had to remain in Yalta, on the Black Sea, under treatment for tuberculosis, Mandelstam wrote to her from Leningrad on 23 February 1926 to provide comfort and encouragement: 'Nadyushok, we'll be together again on May first in Kyiv, and we'll climb that old Dniepr mountain. I'm so glad about this, so glad!' (MR, 92; CC, 514) Every love affair has its intimate topography. In this case, it was the Kyiv 'KHLAM' and the Vladimir Hill on the river Dniepr.[4]

The eccentric poet Makkaveisky, who came from a family of priests, married them without further ado in a grotesque ceremony in the 'Greek café', which was not far from 'KHLAM'. They exchanged two cheap blue rings. 'So began our marriage, or sin, and neither of us dreamt that it would last a lifetime.' But the very next day Mandelstam was inspired to write a wedding poem, out of sheer happiness. It was a meditation on the origins of Western lyrical poetry, on Sappho, the poet who lived on Lesbos, and on Terpander, the inventor of the seven-stringed lyre. He also ingeniously wove themes from Sappho's 'Wedding Songs' (*Epithalamia*) into the poem. The Symbolist and classical philologist Vyacheslav Ivanov had published a collection of poems entitled *Alcaeus and Sappho* in Moscow in 1914. In the blood-drenched Kyiv of 1919, this book finally came into Mandelstam's hands in Nadezhda's room. The prominently domed forehead of Mandelstam's new girlfriend shines out in this poem:

> And a tall cold breeze blew
> From a girl's high forehead …
> Spring runs through the meadows of Hellas,
> Sappho is wearing her gay-coloured boots,
> And cicadas bang tiny hammers, forging
> A gossamer ring.
> (TR, 69; CP, 103–4)

Here, Sappho celebrates her poetic resurrection in the middle of the Russian Civil War, lit only by her coloured shoes and a girl's forehead. The last stanza of the poem refers back to the 'island of the blessed' seen in the poems of Hesiod, Pindar and Horace, an island which always has the additional significance of a profound desire for peace. The

4 M. returns to Kyiv, where he meets Nadezhda for the first time: N. Mandelstam, *Hope Abandoned*, 28–38 ('The Stampede' and 'We').

twenty-eight-year-old Mandelstam thus wove a great quantity of classical poetry into the verses he produced in civil-war-dominated Kyiv, a town which did not in the least resemble an 'island of the blessed'.[5]

Osip had a great liking for 'KHLAM', as it reminded him of his own earlier days as an insouciant young man in the Petersburg 'Stray Dog'. All around him, the students of the avant-garde artist Alexandra Exter were letting off steam. They had decorated the place in honour of the First of May holiday. Nadezhda often came into 'KHLAM' with her clique of friends. These young men loved Mayakovsky's 'Left March'; they were 'lefter than left'. They had long become accustomed to the gunfights of the period of revolution and civil war. 'We moved through the streets while people were shooting, and we ducked into doorways.'[6]

Mandelstam was as merry as the others, but he also differed profoundly from everyone else. He was not led astray by the harsh and violent atmosphere. He had a 'profound aversion to execution and torture'. Terror of any kind was unacceptable to him. And both the Reds and the Whites committed terrorist acts. Ilya Ehrenburg worked with Mandelstam in Kyiv at the department of the Commissariat of Social Welfare for the 'aesthetic education of children' located on Sadovaya Street. The provincial Cheka was accommodated in the house next door: 'A thin fence divided our garden from theirs, where every night innocent people were being tortured and murdered.'[7]

On 31 August 1919 Petliura's Ukrainian Nationalists and parts of Denikin's 'Volunteer Army' overran Kyiv. Before they left, the butchers of the Cheka hurriedly shot all their hostages. The torture and execution cellars overflowed with corpses. The 'White' conquerors opened up these places of horror to public view, as a measure of deterrence and a warning against supporting the Reds. Shocked and bewildered, Kyivians came to look for the bodies of friends and relatives who had disappeared. Nadezhda remembered a horse-drawn cart full of naked corpses driving out of the city. Furious mobs, in search of a red-haired Chekist named 'Chekist Rosa', indiscriminately lynched many women with red hair … In her memoirs,

5 Nadezhda's friend Makkaveisky conducts a form of 'wedding ceremony' for them: Mandelstam, *Hope Abandoned*, 134; Sapphic motifs in M.'s 'wedding song': K. Taranovsky, *Essays on Mandel'shtam*, 83–98.

6 Mandelstam, *Hope Abandoned*, 28.

7 Ehrenburg on their Chekist neighbours: commentary section of N. Mandelstam, *Vtoraia Kniga*, 635.

Nadezhda writes of the 'savagery' induced by the civil war which took place before her eyes.

Almost two decades later, in April 1937, during his period of exile in Voronezh, Mandelstam continued to remember the traumatising excesses of the civil war and the retreat of the Reds from Kyiv:

> Some wife, I don't know whose, searches
> The streets of the monster Kyiv for her husband.
> And on her waxen cheeks
> Not one tear drop has streaked.
>
> Gipsy girls don't tell fortunes for beauties.
> The violins don't play in the Kupechesky Park
> Horses have fallen in Kreschatik
> And the aristocratic Lipki smells of death.
>
> The Red Army soldiers have got
> Right out of town on the last tram.
> And a soaked greatcoat cried out:
> 'We'll be back. Just you wait!'[8]

The 'smell of death', the smell of blood and decaying bodies, hung over the 'Lipki' district of Kyiv after the hurried shootings in the Cheka's cellars. On 31 August 1919, Mandelstam left the city, having stayed there for five months. As usual, he wanted to go to the Crimea. His nineteen-year-old art student girlfriend Nadezhda remained in Kyiv. She was unwilling to travel with him, because 'blood was flowing everywhere beyond the threshold of the house'. Shortly afterwards, communication between Kyiv, the Crimea and other cities was completely cut off. For more than eighteen months, the two lovers were kept apart by the civil war. They were divided by front lines which were not of their making. Nadezhda gave Osip a present when he left. It was a photograph showing her as a schoolgirl, and she wrote on the back: 'To dear Osia, in memory of our future meeting.'

By the middle of September, Mandelstam had got as far as the Crimea, an area the 'Whites' had held since June. In the dossier from the state

8 WH, 205; O. Mandelstam, *Voronezh Notebooks*, 82. This work will henceforth be referred to as VN.

security service which led in 1938 to his final arrest, this journey to the Crimea was noted as a journey 'into White territory'. What drove him to do this? Was it disgust, and fear of the Red terror? Was it a yearning for 'his' Crimea, an emotion he had felt since summer 1915? Or was it the hope of finding work and food there? In her memoirs, Nadezhda insisted that it was right for Mandelstam to leave Kyiv 'where no-one knew him, and where he constantly attracted the furious attention of the mob and its leaders, whatever their political colour'.

For almost a year, Mandelstam would remain in the Crimea, either in the port of Feodosiia or in Koktebel at Voloshin's house. He had scarcely set foot in his 'promised land' when he struck up a song of poetic jubilation. The view of the bleak slopes of Kara-Dagh, behind Koktebel, made him think of the hills of Siena – a bold association indeed. He dreamed of Sienese painting, and the sound of Palestrina and the music of the organ filled his ears. He wrote a poem full of Christian themes which conjures up a moment of mercy in the troubles of the civil war: 'And down the Christian hills, through space that is astounded / Like Palestrina's song, the grace of God descends' (TR, 73). It is, for the moment, Mandelstam's last intellectual reversion to the 'cool mountain air of Christianity', to his 'Catholic phase' of 1913–1915, and to the essays 'Chaadaev' and 'Pushkin and Scriabin', written in defence of Christian art.

But, since 1 May 1919, he had been united with the Jewish Nadezhda Khazina, in a love which soared above the division into Red and White fronts. He sent a letter to her from Feodosiia on 5 December 1919:

> My darling child!
>
> There is almost no hope that this letter will reach you … I pray to God that you will hear what I say: my dear child, I cannot live and do not want to live without you. You are all my joy, you are my own. For me that is as simple as God's day. You have become so dear to me that I constantly talk to you, call you, complain to you. It is only to you that I can tell everything, everything … I rejoice and thank God that He gave you to me. With you nothing will be frightening, nothing will be difficult …
>
> Nadyusha! If you should suddenly appear here this minute, I would cry for joy. Forgive me, my beastikins! Let me kiss your dear little brow. Your plump, childish, dear little brow! My daughter, my sister, I smile with your smile and I hear your voice in the silence …

> Nadyusha, we shall be together at any cost, I shall find you and live for you because you give me life, without knowing it yourself. (MR, 27–8; CC, 484–5)

Here we are already reminded of the main themes of their future love letters, and the fateful phrase is uttered: 'With you nothing will be frightening.' Despite their separation by the civil war, Mandelstam continued to meditate on their relationship. Having written the 'Wedding Song' of 2 May 1919, inspired by Sappho, he wrote a 'cruel and strange' poem in the spring of 1920 which records his view of Nadezhda's destiny. He does not ascribe to her the role of the beautiful Helen; she will not be illuminated by the light of Ilion (Troy) but will stay in that 'yellow twilight' which remained so alien to him throughout his childhood, and which is his metaphor for Jewishness. What he has in mind for Nadezhda is rather the role of the biblical Leah, the daughter of Laban, who faithfully served her first husband Jacob (Genesis 29–31), but had to accept her beautiful sister Rachel as her rival:

> But a fateful change
> Must be fulfilled in you:
> You shall be called Leah – not Helen –
> Not because imperial blood
>
> Flows heavier in those veins
> Than yours.
> No, you shall fall in love with a Jew
> And dissolve in him. The Lord be with you.
> (TR, 77; EW, 56)

In a chapter of the second volume of her memoirs, headed 'Our Alliance', Nadezhda Mandelstam provides a detailed commentary on this poem about her destiny:

> Our relationship must have aroused in him a keen awareness of his Jewish roots, a tribal feeling, a sense of kinship with his people – I was the only Jewess in his life … I was the daughter, who, having fallen in love with a Jew, was destined to renounce herself and be dissolved in him … From me he wanted only one thing: that I should give up my life to him, renounce my own self, and become a part of him.

The poem expresses Mandelstam's patriarchal, biblically inspired image of the future marriage of two people who are at present kept apart by the civil war. But Mandelstam's 'alliance' with Nadezhda cannot be assimilated to a conventional model. It was an extremely unusual symbiosis between two human beings during a cruel epoch.[9]

Most of Mandelstam's year in the Crimea was spent in the town of Feodosiia, a port with a rich cultural inheritance which lay on the southern shores of the peninsula. It had been founded, as Theodosia, by Greek colonists in the sixth century B.C.E. In the Middle Ages, in 1266, it came under the rule of Genoa. It was the centre of Genoese trade in the Black Sea region. Now, though, the Crimea functioned as a rear base for the 'Whites', who were under greater and greater pressure from the Red Army. Large parts of the 'Volunteer Army' had been destroyed. At the beginning of April 1920, General Denikin abandoned the fight, handed over the supreme command to General Wrangel and went into exile.

Mandelstam lived frugally in Feodosiia, relying on the generosity of liberal lawyers, Jewish merchants and poetry lovers. In short, he lived off begged-for and borrowed money. Ilya Ehrenburg reports a telling anecdote on the subject:

> He gathered some rich 'liberals' in Feodosiia and told them severely: 'At the Last Judgement you'll be asked whether you understood the poet Mandelstam, and you'll say: no. You'll be asked whether you gave him to eat, and, if you reply yes, much shall be forgiven you.'[10]

Mandelstam, who throughout his life could only be a poet and nothing else, could not survive just on the magic of his poetry. He often needed his eloquence as well, to obtain funds by begging and borrowing.

A modest literary life existed in Feodosiia, despite the civil war. A small poetry group organised public readings. Mandelstam read by himself on 24 January 1920, and then on 1 March as part of a group of poets. A journal, *K Iskusstvu!* (To Art!), and an almanac, *Kovcheg* (The Ark), were published, and they included many of Mandelstam's poems. The poets met in a cellar or in the Fountain Café and tried to forget the civil war by composing poetry. In 1924, Mandelstam would write four autobiographical sketches under the title *Theodosia*. They are affectionate portraits of the

9 'Leah' poem: Mandelstam, *Hope Abandoned*, 266–7 ('Our Alliance').

10 M. in Feodosiia: I. Ehrenburg, *Men, Years – Life*, 104–9.

town, which was attempting to bear its occupation by the White generals in a dignified manner.

> It was the particular quirk of the city to pretend that nothing had changed, that everything remained just exactly as it always had been. And in old times the city resembled not Genoa, that nest of military and mercantile predators, but gentle Florence … But it was not easy for Attic Theodosia to adjust herself to the severe rule of the Crimean pirates. (RZ, 108–9; NT, 122–3)

Mandelstam endeavoured to find a refuge in this 'gentle Florence', which now had to adjust itself to the harsh laws of civil war. In the search for somewhere to stay at night, the homeless vagrant knocked on many different doors. The four *Theodosia* sketches describe his temporary shelters: with the harbour master Alexander Alexandrovich, who was secretly preparing his own evacuation ('The Harbour-Master'), with an old woman in the quarantine quarter ('The Old Woman's Bird'), with a poetry-writing officer of the Volunteer Army by the name of Tsygalsky ('The Royal Mantle of the Law') and with an eccentric artist ('Mazesa da Vinci') who considered himself to be a Leonardo, and only painted self-portraits.

The depiction of his night-time shelters in the *Theodosia* sketches is a pretext which allows him to portray the atmosphere of the civil war. 'Warm and gentle, the sheep-spirited city was turned into hell' (RZ, 112; NT, 124). The frightful suffering of the epoch is evident in all four sketches: 'one began to sense with physical clarity the plague that had descended upon the world, a Thirty Years' War, with pestilence, darkened lamps, barking of dogs, and, in the houses of little people, appalling silence' (RZ, 115; NT, 126). The portrait of the old woman with whom Mandelstam took refuge in the icy January of 1920 contains this bitter comment: 'At that time it was better to be a bird than a man, and the temptation to become the old woman's bird was enormous' (RZ, 114; NT, 125). Hell, plague, the misfortune of being human! Meanwhile, the power of the soldiers was evident every day on the streets of the town:

> The city was older, better and cleaner than anything that was going on in it. No dirt stuck to it. Into its splendid body bit the pioneers of prison and barracks, along its streets walked cyclopes in black felt cloaks, Cossack lieutenants smelling of dog and wolf, guardsmen of the defeated army

> wearing service caps and charged to the soles of their shoes with the foxy electricity of health and youth. On some people the possibility of committing murder with impunity acts like a fresh mineral bath, and for such people, with their childishly impudent and dangerously empty brown eyes, the Crimea was simply a spa. (RZ, 117; NT, 126–7)

The 'possibility of committing murder with impunity' was equally repellent to Mandelstam whether in relation to the Reds or the Whites. His new Crimean poems are imbued with reflections on the death that lurks all around. In March 1920, he writes:

> Heaviness and tenderness, you're sisters with the same device,
> Bumblebees and wasps both suck the heavy rose,
> Man dies, warm sand cools down,
> And yesterday's sun is borne away on a black bier.
> (TR, 75; FP, 48)

In this spring of 1920, he also produced a darkly magical poem about Venice, a bewitchingly beautiful, but also cryptic vision of the Serenissima. He occasionally tried to work as a day labourer in the vineyards around the village of Otuzy, 'for a piece of sheep's cheese and a jug of water'. The poet Emily Mindlin recalls that one evening, Mandelstam returned sweating from his labours in the vineyard and recited to him the seven magnificent stanzas of the Venice poem. It was his vision of human death, of death in Venice, which was also a mask for dying Petersburg, the 'Venice of the north'.

> Subtle leather smell. Dark blue veins.
> White snow. Green brocade.
> Everyone put in sedans of cypress wood,
> Taken warm and sleepy from his cloak.
>
> And candles burning, burning in their baskets
> Like the dove flown back into the ark.
> On the stage and in the idle
> Assembly, man is dying.[11]

---

11 TR, 85; C. Brown, *Mandelstam*, 87. Mindlin on the emergence of M.'s poem about Venice: V. Kreid and E. Necheporuk, *Osip Mandel'shtam i Ego Vremia*, 218.

'Man is dying', 'a man will die': death is ever present on this peninsula during the civil war. But, in Feodosiia, Mandelstam could dream of the 'green Adriatic' and of Venice, just as when he arrived in Koktebel he rapturously dreamed of 'Siena's hills'. On the Crimean coast, he felt he was in Italy. Siena and Venice – towns he had never seen – lived in his imagination.

He was no doubt very fond of the town. In June 1920, he dedicated a five-stanza poem to it, which appears strangely divorced from the troubles of the civil war, and in which he dreams of ordinary and peaceful daily life.[12] In it, Feodosiia continues to exude animal warmth and a wealth of different colours.

> Ringed round by high hills
> You run down from the mountain like a flock of sheep,
> And you sparkle with pink and white stones
> In the dry, transparent air.
> The pirates' feluccas sway,
> The poppies of Turkish flag burn in the port,
> The canes of masts, the elastic crystal of a wave
> And boats like hammocks on hawsers.
> (TR, 79; OM, 59)

The town lived from its lazily conducted trade, reminiscent of the East, and it housed a peaceful population which included musicians, pilgrims, Turks, a cook, old maids and admirals … 'O joyful Mediterranean menagerie!' he wrote. Mindlin tells us that Mandelstam often dreamed of taking journeys at that time, to the Bosphorus, or the Greek islands. But he never had the money to spend on travelling. At the end of the poem, he appears to have resigned himself to the situation:

> The distance is transparent. Some vines.
> And the fresh wind always blowing.
> It is not far from here to Smyrna and Baghdad
> But sailing is an effort and the stars are everywhere the same.
> (OM, 61)

12 The Feodosiia poem: R. Dutli, *Ein Fest mit Mandelstam*, 59–64.

The poem contains just one disturbing message, in verses 11 and 12: 'The wind carries away the golden seed / It is lost and will not return.' What is meant here is not just the golden seed of daily happiness, but the emigration of the intellectual and artistic elite, the people who sailed from Black Sea harbours in 1920, leaving Russia forever. Vladimir Nabokov, the other famous alumnus of the Tenishev School, had already left the Crimea with his family on 5 April 1919 on a Greek ship called *Hope*, which was heading towards Istanbul. In November 1920, when General Wrangel finally had to abandon the Crimea to the Red Army, he evacuated 130,000 'White' refugees. Even then, the haemorrhage from Russia was not yet at an end: in the autumn of 1922, Lenin would order the secret police (*Gosudarstvennoe politicheskoe upravlenie* – GPU) to arrest 170 leading members of the intellectual elite, professors, scientists and artists (among them the philosophers Nikolai Berdyaev and Sergei Bulgakov), put them on board a ship and remove them from Russia. Mandelstam could not have known anything of this 'ship of the 170 philosophers' in the spring of 1920, but his dream about the 'golden seed' which 'will not return' is also addressed to them.

Mandelstam was certainly no supporter of the 'Whites'. His view of the bloodthirsty Cossack cyclopes is unambiguously clear. There is a poem about the 'forgotten suckling babes of dark' who have 'fallen from the tree of life' (TR, 187; FP, 49). But it concludes by saying that the 'undying nations are condemned, they're fated for the stars', that is, the symbols of the young Soviet state. While in Feodosiia, Mandelstam entered into contact with the Red underground, and, in his constant search for a night-time refuge, he was also sheltered by a Bolshevik named Kamensky.

The poem 'Actors and Workers' (TR, 189), which Mandelstam wrote in summer 1920 for the opening of a café cabaret by the seashore in Feodosiia, also shows 'Red' sympathies. It invokes the unity of artists and workers, who are jointly engaged in a journey to the future. It is characteristic of Mandelstam's idiosyncratic attitude to the new reality that in November 1917, surrounded by Bolsheviks, he wrote three poems in defence of the 'losers of the revolution', whereas in summer 1920, surrounded by Wrangel's 'Whites', he wrote two 'Red' poems of pro-Soviet inspiration. It was as if he had got it into his head that he should stand between the fronts, and always take the other side, honouring the defeated.

He was doubtless aware of the massacres committed by the 'Whites' in the civil war against the Jewish population of the Ukraine. For many military men, the Jews were simply Bolsheviks, and their fight against the latter offered an excuse for pogroms. The deplorable result was that between 1917 and 1921 there were 1,236 pogroms, resulting in 60,000 murders of Jews, while half a million lost their possessions and their homes. Arno Lustiger writes:

> Never before in the pain-filled history of the Russian Jews had there been massacres on this scale … The propagandists of the 'Whites' and the Ukrainian Atamans claimed that the Jews were responsible for the Bolsheviks and their crimes. The age-old battle-cry 'Kill the Jews and save Russia' was heard again … The victory of the White Guard armies could have led to the complete annihilation of Russian Jewry.[13]

Admittedly, Jews were murdered by the Reds as well. On the Polish front, in Galicia, Podolia and Volhynia, the troops of General Budyonny rampaged furiously amid the Jewish population. Isaac Babel's *Red Cavalry* stories and his *1920 Diary* depict these terrible events. On 18 July 1920 Babel wrote in his diary: 'The Jewish cemetery behind Malin … has seen Khmelnytsky and now Budyonny. The unfortunate Jewish population, everything repeats itself … it repeats itself with alarming exactness'. Even so, many Jews were forced to see the Bolsheviks as the lesser evil. In July 1918, in order to put a stop to pogroms carried out by Red Army troops, the Council of People's Commissars sent a telegram, signed by Lenin, ordering all provincial Soviets 'to take decisive measures to stamp out the anti-Semitic movement and its roots'.

Mandelstam had good reason to fear the 'Whites'. As Voloshin recalls, 'he once came to see me in a state of great unease, and he said: "Max Alexandrovich, a Cossack captain has arrived and he wants to arrest me. Please come with me. I fear I may disappear somehow. You know what the Whites do to Jews."'[14] This first arrest went fairly well. Mandelstam was brought before a certain Colonel Zygalsky, who himself wrote poems and admired poets. One of the *Theodosia* sketches, 'The Royal Mantle of the Law', (RZ, 116–19; NT, 126–8) is a portrait of him.

---

13 Pogroms against Jews committed by the 'Whites' during the Civil War: A. Lustiger, *Stalin and the Jews*, 58–60.

14 Voloshin on M.'s fear of the 'Whites': Kreid and Necheporuk, *Osip Mandel'shtam i Ego Vremia*, 114.

Mandelstam was not completely alone in the Crimea. He had close friends, and he was soon in great need of their help. Unfortunately, it was in precisely July 1920 that a quarrel blew up between himself and Voloshin. It arose over a copy of Dante's *Divine Comedy*, which Mandelstam had borrowed from him. He had either lost it (his own version) or stolen it (Voloshin's version). Mandelstam was so angry about the suggestion that he had plundered Voloshin's library that, on 25 July 1920, he wrote an insulting letter in which he called him 'a scoundrel and a slanderer' (MR, 29). But it is not entirely certain that he was innocent: several of his contemporaries have confirmed that he had a negligent attitude towards any kind of property, whether his own or someone else's.[15]

Shortly afterwards, at the end of July 1920, he was arrested in Feodosiia by General Wrangel's counter-intelligence service as an alleged 'Bolshevik spy'. Was it his contacts with members of the Red underground that led to his arrest? Or was it the pro-Soviet poem 'Actors and Workers', which he had read out in public? He was most likely the victim of a denunciation. Emily Mindlin writes in his memoirs: 'Everyone always saw Mandelstam as a suspicious character, probably because of his appearance, which resembled that of a provocatively arrogant beggar.'

Mindlin, along with Maria Kudasheva, rushed immediately to Voloshin, to ask him to put in a word for the imprisoned poet. But it was not until Ehrenburg gave his backing that Voloshin was prepared to send a letter to the head of Wrangel's counter-intelligence in which he emphasised Mandelstam's 'honoured place' in Russian poetry. He was released the next day. Voloshin wrote in his memoirs that despite Mandelstam's insulting letter, he had no choice: he had to use his influence on behalf of the imprisoned poet. He was a person of integrity, who, as Marina Tsvetaeva wrote in her obituary of him, 'A Living Word About a Living Man' (1933), saved 'Reds' from the 'Whites' and 'Whites' from the 'Reds'. He was quick to recognise Mandelstam's literary significance. He regarded him as 'the most musical of contemporary poets', and he made an observation about Mandelstam that has become well known: 'He is goofy, like all genuine poets.'

Mandelstam described his first stay in prison in a prose text, 'The Mensheviks in Georgia' (1923):

---

15 M.'s quarrel with Voloshin: V. P. Kupchenko, 'Osip Mandel'shtam v Kimmerii', 176–83. Voloshin's observations about M.: V. P. Kupchenko, 'Osip Mandel'shtam v Kimmerii', 193 and 198.

> Iphigenia's motherland had collapsed under the soldier's heel. And I had to gaze on the beloved, dry wormwood hills of Theodosia, in the Cimmerian hills, from a prison window, and stroll about a parched little courtyard where frightened Jews huddled. (RZ, 154; CC, 225)

According to Ehrenburg's memoirs, Mandelstam banged on the door of his cell and cried: 'You've got to let me out, I wasn't made for prison!' He is said to have interrupted his interrogator with the words: 'But please tell me, do you release innocent people or not?' These utterances, which have an air of absurdity in that time of violence, are typical of him. It was not the last time this poet, who was 'not made' for prison, would make his acquaintance with the inside of a jail.

After his release, he was expelled from White territory. But there was only one way to leave the Crimean Peninsula, cut off as it was from the mainland: across the Black Sea. On 7 September, therefore, he embarked on a decrepit cargo vessel, which took five days to cross the storm-tossed sea to the port of Batumi, on the south-eastern Black Sea coast of Georgia, where the Mensheviks had set up an ephemeral socialist republic. In an autobiographical text entitled 'The Return' (1923), Mandelstam describes the rough crossing:

> For five days and nights our tiny boat, accustomed only to the Azov Sea, plied the warm, salt waters of the Hellespont. For five days and nights we crawled on all fours across the deck to obtain boiled water, for five days and nights fierce Dagestanis cast suspicious glances our way. (RZ, 145; CC, 219)

When the seasick refugee had firm ground under his feet again, he was at first enraptured by the town, as the beginning of 'The Mensheviks in Georgia' suggests:

> A greenhouse. A humming-bird city. A city of palm trees in tubs. A city of malaria and gentle Japanese hills. A city that resembles a European district in any colonial country, that rings with mosquitoes in the summer and offers fresh mandarin oranges in December. Batum, August 1920. (RZ, 152; CC, 224)

But the enchantment did not last long. Three days after his arrival, Mandelstam was again arrested, this time as an alleged 'White' and 'Bolshevik' double agent (as before, the poet was caught between the fronts), and brought before the military governor of the town, who wanted to send him back to the Crimea. 'Sinister people' were wandering around the room, and out of the torrent of Georgian speech Mandelstam could only distinguish the word 'Bolshevik'. He was finally thrown into the prison, which was located by the town's harbour: 'People are lying on the floor. It is as crowded as a chicken coop' (RZ, 157; CC, 227).

The poet had to go into the town to procure bread; he was accompanied by a guard armed with a rifle, whose name was Chigua. Quite unexpectedly, the guard said to him: 'I love the Bolsheviks. Perhaps you are a Bolshevik?' Mandelstam adds: 'I had the ragged look of hard labour, and a torn trouser leg' (RZ, 158; CC, 227). With the guard's permission, he entered the premises of a Russian newspaper, whose editor notified the civilian governor, Chikvishvili. As a result, Mandelstam was released on 14 September 1920 and permitted to travel on to Tbilisi, although, according to other sources, it was two Georgian poets, Titsian Tabidze and Nikolo Mitsishvili, who had pleaded for him to be set free. On 26 September, he appeared together with Ilya Ehrenburg at a literary evening in the Tbilisi Conservatory. At the beginning of October, the two poets returned to Moscow in an armoured train. Ehrenburg had been ordered back to the capital as a diplomatic courier carrying official mail, and he obtained travel permits for both of them.

Mandelstam did not want to leave Tbilisi without offering a merry poem to his friends, the poets of Georgia. It was a playful little hymn to the proverbial Georgian sociability and pleasure in drinking, which Mandelstam had enjoyed during the two weeks of his stay. It celebrated Georgian varieties of wine, pilau rice, spit-roasted shashlik and inns beside the river Kura. Here are the last two stanzas:

Ask for Teliani
And there's always someone to drink with, even
In the smallest *dukhan*.
Tiflis will start to float in fog,
You and the *dukhan* will start to float, too.

A man can be very old
And a lamb very young,
And under a lean new moon
Rose-coloured wine-steam will stream up,
Mixing with *shashlik* smoke.
(TR, 83; CP, 112)

A sigh of relief can be perceived in this poem, after two periods of imprisonment, a dangerous crossing of the Black Sea and a general feeling of uncertainty and anxiety. It is the work of a fun-loving poet, someone who was, until recently, a 'ragged convict', who can now again get a nourishing meal – perhaps his last chance of this for a long time to come – and who is enjoying his present freedom.

The return journey to Moscow was fraught with risk. The travellers repeatedly noticed how the front lines of the civil war were constantly shifting. After they had gone through the town of Vladikavkaz, the train came under fire from 'White' troops. Rifles were distributed to the passengers, and they were asked to use them. Ehrenburg reports: 'Osip Emilevich, who had an insuperable aversion towards any kind of weapon, was brought to utter distraction by these instructions.' Then, between Rostov and Kharkov, the train was approached by the marauding troops of the anarchist Makhno. But the passengers finally reached Moscow in safety, despite these vicissitudes.[16]

16 M.'s second arrest, this time in Batumi; the intercession of two Georgian poets in his favour; journey to Tbilisi; return to Moscow: Ehrenburg, *Men, Years – Life*, 113–22.

11

I Shall Pray in the Soviet Night

(Petrograd, Tbilisi, Batumi 1920–1921)

The spectre of violence, which had led Mandelstam to flee to the south two years previously, seemed to be waiting in Moscow to receive him. He and Ehrenburg alighted from the armoured train, separately looked for a place to stay, and arranged to meet in the evening at the 'House of the Press' on Nikitsky Boulevard. The literati assembled there were arguing at that time over the kind of poetry best suited to the new reality: that of the Futurists around Vladimir Mayakovsky and Alexei Kruchonykh, or that of the Imaginists. The poetry of the Imaginist movement, which was founded in January 1919 by Vadim Shershenevich, Anatoly Mariengof and the former peasant poet Sergei Yesenin, placed new, glaring, shocking images at its centre. The Imaginists were expert at creating noisy scenes, and they provoked their audiences with scandalous assertions, such as this one: 'The best supporters of our poetry are prostitutes and gangsters.'

On his first evening in Moscow, at the beginning of October 1920, Mandelstam was again threatened by the Chekist Blumkin. Ehrenburg recalls:

> Mandelstam was sitting in another corner of the room. Suddenly Blumkin leapt to his feet and began to shout: 'I'm going to shoot you!'

> training his revolver on Mandelstam, who cried out. The revolver was knocked out of Blumkin's hand, and everything ended well.[1]

The first clash with Blumkin had created a trauma which was barely healed, and this fresh incident led Mandelstam to avoid Moscow for some time. The way to the south was now barred, so he travelled on to Petrograd, the city of his childhood.

It was still October when Mandelstam rented a tiny, unheated room in Petrograd in the basement of the 'House of the Arts' at 59 Moyka Embankment. Before the revolution, the building had belonged to the Yeliseev family, a dynasty of rich merchants and delicatessen suppliers. It now sheltered a crowd of permanently hungry painters, poets and scholars. Mandelstam depicts the strange atmosphere of this house, called 'the ship of fools' by contemporaries, in his essay 'The Fur Coat' (1922):

> We lived in the shabby splendour of the House of the Arts, the Yeliseev House, which occupies the corner of Morskaia, Nevsky and Moyka. We were poets, painters, scholars, a peculiar family, run wild, completely obsessed with our food rations, and constantly sleeping. The state did not know why it ought to feed us, and we were doing nothing. (RZ, 129)

Mandelstam tells us of the hunger and cold they suffered in this 'last harvest winter of Soviet Russia', and of a mysterious second-hand fur coat he bought in Rostov on Don for three roubles, which was 'cheaper than a boiled turnip'. According to Nadezhda, it was a reddish racoon coat with a lot of moth holes, which the freezing poet had bought from an old deacon:

> Why am I uncomfortable in my fur coat? Does this chance purchase perhaps fill me with anxiety? Someone else's fate has jumped from his shoulder to mine and now sits on it. It says nothing, and has made itself comfortable for the moment. (RZ, 129)

The theme of the strange and sinister overcoat would run through Mandelstam's autobiographical writings of the 1920s. It would surface in various manifestations in *The Noise of Time* (1925) and *The Egyptian*

1 Blumkin again threatens M. with his revolver: I. Ehrenburg, *Men, Years – Life*, 123.

Stamp (1928), until the poet, in utter fury, would himself tear the 'overcoat of literature' from his own shoulders in the *Fourth Prose* (1929–1930).[2]

'The Fur Coat' also includes portraits of his neighbours in the House of the Arts, the poet Vladislav Khodasevich and the literary theorist and writer Viktor Shklovsky ('a real literary steamroller, with enough temperament for ten people'). Shklovsky, for his part, recalled Mandelstam's behaviour in the House of the Arts in *Sentimental Journey* (1923), painting a strange portrait which was full of sympathy but also acknowledged his eccentricity:

> Osip Mandelstam grazed in the house like a sheep and wandered through the rooms like Homer. He's an extremely intelligent man in a conversation. The deceased Khlebnikov named him the 'marble fly' … Mandelstam loved sweets to distraction. Living in extremely difficult circumstances – without boots, without heat – he contrived to be treated like a spoiled child. He was as disorganized as a woman and light-minded as a bird – and not entirely guileless in this. He had all the habits of the true artist. An artist will even lie to free himself for his all-important work. He's like the monkey, who, according to the Hindus, keeps quiet so that he won't be put to work.[3]

Nowhere else is there a reminiscence of this kind, in which the poet Mandelstam is simultaneously likened to Homer, a sheep and an Indian monkey! He had been given room 30a in the basement, which was occupied by Yeliseev's servants before the revolution. His Homeric wanderings through the house were a flight from the cold and a search for warmth and food. Shklovsky's wife Vasilisa was happy to feed him, and often did so. The Shklovskys will repeatedly emerge as good fairies in Mandelstam's life.

On 21 October 1920, Mandelstam gave a reading in the 'Poets' Club' on Liteiny Prospekt alongside other poets, and he impressed the Symbolist Alexander Blok, who was normally very hostile towards the Acmeists around Gumilyov. The entry in Blok's diary for 22 October, however, also

2 The fur coat theme: appendix to O. Mandelstam, *Das Rauschen der Zeit*, 332–4; N. Mandelstam, *Hope Against Hope*, 193–4 ('Cycle').

3 Shklovsky recalls M.'s time in the 'House of the Arts': V. Shklovsky, *A Sentimental Journey*, 237–8. Vasilisa Shklovskaia's recollections: O. S. Figurnova and M. V. Figurnova, *Osip i Nadezhda Mandel'shtamy v Rasskazakh Sovremennikov*, 98 and 104.

contains a poisonous and lamentable anti-Semitic remark, which was always excised from Soviet bloc editions of his work:

> The event of the evening was I. Mandelstam … His poetry has got much stronger. It was at first unbearable to listen to the general sing-song delivery, in the style of Gumilyov. But you gradually get used to it, the 'little Jew' disappears, and the artist comes into view. His poems emerge from dreams – very individual dreams which are located exclusively in the artistic realm.[4]

A poem by Mandelstam which he produced shortly after this, on 25 November 1920, conjures up a particular dream-like vision. It refers to a burial in Petersburg, a meeting in the future and the possibility of return. According to Nadezhda Mandelstam, the 'we' of the poem means his fellow poets, those close friends and 'conspirators against emptiness' who had joined together on the eve of the First World War to form the Acmeist group: Nikolai Gumilyov, Anna Akhmatova and Mandelstam himself:

> In Petersburg we will gather anew
> As if we had there buried the sun,
> And for the first time we will pronounce
> The blessed, senseless word.
> In the black velvet of the Soviet night
> In the velvet of universal emptiness,
> The dear eyes of the blessed women sing on,
> Immortal flowers ever bloom.[5]

The 'burial of the sun' points to the death of poetry, which Mandelstam often associated with the violent death of Alexander Pushkin. In the essay 'Pushkin and Scriabin' (1916), he writes of the 'solar body' of the poet, which was buried at night (GP, 62–3; SE, 136). The poets will die, no doubt, but they will return, because 'blessed women' will perform the loving service of preserving them: 'Maybe centuries will pass / And the

4 Blok's diary entry for 22 October 1920: A. Grishunin, 'Blok i Mandel'shtam', 155–6. The meaning of 'We' in the 'Petersburg Poem': N. Mandelstam, *Hope Abandoned*, 74–5 ('Return').

5 TR, 97; S. Goldberg, 'To Anaxagoras', 298. This article will henceforth be referred to as TA.

dear hands of blessed women / Will gather our light ash' (TR, 97; TA, 298). In the present, though, fear reigns in Petrograd, and a wide-awake poet and night-time reveller utters his anxious prayer for the 'blessed, senseless word' of poetry:

> The capital arches like a wild cat
> A patrol stands on a bridge,
> Only a wicked motor car will rush through the darkness
> And cry out like a cuckoo.
> I don't need a night pass,
> I do not fear the watchmen:
> I will pray in the Soviet night
> For the blessed, senseless word.
> (TA, 298)

Unfortunately, the reference to the 'blessed, senseless word' turned out to be all too true. When Mandelstam produced the last volume of poetry published during his lifetime (1928), the censor insisted on replacing the phrase 'Soviet night' with 'January night' and the poem was placed alongside verses written *before* the October Revolution. In a country where the 'sun of the future' was supposed to be shining, the expression 'Soviet night' was heretical.

In autumn 1920, Mandelstam made the acquaintance of the beautiful Olga Arbenina, an actress of the Alexandra Theatre, through his friend and fellow poet Nikolai Gumilyov, and he fell head over heels in love. He wrote a handful of love poems for her, which are among the most magical examples of Russian lyric poetry. The poem 'For Joy's Sake' is nourished by classical images, by the analogy Plato makes between poets and bees in his dialogue *Ion* and by the identification of poetry with honey. The bees were creatures sacred to the underworld goddess Persephone, the spouse of Hades. According to the myth, the gift of poetry is closely associated with death. In those days of hunger and cold, Mandelstam speaks of anxiety and death – but also of kisses, sunshine and poetry.

> Take, for joy's sake, from these hands of mine
> A little honey and a little sunlight
> As the bees of Persephone once ordered us to do.

We cannot cast adrift an unmoored boat,
Nor hear a shadow shoed in fur,
Nor conquer fear in this tangled dreaming life.

All we have left to us is kisses
Sheathed in down like tiny bees
That die as they scatter from the hive.

They rustle in the translucent recesses of the night,
Their homeland is Taigetos' tangled woods,
Their food is honeysuckle, time, and mint.

So take, for joy's sake, this wild gift of mine,
This uninviting desiccated necklet
Made of dead bees that once turned honey into sunlight.
(TR, 91; FP, 50)

Mandelstam went with Olga Arbenina to see the opera *Orpheus and Eurydice* (1762) by Christoph Willibald Gluck in the Marinsky Theatre, in a 1911 production by Meyerhold, which was re-created in 1920. One of Mandelstam's poems evokes the shadow choirs and arias of this performance (TR, 93). Gluck's opera would always remain his favourite, and the myth of Orpheus, including his descent into the underworld, would retain a central significance in his poetry.

The girlishly slim Arbenina, to whom the enamoured Gumilyov also dedicated a poem ('Olga'), is associated with the beautiful Helen, with Eurydice and with Psyche, who personified the soul in ancient times. Two of Mandelstam's poems, the 'Lethe poems' (TR, 87 and 89) written in October and November 1920, speak of the journey of the soul and the word into the underworld. The ancient Greeks imagined the soul as a young woman with butterfly wings, or as a swallow. Mandelstam identifies the poet's word with this swallow and with the 'mad Antigone':

I have forgotten the word I wanted to say.
On severed wings, to play with the transparent ones,
The blind swallow flies back to her palace of shadows.
Night songs are sung in frenzied absentmindedness.
(TR, 89; EW, 58)

According to this myth, the word must descend into darkness and death if it wants to return someday, in memory of death and the dead: 'And on my lips the black ice burns, / The recollection of Stygian clamour' (EW, 58).

Mandelstam also went with Olga on 8 December 1920 to a performance of Stravinsky's ballet *Petrushka*. After this there were poems of departure and separation. He was hopelessly in love, so much so that his memory of the meeting with Nadezhda in Kyiv in May 1919 was almost obliterated. Mandelstam did not possess the qualities of a lady-killer or a Don Juan; his unique charm was inseparable from the magic of his poems. In one of them (TR, 101) the loving Self is an Achaean speaking from inside the Trojan horse: this looks back to the account by Menelaus in the *Odyssey* (Book 4, 277–84). The beautiful Helen slipped out of his hands all too quickly. Arbenina's beauty now finally became the subject of a poem. The passion-struck poet confesses that: 'My blood has been changed / For something wild and strange' (TR, 111; FP, 53). At the end of the 'Arbenina cycle', the poet proclaims his continuing love and promises to stop being jealous: he swallows 'the coals of jealousy' (TR, 115). Even the playful irony of the poem 'I'm Sorry That It's Winter Now' (TR, 107) is unable to conceal his melancholy:

> To tell the truth, it's not your fault,
> Why weigh things and turn things inside out?
> You were created as though on purpose
> To squabble in comedies on the stage.
> …
> So give up trying to be cleverer,
> You're all caprice, all instantaneous.
> Even the shadow of your hat
> Is like the carnival mask in Venice.[6]

Gluck's opera, Stravinsky's ballet, Venice's carnival: the starving inhabitants of Petrograd flocked to dazzling spectacles like drowning people grasping at straws. Poetry readings were also ritual occasions during this period of constantly gnawing hunger. On 18 November 1920 Mandelstam declaimed his verses in the 'House of the Arts'. He was introduced

6 TR, 107–9; C. Brown, *Mandelstam*, 249.

by the literary scholar Viktor Zhirmunsky. During the harsh winter of 1920–1921, readings like this brought in a little bread, at a time when the poet was greatly in need of it.

The Bolshevik policy of forcibly requisitioning produce from the peasants had almost brought agricultural production to a standstill, owing to the exorbitant and arbitrary way in which it was implemented. The outlines of an economic catastrophe started to be visible. On 22 January 1921, the bread ration in the cities had to be reduced by a third; this was followed by a fuel crisis. The urban workers were hungry and cold and had no work. A wave of strikes developed. Zinoviev, the head of the Petrograd party organisation, proclaimed martial law in the city on 24 February and ordered the military to intervene against the strikers. There followed an extremely tragic and revelatory episode. The Kronstadt sailors declared their solidarity with the Petrograd workers and on 28 February 1921 they voted for a resolution which called for fresh elections and the restoration of fundamental freedoms for the 'workers and peasants, and the Anarchist and Left Socialist parties'. This was a protest by proletarian revolutionaries against autocratic Bolshevik rule. But the Bolsheviks could not tolerate any opposition; the Red Army was sent in, under the command of General Tukhachevsky. By 18 March, Kronstadt had been recaptured, after a severe struggle, followed by indiscriminate shooting of the insurgents. Bolshevik propaganda attempted to present the rebellion as a 'White Guard conspiracy', but with the liquidation of the proletarian rebels the holders of power had given their subjects a foretaste of the future.

In the politically catastrophic month of March 1921, Mandelstam returned to Kyiv. His parting impression of Petrograd was the thunder of cannons which could be heard from the direction of Kronstadt. He had obtained Nadezhda Khazina's new address in Kyiv from Ehrenburg's wife. He had not seen her since the end of August 1919. The troubles of the civil war had driven them apart. But now he travelled to Kyiv, catching her unawares with a renewed affirmation of his love. She agreed to travel to Moscow with him. Her parents had twice been driven from their house by semi-official expropriations. When Mandelstam arrived, a crowd of female arrestees had just been pushed into the now empty apartment to sweep the floors. Osip and Nadezhda stayed in Nadezhda's room for two hours as a protest, and he recited his latest poems to her. Shortly afterwards, they travelled to Moscow, and as Nadezhda recalls: 'we were never again separated, until that night of the First and Second May 1938 when the soldiers of the guard led him away'.[7]

Even before his journey to Kyiv, it became clear to Mandelstam that he had to take his departure in another sense as well, to make his exit from the 'old' world, as already predicted in his 1918 poem 'Tristia'. On 14 February 1921, there was a requiem mass in the Petrograd Cathedral of Saint Isaac in memory of Alexander Pushkin. Mandelstam recorded the event in a poem. As if in a final affirmation of his fascination with Christianity, a faith he says he 'will never abandon', he evokes the splendid interior of the cathedral, which was built by Montferrand. It is Mandelstam's last truly religious poem, and it closes a cycle of poems dedicated to churches and sacred spaces, the spiritual centres of Orthodoxy and Catholicism:

> Hagia Sophia and Saint Peter's –
> Eternal barns of air and light,
> Storehouses of everlasting goods,
> Granaries of the New Testament.
> (TR, 117; EW, 62)

As if to banish all anxiety over what is to come, the poem includes the adjuration: 'Free is the slave who once has conquered fear.' Fear would be a constant theme of Mandelstam's work during the 1920s. In her memoirs, Nadezhda writes that as a person with inner strength, he was not anxious, because he was 'free'. But it is impossible to overlook how frequently the theme of fear surfaces in his poetry, even if only as a magical incantation which claims to banish it.[8]

---

7 M. joins Nadezhda again in Kyiv: Mandelstam, *Hope Abandoned*, 36 ('The Stampede').

8 M.'s freedom from fear, according to Nadezhda: Mandelstam, *Hope Abandoned*, 202 ('Fear'). For the recurrent theme of fear in M.'s poetry and prose during the 1920s, see these poems: 'Venetian Life' (TR, 85: 'For there's no salvation from love and terror'); 'For Joy's Sake from My Hands' (TR, 91: 'Not to be silenced, life's dark terrors'); 'In Petersburg We Will Gather Anew' (TR, 97: 'I don't need a night pass / I do not fear the watchmen'); 'Now No Different from the Others' (TR, 113: 'The fear I feel without you here'); 'I Love under the Vaults of the Grey Silence' (TR, 117: 'Free is the slave who once has conquered fear'); 'Concert at the Railway Station' (TR, 121: 'I'm late. I'm afraid. This is a dream'); and 'The Slate Ode' (TR, 155: 'Here terror writes'). See also the novel *The Egyptian Stamp* (1928): 'Terror takes me by the hand and leads me. A white cotton glove. A woman's glove without fingers. I love terror, I respect it. I almost said "With it I'm not terrified"' (RZ, 240; NT, 162). The theme of fear is continued in the poetry of the 1930s: 'Our close alliance

In May 1921, one of Mandelstam's most important essays, 'The Word and Culture', appeared in the Petrograd almanac *The Dragon*. He begins with the laconic assertion that 'culture has become the Church' (GP, 83; SE, 67). His essay was a provocative contribution to the ongoing dispute between the Futurists and the Imaginists. He praised the Culture Church and classical poetry ('Classical poetry is the poetry of revolution'). And he delineated an idiosyncratic future-oriented classicism which, while not denying the past, recognised the cyclical character of human experience. The 'new poets' of Mandelstam's dreams were entirely different from both the Futurists and the Imaginists:

> One often hears: that might be good, but it belongs to yesterday. But I say: yesterday hasn't been born yet. It has not yet really come to pass. I want Ovid, Pushkin, Catullus afresh, and I will not be satisfied with the historical Ovid, Pushkin, Catullus … Not a single poet has yet appeared. We are free of the weight of memories. For all that, how many rare presentiments: Pushkin, Ovid, Homer. (GP, 84–5; SE, 69)

For Mandelstam, the 'synthetic poet of modern life' is 'a kind of Verlaine of culture': 'For him the whole complexity of the old world would be like that same old Pushkinian reed. In him, ideas, scientific systems, political theories would sing, just as nightingales and roses used to sing in his predecessors' (GP, 88; SE, 71). Mandelstam thought he himself was the nearest approximation to this new Verlaine of culture, with his combination of musicality and complexity …

In 'The Word and Culture', Mandelstam compares poetry to a plough, which turns up the virgin soil of time in such a way that its deeper layers will come to the surface (GP, 84; SE, 68). But this essay by the 'ploughman of time' cannot be understood without taking into account its background, its dominating, pitiless background: hunger. It is against the background of hunger under 'War Communism' that Mandelstam invests daily life and culture, bread and the word, with an aura of sacredness.

---

holds anxiety' (MM, 7); 'Help me, O Lord, to live through this night / I fear for life, for Your handmaiden' (MM, 51; MN, 36); 'The Horse-cart Driver' (MM, 95; AA, 131; MN, 50: 'Now I suffered all the terrors / That are contained within the soul'); 'The Apartment' (MM, 161; MN, 71–2: 'The gush of age-old terror'). There are many other examples.

> A heroic era has begun in the life of the word. The word is flesh and bread. It shares the fate of bread and flesh: suffering. People are hungry. Still hungrier is the state. But there is something even hungrier: time. Time wants to devour the state. (GP, 86; SE, 69)

This was a provocative remark. A further provocation by Mandelstam was his attitude to the relationship between the state and culture. The state was already trampling culture underfoot, but its 'exclusion from cultural values' placed the state 'in full dependence on culture' (GP, 84; SE, 68). He concluded by radically dividing his contemporaries into 'friends' and 'enemies' of the word; this distinction would imbue his future attitude to the holders of power.

By 1921, the 'hungry Soviet state' had reached a dead end in its dealings with the burdensome food problem. It had no option but to return to the previous system: at the Tenth Party Congress in March 1921 Lenin personally proposed the 'New Economic Policy' (NEP). Under this, private trade within the country was again permitted and leases were to be granted to private entrepreneurs, including those from abroad. This was a step back to the capitalist economy which many revolutionaries regarded as a shameful surrender. But the measure was justified by its success. The years that followed saw a loosening of hunger's cruel grip.

In June 1921, Mandelstam travelled with Nadezhda to Rostov on Don, where he happened to meet the painter Boris Lopatinsky, with whom he had collaborated in 1918 in the People's Commissariat for Enlightenment. His former colleague was now the head of the Central Evacuation Authority, an organisation which provided aid to refugees in the Caucasus region, and he unhesitatingly took the couple with him on a tour of service, which embraced Kislovodsk, Baku (Azerbaijan), Tbilisi (Georgia) and Batumi (also Georgia).[9] The Mandelstams made their journey in a railway carriage provided 'for mental cases', and they were eyed mistrustfully by 'genuine' functionaries who were on official missions. Despite the incidents that took place – in Baku, for instance, there was an outbreak of cholera on the train – this 'tour of service' was a stroke of luck. Daily life in Moscow had become so difficult that they greeted the prospect of a journey into southern climes as manna from heaven. In Kislovodsk, there was at least unleavened bread and rice, wrote Nadezhda. And 1921 Georgia

9 A 'tour of service' through the Caucasus in June 1921: Mandelstam, *Hope Abandoned*, 46–7 and 82 ('Disintegration').

was 'another world', quite different from 'gloomy, dirty Moscow', where to find a handful of flour from Ukraine counted as a miraculous event.

Before they set off, Mandelstam wrote to Nadezhda's mother Vera Khazina to say that he had 'made an application to the Lithuanian embassy' (MR, 31). We know what this involved from her memoirs: the Lithuanian poet Jurgis Baltrušaitis, who had misgivings about Mandelstam's future fate, had implored him to apply for Lithuanian citizenship (Mandelstam's parents came from Lithuania), so as to keep open the possibility of leaving Soviet Russia. Mandelstam acquired the necessary papers, but eventually gave up on the idea of securing foreign citizenship and travelling abroad 'because one cannot avoid one's fate'.[10]

He would soon see how cruel this fate could be for Russian poets. On 7 August 1921, Alexander Blok died in Petrograd, officially from 'general nervous exhaustion' but in reality because he was morally broken and disappointed by the 'music of the revolution' he had once celebrated. The collapse of culture prophesied in Blok's later essays was now well underway. Mandelstam was in the Georgian town of Batumi when the news was announced, and he was asked to give a lecture on the dead poet. This lecture was the basis for his later assessment of Blok, published in the essay 'Badger's Burrow' (GP, 139–44; SE, 105–9). The poem 'Concert at the Railway Station' was also a reaction to Blok's death, to his theme of the poet's shortness of breath and to the silencing of music. Mandelstam casts his mind back to the concerts of his childhood in the railway station at Pavlovsk, that architectonic mixture of iron and glass, which bore witness to the jarring collision between music and technological progress, Tchaikovsky and the sound of train whistles. The poem starts with the observation 'Can't breathe. And the earth seething with worms' and ends with the disappearance of music.

> And I think, how like a beggar the iron world
> Shivers, covered with music and froth.
> And I go out through the glass passage. The steam
> Blinds the pupils of the violin bows. Where are you off to?*
> It's the funeral feast of the beloved shade.
> It's the last time the music sounds for us.
> (TR, 121; CR, 51)

10 M. abandons his application for Lithuanian citizenship: Mandelstam, *Hope Against Hope*, 27 ('Public Opinion').

Then a second event took place, even more shattering for Mandelstam. Nikolai Gumilyov, his friend, fellow poet and founder of Acmeism, was shot in Petrograd as a 'counter-revolutionary'. He had allegedly participated in a 'monarchist conspiracy', along with sixty-one other co-defendants. The execution of the thirty-five-year-old Gumilyov was the first murder of a poet committed by the Bolsheviks, and it was a warning sign. The deaths of Blok and Gumilyov in August 1921 provided a significant impulse to emigration for a range of different writers. The poet Nikolai Otsup wrote: 'After August 1921 you couldn't breathe in Petersburg, it was impossible to remain; the mortally ill city died when Blok and Gumilyov took their last breath.'[11]

After the execution of Gumilyov, Mandelstam's beloved city was now 'a town of the dead'. The fact that his friend and fellow Acmeist was the first victim inevitably upset him greatly. The event was a demonstration of what refractory poets could expect from the regime. The crushing character of this blow for Mandelstam can be seen from a letter he would write to Anna Akhmatova in 1928, on the seventh anniversary of Gumilyov's murder: the conversation with 'Kolya' had 'never been broken off', nor would it ever be (MR, 145).

During the months of July and August 1921, Mandelstam found accommodation in the 'House of the Arts' in Tbilisi. There, Boris Legran, the Russian Ambassador to Georgia, informed him of Gumilyov's execution. His reply was a short, bitter poem which conjures up the stars, the 'salt' of their fateful power and the 'axe', used as a metaphor for violence and execution. It ends with a harrowing face-to-face confrontation with death and misery:

> I was washing at night in the courtyard –
> The sky's harsh stars shone out,
> Starlight, like salt on an axe-head –
> The rain-butt, brim-full, had frozen.
>
> The gates are locked,
> And the earth in all conscience is bleak.
> There's scarcely anything
> Purer than the truth of a clean towel.

11 Nikolai Otsup's view of the impact of the events of August 1921: J. Kusmina, *Anna Akhmatova*, 124. M. is informed while in Georgia of the execution of Gumilyov: Mandelstam, *Hope Abandoned*, 86–7 ('Disintegration').

A star melts, like salt, in the barrel
And the freezing water is blacker
Death more lucid, misfortune saltier,
And the earth more truthful, more awful.
(TR, 123; EW, 64)

According to Nadezhda Mandelstam, a 'new voice' is now perceptible in Osip's poetry. The poem marks a turning point, showing that he has attained the world view of a 'mature human being'.[12] The poem that followed this one, in January 1922, 'Winter for Some Is Arak Spirit', already indicates a stoic approach to that season: 'To starve like an apple-tree in its winter binding; / Senselessly drawn by tenderness for everything alien, / Fumbling through emptiness, patiently waiting' (TR, 125; EW, 64). The poem again speaks of the 'salty decrees of the cruel stars'. Several of Mandelstam's poems are imbued with hostility and mistrust towards the stars and their 'decrees'; and the red star is also a symbol of the Soviet state! And yet, despite the frosty misery of winter, the poem can still conjure up a sparse and modest dose of animal warmth, and it contains the unconditional affirmation: 'I'd give the lot for life.'

From September to December 1921, Mandelstam lived with his future wife in Batumi, on the Black Sea, and busied himself with Georgian poetry. He translated the lyric poetry of his Georgian contemporaries, and the epic poem *Gogotur and Apshina* by the classic Georgian poet Vasha Pshavela (1861–1915), with the help of the poets Titsian Tabidze and Paolo Iashvili. The latter was the leader of the 'Blue Horns' group. Mandelstam's stay in Tbilisi and Batumi also bore fruit in the essay 'A Word or Two about Georgian Art'. In it he investigates the myth of Georgia and the Caucasus in the works of the Russian poets Pushkin and Lermontov and outlines a cultural philosophy of ageing and maturing, ferment and intoxication, with reference to Georgian wine culture: 'Yes, culture intoxicates us … Wine ages – therein lies its future; culture ferments – therein lies its youth' (GP, 95, 99; CC, 160, 163). Culture had already become Mandelstam's final 'church'. It was an intoxicating viaticum, a way of lasting out the winter.

At the end of December, Osip and Nadezhda left Batumi by steamer. They celebrated the new year in the port of Sukhumi. When they returned to the ship, they saw traumatised civil war soldiers, and they asked

12 The poem 'I Was Washing at Night in the Courtyard' as a turning point in M.'s work: N. Mandel'shtam, *Kniga Tret'ia*, 49–50.

themselves 'what had they been fighting for?' They eventually reached Rostov on Don, after calling at Novorossiisk, another port on the Black Sea, and Ekaterinodar. Mandelstam was pleased to hear Russian spoken again, after spending six months in Azerbaijan and Georgia. In January 1922, the Rostov newspaper *Soviet South* published several prose texts he had written, including 'The Bloody Mystery-Play of January Ninth', a commemoration of the massacre of 'Bloody Sunday' during the defeated revolution of 1905: 'No-one heard the last clarion call of imperial Russia – its death-agony, its dying groan – resound in the frosty January air. Imperial Russia died like a wild beast – no-one heard its final wheeze' (GP, 91; CC, 237).

Any nostalgia for Tsarist Russia is completely absent from this text. For Mandelstam, there was no way of going back to the time before the revolution. He was in the middle of a historical tragedy, and he could not leave the theatre during the performance. Nor did he want to. He finally abandoned the idea of emigration during the cruel year of 1921 – the year of the suppression of the Kronstadt rebellion and the shooting of Gumilyov – because 'one cannot avoid one's fate'. Death had now become cleaner, and misery bitterer, while 'the earth, though grimmer, was more just'.

12

My Time, My Beast

(Moscow 1922–1923)

Mandelstam stayed in Russia. He could no longer imagine a life separated from the Russian language and Russian culture. After all his intellectual sojourns in Western culture, he had found 'the road back' (GP, 61; SE, 120), just like his model Chaadaev. He also lacked the means to emigrate: he had neither family jewels nor connections which might have made it possible to start again somewhere else. In addition to this, he was no longer alone, but joined by his partner Nadezhda, whose name means 'hope' in Russian. A modest but not an unreal foundation for the future.

In March 1922, the pair were again in Kyiv, Nadezhda's hometown, where they had first met on 1 May 1919. They exchanged marriage vows quickly and unceremoniously by signing an official register. Their best man was Mandelstam's friend, the Futurist poet Benedict Livshits. They did not have the money to buy wedding rings. They had no interest in bourgeois accessories. It was not the right time for such things. On 7 March, Mandelstam gave a lecture in the Kyiv Philosophical Academy on the theme 'Acmeism or Classicism? Inner Hellenism in Russian Literature', which was to be the basis for one of his most important and brilliant essays, 'About the Nature of the Word'. In June 1922, it would be published in Kharkov as a brochure.

The essay is an attempt to recover unity, wholeness and continuity in the whirlwind of events, during an epoch of frantic acceleration. It is a survey of Russian poetry, going all the way from the *Tale of Igor's Men* (at the end of the twelfth century) to his admired contemporary, the Futurist Velimir Khlebnikov. But it is more than that: it contains fundamental reflections on the value and dignity of Russian culture. Mandelstam's intellectual lodestar is now the French (and Jewish) philosopher Henri Bergson, whose main work, *L'Évolution créatrice* (Creative Evolution), he had discovered in 1907–1908 during his studies in Paris. Bergson's search for the 'inner connection between phenomena' now becomes Mandelstam's own. The philosopher Chaadaev, whom he had admired since 1914, had in his criticism of Russia's lack of culture and history left out of account an element which he now considered to be of central importance: the Russian language. 'Such a highly organised, such an organic language is not merely a door into history, it is history itself' (GP, 117; SE, 87). Mandelstam goes on to present to the reader an intellectual genealogy of the Russian language, starting with classical antiquity and passing through Byzantium to the present-day writings of Khlebnikov. The Russian language, he says, is 'a Hellenic language'. Thanks to this inheritance, it has become 'sounding and speaking flesh' (GP, 115; SE, 85).

It is clearly apparent from this essay that Mandelstam was seeking a new spiritual home in those years of unrest; his answer is an 'inner, domestic Hellenism'. He had left behind the apocalyptic emotionalism of the epoch and was offering a new approach to the essence of culture:

> Hellenism is a baking dish, a pair of tongs, an earthenware jug with milk; it is domestic utensils, crockery, the body's whole ambiance; Hellenism is the warmth of the hearth felt as something sacred; it is any personal possession that joins part of the external world to man, any clothes placed on someone's shoulders ... Hellenism means consciously surrounding man with utensils instead of indifferent objects; the metamorphosis of these objects into the utensil, the humanisation of the surrounding world; the environment heated with the most delicate teleological warmth. (GP, 124; SE, 91)

A modest infusion of the sacred into everyday life and a straightforward secularisation of culture are only apparently contradictory aspects of Mandelstam's search for a minimum of warmth. They are precautions taken to prevent the loss of inner stability and mental equilibrium in an epoch of hunger, cold and violence. The essay also presents a renewed conception of Acmeism as a 'moral force' (GP, 129; SE, 95). Mandelstam would soon be in dire need of this.

At the end of March 1922, the newly married pair returned to Moscow. In April, Mandelstam managed to find a small room in the left-facing wing of the 'Herzen House' at 25 Tverskoy Boulevard. This building, renamed in 1920 in honour of Alexander Herzen (1812–1870), the political writer and opponent of Tsarist autocracy, was the literary centre of Moscow, the official headquarters of the All-Russian Writers' Union. Visitors noticed the rudimentary way Mandelstam's room was furnished. In the middle there was a mattress, which served several purposes. The only piece of personal furniture was a small chest, in which manuscripts, photographs and letters were stored. Possessions did not interest him. Now he had a roof over his head, at least for a few months. He had found his real, his intellectual, dwelling place elsewhere.

On 10 November 1921, a 'Central Commission for the Improvement of the Living Conditions of Scholars' (TseKUBU) had been set up. For many intellectuals, it provided a life-saving minimum supply of provisions. On his return to Moscow, Mandelstam was allotted a 'second-category food ration'. The ex-Symbolist Valery Bryusov, now a Bolshevik literary functionary, had successfully argued against placing Mandelstam in the first category. But, as Nadezhda points out, even the few modest items of food in the smaller ration constituted 'wealth' for the Mandelstams. Once a month, they received a bag of grapes, flour and sugar, a piece of butter and a 'disgusting pig's head'.

Despite receiving this 'wealth', the poet Mandelstam was still a beggar, who only possessed the clothes he was wearing. After his return to Moscow, an appeal was made to Maxim Gorky, who was in charge of the distribution of resources to writers, to ask him to allocate a pair of trousers and a pullover, on the grounds that he had been arrested twice, by both the 'Whites' and the Mensheviks. Gorky struck out the trousers, as, in his view, Mandelstam's 'services to society' only entitled him to a pullover.[1] But Nikolai Gumilyov gave his friend his second pair of trousers.

---

1 Bryusov's refusal to place M. in the first ration category: N. Mandelstam, *Hope Abandoned*, 101–2 ('Some Contemporaries'). Gorky's refusal to assign a pair of trousers to M.: ibid., 81 ('Return').

The hungry Khlebnikov was a frequent guest of the Mandelstams in their room in the 'Herzen House'. They shared their food ration with him. The Futurist poet, who had been challenged to a duel by Mandelstam in November 1913 over the Beilis Affair, now sat, mainly sunk in meditative silence, eating a meagre portion of buckwheat porridge with his frustrated former duellist. Mandelstam tried to get hold of a room for the homeless Khlebnikov, and he turned for help to the philosopher Nikolai Berdyaev, who was, at that point, chair of the Writers' Union (although he would be forced into exile later in 1922). The furious Mandelstam, writes Nadezhda, demanded a room of 'at least six square metres' and described Khlebnikov as 'the greatest poet in the world'.[2] But all the rooms had already been allotted to 'more important' writers. And Khlebnikov, who did not have the support of any writers' organisation, was finally driven out of Moscow – to begin his final odyssey. The Futurist 'president of the globe' who wanted to 'be on first-name terms with the stars', and had worn himself out with his high-flown mathematical visions and audacious linguistic experiments, died exhausted and alone on 28 June 1922 in the village of Santalovo, in the governorate of Novgorod. Thus, the poetic death toll continued to increase: after Blok and Gumilyov the most eccentric of the Cubo-Futurists now took a premature departure. In the essay 'Literary Moscow' (1922), Mandelstam vehemently expressed his fury over the lukewarmness of the obituaries for Khlebnikov, that 'great archaic poet'.

On 26 March 1922, Lenin suffered a stroke and had to withdraw from the leadership of the state and the party. As a result, 'the fight for Lenin's inheritance' began behind the scenes. In May 1922, Stalin was appointed General Secretary of the party. A strange chronological coincidence: while Stalin and Trotsky were jockeying for power, Mandelstam the poet was struggling in May 1922 to bring to a wider audience his conception of the European inheritance after the October Revolution. To this end, he wrote a poem and an essay. The essay, 'Human Corn', appeared on 7 June 1922 in *Nakanune* (On the Eve), a leading organ of the Russian émigré community in Berlin. The contemporary background was the World Economic Conference in Genoa and the Rapallo Agreement of 16 April 1922 between the Russian Soviet Republic and Germany, which marked a rapprochement after years of sanguinary discord. Mandelstam's essay took the current international situation as its starting point but went beyond

2 Khlebnikov as M.'s guest: ibid., 111–13 ('Khlebnikov').

this to mount a plea for the 'universal hearth and home' and 'worldwide domesticity'. It sharply attacked nationalism and messianism and it contained this core statement affirming his commitment to Europe, his vision of the continent's future:

> In present-day Europe every national idea is condemned to futility, as long as this Europe has not found its vocation as a unified whole and grasped its character as a moral personality. No small-scale national existence is possible any longer outside a common European consciousness, to which it relates in a sense as to a mother. The way out of national ruin, out of the situation of a grain in a sack of corn, to international unification, leads through a rebirth of European consciousness, through the revivification of Europeanism, of the sense of belonging to our great European community of peoples. The 'feeling for Europe', that feeling which has been muffled, suppressed, and held down by war and fraternal strife, is returning to the sphere of active, effective ideas. (GP, 135)

Mandelstam's essay was also directed against Oswald Spengler's *The Decline of the West*. In deliberate contrast to Spengler, he described Europe as the 'youngest, tenderest and most historic continent, whose skull, like the skull of a small child, has not yet hardened' (GP, 133). Mandelstam was not seduced for one moment by Spengler's theories, writes Nadezhda in her memoirs. His image of Europe is characterised simultaneously by an age-old cultural memory, reaching far back into classical antiquity, and a paradoxically youthful freshness. As the title 'Human Corn' indicates, a poetically figurative structure of corn, wheat and bread metaphors pervades the text. This structure is an essential component of Mandelstam's work between 1921 and 1923, as well as evidence of the epoch's domination by the trauma of famine and starvation.[3]

The poem 'Europa' (TR, 127), which was written at this time, is a meditation on the myth of Europe's origin, namely the abduction of Europa, the daughter of the King of Phoenicia, who was taken to Crete by her lover Zeus, who changed himself into a bull for the purpose. It is a fabric of sense impressions, a sensuous representation of Europa's anxious journey. The poem is erotic in nature ('Europa's gentle hands: take them!

---

3 M.'s essay 'Human Corn' and his use of corn and bread metaphors, 1921–1923: E. A. Toddes, 'Stat'ia "Pshenitsa Chelovecheskaia" v tvorchestve Mandel'shtama'; R. Dutli, *Europas zarte Hände*, 124 and 144–51.

Take everything!'), with its subtle allusion to Sappho, the first poetess of the West (who flourished around 600 B.C.E.), and her characterisation of Eros as 'a bitter-sweet torment'. It was inspired by the famous painting done in 1910 by the Russian artist Valentin Serov, *The Abduction of Europa*. Yet the poem did more than evoke a myth and a painting; it was more than the sensuous and erotic actualisation of Europa's anxious journey into the unknown. Nadezhda Mandelstam notes that because of a certain similarity between Serov's *Europa* and herself, a quiet, private myth developed among the newly married Mandelstams. She writes that the poem demonstrates sympathy for the girl and the woman. Mandelstam understood very well that she would rather lead a peaceful existence with an ordinary husband and breadwinner than be abducted by this bull, this 'feckless vagabond' who would drag her with him from place to place. With the European Mandelstam, a poet who in Soviet Russia would very soon have difficulties with the ruling regime, it would not be possible to have a calm and peaceful life.[4]

In August 1922, Mandelstam's second great collection of poems, *Tristia*, came out in Berlin, under the imprint of 'Petropolis', which was one of the numerous publishing houses run by Russian émigrés. The Moscow censorship had prevented its publication at home, so it was brought out by the firm's Berlin branch. Owing to Mandelstam's absence in Georgia, the volume was put together without his assistance. The poet Mikhail Kuzmin, who worked for 'Petropolis', chose the title *Tristia* because Mandelstam had already written a poem of that name in 1918 under the inspiration of Ovid's *Tristia*. Mandelstam was displeased with the arrangement of the book, because of the arbitrary way it mixed up poems from the period of the October Revolution and the civil war with the products of his earlier creative period, which had already been published in *Stone*.

Notwithstanding his reservations, he remained for a long time the poet of *Stone* and *Tristia*, and it was these two collections that shaped his contemporary image. In any case, most of the late poems of the thirties would not be published until many years after Mandelstam's death, and were at first only available in the underground. Viktor Zhirmunsky, who had already come out in support of the Acmeists in his 1916 essay 'Those Who Have Overcome Symbolism', wrote a review praising *Tristia*.

4 The poem 'Europa' and Sappho's 'bitter-sweet torment': Dutli, *Europas zarte Hände*, 133–43. The private myth identifying Nadezhda with Serov's *Europa* abducted by a 'feckless vagabond': N. Mandelstam, *Hope Abandoned*, 139.

He stated that the author of the collection had a 'sublime vision of linguistic images' and noted his 'ever freer and bolder flights of metaphor', which were held in check by 'classically strict and precise epigrammatic formulae'. This was the last benevolent review he ever received. It was written by a connoisseur of poetry whose views were not distorted by ideology.[5]

The poems in the *Tristia* volume audaciously blended images and themes from classical antiquity with features of Russia's present. Mandelstam employs the cities of the past, Jerusalem, Troy, Rome, Venice, as a mask for Petropolis-Petersburg, which enables him to do justice to the historic magnitude of the upheaval and the fall of the old order. *Tristia*'s colour is the colour of mourning. The 'black sun' of the apocalypse shines over everything. Death is ever present, whether it is his mother's, his own, another's or Petersburg's. The volume speaks of departure, guilt and exile. But *Tristia* also signifies resistance against the death of culture; it is an attempt to appeal against the powers of destruction and oblivion. Myths about loyalty, morality and remembrance are scattered throughout the poems. Penelope, the wife of Odysseus, the incarnation of loyalty, is as much an emblem of these poems as is Sophocles' Antigone, who demands a burial for her brother in defiance of Creon's decree.

Mandelstam put odd details into *Tristia* in order to bring alive the cultural cargo of the West as a heightened present and a cultural 'device' for future use. He outlined a supra-temporal network of literary associations and cultural relations throughout history, he unified contradictory elements, he interlaced everyday language with archaisms, he referred formally to the odes and elegies of the Russian classics Derzhavin, Batyushkov and Pushkin, yet, despite this, he was able to instil modernity into his verses by the boldness of his metaphors.[6]

Notwithstanding all his invocations of Western tradition and cultural continuity, it was impossible to ignore the great break that had come about. During the night of 8 to 9 October 1922, only two months after the publication of *Tristia*, he produced a programmatic poem in which his epoch is addressed as a time-beast with a broken backbone, as a 'weak and cruel' beast, which looks back on its own tracks:

5 Zhirmunsky's review of *Tristia*: V. Zhirmunsky, 'Preodolevshie simvolizm', 141.
6 On the *Tristia* volume of poems: appendix to O. Mandelstam, *Tristia*, 278–95.

My time, my beast, who will be able
To peer into your pupils
And with his own blood glue together
The vertebrae of two centuries?
…
Buds will swell again as always
And green shoots will spurt,
But your backbone has been broken,
My wonderful, pitiful time!

And within a meaningless smile
You look backward, cruel and weak,
Like a beast that used to be agile,
On the tracks of your own feet.
(TR, 139–41; PO, 14–15)

The broken backbone, the evocation of a human sacrifice (a child's), the viper as the 'golden measure of the age': the images of this poem do not bode well for the future. The comparison of the epoch with a beast points forward to the 'wolfhound century' in Mandelstam's famous poem of March 1931 (MM, 57), which would lead among other poems to his arrest.

In August 1922, Mandelstam visited a man who was right at the centre of power in Soviet Russia: Nikolai Bukharin. This was not the last time his name would appear in the poet's life. Leading Bolshevik theoretician, head of the Communist International, member of the Central Committee and the Politburo and author of an *ABC of Communism*, he also enjoyed the confidence of Lenin, who would describe him in his testament as 'the darling of the whole party'. Mandelstam's aim in seeking out the cultivated Bukharin was to appeal for support in the case of his brother Yevgeny, whom the authorities had confused with another Mandelstam, a Menshevik, and who had just been arrested for the second time. Bukharin used the opportunity to ask Mandelstam to write a poem, which he would print in the government newspaper *Izvestiia*, so as to show that the poet stood on the 'right side', the side of the revolution.

What did Bukharin expect? A eulogy of the Bolsheviks, the holders of power, or a satirical attack on the 'old world' which had recently gone under? Mandelstam was too recalcitrant to be useful as a political propagandist. What Bukharin received from him instead was a strange and enigmatic poem about bread ('the leaven swells') full of religious symbolism, with cherubim, church domes and 'Sophias of bread' which called up in the reader's mind the image of the Cathedral of St Sophia in Kyiv or the Sophia in the Novgorod Kremlin.[7]

> As if Sophias of bread
> Raise cupolas of rounded ardour
> From a table of cherubim
>
> And to coax a miraculous surplus
> With force or caresses
> The kingly herd-boy, time, seizes the loaf, the word.
> (TR, 131; EW, 66)

According to Nadezhda, Mandelstam was delighted that he had been able to place a poem with religious symbolism in the government newspaper of a state which was enforcing atheism by decree. At a time when the churches had been demolished or converted into garages, warehouses and cinemas, the poem was blatantly provocative. Nevertheless, Bukharin was well mannered enough to keep his promise and really have the poem printed, even though it was diametrically opposed to the new age and its newspaper. It appeared in *Izvestiia* on 23 September 1922 as a facsimile, in Mandelstam's handwriting. If there was ever any surrealism in the Soviet Union, this page of newsprint was it!

Mandelstam wrote his essay 'Humanism and Modern Life' during the early onset of winter in 1922. It was printed on 20 January 1923 in the Berlin émigré newspaper *Nakanune*, where 'Human Corn' had already appeared (on 7 June 1922). His affirmation of faith in Europe was now supplemented with a plea for European humanism. He warned his contemporaries against a regime that employs violence and despises human beings, a social order with affinities to Babylon and Assyria. And, in disquieting fashion, he foretold the shape of Stalinism, already anticipating the arrival of the 'wing of oncoming night':

---

7 Poem about 'Sophias of bread': C. Brown, *Mandelstam*, 100; Dutli, *Europas zarte Hände*, 147–51.

> There are certain periods that say they have nothing to do with man: that say he should be used, like brick, like cement; they say he should be built from, not for. Social architecture takes its measure from the scale of man. Sometimes it becomes hostile to man and nourishes its own majesty by belittling and depreciating him.
>
> …
>
> Everybody senses the monumentality of form of the oncoming social architecture. The mountain is still not visible, but already it casts its shadow over us, and we … move about in this shadow with fear and perplexity, not knowing whether it is a wing of oncoming night, or the shadow of our native city that we are about to enter …
>
> If an authentically humanistic justification is not at the base of the coming social architecture, then it will crush man as Assyria and Babylonia did. (GP, 175–7; SE, 165–6)

With despairing optimism, Mandelstam appealed for support to the values of European humanism, which would come back into force, he prophesied, 'when the time has come'. Thus, the prophetic utterances of 'Humanism and Modern Life' envisaged not only the coming of Stalinism but the fall of the Soviet system …

Mandelstam had a clear-sighted perception of the essence of the totalitarian social order, even during Lenin's lifetime. The 'Red terror' against all 'counter-revolutionary forces' decreed by Lenin in September 1918 was a warning signal. The party leader went on to demonstrate his fundamentally distrustful attitude towards intellectuals by the forcible expulsion of part of the intellectual elite in autumn 1922 on the 'ship of the 170 philosophers'. The foundation stone of the 'Gulag Archipelago' had already been laid in 1923, on Lenin's instructions, when the Solovki prison camp for enemies of the regime was established on the Solovetsky Islands in the White Sea. The measure was aimed at the rigorous suppression of any form of opposition. The propaganda of the regime presented Solovki as a defensive measure by the young Soviet system, but Mandelstam was suspicious of these attempts at embellishment, and he told Nadezhda that he had never *seen* any convict who had returned from Solovki, and that until he did, he would put no credence in the state's claims.[8]

---

8 M. disbelieves the propaganda issued about the Solovki prison camp: Mandelstam, *Hope Abandoned*, 154.

The wave of repression against SRs and Social Democrats (Mensheviks) again struck Mandelstam's brother Yevgeny, who was arrested for the third time in spring 1923 in Petrograd. Mandelstam again intervened in favour of his younger brother. He went to Bukharin and asked him to use his influence with Zinoviev, the head of the party in Petrograd. There is a letter from Mandelstam to his father (MR, 36) telling him about this attempt to intercede, which was in fact successful, as Yevgeny was set free.

Mandelstam felt that he was alone in expressing his forebodings about the 'oncoming night' in 'Humanism and Modern Life'. By 1923, he had already chosen to go into 'inner exile', even before he began to be ostracised in *Soviet* society. Nadezhda Mandelstam writes: 'The isolation chosen by Akhmatova and M. was the only possible course. It was the beginning of an age during which a few lone figures held out against a vast, organised mass.' It was a fateful choice.[9]

On 23 May 1922, Mandelstam presented to the State Publishing House an anthology of fragments from Old French epic poems which he himself had translated, including an extract from the eleventh-century *Chanson de Roland*. The project was rejected. But these translations were a personal confession of faith, and 'destiny spoke' in them, according to Nadezhda. The *Aliscans* fragment, she wrote, was an 'oath' never to hide if the defence of life was at stake. The passage from the twelfth-century *Life of St Alexius* was Mandelstam's 'vow of poverty'. It was a hidden, personal oath, not a public declaration. A lack of material possessions, social isolation and loneliness would remain constant features of Mandelstam's life right to the bitter end.[10]

Mandelstam also remained an outsider in literary terms. In 1916–1917, his colleague Nikolai Gumilyov had attempted to revive the 'Poets' Guild' of 1911, and he tried a second time in 1921. But Mandelstam did not believe in revivals. In contrast to Gumilyov, who was a born teacher, he needed no pupils. He continued his commitment to Acmeism, the 'we-feeling' of 1913, for the whole of his life, but he did not support its re-animation in any form. He had internalised Acmeism, he had made it his own personal 'school'. A young poet, Lev Gornung, sent him his poems. In July 1923 he wrote in reply:

9 The 'outsiders' go into 'inner exile': ibid., 145 ('Living Space in the Superstructure').

10 M.'s confession-like translations of the *Chanson de Roland*, *Aliscans* and the *Life of St Alexius*: N. Mandelstam, *Hope Against Hope*, 240 ('The Bookcase'); R. Dutli, *Ossip Mandelstam*, 257–72.

> The Acmeism of 1923 is not that of 1913. To be more precise, there is no such thing as Acmeism. It aimed simply to be the 'conscience' of poetry. It is a court pronouncing judgement on poetry, not poetry itself. Do not despise the poets of the present. They have the blessing of the past. (MR, 38)

Connoisseurs of poetry continued to value Mandelstam, but by 1923, the representatives of 'revolutionary art' thought he was destined for the scrap heap. At the end of May 1923, the Moscow publisher 'Krug' (The Circle) issued *The Second Book*, a volume of poems dedicated to Nadezhda Mandelstam, which was an improved edition of *Tristia*, this time put together by the author himself. But now Mandelstam could not count on sympathetic reviewers like Zhirmunsky. It was a particularly bitter blow that one of the leading literary figures of the former era, the ex-Symbolist Valery Bryusov, who had offered his services to the Bolsheviks after the revolution and now headed the literature section of the People's Commissariat for Enlightenment, denied that Mandelstam's work had any contemporary relevance at all. Writing in the journal *Press and Revolution* (no. 6, 1923), he tore the book to pieces:

> Detached as it is from social life and social and political interests, from the problems of modern science and the search for a contemporary view of the world, the poetry of Mandelstam feeds only on the subjective experiences of the poet and on abstract 'eternal' questions of love, death and so on, which in their entirely metaphysical aspect have long been hollowed out and emptied of any real content.

It is true that a third and considerably expanded edition of *Stone* was published in July 1923 by the State Publishing House, but the volume demonstratively bore the same title as before, even though the content was supplemented by more recent poems. People were inevitably reminded that this was a re-edition of two pre-revolutionary collections of the same name, issued in 1913 and 1916. It was hardly a proof of contemporaneity. The duty to be contemporary at any price was a heavy burden for Mandelstam, until he wrote a poem in which he expressed his complete rejection of the world of contemporaneity.

13

No, Never Was I Anyone's Contemporary

(Moscow 1923–1924)

The year 1923 witnessed quarrels between numerous artistic groupings over the privilege of representing true revolutionary art. No longer, as in 1919, were the parties to the conflict the Futurists and the Imaginists. The latter were close to dissolution. If the image-obsessed Sergei Yesenin had not belonged to the group, it would hardly be worth a mention for posterity. But, in 1923, Vladimir Mayakovsky, the former Futurist, formed the group LEF ('Left Front of Art'). LEF claimed to be creating the revolutionary art of the future. It was attacked by two groups of proletarian writers, 'the Smithy' (*Kuznitsa*) and 'October', which were themselves in competition with each other. Since 1920, there had been an umbrella group of proletarian writers' groups, usually referred to by the abbreviation VAPP ('All-Russian Association of Proletarian Writers'). Its journal *Na postu* (On Guard) was a polemical instrument in the fight against all those who were unwilling to conform to the ideal of a unified proletarian art in the Soviet state.

The essays Mandelstam wrote between 1922 and 1924 were lively commentaries on modern Russian poetry after Symbolism, including sharp-tongued and at times brilliant polemics. For him, the sweaty and bombastic proletarian writers were not worth discussing. He simply ignored them. With the more discriminating representatives of LEF, on the other hand, he was prepared to engage, though he gave them plenty of hard knocks. The work of Mayakovsky, the former 'drummer of the revolution', is briefly summed up in the essay 'Storm and Stress' (1923) as the 'poetry of common sense', which endeavours to teach lessons, and is nothing more than a tool of pedagogy (GP, 196; CC, 178). In 'Literary Moscow' (1922), Mandelstam had already cast doubt on Mayakovsky's project of a 'poetry for everyone', a 'poetry liberated from all culture'. Mayakovsky, he said, 'impoverishes his poetry in vain' (GP, 149; CC, 147). In this polemic, Mandelstam had put his finger on a sore point: Mayakovsky, the brilliant and impetuous Futurist of the early days of the avant-garde, had become a copywriter for the young Soviet state, and the prophet of a glorious future, who composed publicity verses for contemporary Soviet products such as synthetic rubber galoshes, which appeared in the windows of the telegraph agency ROSTA. These missteps were typical of this talented man, whose poetic voice never recovered for the rest of his life. He committed suicide in 1930. There was only one Futurist of whom Mandelstam had a high opinion. That was Khlebnikov. But Khlebnikov was already dead.

In the essay 'Literary Moscow', Mandelstam uses the example of the machine poetry of Nikolai Aseev to dismiss the enthusiasm for technology and the utilitarianism of LEF and the Constructivists as sterile and absurd:

> A purely rationalistic, electro-mechanical, radioactive and in general technological poetry is impossible, for a single reason that should be equally close to the poet and the mechanic: rationalistic mechanical poetry does not store up energy, gives it no increment, as natural irrational poetry does; but only spends, only disperses it. The discharge is equal to the windup. As much comes out as is wound up … That is why Aseev's rationalistic poetry is not rational, why it is sterile and sexless. A machine lives a deep and animated life, but it gives forth no seed. (GP, 149; SE, 148)

A culture of polemic belonged as much to Mandelstam's argumentative nature as it did to the epoch. In his essay 'About the Nature of the Word' (1922), he writes that the 'frail boat of the human word' is borne into 'that open sea of the future, where there is no sympathetic understanding, where dreary commentary replaces the fresh wind of hostility and sympathy of one's contemporaries' (GP, 130; SE, 95). Evidently, the 'fresh wind of hostility' was just as valuable to this poet as 'sympathy'. No more needs to be said about his attitude to polemic.

Sometimes, his polemical exaggerations overstepped the mark. Even the two female colleagues who had been close to him in such significant phases of his life as 1916 and 1917–1918 were assailed with harsh invective in these intellectual exercises. In 'Literary Moscow', he writes of the 'domestic needlework' of Marina Tsvetaeva's poetry, and of the 'tastelessness' and 'historical insincerity' of her poems about Russia, crudely denigrating her writings as 'feminine poetry' (GP, 146; SE, 146), while Anna Akhmatova, whose poetry he had praised in 1916 as 'one of the symbols of Russia's greatness' (GP, 73), is described simplistically in *Notes About Poetry* (1923) as a 'Stylite' standing on a 'parquet floor' (GP, 181; SE, 98). The polemicist's mischievous pleasure in being unjust led him to make unfair attacks on his colleagues. Nadezhda wrote in 1958 to Anna Akhmatova that her husband was no longer himself in that period of 'suffocation': a 'mass of erroneous judgements and stupid ideas' had crept into his thinking.[1]

Even so, in other cases, Mandelstam was astoundingly capable of recognising the importance of work diametrically opposed to his own. The best examples of this are his evaluations of Velimir Khlebnikov and Boris Pasternak. Mandelstam's remarks about them, for example in the essays 'Notes About Poetry' and 'Storm and Stress' (1923), are some of the most appropriate comments that could be made about these two poets who were so dissimilar from him. Mandelstam never tired of praising the language experimenter and visionary Khlebnikov, 'who immerses us in the very thick of Russian root words, in the etymological night dear to the mind and heart of the clever reader' (GP, 114; SE, 85). He likened Khlebnikov to 'a mole who provides for the future by burrowing enough passageways in the earth to last for a whole century' (GP, 117; SE, 86–7) and described him as a 'great archaic poet' (GP, 146; SE, 145), and an 'idiotic Einstein' in the 'authentic, innocent Greek sense of the word' (GP, 195; SE, 162). Khlebnikov, he said, had created 'a huge all-Russian prayer-and-icon book, from which for century upon century everyone who has the requisite energy will be able to draw' (GP, 196; SE, 162).

In Mandelstam's *Notes About Poetry*, Pasternak's work receives a degree of commendation which can only be compared with Marina Tsvetaeva's enthusiastic essay 'A Flood of Light' (1922): 'To read Pasternak's verses is to

1 Nadezhda Mandelstam's 1958 letter to Anna Akhmatova: N. Mandelstam, 'V etoi zhizni menia', 99.

clear one's throat, reinforce one's breathing, renovate the lungs; such verses must be a cure for tuberculosis. We do not have any healthier poetry now. It is *koumiss* after powdered milk' (GP, 184; SE, 100). And Mandelstam's encomium of Khlebnikov and Pasternak is vigorously formulated: they are the 'secularisers of poetry' who have done 'first-rate work' (GP, 180; SE, 98).

He generally starts off his polemical essays by criticising Symbolism. Even so, he does admit in the essay 'Attack' (1924) that the whole of contemporary Russian poetry 'came out of the womb of Symbolism' (GP, 246; SE, 73). The same text also bemoans the 'ungratefulness' of the epoch towards its poets, which is why he is prepared to judge his literary fathers more mildly from a distance. The emotion of gratitude ran counter to the polemical impulse; it prohibited harsh and discordant language. In several essays of the years 1923 and 1924, such as 'An Army of Poets' and 'Attack', Mandelstam regretted the emergence of a throng of new poets, the disappearance of a cultivated reading public and the widespread 'poetic illiteracy' of the time (GP, 247; SE, 74). In the essay 'Literary Moscow', he had already lamented the insouciance of contemporary poets, whose cultural revolutionary posturing had led them to forget the most important rules of poetry:

> Inventiveness and remembrance go hand in hand in poetry. To remember means also to invent. He who remembers is also an inventor. The radical illness of Moscow's literary taste lies in forgetting this double truth … Poetry breathes through both the mouth and the nose, through remembrance and inventiveness. One needs to be a fakir in order to deny oneself one of these modes of breathing. (GP, 147; SE, 147)

Mandelstam mainly reproached the future-intoxicated cultural revolutionaries for their neglect of 'remembrance'. But he also protests, in 'Attack', against attempts by the holders of power to appropriate and regiment poetry:

> Poor poetry! Under the muzzle of these many revolvers now levelling unmitigated demands at her, she shies. What should poetry be like? Well, maybe poetry shouldn't be like anything, maybe poetry doesn't owe anybody anything, and maybe these creditors of hers are all fraudulent! (GP, 244; SE, 72)

The ghostly shadow of Blumkin's threatening revolver now seemed to be appearing everywhere, as a whole collection of revolver muzzles! No poet of this epoch demanded poetry's freedom and independence more emphatically – and indeed more anachronistically! – than Mandelstam.

His confrontation with the epoch is reflected in the series of poems which followed 'My Time, My Beast' (October 1922). Mandelstam's poem 'The Finder of a Horseshoe' appeared in number 2 of the journal *Krasnaia nov'* (Red Virgin Soil), March–April 1923.[2] It was in free verse, and it bore the subtitle 'A Pindaric Fragment'. It is certainly nourished by memories of the Greek poet Pindar (c.520–446 B.C.E.) and his victory odes celebrating athletic triumphs in the Panhellenic Games. But, in contrast to Pindar's intact world, in which events are made meaningful by being embedded in myth, by being raised to a divine level, Mandelstam demonstrates a fractured modernity. The poem tells us of broken carts and a dying horse. It was not Pindar's vaunted racehorse, but the horse named Russia which was moribund. In the background, though, there lay an allusion to Peter the Great on horseback, as displayed in Falconet's famous equestrian statue in St Petersburg's Senate Square. The old world no longer exists, and the broken spinal column of the time-beast has long since been in a stranger's hands: 'Children play at knucklebones with the vertebrae of dead beasts / And the fragile chronology of our era is coming to an end.'

But in 'The Finder of a Horseshoe' the poet's role is to protect the fragments left by the past, and to preserve the memory, the relics, of a cultural inheritance, which the 'horseshoe' symbolises. The past is present even in death, even in the last gesture, the final word:

> The horse foams in the dust.
> But the acute curve of his neck
> Preserves the memory of the race with outstretched legs.
> ...
> Human lips which have nothing more to say
> Preserve the form of the last word said.
> And the arm retains the sense of weight,
> Though the jug splashed half empty on the way home.
> What I'm saying at this moment is not being said by me
> But is dug from the ground like grains of petrified wheat.
> (TR, 151–3; EW, 69–70)

2 The poem 'The Finder of a Horseshoe': S. Broyde, *Osip Mandel'shtam*, 169–99.

Mandelstam assigns an archaeological mission to his poetry, but the Self of the poem is itself threatened by time, subjected to wear and tear: 'Time pares me down like a coin / And there's no longer enough of me for myself.'

The image of the horseshoe suggests that, in 1923, Mandelstam is summoning up the power of poetry by writing magical, 'talismanic' poems which are intended to outlast a destructive epoch.[3] They plainly proclaim the imperative of remembrance. The 'Slate Ode', composed in March 1923, is a modern, combative echo of the last ode written by the Russian poet Gavril Derzhavin (1743–1816), 'The Flow of Time' (6 July 1816), which he scratched on a slate with a slate pencil. It was a lament about the impermanence of things, the 'current of time's river' which carried off all human deeds into 'the abyss of oblivion' in which everything had to disappear. Mandelstam opposes the pathos of impermanence by calling up the 'talismanic' power of the poetic word. His ally is again the exiled Ovid, who in his *Epistulae ex Ponto*, written between the years 12 and 17 C.E., insists on the power of the poet's word to resist the destructive work of time: 'Voracious time therefore destroys / But death delays, defied by my toughness' (Book 4, 10, lines 7–8).

Mandelstam's 'Slate Ode' is a raging nine-stanza stream of images, a complex message in a bottle for the future. It is the unwavering self-affirmation of a poet who has become disconnected from his age:

A mighty junction of star with star,
The flinty path in an older song
In language of flint and air combined:
Flint meets water and ring joins horseshoe;
On the soft shale of the clouds
A milky slate-grey sketch is drawn:
Not the discipleship of worlds
But the delirious dreams of mooning sheep.
…
Here terror writes, here writes displacement
In a milky lead-pencil hand;
And here is shaped a rough-draft version

3 The magical, 'talismanic' function of M.'s poetry of 1923–1924: O. Ronen, *An Approach to Mandel'shtam*, 6–13.

Of running water's own disciples.
…
It's only from the voice we'll know
That there was scratching and conflict there;
So we draw the hard pencil in the one direction
Indicated by the voice.
I tear the night, the burning chalk,
For the sake of an instantaneous record.
I change for noise the song of arrows
And for order the clatter of bustards' wings.
…
Who am I? Not a real stone mason,
No shipwright I, I don't roof buildings,
I'm a double-dealer with a double soul
The friend of night, the day's assailant.
(TR, 155–9; SE, 61–2)

The confession that 'here terror writes' sounds unusually direct. The 'Slate Ode' bears witness to the loneliness of this poet in his epoch by reminding us of the first verse of Mikhail Lermontov's famous poem 'Alone I Set Forth on the Road' (1841): 'The star to the star'. But it also includes powerful magical images, which proclaim the necessity of uninterrupted creation.

Mandelstam was urgently in need of the magical power of these verbal talismans, which might serve to counteract the fear and loneliness he suffered. He was already in conflict with officialdom in 1923. This led to his resignation from the All-Russian Writers' Union. It was a precursor of the irrevocable break of 1930. In a letter written on 23 August 1923, Mandelstam announced his resignation from the Writers' Union, protesting against the inefficiency, arbitrariness and violence that prevailed in the House of Writers at 25 Tverskoy Boulevard. It was a place where 'writers' who had no talent but were close to those in power were able to strut around as miniature potentates, a place from which real artists were driven out. (Mandelstam had failed in his attempt to get a room there for the homeless Khlebnikov.) Thenceforth, it was the fate of the ghost of the 'Herzen House' to wander through Russian literature. It appears as the 'Griboedov House' in Mikhail Bulgakov's epoch-making novel *The Master and Margarita*, in which he unleashes Woland, his Moscow Satan in disguise. In his angry *Fourth Prose* (1929–1930), Mandelstam would describe it as 'that obscene building on the Tverskoy Boulevard', where the 'clinking of pieces of silver' could be heard. It was a place where the Judases of the literary profession put their dignity up for sale (RZ, 268; NT, 187). No one would claim that Mandelstam was an undemanding contemporary who adapted himself to the conditions of the time without complaint. His uncompromising stance in moral and artistic matters is already evident from his resignation from the Writers' Union in August 1923. Further conflicts with official bodies could be expected.

Now he was homeless again; he entrusted his few belongings to his brother Alexander and on 10 August 1923 he travelled with Nadezhda to the Crimea, to Koreis, near Gaspra, where he found shelter in a rest home run by TseKUBU as a qualifying individual in the 'second category'. He was lucky to be permitted to make a summer trip to the Crimea, and he owed his good fortune to the publication of two prose texts he had written, 'Cold Summer' and 'The Sukharevka', in the Komsomol newspaper *Ogonyok*, on 15 and 28 July respectively. These pieces were parts of a portrait of the city of Moscow that was poetic in character, but with a political edge. They also cast a critical eye on the new 'revolutionary' and functional architecture:

> Symmetrical as a honeycomb, an accumulation of measurements devoid of all majesty. Moscow's deathly boredom first paraded itself as enlightenment, then as a smallpox vaccination; and as soon as it begins to take shape it will no longer be able to stop but will rise like leavened dough. (RZ, 164; CC, 242)

On the journey to Gaspra, the Mandelstams shared a compartment with an 'amiable' fellow passenger, Andrei Vyshinsky, who was not at all prominent then, but would later enter history as an unscrupulous state prosecutor in the Moscow show trials of 1936 to 1938. During this epoch, the paths of the later victims often crossed those of the executioners in harmless settings. Only in retrospect did these accidental meetings take on their spectral character.[4]

The '*Ogonyok* money' was just enough to cover the railway tickets to Gaspra. Mandelstam's extreme lack of financial resources is evident from a begging letter he sent on 21 September 1923 to his father. He could not

4 M. shares a train compartment with Andrei Vyshinsky: N. Mandelstam, *Hope Abandoned*, 220 ('A Honeymoon').

afford tickets back to Moscow, and it was no longer possible to borrow money: 'We are in a hopeless situation', he wrote (MR, 44). Many of his contemporaries have described his constant money troubles. But they also mention his mania for borrowing money from everyone … money which perhaps never came back to the lender. Mandelstam self-mockingly recorded this irksome side of his life in a jocular, pseudo-classical epigram:

> And if you mourn that I owe you eleven thousand roubles
> Just think, it might well have been twenty-one thousand.
> (BT, 121)

But that summer was not dominated exclusively by problems with money. It was in Gaspra that Mandelstam began work on an autobiographical text, which was published in 1925 under the title *The Noise of Time*. The fourteen chapters of this book (to which the four *Theodosia* sketches about the civil war period were added in summer 1924) brought together an abundance of memories of his childhood and youth in Petersburg. The book condensed a whole epoch into a series of details which often appeared bizarre. It was an atmospheric portrait of pre-revolutionary Russia, and of its 'sickly calm' before the great storm of the revolutions of the twentieth century. Mandelstam did not preach nostalgia, however. The old Russia had to perish, there was no doubt about that. His rejection of nostalgia was accompanied by a rejection of 'autobiography' or 'talking about yourself':

> My desire is not to speak about myself but to track down the age, the noise and the germination of time. My memory is inimical to all that is personal … My memory is not loving but inimical, and it labours not to reproduce but to distance the past. A *raznochinets* needs no memory – it is enough for him to tell of the books he has read, and his biography is done. (RZ, 88; NT, 109–10)

The Noise of Time is an attempt at a calm farewell, and it supplements the complicated goodbye rituals presented in the time poems 'Tristia' and 'The Finder of a Horseshoe'. Even so, it contains political dynamite. Although Mandelstam claims, at the end of the piece, to be speaking about 'the nineteenth century', he also unmistakably has the new century in mind when he refers to the 'measureless cold, which welded decades together into one day, one night, one profound winter, within which the terrible power of the State glowed, like a stove, with ice' (RZ, 102; NT, 117). This was an early evocation of the 'frosty state' with its 'terrible power', a vision of the new state's all-encompassing glaciation.

On 6 October 1923, Mandelstam and his wife returned to Moscow with borrowed money, breaking their journey in Kyiv. He again had no roof over his head. Under protest, he gave back the room in the Writers' House on the Tverskoy Boulevard. To his father he wrote: 'I have lost my head a little … No work, no money, nowhere to live' (MR, 46). At first the couple found accommodation with Nadezhda's brother Yevgeny Khazin on the Ostoshenka. At the end of October, thanks to Yevgeny's help, they found a room at 45 Bolshaia Iakimanka for a few months, in the 'house of a professor', which seemed to them to be like 'paradise': 'Light … calm … No-one calls on us. Our own kitchen … Firewood … Peace and quiet … In a word: paradise' (MR, 46). But it was only one more halting point on their eternal trek from one furnished room to the next.

Mandelstam's professional situation was deeply depressing:

> What am I doing? I'm working for money. The crisis is grave … There were more translations, articles, and so forth. "Literature" is loathsome to me. I dream of quitting this nonsense. The last time I worked for myself was in the summer. (MR, 47; CC, 489–90)

What he meant by 'work for myself' was producing *The Noise of Time*, written while he was in Gaspra. His breadwinning activities included translations of the works of third- or fourth-rate 'progressive' writers such as Toller, Daudistel, Barthel and Barbusse. The term 'internal emigrant' was already in use by 1923, and it was applied to Mandelstam. According to Nadezhda's memoirs, by 1923 he had already been removed from the list of approved contributors to Soviet journals.[5] She perhaps placed the date one year too early, because many of Mandelstam's essays and journalistic texts were in fact published in 1923. An essay on Auguste Barbier, the poet of the badly led Paris Revolution of 1830, was published on 15 August 1923 in the journal *Searchlight*, together with Mandelstam's translation of Barbier's poem 'La Curée' (The Spoils). The Barbier essay ambiguously referred to a 'classically unsuccessful' and 'cynically abused'

5 M.'s name is removed from the list of approved contributors to the journals: ibid., 145 ('Living Space in the Superstructure').

revolution (GP, 213; CC, 184). The similarity with a more recent revolution was certainly no accident.

Mandelstam even became a roving reporter for the Komsomol paper *Ogonyok* (The Spark), and he sent in an account of the first international peasants' congress, which took place in Moscow in October 1923 and had the German communist Clara Zetkin as its guest of honour. In December 1923, he interviewed a man called Nguyen Ai Quoc, who later became the president of the Democratic Republic of Vietnam under the name Ho Chi Minh. The picture Mandelstam presents of his interviewee, who was almost the same age as him and of youthful appearance, is marked by considerable sympathy (GP, 235; CC, 249–51). Mandelstam face to face with Ho Chi Minh: another surreal aspect of the history of the twentieth century.

Lenin died on 21 January 1924. Mandelstam became a reporter once again for a Moscow newspaper, and he wrote a short nocturnal mood picture of the queue of people heading for the white-pillared hall of the House of the Trade Unions where Lenin's body was lying in state.

> Oh revolution, how accustomed you have become to queues! You have sweated and strained and walked bent over in the queues of the nineteenth year and the twentieth year; now comes your biggest queue, your last waiting line on the way to the night-time sun, the night-time coffin …
>
> Dead Lenin in Moscow! Oh to feel Moscow at this moment! Who would not want to see it, the dear face, the face of Russia?
>
> What time is it? Two, three, four o'clock? How long will we stand there? No-one knows. We've lost all sense of time. We are standing in a wondrous, nocturnal human forest. And there are thousands of children with us. (GP, 239–40)

The image of the laid-out body of the 'night-time sun' had until then been reserved for poets like Alexander Pushkin. Mandelstam's text bears witness to the apocalyptic perception of Lenin's death which prevailed at the time. The death of the founder of the state, whom many people had considered immortal, signified more than the end of an epoch. Mandelstam's reportage betrays how moved he is, or at least it is evidence of an attempt to come to terms with his epoch. But, in talking to Nadezhda, he adopted a different tone, a tone of complete disillusionment: 'They've come to complain to Lenin about the Bolsheviks … But it's a vain hope: it won't do any good.' Boris Pasternak also stood with the Mandelstams in the queue of hundreds of thousands of people. Together they went past the open coffin of the dead Lenin. On the way home, Mandelstam expressed his amazement at old-fashioned Moscow: 'It is as if they were burying a Tsar.' Lenin's burial was the last eruption of the popular uprising, Nadezhda commented. She had seen that Lenin's popularity was not based on fear, as was Stalin's later 'deification', but on the hopes that the people attached to the head of state.[6]

Film shots of the funeral ceremony show the broad face of Stalin over Lenin's coffin. This was the man of whom Lenin had warned in his testament: 'Comrade Stalin has concentrated enormous power in his hands; I am not sure whether he always knows how to use that power with sufficient caution.' But it was too late – Stalin could no longer be dislodged from the position of General Secretary of the party. He was saved by Lenin's third stroke, which occurred on 9 March 1923, and he was the main speaker at Lenin's funeral. As a former pupil at the Theological Seminary in Tbilisi, he knew how to exploit the suggestive power of liturgical incantations: 'We vow to thee, Comrade Lenin, that we shall honourably fulfil thy commandment.' Stalin was certainly not referring to Lenin's testament when he spoke of his 'commandment' …

Mandelstam celebrated the New Year of 1924 in Kyiv with Nadezhda. There, he wrote one of his more important poems about the epoch; it was completed towards the end of January under the impression of Lenin's 'epoch-making' death, and it was entitled 'The First of January 1924'. In nine long stanzas, he speaks of time falling asleep and of the 'senile son' of the age.

Whoever kisses time's ancient nodding head
Will remember later, like a loving son,
How the old man lay down to sleep
In the drift of wheat outside the window.
He who has opened the eyes of the age,
Two large sleepy apples with inflamed lids,
Hears forever after the roar of rivers
Swollen with the wasted, lying times.

6 M. on Lenin's death and lying in state, and on complaints about the Bolsheviks: ibid., 237 ('Interlude').

The age is a despot with two sleepy apples
To see with; and a splendid mouth of earth.
When he dies he'll sink onto the numb
Arms of his son, who's already senile.
I know the breath growing weaker by the day.
Not long now till the simple song
Of the wrongs of earth is cut off,
And a tin seal put on the lips.

O life of earth! O dying age!
I'm afraid no one will understand you
But the man with the helpless smile
Of one who has lost himself.
O the pain of peeling back the raw eyelids
To look for a lost word, and with lime
Slaking in the veins, to hunt
For night herbs for a tribe of strangers.
(TR, 163; CR, 51)

The poem 'The First of January 1924' is an unsparing confrontation with the 'wasted, lying times', an interrogation of his own epoch which does not shrink from posing direct questions: 'Who else will you kill? Who else will you worship? / What other lie will you dream up?' A tremendous poem by a poet who resists his gloomy vision ('What more do you want? They won't touch you, won't kill you.') but at the same time already has a clear idea of his eventual doom: 'Not long now till the simple song / Of the wrongs of earth is cut off / And a tin seal put on the lips.'

This is not Mandelstam's first premonition of his own execution. As early as 1922, in a poem entitled 'The Scalp Tingles with Cold', he writes:

It's plain that some purpose
Is moving these lips
The tree-top laughs and plays
Into the day of the axes.
(TR, 129; SP, 66)

The poem 'The First of January 1924' takes its reader on a journey through night-time Moscow, evoking arbitrary justice, rattling Underwood typewriters, decrees and denunciations, but, as Paul Celan wrote, despite all these premonitions it manages to 'triumph over contingency with laughter'. 'And from the sick son's blood the lime will vanish / And there will be sudden, blessed laughter.'[7]

Rooted though it is in its epoch, the poem demonstrates an astonishing sense of separation from it, and a poem written shortly afterwards brings this to a culmination by denying any kind of contemporaneity. In an age when to be at one with one's contemporaries was an imperative requirement, when a person had to identify unconditionally with the 'new' epoch, this was a provocation, a form of sacrilege:

> No, never was I anyone's contemporary –
> Not for me such honour.
> O how despicable that namesake of mine.
> That wasn't me, that was someone else.[8]

Not until seven years later, in May 1931, would Mandelstam apparently retract this statement, and in 'Midnight in Moscow' (MM, 79) proclaim: 'It's about time you knew, I too am a contemporary!' But the 1924 poem already contains a concession to the peremptory requirements of the age, striking a note of resignation: 'Well if we're not to hammer out another / Let us live this age we've got!'

The cycle of five great poems about his epoch was now complete: 'My Time, My Beast', 'The Finder of a Horseshoe', 'The Slate Ode', 'The First of January 1924' and 'No, Never Was I Anyone's Contemporary'. They are among the most important he ever wrote. They provide the key without which it is impossible to understand this poet. Despite his self-imposed injunction 'Let Us Live This Age We've Got', Mandelstam gradually adjusted himself between 1922 and 1924 to a kind of hibernation. He no longer expects the 'wasted, lying' times to comprehend him; he places his faith instead in the future impact of his poetry, perhaps even its posthumous impact.

Mandelstam refers to this 'future' amazingly early in some of his prose pieces. In 'About the Interlocutor' (1913), he saw the ideal reader as a 'providential interlocutor' of the future. In the 1922 essay 'About the Nature of the Word', he likens a poem to an Egyptian boat of the dead on

7 Paul Celan on the poem 'The First of January 1924': LG, 81.

8 TR, 169; C. Brown, *Mandelstam*, 117.

its journey into the beyond: 'Once more I compare the poem to an Egyptian boat of the dead. In this boat, everything is equipped for life; nothing is forgotten' (GP, 130; SE, 95). At the end of the essay 'Attack' (1924), he compares the Russian poets 'who have not yet found their readers' with stars 'that have already sent out their rays of light to this distant and as yet unattained destination'. Perhaps the poems will only reach their goal after 'the poetic luminaries have become extinct' (GP, 248; SE, 74): an astronomical metaphor for a seemingly untimely but also tragically misjudged *oeuvre*.

He may have been a literary outsider, but, for representatives of the Communist Party, he was a typical 'fellow-traveller'. This was a term coined by the first People's Commissar for Enlightenment, Anatoly Lunacharsky, and Trotsky employs it in his polemical collection of essays *Literature and Revolution* (1924). It refers to non-communist writers who accepted the October Revolution but insisted on the independence of literature, and did not want it to be exposed to the 'dictatorship of the proletariat'. In the course of the 1920s, the 'fellow-travellers' were subjected to increasingly vitriolic attacks by the proletarian writers' groups.

Mandelstam was one of the writers who signed a collective letter delivered to the press section of the Central Committee of the Communist Party on 9 May 1924. At that time, a conference was about to be held to lay down the rules for the party's future policy towards literature. The outcome of this conference was that, on 18 June 1925, the Central Committee issued the resolution 'On the Policy of the Party in the Field of Fine Literature', which was intended to regulate the co-existence of the 'proletarian writers' with other literary groupings. It reflected Bukharin's ideas on the subject, and its aim was gradually to bring the 'fellow-travellers' and the peasant writers into line with the goal of creating a 'proletarian' Soviet literature.

The signatories of the letter of 9 May 1924 made this statement:

> We believe that literature must reflect the new life which surrounds us, in which we live and work. On the other hand, however, literature must be the creation of an individual author who perceives and reflects the world in his own way. (MR, 51–2; CC, 576)

It was signed by thirty-six people, among them important prose writers such as Isaac Babel, Boris Pilnyak and Mikhail Zoshchenko, and the poets Yesenin and Mandelstam.

One party official and critic who came out against proletarian dictatorship over art and literature was Alexander Voronsky, who recognised the talent of the 'fellow-travellers' and promoted their work, particularly in the journal *Red Virgin Soil* which he had founded in 1921. A further volume of Mandelstam's poetry, *The Second Book*, was issued in 1923 by the 'Krug' publishing house, which was headed by Voronsky. Between 1925 and 1927, Voronsky was a supporter of Trotsky, at a time when the latter was already unable to achieve anything against the provisional triumvirate of Stalin, Zinoviev and Kamenev. Voronsky was arrested in 1927, expelled from the party and executed ten years later. The epoch of the 'fellow-travellers' was very short-lived.

At the end of July 1924, Mandelstam moved from Moscow to Leningrad. This was yet another of his repeated changes of residence, dictated by the everlasting housing shortage. The city of his childhood, the propagandistically celebrated 'cradle of the revolution', had just been given a new name, in memory of Lenin. Mandelstam continued his attempts to stay above water financially with translations and reviews for publishing houses. Almost none of his work now appeared in the journals. The rumour spread that Mandelstam had stopped writing poetry and had become a translator. Even the well-disposed Bukharin, who, among other things, was chief editor of *Pravda*, told him that he would no longer be able to print any of his poems, though he could still print his translations. This was a time 'of sharpening class struggle'.[9]

Mandelstam hardly wrote any poems after his rejection of contemporaneity ('No, Never Was I Anyone's Contemporary'), and he fell silent completely in the spring of 1925. One magical exception, a poem full of strange details about an unusually mild Petersburg winter, is dated 17 December 1924: 'Oh you houses, not too tall, with square windows – / Greetings! Winter in Petersburg, you've turned out so mild!' (TR, 171). Mandelstam evidently cannot bring himself to utter the majestic new appellation 'Leningrad'. But the tone of the poem is surprisingly lighthearted; it shows us unused skates, unfrozen canals, mandarin oranges and mocha coffee (luxury products, signs of the improvement in supplies during the NEP era), old periodicals in doctors' waiting rooms and, finally, trams, which possessed a special aura for Mandelstam. As we shall see, he

9 From now on, Bukharin will only be able to print M.'s translations, not his poems: Mandelstam, *Hope Abandoned*, 234 ('Interlude').

would even devote one of his children's books to a tram. The conclusion of the poem evokes a search for warmth, because the cold still dominates, despite everything: 'After the baths, after the opera, it doesn't matter where or when – / The headlong flight to the warmth of the tram.'

But, for Mandelstam, the harmless tram always had a threatening aspect. At the start of the 1930s, he would say reflectively to Nadezhda: 'We always think everything is all right just because the streetcars are running.' The streetcar, he implied, was nothing but an emergency regime's way of simulating normality.[10]

10 M. on the streetcar as a simulation of normality: ibid., 217 ('A Honeymoon').

14

Nadezhda by the Black Sea

(Leningrad and Yalta 1925–1926)

In mid-January 1925, Mandelstam happened to meet Olga Vaksel on a Leningrad street. She was an elegant beauty and an actress who dreamed of appearing in films. She had already gone through a failed marriage and she had a one-year-old son to take care of. Mandelstam was already acquainted with her: in the summer of 1916, when she was thirteen, and a year later, at fourteen, she had visited Maximilian Voloshin, accompanied by her mother, at a time when Mandelstam too was in Koktebel. Now twenty-two, she had the fragile charm of an unhappy young woman, whose aspirations for life and dreams of stage success were not being fulfilled. Mandelstam brought Olga home to meet Nadezhda. But what started as a three-way friendship ended as the worst crisis in their marriage. Mandelstam almost immediately fell in love with Olga, passionately at first, then insanely.

Triangular relationships were not unusual in the early Soviet years. They were regarded as chic and progressive, because they were considered anti-bourgeois. The unhappy hero of the most famous 'ménage à trois' of the epoch was the 'drummer of the revolution' himself: Vladimir Mayakovsky. For years, he was the third person in the marriage of Lilia and Osip Brik. Mayakovsky suffered misery for the whole of his life owing to his love for Lilia. As far as the Mandelstams were concerned, Nadezhda seemed at first to be quite happy with the way the triangular relationship was working out. She jokingly described her husband as 'a Mormon' and did not object to his rather chimerical plan for the three of them to take a trip to Paris. But the erotic dynamite in the relationship quickly got out of control.

'A Case of Touch and Go', a bitterly angry chapter in the second volume of Nadezhda's memoirs, gives some impression of the seriousness of the catastrophe. As late as 1970, when she was writing the book, she still felt as if her pen was guided by unbridled jealousy. Almost every day, the young beauty came to see them and 'carried Mandelstam off' in her presence.[1] The situation would have been utterly banal, if Mandelstam had not written two of his finest poems for Olga in those first few months of 1925, which he wisely concealed from Nadezhda. (In 1935, while in exile in Voronezh, he was informed, long after the event, of Olga Vaksel's suicide in Oslo, and he added two further poems.) These are the verses of a deeply enamoured poet who is already involved in telling lies and making excuses to his wife and cannot see a way out of the situation. His life had gone into freefall:

> Like summer lightning a life fell away,
> As an eyelash into a tumbler falls,
> Life lied to the bitter end
> I don't accuse, I don't defend.
> (TR, 195, 197; FP, 66)

The poem projects a utopia of absolute love. The 'golden fleece' wrapped round the beloved is the garment of an unprecedented myth of love. An imaginary pair of lovers is introduced, who leave everything else behind. The fascination of the poem lies in the tension between the myth of an erotic utopia and the tiny, unpretentious details of everyday existence:

> Do you want an apple in the night?
> Do you want hot honey, fresh and light?
> Do you want me to take your boots off,
> To lift you like a fleck of fluff?

1 The affair with Olga Vaksel: N. Mandelstam, *Hope Abandoned*, 240–51 ('A Case of Touch and Go').

Angel clad in a golden fleece
Standing in a web of light,
The lamplight plays upon your face
And lights the shoulders I've embraced.
…
As you stuttered foolishness,
Lied and smiled with tenderness:
A blush flooded your face
With clumsy beauty and awkward grace.

Behind a tower on a palace,
Behind the garden cuckoo spit;
In that beyond-the-eyelid life
You will surely be my wife.

So putting on my dry felt boots
And donning golden sheepskin coats,
Let us set off hand in hand
Down the same road to the distant land,

Without a backward glance, no hindrance and no fear,
Toward that shimmering frontier:
Where from dusk to the pre-dawn glow
Streetlamps with light overflow.
(TR, 195–7; FP, 66–7)

Even the apple in the Garden of Eden is included … Mandelstam used to meet Olga in the 'Astoria', a Leningrad hotel, and he temporarily rented a room in the 'Angleterre' (the hotel where Sergei Yesenin would commit suicide in December of that same year, 1925). He also occasionally hired a *droshky*[2] so that he could declaim his poems to her while they were riding around, and they travelled together from Bolshaia Morskaia Street to Tavricheskaia Street, where she lived with her mother and her little son. But Nadezhda could no longer stand Olga's increasingly frequent 'abductions' of her husband, and so she packed a suitcase. The well-known avant-garde painter Vladimir Tatlin (who is only identified in

2 Low four-wheeled open carriage.

her memoirs with the initial T.) had courted her, and he now offered to be her saviour. But when, by chance, Mandelstam arrived back sooner than expected and found Nadezhda waiting with her suitcase, he returned to his senses. Shortly afterwards, Tatlin rang the bell, having arrived to pick her up. Mandelstam opened the door and announced: 'Nadia will stay with me.' He threw Nadezhda's goodbye letter into the fire, telephoned Olga, and 'rudely and abruptly' informed her that the relationship was at an end. That was in the middle of March 1925. Nadezhda's astonishment that the accidental return of Mandelstam and the sight of her packed suitcase should have had such a fateful effect on her life still resonates in the memoirs she published in 1970.

The nightmarish situation had lasted for roughly two months. In Nadezhda's account, it was definitely Olga who threw herself at Mandelstam. In Olga's more detached memoirs, it was the poet who was madly in love: he fell to his knees before her, he cried and told her hundreds of times that he could not live without her.[3] Where the truth lies is hard to say, in the kingdom of Eros, and with two jealous witnesses. But the impression of a poet who was hopelessly in love is not at all far-fetched, in view of the poem 'Like Summer Lightning a Life Fell Away'. In her memoirs, though, Nadezhda voiced the well-founded suspicion that Mandelstam was only using the affair as a means of creating the two unbelievable poems … By the time the treacherous verses had been written, the crisis had already been overcome. From the land 'beyond the eyelids', the kingdom of erotic utopia, Mandelstam was now able to return to sober reality.

The second poem dedicated to Olga Vaksel recounts the mad dash of a poet who has become a nomad, with no fixed abode, through the dark streets of the town. A boundless sense of loss is perceptible. The stars, which are always cruel ('prickly') in Mandelstam's poetry, again become involved: 'The only light is in the stellar, prickly untruth.' And the painful conclusion is reached: 'Life will float by.' Even the erotic motifs of the poem: locks of hair, lips, pupils of the eye, the 'rose-coloured skin', are a bitter yet sensual elegy:

> I will race through the dark street's bivouac
> Behind the bird cherry branch in a black sprung carriage,
> Behind the hood of snow, the eternal, the millwheel noise …

3 Olga Vaksel's memoirs: A. Smol'evskii, 'Ol'ga Vaksel', 167–8.

I remember only the misfires of chestnut locks
Smoked with bitterness, no, with formic acid;
They leave on the lips an amber dryness.
At such minutes the air seems to me hazel,
Fringed with such brightness the rings of pupils,
And that which I know of the apple – the rose-coloured skin.
(TR, 175; OM, 95)

On 25 March, as if he wanted this time to abduct Nadezhda, Mandelstam fled with her from Leningrad, the scene of these demoralising occurrences. They went to Detskoe Selo, formerly Tsarskoye Selo ('the Tsar's village'), which was thirty kilometres away. The little town had acquired its new name, 'Children's Village', in 1921, because orphans of the civil war were housed there. In Detskoe, the Mandelstams were accommodated in the small private hotel 'Zaitsev', which occupied the building of the Lyceum. That was the site of the renowned school attended by Alexander Pushkin between 1811 and 1817, the place where he wrote his first verses. But literature was far from their thoughts; they were concerned with their own relationship. At the beginning of April 1925, while they were still in Detskoe, Mandelstam's autobiographical book *The Noise of Time* was brought out by the Leningrad publishing house 'Vremia'. In it, he said goodbye to his childhood and to old, pre-revolutionary Russia.

Mandelstam wanted to start life afresh with his wife after their period of crisis. Nadezhda had been hit hard by what had happened. Her health, too, was deteriorating steadily. She suffered from fever attacks and was in a debilitated condition. She begged to be given her freedom: 'What do you need me for? Why are you keeping me? What's the point of living in a cage like this? Let me go.' Osip suffered his first heart attack during that spring of 1925 – the precise date is unknown – and would henceforth be afflicted more and more frequently by physical complaints and breathing difficulties. Damaged in morale and health, but reconciled for the moment, the pair ended their quarantine in Detskoe and returned to Leningrad on 24 April.[4]

Posterity has constructed a mythical picture of the Mandelstams. Joseph Brodsky saw them as a modern incarnation of Orpheus and Eurydice,

4 The Mandelstams stay in Detskoe after the affair has ended: Mandelstam, *Hope Abandoned*, 251 ('The Beggar').

though with roles reversed. The pair seemed to be bathed in radiant light, thanks to Nadezhda's heroic role in preserving Mandelstam's poems and the superb memoirs she wrote. Yet their life together was marred by frequent quarrels, as is pointed out emphatically in 'First Quarrels', which was a chapter of the second volume of her memoirs. The story of the Mandelstam pair should not be presented as entirely idyllic.

Right from the start, Osip behaved like a jealous patriarch. He did not let Nadezhda look for work, he prevented her from going anywhere, and he demanded that she completely subsume her life in his (he had already envisaged this kind of relationship in the 'Leah' poem of 1920). Nadezhda was also the irreplaceable amanuensis to whom he dictated his texts. Mandelstam almost never wrote anything down on paper. Instead, he walked around the room, muttering incomprehensibly at first, and listening to the 'inner image' which in his view should precede the written poem and be 'felt' aurally by the poet. 'Not a single word has appeared, but the poem already resounds' – that is how the mysterious process is presented in the essay 'The Word and Culture' (1921) (GP, 87; SE, 70). When the words finally came, he did not write them himself but dictated them feverishly, according to Nadezhda.

She was, in a sense, his human dictaphone, and she had to be permanently available. The prose pieces were also dictated. Nadezhda describes how *The Noise of Time* emerged, in Gaspra on the Crimean Peninsula, during the summer of 1923. Mandelstam first spent an hour walking around by himself, then returned, 'tense and bad-tempered', to demand that she sharpen her pencils, start work immediately and write down what he said. He dictated very quickly, usually covering a whole chapter of this dense piece of prose in one sitting. If she wanted to interject with a remark, Mandelstam called her to order: 'Ssh! Don't interrupt … You don't understand, so keep quiet.' Furious quarrels were not unusual during these sessions.

To outsiders, Mandelstam's tyrannical attitude while dictating his work inevitably appeared bizarre and repellent. It was hard to understand that he himself was under pressure: he was under the imperious dictatorship of his emerging inspiration. As a writer, he was not in the least prolific; phases of feverish creation alternated with long stretches of silence. If words then came to the surface, delay was out of the question. The Mandelstams' contemporary Emma Gerstein has described the harsh dictation procedure as a 'sadistic ritual'.[5] But married couples have complex interconnections, they are phenomena difficult for outsiders to comprehend. At a moment's notice, when the creation of his work was not involved, Mandelstam could start to be movingly concerned about Nadezhda. In the chapter 'A Honeymoon', she describes an episode which occurred when they were spending the night on a terrace in Batumi, the Georgian town on the Black Sea coast. Nadezhda woke up several times, and she saw Mandelstam sitting on a chair next to her bed. He was waving a piece of paper to chase away the mosquitoes. And she adds this comment: 'How well we got on – if only we had been allowed to live out our lives together.'

The jealous patriarch, the tyrant of the dictation sessions, the movingly solicitous mosquito chaser: this is the multiplex reality of married life. Even so, it was amazing that they stayed together, because as a young woman Nadezhda had mixed in revolutionary Kyiv in circles of uninhibited art students who were thirsty for new experiences, and she wanted to keep her independence and be subordinate to no one. By character, she was not gentle, nor patient, nor particularly faithful; she had always had a taste for adventure, and she could quarrel as much as her husband. How Mandelstam managed to bind her to himself despite this is a mystery which would continue to preoccupy the author of the chapter 'First Quarrels'.

In a television interview given in 1973, Nadezhda insisted that while they had often quarrelled during the day, 'the nights were good, we always made love at night'. The two partners must have been strongly attracted to each other sexually. According to the memoirs, Mandelstam did not think the 'physical success' of this relationship reduced their love to a lower level, rather the opposite. Unlike Alexander Blok, who yearned after an ethereal and beautiful lady in his myth of love, Mandelstam wanted to have a loving relationship with an 'unsophisticated girl' (*devchonka*), with whom 'everything would be a laughing matter, simple and crazy', but with whom an 'extreme closeness' would gradually develop, which would make it possible to say: 'with you I am free'.

Sexuality for Mandelstam was inextricably associated with life; it signified vitality. The 'sexless space' metaphor in one of his 1935 Voronezh poems ('No, Not a Migraine': WH, 55) referred to death. Sexlessness denoted indifference, an inability to choose, to make a moral judgement.

---

5 M. dictates *The Noise of Time* to Nadezhda in Gaspra: ibid., 226–7 ('A Honeymoon'). The allegedly 'sadistic ritual' of M.'s dictation procedure: E. Gerstein, *Moscow Memoirs*, 393.

Erotic matters are treated in a reserved manner in Mandelstam's writings, but it is unmistakably clear that they are also nourished by the fire of love. In the poems he wrote for Marina Tsvetaeva, Salomeia Andronikova, Tinatina Dzhordzhadze, Olga Arbenina, Olga Vaksel and Maria Petrovykh, but also for Nadezhda ('Europa's gentle hands: take them! Take everything!' TR, 127), the erotic aspect emerges in the way apparently incidental matters are called to mind, and in the restrained and tender evocation of bodily details (brows, pupils, eyelashes, neck, shoulders, hands and skin). Here, there is no eye-catching exhibitionism, but rather sublimated erotic suggestiveness.

The Mandelstams gradually grew together into a strong and inseparable pair. Their continued love for each other always astonished their mutual friend Anna Akhmatova, whose three marriages all ended in divorce: 'Osip's love for Nadia was unbelievable, unimaginable … I never again met anything comparable in the whole of my life.' Anyone who only sees Mandelstam's dictatorial harshness, the allegedly 'sadistic ritual' which is so hard for outsiders to understand, is bound to miss the essence of their life together. After the great crisis caused by the Vaksel affair, their love would soon be offered an excellent chance to prove itself.[6]

In September 1925, the doctors established that Nadezhda had tuberculosis, and they urgently advised her to live in the south for some time, and to go to Yalta, the town on the Crimean Peninsula where Anton Chekhov had once attempted to cure the same ailment. We owe to these many months of absence a bundle of approximately fifty love letters, which show a caring, loving Mandelstam making daily gestures of tenderness. He stayed in Leningrad, attempting to provide a material basis for Nadezhda's stay in the Crimea by doing gainful work such as translations and reviews for publishers. There was no professional body or insurance company to take over the cost of the cure; since his resignation from the Writers' Union in August 1923, Mandelstam had depended entirely on his own resources. Nadezhda travelled to Yalta on 1 October 1925, and Mandelstam took a small room in the house of his brother Yevgeny on Vasilyevsky Island, which was house number 31 on Street Line 8. After the early death of Yevgeny's first wife Nadezhda Darmolatova, the household now consisted

6 The 'physical success' of the couple's relationship, their 'extreme closeness': Mandelstam, *Hope Abandoned*, 280–1 ('Veiled Admissions'). Sexuality as vitality; the 'sexlessness' of death: ibid., 442 ('The Unbroken Flow'). Akhmatova on M.'s 'extraordinary and unbelievable love' for Nadezhda: A. Akhmatova, *My Half Century*, 96.

of Yevgeny himself, his mother-in-law, his five-year-old daughter Tatka (Natasha) and Osip and Yevgeny's father, Emil.

Mandelstam's letters to Nadezhda during 1925 and 1926 largely consist of reports about his gruelling struggle to obtain money, garnished with stories of the amounts of roubles he expected to acquire through literary drudgery. They also include repeated declarations of love, in each of which he endeavours to outdo the previous one. Using a range of diminutive forms and modifications of the name Nadezhda (the Russian word for 'hope') Mandelstam runs the whole gamut of linguistic tenderness, calling her Nadia, Nadka, Nadinka, Nadiushka, Nadichka and so on. He also often used names which in a grammatical sense were undoubtedly male: Nadik, Nadiushok, Nadionish. Only the Russian language is capable of producing these gruffly tender nuances. Gender-switching is in fact a leading characteristic of these love letters. Thus, Mandelstam would very often give himself the female nickname 'Niania' (children's nurse), but sometimes would hop back into a distorted male form of the word: 'Your Nian.'

He also applied a legion of pet names to Nadezhda: 'little animal', 'little dove', 'little swallow', 'little sheep', but also 'little sun', 'tiny little bent legs', 'little bandy-leg', 'my little stutterer'. Her facial features are repeatedly brought into the game: her broad mouth, her domed child's forehead, but also other parts of the body: 'little hair', 'little paw', 'little eye', 'little shoulder', 'little leg', with the mindless absurdity characteristic of lovers. The rich morphology of the Russian diminutive moulds this everyday version of the Song of Songs: 'I kiss your little pomegranates' (MR, 104).

They tossed all possible family roles back and forth in these letters; neither of them had any children. She is his child, his little child, his little daughter, his little sister, but also (once) his 'little son' (MR, 116). He is her 'friend', 'brother', 'husband' but also her 'Niania', her nurse. For him, Nadezhda was simply 'my life: please understand that you are my life!' (on 11 November 1925). On one occasion, he postulated that the two lovers were identical: 'That I am you through and through and am around you' (12 February 1926), on another that they were breathing the same air (10 March 1926). He repeatedly invokes the protection their love gives to both of them: 'Love shall preserve us, Nadia. We have nothing to fear, my joy!' (7–8 February 1926) And he reaches this conclusion: 'To love you so makes life worth living, Nadik-Nadik!' (5 March 1926)[7]

7 M.'s love letters to Nadezhda: CC, 484–582.

Mandelstam tried to console her. He himself suffered severely from the separation which was necessary for her health. The letters to Nadezhda were pauses for breath in the struggle for the smallest bit of money. But their tone is mostly a happy one. They repeatedly bear witness to a boundless *joie de vivre*. Mandelstam was a poet whose face was turned towards life and its small enjoyments, and he invited Nadezhda to adopt this philosophy as well: 'Did you buy a melon in Melitopol? My little child, enjoy life, we are happy, look forward to our next meeting, just as I do' (on 15 October 1925). In her memoirs, Nadezhda would repeatedly express her astonishment at Mandelstam's 'boundless love of life' and his 'spiritual serenity', given the tragic circumstances of his life.[8] It was a puzzle.

He made several journeys to the Crimea to see her. The first was in mid-November 1925. They met again at the end of March 1926 in Kyiv, then once again a month later in Yalta. On the first occasion, Mandelstam was at the railway station in Moscow when he had a recurrence of his heart trouble and a severe attack of dizziness (MR, 64). His brother Alexander had to collect him. He set his father's mind at rest by writing from Yalta: 'I am able to work and am definitely not an invalid yet' (MR, 66). He was thirty-four years old. In letters sent in February and March 1926, he repeatedly expresses the hope that he will be able to be with Nadezhda in Kyiv on the First of May ('our magic date') at the same place where they got to know each other in 1919. On 23 February 1926, he writes: 'Nadiushok, on the First of May we shall again be together in Kyiv and we shall climb our old hill on the Dniepr. I am so happy about this, so happy!' (MR, 92) But Nadezhda's health was too weak to allow her to make a journey at that time, so they met again in Yalta.

In Yalta, they worked together on Mandelstam's translation projects, when Nadezhda's state of health permitted. She continued to suffer frequent attacks of fever, which made her feel dizzy and weak. She was severely emaciated. Her tuberculosis was not yet healed, and this necessitated a further stay in the Crimea. At the end of May, she was able to return, but only temporarily, from Yalta, and spend the summer with Mandelstam in two furnished rooms in the 'Chinese Village' in the park at Detskoe Selo. Their friend Benedict Livshits, who had acted for them as best man at their wedding in 1922, also lived in the neighbourhood. In

8 The mystery of M.'s 'boundless love of life' and his 'spiritual serenity': N. Mandelstam, *Hope Against Hope*, 56–7 ('The Leap'); Mandelstam, *Hope Abandoned*, 152 ('On the Threshold'); ibid., 208–9 ('Stray Recollections'); and in other places in both volumes.

mid-September, however, Nadezhda had to return to the Crimea, because to spend the winter months in the northern climate would be inadvisable. The fragility of her health would remain a constant and excruciating source of anxiety.

After the spring of 1925, when he had written the two poems dedicated to Olga Vaksel, Mandelstam entered a period of poetic silence which lasted for more than five years. The need to do intensive paid work to make possible Nadezhda's stay in the Crimea was only one of the reasons for this. After his rejection of contemporaneity in 1924 ('No, Never Was I Anyone's Contemporary'), he had consciously chosen silence in his confrontation with the epoch. The publication of *The Noise of Time* in April 1925 met with an ambiguous response. A review in the journal *Press and Revolution* (no. 4, 1925) was typical: the brilliance of the style was noted, but even this was dismissed as 'old-fashioned and untimely'. The book was also reviewed in the Berlin, Brussels and Paris publications of the Russian emigration. Dmitry Sviatopolk-Mirsky, writing in the Paris *Sovremennye Zapiski* (no. 25, 1925), praised it as one of the 'three or four most significant books of recent times'. But his enthusiastic evaluation referred only to Mandelstam's depiction of his childhood and youth, and it strictly excluded the *Theodosia* sketches about the civil war period in the Crimea.

The reaction of a fellow poet to his book brought some consolation. In a letter sent to Mandelstam on 16 August 1925, Boris Pasternak indicated that he was very impressed: '*The Noise of Time* has given me an exceptional amount of enjoyment, something I have not felt for a long time.' The book, he added, had 'felicitously expressed many scarcely perceptible and fleeting experiences'. But then came the big question: 'Why don't you write a big novel?'[9] To write a big novel was Pasternak's personal wish, which he ultimately fulfilled with *Doctor Zhivago*; but it did not fit in with Mandelstam's own conception of art. He had already buried any such idea in his 1922 essay 'The End of the Novel'.

He did, however, step forth in 1925 and 1926 as the author of four small children's books: *The Two Trams*, *The Primus Stove*, *Air Balloons* and *The Kitchen*. During the 1920s, the writing of children's books helped a fair number of Soviet poets to survive materially and sometimes also spiritually. Daniil Kharms and Alexander Vvedensky are just two prominent examples. In Mandelstam's case, the verses in his first children's book,

9 Boris Pasternak's letters to M.: E. V. and E. B. Pasternak, 'Koordinaty', 48–50.

The Two Trams, which was published in January 1925 by the State Publishing House with illustrations by Boris Ender, cannot be seen merely as a harmless appendage to his actual poetry. They are a coded expression of his continued appreciation of his friend Nikolai Gumilyov, who was shot in 1921 as a 'counter-revolutionary', and of his grief over Gumilyov's death. The latter's most famous poem was 'The Streetcar Gone Astray' (1921). Hence, in order to pursue a posthumous dialogue with his friend, Mandelstam chose his emblematic streetcar theme, transforming it into a universal child's theme: Tram is looking for his lost brother Klik. He finally finds him, lost and exhausted, and together they drive back to the tram depot: 'And one says, leaning on the other / O Klik, how I have yearned for you! / It makes me feel so very pleased / Just to hear your clanging bell' (BT, 33). By 1925, it would already have been completely impossible to write a text in memory of the executed Gumilyov. The loophole provided by a children's book was therefore a way of getting round the censorship.[10]

Two other children's books by Mandelstam appeared in 1925–1926: *The Primus Stove*, with illustrations by Mstislav Dobuzhinsky, and *The Kitchen*, illustrated by Vladimir Izenberg. They display objects of everyday life and they allow us to imagine Mandelstam's dreams of comfortable accommodation, which would promise warmth, and food that was properly cooked and palatable. The kitchen was his favourite room wherever he lived. But the books also contain hints of loneliness, fear and violence: the ringing telephone which no one can get to: 'Suddenly it becomes dumb and motionless / Because no one wants to pick it up' (BT, 13); the sugar loaf, which can already guess its fate: 'The sugar loaf, the sugar loaf / Is white with fear, it wants to scream / They have made fresh tea / So sugar must be put in it!' (BT, 11); and the sufferings of the smoothing iron: 'If you only knew how painful it is / When I have to stand on the fire' (BT, 17).

Even the apparently harmless children's book *Air Balloons*, which was published by the State Publishing House in 1926, contains hidden political dynamite. 'I the Green have trouble with … the dreadful Red' (BT, 37). Could a colour scheme still be innocent in the mid-twenties? Since the Russian Civil War, political struggles between the Bolshevik 'Reds' and the Tsarist 'Whites' had found expression in colours. The sacred character of the colour red had been established early in Soviet times. In this children's book Mandelstam's sympathy is not with 'Red' ('the braggart, the

10 M.'s children's book *The Two Trams* as a coded threnody for Gumilyov: E. Zavadskaia, 'Tramvainoe teplo', 55.

loudmouth') but with 'Green', the insecure 'foundling' and 'foster-child'. In the political conflicts of recent years, green was the colour of the anarchists! The theme of freedom also flares up suddenly in the book. A boy presents little Green with freedom – 'What should you do, you idiot? / Creep around like a snail? / No, fly into the air / With the cord still round your tummy!' (BT, 45) – while the 'dreadful loudmouth Red' is still chained up and has to wriggle around at the end of his cord.[11]

The Mandelstams had no children. According to Nadezhda, they made a deliberate decision not to bring up a child in that cruel epoch. But Mandelstam got on very well with children, and children's books were a good opportunity to speak to them. Tiny, precocious Tatka, the daughter of his brother Yevgeny, was a discerning reader of his books. For Mandelstam, in the mid-twenties, children's verses did not amount to a real way out of the impasse he was in, but they did constitute a modest compensation for the poetry that was missing. Soon, though, even the freedom to create children's literature began to be restricted. In 1927, it was Lenin's widow, the sacrosanct Krupskaya herself, who engineered a propaganda campaign against 'ideologically unreliable' and 'harmful' fairy tales for children. Kornei Chukovsky's magnificent children's books were her main target. In 1928 his story *The Adventures of Crocodile Crocodilovich* was banned. The authorities searched through all 'harmful' children's books for the dangerous political allusions they might contain. Their authors were rigorously 'unmasked' at a time of heightened 'ideological vigilance' and intensified 'class struggle'. With his four tiny contributions, Mandelstam was too marginal a children's author to suffer much damage from this campaign. But, in 1927, he wrote a short satirical text about children's literature for his own use. It was a protest against the political instrumentalisation of children and their incorporation into the class struggle (GD, 35–6; BT, 165–6; CC, 280–1).

Even during his 'period of silence' between 1925 and 1930, therefore, Mandelstam did at least write children's verses, as well as prose. His journalism of the period includes two texts which provide some insight into the development of his attitude towards his own Jewishness. In the prose sketch 'Kyiv' (1926), which was a portrait of 'an indomitable city', he has a section on the Jewish traders and artisans who lived in the lower part of town, known as the Podol.

11 M.'s books for children: appendix to O. Mandelstam, *Die beiden Trams*, 213–31.

> I hear some muttering just underfoot. Can it be a cheder? No … It's a basement synagogue. A hundred venerable old men in striped talesim are seated like school-children behind narrow yellow desks. No-one pays any attention to them. If only Chagall were here! … And in the evening, the attentive passer-by may glimpse through an open window the frugal supper of some Jewish family – a loaf of challah, some herring and a pot of tea …
>
> The Podol has always paid for the splendour of the upper city. The Podol has burned. The Podol has been flooded. The Podol has been ravaged by pogroms. (RZ, 173, 176; CC, 252, 254)

At the end of March 1926, Nadezhda made the journey from Yalta and they were able to meet in Kyiv. Osip attended several plays put on by the State Jewish Theatre (GOSET), which had been founded in 1919 as the Moscow Jewish Chamber Theatre by Alexei Granovsky. Between 1919 and 1922, Marc Chagall played a part in establishing the theatre's ambiance by creating the décor and stage scenery. His role was later taken over by another artist, Natan Altman. The repertoire included plays in Yiddish by Sholem Aleichem, Yitskhok Leybush Peretz, Abraham Goldfaden and others.

While in Kyiv, Mandelstam was greatly impressed by the Jewish actor Solomon Mikhoels (1890–1948), and he immediately wrote a character sketch of him. On the return journey to Moscow, the train halted for some time in a Belarusian *shtetl*. Mandelstam had separated himself from Jewishness early in his life, with the help of his assimilated mother, and seemed to have become completely absorbed in the culture of Russia, but his experiences on this journey made a lively impression on him. On looking through the carriage window he saw a rabbi in a long frock coat making his way forward through the gurgling mud 'like a black beetle'. His gestures 'expressed aloofness from his environment, combined at the same time with such a knowledge of his route' that the assimilated townsman Mandelstam was amazed. The rapidly moving rabbi remained 'stuck firmly in my mind' because 'without him this modest landscape appeared devoid of meaning' (GD, 30; CC, 260). Did he suddenly remember his forefathers, who came from Shagory, which was a *shtetl* of identical character? In any case, Mikhoels's acting skill also stimulated thoughts about Jewishness which had previously hardly entered his mind.

> The plasticity and power of Judaism comes from its having managed to develop and perpetuate down through the ages a feeling for form and movement which governs all aspects of style, making it permanent, millennial … I am speaking here not of the cut of a man's coat, something which is always changing and which it is pointless to evaluate, nor have I taken it into my head to justify on aesthetic grounds the ghetto or the village life-style. Rather I am speaking about the inner plasticity of the ghetto, about that immense artistic power, which is surviving the ghetto's destruction, and which will emerge completely only after the ghetto is destroyed. (GD, 31; CC, 261)

It was this 'immense artistic power' which continued to tie Mandelstam to Jewishness, a connection which would grow ever stronger. He reviews the theatrical art of Mikhoels with deep sympathy, and he places it on an equal level with the great artists of antiquity ('the Jewish Dionysius'):

> Standing stock still for a fraction of a second, he suddenly becomes intoxicated … the Jewish Dionysius is not demanding, and immediately offers him the gift of gaiety …
>
> Mikhoels's face takes on the expression of world-weariness and mournful ecstasy in the course of his dance, as if the mask of the Jewish people were drawing nearer to the mask of Classical antiquity, becoming virtually indistinguishable from it.
>
> The dancing Jew now resembles the leader of the ancient Greek chorus. All the power of Judaism, all the rhythm of abstract ideas in dance, all the pride of the dance, whose single motive is, in the final analysis, compassion for the earth – all this extends into the trembling of the hands, into the vibration of the thinking fingers which are animated like articulated speech. (GD, 32; CC, 261–2)

Publications like the *Encyclopaedia Judaica* (Jerusalem 1971) and the *Neues Lexikon des Judentums* (Gütersloh 2000) have spread the cliché that Mandelstam was a 'representative of Jewish self-hatred'.[12] This crude label could only be attached to the poet by someone who is unaware of

12 M. as an alleged representative of 'Jewish self-hatred': *Encyclopaedia Judaica*, Jerusalem 1971, vol. 11, 866: 'a painfully neurotic self-hating awareness of his Jewish antecedents … Yet he never attempted to conceal his Jewish origin, but continued to brood and write about it.' Also *Neues Lexikon des Judentums*, ed. Julius H. Schoeps, Gütersloh

his articles 'Kyiv' and 'Mikhoels'. In a letter sent on 17 February 1926 to Nadezhda, Mandelstam writes about a meeting he had with the orientalist Shileiko: 'And I said to him, I only love you … and *Jews*' (MR, 84; CC, 506). In 1926, Mandelstam's rapprochement with the world of his ancestors still had some way to go. Later, in his polemical, anti-Stalinist *Fourth Prose* of 1929–1930, he speaks of the 'honourable title of Jew, of which I am proud', and of his 'blood, burdened with its inheritance from sheep breeders, patriarchs and kings' (RZ, 265; NT, 186). In the 1931 poem 'Canzone' (MM, 75) the 'prodigal son' would confirm his return home. Mandelstam's relation to his own Jewishness was complex. It was a profound personal confrontation which cannot be grasped by applying simplistic categories.

It is true that in 1925, in *The Noise of Time*, he was still describing his father's world, with its strongly Jewish character, as a sphere which was alien and seemingly threatening to him as a child. But in 1926, while he was writing the prose texts we have just mentioned, which displayed a highly sympathetic attitude towards Jewishness, his letters to his father also demonstrate an increasing closeness to his Jewish background. Emil Mandelstam was evidently angered by the way Osip had depicted 'his' world in *The Noise of Time*. In a letter sent from Yalta at the end of April 1926, Osip says: 'As far as my "memories" of you are concerned, you are absolutely wrong: I have not cast them aside or pushed them away. The bond between us is stronger than you imagine!' (MR, 114) What a difference there is between Osip Mandelstam's letters to his father and Franz Kafka's *Letter to His Father*! From alienation to a renewed understanding: that is the path travelled by Mandelstam in relation to both his father and his own Jewishness. Thus, he was a poet who gradually integrated his father's initially repressed spiritual inheritance into his work, thereby enriching it.

Nadezhda suffered increasingly both from the pain of separation from her husband and from loneliness by the shores of the Black Sea. Likewise, Mandelstam writes on 1 October 1926: 'My dearest little child, my sunny Nadik! Why did I send you away to the sea as if you were some kind of Ovid? Do you want to come home to your Nanny and the cat …?' (MR, 116; CC, 525) Then on 3 October: 'My darling wife, I can't go on any longer without you, my sunny Nadik. Why did I let you go? I know that it was necessary, but I'm so depressed, so depressed' (MR, 119; CC, 527). For

2000, 544: 'Although he was Jewish, Mandelstam's writing and his attitude of mind were alien to Judaism. He can be seen as a representative of Jewish self-hatred.'

a short period, Nadezhda rented a room in Koktebel, the Crimean town which had an almost mythical status for Mandelstam, the place where he had once felt so happy: 'I can't believe that this time you are in Koktebel without me', he wrote (MR, 120; CC, 528). In other letters to his 'poor shining beggar-girl', he attempts to comfort her, oscillating between the rational approach, which required that Nadezhda remain in the Crimea, and the ardent wish to have her with him again every day.

Alongside his exhausting round of paid literary work, Mandelstam was also trying to find a place to live. In October 1926, after several failed attempts, he moved into a bright, roomy flat in the Lyceum building at Detskoe Selo, where accommodation was cheaper than in Leningrad. He had to pawn Nadezhda's watch, and to sell a few other items, because the need for money continued to be acute. But the new flat constituted a distinct improvement in living conditions, and Mandelstam practically raved about it in his letters. 'Everything is very clean, bright and comfortable', he wrote at the beginning of November (MR, 130). It was a three-roomed flat with a kitchen and a bath, and it was the greatest degree of (very relative) 'luxury' the Mandelstams would ever enjoy. This comfortable existence would last only for a short time, barely two years, and even then it was interrupted by the need for Nadezhda to return periodically to the south. The doctors had warned her urgently against returning to wet, cold Leningrad, but the Mandelstams could no longer stand the situation they were in. In December 1926, Nadezhda returned from the Crimea to Detskoe.

15
The Brassy Taste in My Mouth
(Detskoe Selo 1927–1928)

Mandelstam was happy that Nadezhda had returned. The fact that they were together again had the effect of somewhat reducing the pressure to concentrate on earning money, so that in 1927 Mandelstam was able to draw up publication plans and make a start on several book projects. In February, he signed a contract with the publishing house 'Academia' to produce a volume of collected essays entitled *On Poetry*. On 21 April, there followed a contract with the 'Priboi' publishing house for a novel with the title *The Adventures of Valentin Garkov*, which was published eighteen months later in an altered form as *The Egyptian Stamp*.

In summer 1927, Mandelstam worked hard on the *Egyptian Stamp* project, which was not intended to be a novel but rather to demonstrate the 'pulverisation' of the genre, as foreseen in the 1922 essay 'The End of the Novel'. Nadezhda was not keen on this text. She regarded it as the hybrid fruit of a crisis, a manifestation of inner weakness and a concession to the epoch and its demand for large-scale works. Above all, though, the text did not offer a way out of the crisis; it did not clear a free path which would allow Mandelstam to return to creating poetry. It was only the trip to Armenia that would bring about this miracle.[1]

1 Nadezhda's objections to *The Egyptian Stamp*: N. Mandelstam, *Hope Abandoned*, 215–16 ('A Honeymoon').

Even so, *The Egyptian Stamp* was not merely the enforced product of a period of silence, nor was it the fruit of a personal and creative crisis. On the contrary, it was one of the boldest and most original prose texts of the Soviet 1920s, rich as that period was in experimental creations. The most bizarre of all Mandelstam's prose writings, it follows in the footsteps of Gogol's story 'The Overcoat' and Dostoevsky's *The Double*. It is ostensibly the story of the experiences of a little man, Parnok, during the summer of 1917, between the February and October Revolutions, whose frock coat had been repossessed by the tailor Mervis because the customer had not paid for it.[2]

This article of clothing is also a symbol representing freedom and democracy. And the whole story is an outcry against arbitrary rule and violence. While he is vainly searching for his suit, Parnok notices an angry mob of people, and he is the only bystander who tries to hold them back from a lynching. He attempts to call the police, to sound the alarm to the state – but 'the state had vanished, and was sleeping like a carp' (RZ, 209; NT, 145). All his efforts are in vain; there is nothing in the text to indicate that Parnok succeeded. The suit disappears into Captain Krzyżanowski's trunk, and we must assume that the lynch mob eventually had its way. Parnok is a descendant of the harassed 'little men' who were celebrated in nineteenth-century Russian literature. He can neither hinder nor prevent anything from happening. He himself is a man under threat and a loser. He is the embodiment of the endangered individual, the helpless outsider. He is the 'Egyptian stamp', whose fate it is to be franked, stained and devalued. His expulsion from society is as pre-ordained as his destruction in the black Petersburg night. Parnok is the 'lemon seed' (RZ, 212; NT, 147) thrown into a crevice in the granite walls of Petersburg, a tiny creature who yearns for the south, for sunlight and warmth. Mandelstam's eternal dream.

The form of this piece is dictated by an 'influenza dream'. It is described on one occasion as a product of 'delirium' (RZ, 238; NT, 161). It is a tangled mass of wild associations, fragments of memory and clusters of oddly perceived events and objects. Whose nightmares are these? Whose memory? An author seems to be fighting with his alter ego: 'Lord, do not make me like Parnok! Give me the strength to distinguish myself from

2 *The Egyptian Stamp*: appendix to O. Mandelstam, *Das Rauschen der Zeit*, 318–25; C. Isenberg, 'Associative Chains in *Egipetskaia Marka*'; D. M. West, *Mandelstam: The Egyptian Stamp*.

him' (RZ, 215; NT, 149). The desperate search for the lost frock coat also signifies the search for identity in a world which is out of joint, in an epoch of shattered meanings, where the dignity of the individual is under threat.

> It is terrifying to think that our life is a tale without a plot or hero, made up out of desolation and glass, out of the feverish babble of constant digressions, out of the delirium of the Petersburg influenza. (RZ, 238; NT, 161)

The Egyptian Stamp reflects the crisis of a person whose biography has been 'pulverised', as the 1922 essay 'The End of the Novel' had ominously pointed out. It is a bitter kind of medicine, an antidote to the fever caused by the whirlwind of events in Petersburg. 'Like powdered aspirin', it leaves 'a brassy taste' in the narrator's mouth (RZ, 229; NT, 156).

The seemingly playful whirl of Parnok's word associations, like those of the narrator, cannot hide the nightmarish atmosphere of the story, which is dominated by terror as well as by irony:

> Terror takes me by the hand and leads me. A white cotton glove. A woman's glove without fingers. I love terror, I respect it. I could almost say 'With it, I'm not terrified.' (RZ, 240; NT, 162)

While the world of *The Noise of Time* was still full of music, despite its approaching end, *The Egyptian Stamp* repeatedly alludes to music's absence, removal and disappearance. The fate of the Italian singer Angiolina Bosio is woven into its kaleidoscope of images. She died of pneumonia in 1859 in St Petersburg, and her death becomes a symbol of the death of song in the freezing cold. *The Egyptian Stamp* also refers to the death of another singer, the poet Alexander Pushkin, who was forced by social intrigues to fight a duel which he did not survive: 'There, with a distorted face, was Pushkin' (RZ, 193; NT, 136). For Mandelstam, this was *the* crime against Russian culture, a crime which prefigured all the later murders of poets. In *The Egyptian Stamp* the death of the singer seems to be a foregone conclusion. If one bears in mind Mandelstam's future fate, the piece's visionary quality is evident. Ten years before the bitter end, his 'expulsion' and 'ruin' are anticipated in a harrowing manner with the use of grotesque images. Perhaps Nadezhda disliked this hallucinatory fruit of Mandelstam's crisis because she feared the excruciating precision of his forecast. Nevertheless, *The Egyptian Stamp* did also contain a confession of faith in which hope was not entirely ruled out: 'Life is both terrifying and beautiful!' (RZ, 212; NT, 147)

The couple spent the summer of 1927 in Detskoe, and they made new friends, people whom Mandelstam valued highly. He got to know the actor and producer Vladimir Yakhontov, who was a graduate of Meyerhold's famous theatre, and had just set up a one-man theatre called *Sovremennik* (Contemporary), which produced original-text montages of the works of classic Russian writers like Pushkin and Gogol as well as a Lenin montage. Mandelstam wrote a prose sketch about Yakhontov, which also contained insights into his own way of dealing with the classics: 'Our classical repertory resembles a powder-keg on the verge of exploding' (GD, 40; CC, 267). Despite political depression and creative crisis, Mandelstam remained a sociable person, and enjoyed making new contacts.

Once the summer had ended, Nadezhda again had to travel south for reasons of health. Mandelstam joined her at the end of October. They travelled together to the Abkhazian town of Sukhumi on the Black Sea and to Armavir on the River Kuban in the Caucasus, where Mandelstam's brother Alexander had found work. Mandelstam was already dreaming of making an excursion to the Caucasus at the beginning of May, when he was briefly in Moscow. He wrote a jaunty letter to his brother:

> I can just imagine you sitting in an Armenian café and wiping the balls off the billiard table. We have found Armavir on the map and are delighted with how far south it is. Like Pechorin [[author's note: from Lermontov's *A Hero of Our Time*]] you at least have travelled to the Caucasus. I, on the other hand, have nothing much to boast of … We have recently revisited the memories of the good old Moscow days. It is as if we had never gone away. We have seen all our eccentric acquaintances. We have travelled enthusiastically by bus and taxi. We have eaten caviar out of paper in a hired carriage, imitating the 'Embezzlers' [[author's note: a novel by Valentin Katayev]] … Why not send everything to the devil and come to us in Detskoe? We have a well-built house there with a bathtub, a maid and a telephone. (MR, 135–6)

Mandelstam's letters were seldom as unworried and relaxed as this one, although the phrase 'I have nothing much to boast of' indicates that the 'period of silence' is still continuing, and no new poems have yet appeared.

He is enjoying travelling by bus and taxi and eating cheap caviar … But the 'New Economic Policy' (NEP) was now rapidly approaching the end. In Detskoe during 1927, the Mandelstams enjoyed a prosperity which was simulated rather than real. They even had a cook 'for the whole of the winter', a strange woman who was a Baptist. She made purchases for the pair, who were completely useless in practical matters, and she was able to cook excellent meals. Never again would they live so well as when under the thumb of the Bible-reading Yelena Ivanovna, as Nadezhda nostalgically recalls in her memoirs. But the modest 'luxury' of Detskoe would not last long. Moreover, Mandelstam felt uneasy there, because he was surrounded by memories of Pushkin's schooldays. His lasting shyness about mentioning that poet corresponded to his discomfort at living in his shadow. 'M. was terribly upset by what for him was almost sacrilege, and at the first pretext he insisted we clear out and revert to our usual homeless existence', remarks Nadezhda reproachfully.[3]

As a writer, Mandelstam was now in a marginal position. He kept his distance from the official euphoria which was *de rigueur*, particularly in 1927, in the atmosphere created by the tenth anniversary of the October Revolution. Sergei Eisenstein had been treated as a star director of Soviet cinema since the triumph of *The Battleship Potemkin*, and he produced his film *October* for the tenth anniversary. Vladimir Mayakovsky joined in the celebrations by writing the poem 'Very Good!' which he himself described as 'The October Revolution, cast in bronze'. But the year 1927 was also remarkable for the power struggle in the Soviet Union, conducted by Stalin with increasing ruthlessness. He, Zinoviev and Kamenev had formed the short-lived triumvirate that dominated the country after Lenin's death, but he soon emerged as the absolute ruler of the party apparatus. In autumn 1927, Zinoviev, Trotsky and Kamenev were removed from the Central Committee, and at the beginning of 1928 they were expelled from the party. Zinoviev and Kamenev publicly repented and survived relatively unscathed – though only temporarily, until the show trial of 1936. Stalin's arch-enemy Trotsky, however, was expelled from the Soviet Union in February 1929, to be assassinated in Mexico in 1940 by one of the dictator's henchmen. As early as 1926, Stalin had already gained control over what would be his most effective instrument of domination: in that

3 The Bible-reading cook: Mandelstam, *Hope Abandoned*, 227–9 ('A Honeymoon'). M.'s inhibitions about living in Pushkin's former lycée: N. Mandelstam, *Hope Against Hope*, 30 ('Interview').

year, shortly before his death, Felix Dzerzhinsky, the head of the secret police (the GPU), handed him supreme authority over that organisation.

What did the sensitive Mandelstam, who had already detected the 'wing of oncoming night' in his 1922–1923 essay 'Humanism and Modern Life', think of Stalin's claim to supreme power, which manifested more and more cynically as time went by? According to the minutes of the interrogation that followed his first arrest, in May 1934, he admitted that during the year 1927 he had 'a not very profound, but sufficiently passionate sympathy for Trotskyism'. In the secret service investigations that led to Mandelstam's second arrest on 2 May 1938, this admission was distorted into the phrase: 'Mandelstam, as he himself confesses, cherished a strong sympathy for Trotskyism in 1927' (MR, 300). These statements were made under considerable psychological pressure and cannot therefore be accepted without reservation. The alleged sympathy for Trotsky probably meant that he found Stalin's political machinations repugnant.[4] One should also bear in mind that Alexander Voronsky was arrested in 1927 as a part of the persecution of the Trotskyist opposition. Voronsky had encouraged the literary 'fellow-travellers' and had published Mandelstam's book of poems, *The Second Book*, in 1923.

Mandelstam's dismay over the apparently inescapable course of events is evident from his story *The Egyptian Stamp*, which he continued to work on until February 1928, with its nightmarish atmosphere and its murderous lynch mob. The poet's 'period of silence' was not just a case of writer's block; it also expressed his consternation over the trend of politics. Yet 1928 also appeared to be a year of triumph for Mandelstam, marked by the publication of three of his books. Admittedly, nothing more would be published during his lifetime. The series opened in May 1928 with the volume *Stikhotvoreniia* (Poems), which appeared under the State Publishing House imprint. It offered an overview of the whole of his poetry to date, and included three sections: 'Stone', 'Tristia' and 'Poems 1921–1925'. The intervention of the censor was clearly apparent, however. The November 1920 verse 'And in the Soviet night I pray / For the blessed meaningless word' (TR, 97) had to be altered to read: 'And in the January night I pray.' The censor struck out most of the poem 'To Cassandra' (TR, 51), which was composed shortly after the October Revolution, leaving only the first stanza, and the ominous title also had to go. It was completely unthinkable

4 The admission of 'Trotskyism' recorded in the minutes of M.'s May 1934 interrogation: V. Shentalinsky, *Arrested Voices*, 177.

to refer to the revolution as a 'plague' and a 'one-armed victory', as he did in the third stanza. (Indeed, the poem was still missing from the highly bowdlerised volume of Mandelstam's poetry issued in 1973, during the Brezhnev era!) The ambiguous poem of May 1918 about the revolution, 'The Twilight of Freedom', was printed without its title or the first two verses because 'twilight' also signified 'fall'. The religious poem of 1921 about the Cathedral of Saint Isaac in Petrograd (TR, 117) was completely unacceptable, and Mandelstam himself did not include it when he put the book together – a clear case of self-censorship.

It was a miracle that the book was able to appear at all. In his 17 February 1926 letter to Nadezhda, who was staying in Yalta, Mandelstam reported that Konstantin Fedin had agreed to the inclusion of a book of his poems in the State Publishing House's 'plan'. But he had no illusions about its future fate: 'it will be sent to Moscow ... and ... struck off' (MR, 84; CC, 506). And, not long afterwards, on 22 February, he wrote: 'My volume of poetry has been done to death' (MR, 90). Its eventual publication, two years later, was entirely due to the influence exerted by Nikolai Bukharin, who in 1922 and 1923 had already supported Mandelstam's efforts to intercede in favour of his arrested brother Yevgeny. On 10 August 1927, Bukharin wrote to Khalatov, the director of the State Publishing House. A week later, Mandelstam received a contract. A 'private' letter from Bukharin had been sufficient.[5] At that time, his official position was still unquestioned. He was a member of the Central Committee and the Politburo, chair of the Communist International and chief editor of *Pravda*. The beginning of the end was not to come until November 1929, when he was removed from the Politburo. In December 1927, the Fifteenth Party Congress had issued 'directives for the establishment of a Five Year Plan for the economy', thereby introducing an accelerated process of industrialisation and ending the relatively liberal NEP era. Along with Rykov and Tomsky, Bukharin had resisted the radical change of course in economic policy associated with the First Five Year Plan (1928–1932), and Stalin had replied by forcing all three into the position of a 'right opposition' and removing them from office.

Bukharin's close involvement in the fate of Mandelstam's book of poetry is also demonstrated by the episode of the five ageing bank employees, whom the authorities proposed to shoot as a measure of deterrence. This

5 Bukharin's letter of 10 August 1927 to Khalatov: *Russkaia Mysl'* (*La Pensée russe*) 4321, 8 June 2000.

was only one of the indications that henceforth a new and biting wind was going to blow where the economy was concerned. Mandelstam had read about the case in *Pravda*, and on 14 April 1928 he wrote to Bukharin to beg him to commute the death penalty. Then, on 18 May, he sent him a copy of his book of poetry, which had just been published, and wrote on the title page as a dedication 'Every line of this book contradicts what you are intending to do.'[6] Shortly afterwards he received a telegram from Bukharin informing him that the death penalty had been commuted into imprisonment. Mandelstam's abhorrence of executions, which Nadezhda had already noticed in May 1919 during the civil war, was still as strong as ever. His poetry therefore continued to be effective against violent death, for one last time. This too would soon change.

The day of 18 May 1928 on which Mandelstam sent his book to Bukharin, including his protest, was also the first day of the trial mounted against the 'wreckers', some engineers who worked at the Shakhty mine. This was a modest precursor of the show trials of the 1930s. But it was not only economic policy that now felt the blast of a harsher wind. On 21 May 1928, there were mass arrests of priests and scholars in the precincts of the monastery located in the town of Sergiev Posad. Among them was the theologian and polymath Pavel Florensky, one of the most important figures in Russian intellectual history. It was his first arrest. For Mandelstam, this news was a 'devastating blow' which threw him into despair.[7] Father Florensky was eventually shot in 1937 in the concentration camp on the Solovetsky Islands. He could not have been saved by the word of a poet; this had long since ceased to have any political impact.

The reviews of Mandelstam's volume of poetry were almost identical in tone. He was berated for his lack of 'genuine contemporaneity' and the 'misunderstanding' of revolution in the poems. The journal *Novy Mir* (1928, no. 8) described the book as an 'interesting and significant, but already outdated, manifestation of Russian poetry'. The journal *Book and Revolution* (1929, nos 15–16) fired with heavier ammunition, drawing in its review on the conventional ideological clichés. Mandelstam, it said, was 'a bourgeois poet through and through'; he represented a bourgeoisie which was 'already fully Europeanised' and 'extremely aggressive'.

---

6 M. dedicates his last published book of poetry to Bukharin with an appeal for the commutation of five death penalties: Mandelstam, 113 ('Transmission Belts').

7 M.'s despair at the arrest of Florensky: Mandelstam, *Hope Abandoned*, 81 ('Return') and 210 ('Stray Recollections').

Words of encouragement and admiration came from Boris Pasternak, as in the case of Mandelstam's earlier book *The Noise of Time*. He wrote in a letter of 24 September 1928: 'How happy and proud you must be to be identical with the author of this book: I know of nothing similar, and nothing to equal it! … These lines are an unalloyed outcry of enthusiasm and amazement.' Pasternak's letter offered some consolation, but it could not drown out the chorus of 'official' criticism. Moreover, according to Anna Akhmatova, Mandelstam had doubts about Pasternak's sincerity. She claims he said to her: 'I'm sure he hasn't read a single line of mine.'[8]

At the end of June 1928, a month and a half after the volume of poetry, Mandelstam's collection of essays *On Poetry* was published by the 'Academia' publishing house. Again, there were clear traces of censorship and self-censorship. If the text is compared with the original versions, published in journals between 1913 and 1924, the distortions and falsifications are strikingly apparent. Here is just one example. The remarkable phrase 'Culture has become the Church' in the 1921 essay 'The Word and Culture' was changed into: 'Culture has become an army camp.' Instead of spiritualisation – militarisation! But even these revised versions gave rise to massive ideological criticism. In the journal *Press and Revolution* (1929, no. 6) Mandelstam is described as 'the last Mohican of Acmeism', who in the twelfth year of the revolution still dares to present a 'hundred percent idealist conception of how to perceive the world', which bears witness to his 'obscurantist and reactionary attitude'. The criticism of the ideologists was resounding ever more loudly.

Mandelstam again spent the summer months of 1928 with Nadezhda in Yalta, in a cheap boarding house called the 'Eagle's Nest', and there he made the final corrections to his book *The Egyptian Stamp*, which was now almost ready. His letter of 25 June to a woman named Korobova, an official in the State Publishing House, shows him to be a nervous writer of prose, who was struggling to achieve a definitive version and did not shy away from agreeing to pay for his alterations to the text, despite his own money problems. His furious determination to have superfluous passages removed sounds panicky: '*Nothing* of what is deleted must be printed, but if 'Encounter in the Editorial Office' and 'Absalom' [[author's

8 Pasternak's letter about M.'s 1928 book of poetry: *Voprosy Literatury* 9, 1972, 162. M.'s doubts about the sincerity of Pasternak's praise for his poems: A. Akhmatova, *My Half Century*, 85.

note: two lost prose texts]] are printed nothing remains except for me to hang myself' (MR, 140; CC, 538).

Mandelstam's uncompromising approach to artistic matters corresponded to his unshakeable loyalty towards his Acmeist friends. On 25 August 1928 he wrote from Yalta to Anna Akhmatova. The date is striking: it was the seventh anniversary of the death of Nikolai Gumilyov, who was shot in Petrograd in 1921. In the letter, Mandelstam affirms: 'You should know that I'm able to conduct imaginary conversations with only two people: Nikolai Stepanovich and you. My conversation with Kolya never was and never will be broken off' (MR, 144–5; CC, 539). The 'We' feeling Mandelstam had experienced in 1912–1913 remained intact.

A telegram of 14 August to Benedict Livshits demonstrates Mandelstam's permanent shortage of money. He again tries to touch his friend for a loan: 'Return to Leningrad more expensive. Help us. Never been in such a situation. Sold things. Both ill' (MR, 144). The letter to Akhmatova also contains the phrase 'I want to go home.' His desperate search for a loan must have paid off once again, as they did manage to get back to Leningrad. The third book of the year was awaiting them. This was *The Egyptian Stamp*, which was issued at the beginning of September 1928 by the Leningrad publisher 'Priboi'. Apart from the eponymous story, it included reprints of *The Noise of Time* and the *Theodosia* prose sketches about the civil war period in the Crimea. *The Egyptian Stamp* story was a 'prose delirium' composed of grotesque images and strange nightmares. Bizarre in both form and content, it continued the bold experiments of the avant-garde while remaining characteristic of Mandelstam. The press reaction was predictable. A certain Tarasenkov let fly in the organ of the proletarian writers, *Na literaturnom Postu* (On Literary Guard, no. 3, 1929):

> Behind this there stands Mandelstam's consciousness of his spiritual and psychological death, the feeling that his existence is completely ruined … The book is simply a demonstration that the writer is infinitely removed from our epoch. His view of the world is entirely rooted in the past.

How did Mandelstam reply to the accusation that he was a 'former' poet, a non-contemporary to whom revolutionary reality was something alien and incomprehensible? One of Mandelstam's rare public expressions of opinion appeared on 18 November 1928 in the newspaper *Reader and*

Writer (no. 45), when he answered a questionnaire on the theme 'The Soviet writer and the October Revolution':

> The October Revolution could not but influence my work, since it took away my 'biography', my sense of individual significance. I am grateful to it, however, for once and for all putting an end to my spiritual security and to a cultural life supported by unearned cultural income … I feel indebted to the revolution, but I offer it gifts for which it still has no need …
>
> I am deeply convinced that, in spite of all the limitations and dependence of the writer on social forces, modern science does not possess any means of causing this or that desirable writer to come into existence. Rudimentary eugenics alerts us to the fact that any kind of cultural interbreeding or grafting may produce the most unexpected results. (RZ, 245; CC, 275)

It is an enigmatic utterance, full of polemical sharpness, and a text of immense freedom. It was *precisely* a writer's intellectual dependence and life as a cultural pensioner which had *not* been abolished ten years after the revolution, but was rather in the course of being officially installed. A minimal amount of talent and a readiness to do literary hackwork were enough to provide a writer with food packages, free housing, dachas, 'official journeys', 'creative holidays' in state rest homes and pensions. Amazingly, one of the few people to take the commandments of the revolution seriously was the 'former' poet Mandelstam. He would have to pay a high price for this in the 1930s: a continuing lack of accommodation and crushing material poverty, but also political persecution, two periods of imprisonment, exile and death in a Siberian labour camp. In Mandelstam's case, the desire to break off intellectual and material dependence and supply was put into effect with terrifying radicalism.

This does not in the least imply that he preferred to be an ascetic, or that he liked to live in poverty. The belief that Mandelstam wanted to be poor fits in well with the legend of his saintliness; but Nadezhda protests against it:

> Mandelstam too liked all the pleasures that money can give. We were not ascetics by nature, and neither of us practiced self-denial for its own sake; we were simply forced into it by circumstances, because the price

> demanded in return for an increase in one's rations was just too high. But we did not *want* to be poor, any more than M. wanted to die in a camp.[9]

Although Mandelstam answered the questionnaire by defining his own work as untimely, he added that it was not fixated on the past, but rather in advance of its time, that it belonged to the future, providing gifts 'for which the revolution still has no need'. Thus, he claimed to represent his own personal 'avant-garde'. That was a bold way of turning around the accusations he was being pelted with. Moreover, the sarcastic remark that the production of 'desirable writers' was undesirable at the present stage of eugenics was a colossal piece of impudence when addressed to people who already wanted to convert writers into 'engineers of human souls' (Stalin's words) who would be permanently at the disposal of the holders of power.

The idyll of relative well-being they enjoyed in Detskoe Selo was now at an end. The apartment in the Lyceum had to be relinquished. Mandelstam thought that he would survive more easily in the capital, and in December 1928 he moved back there. At first, he found accommodation with his brother Alexander, in apartment number 3, 10 Starosadsky Lane, which was a crowded communal dwelling. His return to the city he had described in June 1918 in a poem as 'the capital of filth' (TR, 183) was a symbol of the new, calamitous stage of his life that was now beginning.

9 M.'s rejection of asceticism: Mandelstam, *Hope Abandoned*, 271 ('Our Alliance').

16

Ulenspiegel's Chewed-Up Heart

(Kyiv and Moscow 1929)

The first months of 1929 were again a period of worry and anxiety, dominated by Nadezhda's illness. At the end of December 1928, the pair travelled to Kyiv, where they stayed with Nadezhda's parents. On 20 January she underwent what was classified as a difficult operation on her appendix. The clinicians feared that the tuberculosis she had suffered from for years might have spread to other organs of her body. Money was again in very short supply. Mandelstam had the good fortune to meet a surgeon who had taken part in the meetings of the 'Poets' Guild' in 1912–1913, and had herself written verses. This was Vera Gedroits. In a letter to Mikhail Zenkevich, a fellow Acmeist who had been an editor at the Moscow publisher 'Land and Factory' since 1923 and was an important source of income, Mandelstam asks him to accelerate the payment he is owed for current translation work, and describes their difficult situation:

> We stand here completely penniless. The parents [[Nadezhda's parents: RD]] have no credit. They even have trouble getting together 3 roubles for essential provisions. What is worst of all, though, is that we have *nothing for the treatment*. Good at least that Gedroits is here. (MR, 151)

Despite all their apprehensions, the operation proceeded satisfactorily. In mid-February 1929, Mandelstam wrote to his father:

> The whole thing was very hard for me. We had almost no money. Nadia's parents are completely helpless and desperately poor. Their house is cold and neglected … I had to fight for every cup of meat broth I carried into the hospital … Having received a little room to myself in the hospital I could spend whole days there. I even spent the night there, taking turns with the nurses and the medical orderlies … The frost was extremely severe when I brought Nadia home. She was so weak she could hardly walk. But now she has improved beyond recognition. She is regaining her strength and her will to live increases by leaps and bounds. (MR, 160)

Mandelstam also informed his father of his renewed hope that he would be able to give up his 'prison-style work' of 'assembly-line translation' and 'go over to living human labour'. Isaac Babel, the author of *Red Cavalry* and *Odessa Tales*, was trying to get him a position in the Ukrainian Cinema Administration (VUFKU). His job would be to write reviews of film scenarios. A few texts by Mandelstam on contemporary films have in fact survived. The two films were not outstanding products of Soviet cinema, but lightweight ephemera, *Tatar Cowboys* and *The Heaviest Doll in the World* (GD, 13–16, 59–70). In his letter, Mandelstam enthusiastically looked forward to 'very easy and clean work', paid holidays and the amenities of a regulated working life. These were all dreams, and nothing more!

It is not known why his hopes of film work in Kyiv were dashed, just like all his other attempts to secure employment. Probably because Mandelstam did not belong to the world of cinema, and because he was incapable of doing anything other than his original, distinctive poetic work. Viktor Shklovsky had already offered the friendly suggestion in 1927 that he should make a living by writing film scenarios, something Shklovsky himself did with enthusiasm. Mandelstam replied to this well-meant advice with the witty parody 'I Write a Scenario', in which he immediately pushes every story line straight to absurdity (GD, 37–79; CC, 301–2). The failure of Mandelstam's foray into the world of film was entirely predictable. By the start of April 1929, he had awakened from his Kyivian dreams and was back in Moscow. He found temporary accommodation in a hostel run by TseKUBU (Central Commission for the Improvement of the Living

Conditions of Scholars) at 5 Kropotkin Quay. But the rest of the year was overshadowed by disaster.

The calamity Mandelstam suffered in 1929 originated from the field of activity in which he had earned his bread since 1923: translations of the work of more or less 'progressive' foreign authors. He translated Ernst Toller's *Masse Mensch* (Masses Man), Max Barthel's poetry volumes *Arbeiterseele* (The Worker's Soul) and *Lasset uns die Welt gewinnen* (Let Us Gain the World), plays and stories by the French unanimists Jules Romains and Georges Duhamel and other works which have now been forgotten. We can only guess how galling it was for a first-rate poet in constant need of money and under great time pressure to have to wear himself out by translating third- and fourth-rate authors. Most recently, between 1927 and 1929, Mandelstam's labour power had been poured into large-scale projects such as a Walter Scott edition or the works of the American adventure-story writer Thomas Mayne Reid. He worked on the latter project jointly with his friend Benedict Livshits. There was a certain amount of sharp practice involved here. As both of them knew French better than English, they usually translated the French translation into Russian instead of the original. When this came to the notice of Ionov, the director of the 'Land and Factory' publishing house, he terminated their employment, and, in April 1929, reported both poets to a Court of Honour. Even the hated, soul-destroying hackwork was now under threat.

These translations were not required to be of high quality. What was involved here was the large-scale production of culturally insignificant literature to serve the needs of 'construction' or to provide undemanding reading material for the wider public. Drawing on his own personal experience, Mandelstam wrote numerous newspaper articles against the translation practices of Soviet publishers, which were divorced from all standards of value, and were purely concerned with marketing and securing a mass readership. Thanks to his polemical sally 'Torrents of Hackwork' (GD, 71–9; CC, 283–9), which was published on 7 April 1929 in the highly official government newspaper *Izvestiia*, and an equally trenchant text, 'On Translations', which appeared in July 1929 in the main journal of the proletarian writers, *On Literary Guard*, Mandelstam increasingly gained a reputation as an annoying troublemaker who made a fetish of quality and demanded concrete reforms. Some literary functionaries were just waiting for the opportunity to silence the querulous and argumentative 'former poet'.

In September 1928, the Russian translation of a novel by the Belgian writer Charles de Coster, *The Legend of Thyl Ulenspiegel*, was published in Moscow. This apparently insignificant event would prove to be the beginning of the end for Mandelstam. In May 1927, the 'Land and Factory' publishing house had offered him the task, which he accepted, of revising two Russian translations of the book, by Arkady Gornfeld and Vasily Kariakin, which were already in existence. When the novel was published, Mandelstam's was the only name mentioned on the title page. It was a symptom of the shoddy publishing practices he himself had denounced in his two recent articles. Although he was not the guilty party, he wrote to Gornfeld, who was unaware of what had happened, and offered him in reparation the whole of the fee he had received for the revision. Despite this, Gornfeld felt obliged to write on 28 November 1928 to the Leningrad *Red Evening News* accusing Mandelstam of stealing his work.

Mandelstam replied to the accusation of plagiarism in a letter of 12 December 1928 to the *Moscow Evening News*, expressing his fury 'as a Russian poet and *littérateur*' (MR, 145–9). It was particularly painful that Gornfeld brought up Gogol's story *The Overcoat*, playing it off against him. That hallowed piece of Russian literature was the story of how an insignificant, harassed official named Akaky Akakievich was robbed at night of his laboriously acquired overcoat while crossing a big city square. In his time, Dostoevsky had written that 'we all emerged from Gogol's *Overcoat*'. The accusation of plagiarism had now been made, but it had no immediate consequences. It was not until five months later, on 7 May 1929, a month after 'Torrents of Hackwork', Mandelstam's attack on Soviet publishing houses, had been published in *Izvestiia*, that *Literaturnaia Gazeta* returned to the issue by publishing a provocative commentary headed 'A Simple Plagiarism and an Impudent Bungler'. It was composed by a certain Zaslavsky, who rehashed the Gornfeld episode and accused Mandelstam of plagiarism and shoddy work.

Mandelstam wrote a short reply to Zaslavsky's slanderous feuilleton, which was published in *Literaturnaia Gazeta* on 13 May 1929 along with a letter from fifteen other writers, including well-known individuals such as Boris Pasternak, Boris Pilnyak, Valentin Kataev, Yury Olesha and Mikhail Zoshchenko, in which they declared their solidarity with him. But the journal's editorial board suggested that a Dispute Committee of FOSP (Federation of Organisations of Soviet Writers) should be set up, and that the Mandelstam case should be referred to it. It would await the committee's decision and then publish the result. A whole series of letters show the gruelling and hopeless struggle Mandelstam waged during 1929 to refute the allegation of plagiarism and literary bungling. The way the lawsuit was conducted could have been invented by Kafka: the judge was an interested party and a plaintiff rolled into one. The 'Dispute Committee', which held its first meeting on 22 May 1929, was chaired by Semion Kanachikov, a party official. He was the editor of *Literaturnaia Gazeta*, the journal which had asked Zaslavsky to write the feuilleton, as well as being the official secretary of FOSP – a sinister concentration of authority in one person, which made a mockery of any objective assessment of the conflict. The plagiarism dispute provided a welcome opportunity for the literary functionaries of FOSP to silence a troublesome writer.[1]

1929 was altogether a catastrophic year for Russian literature. It marked the end of early Soviet literature, which had delighted in experimentation, had been nourished by the avant-garde's sense of a new departure and was committed to diversity. Artistic creation now began to be influenced ever more strongly by the 'social task' of contributing to Soviet construction. The dogmatic and defamatory propaganda issued semi-officially by the Russian Association of Proletarian Writers (RAPP) was directed against everything not strictly 'proletarian'. Mikhail Bulgakov, who had shown his scepticism towards the euphoria of progress with the satirical fantasy *The Heart of a Dog*, published in 1925, was one of many victims of RAPP's merciless agitation. The 'Proletarian Writers' also attacked Yevgeny Zamyatin, author of the visionary dystopia *We* (1920), and Boris Pilnyak, who had allowed his revealing novel *Mahogany*, rejected at home, to be published in 1929 by the 'class enemy' in Berlin, which made matters worse. RAPP also turned its attention to the last surviving avant-garde grouping, the Absurdists around Daniil Kharms and Alexander Vvedensky, whose OBERIU (Association of the Art of Reality) was disparaged for its 'literary rowdyism' and forced out of existence in 1930. Even Vladimir Mayakovsky, the 'drummer of the revolution', was attacked ever more fiercely by the proletarian-writer functionaries as a writer 'incomprehensible to the masses' and booed off the stage. He chose an early suicide, in April 1930, and was no longer there to experience the Great Terror of the late 1930s.

---

1 The Ulenspiegel Affair: letters 109, 117–22, 124–7 and 130–1 in O. Mandelstam, *Du bist mein Moskau und mein Rom*; for the commentaries and the afterword to the same volume, 359 and 456–9.

There were various risky ways in which writers under attack could respond to this campaign. Zamyatin wrote to Stalin in 1931 asking for permission to leave the country. This was granted, a highly exceptional concession. Zamyatin died in Paris in 1937. Mikhail Bulgakov, who was also in trouble, wrote a 'Letter to the Government' in 1930, but was not permitted to leave. Pilnyak engaged in a superficial self-criticism, promised to keep to the party line in any future novels, but still included large parts of *Mahogany* in a novel he published in 1930, *The Volga Flows into the Caspian Sea*. He was shot in 1938. Kharms and Vvedensky turned to writing for children. They died miserably in prison in 1942.

Thus Mandelstam was not the only victim of this brutal change of line; the whole of Soviet literature suffered. But his response was not typical of the time. After the dispute with FOSP and *Literaturnaia Gazeta*, the need for self-preservation ought to have induced him to back down by falling silent or to engage in self-criticism. He did neither of these things. He reacted in an entirely un-Soviet manner: he defended himself and insisted on his rights. He chose conflict and eventually made a radical break with the official writers' organisations. On 11 June 1929, he sought the support of the Leningrad writers, describing his situation in all its seriousness:

> After what has been done to me, one can no longer live. Take this badge of shame away. I demand an investigation. They have hunted me like an animal. Words are powerless here. Action must be taken. Proceedings must be brought against the instigators of this smear campaign, against those who tolerated it out of cowardice or false ambition. They should be called to account for their hangman's work backed up by lies. (MR, 175)

But the campaign of slander could not be put into reverse, and the 'Ulenspiegel Affair' could not be stopped in its tracks. In August 1929, admittedly, Mandelstam again found employment, which suggested a certain degree of 'normality', but appearances were deceptive. As usual, the position only lasted a few months. His new job was with the newspaper *Moskovskii Komsomolets*. He edited a weekly literature page and acted as a counsellor to young poets. Despite the burden of the 'Affair', he tried to take the task seriously, and to raise the literary level of the Komsomol poets. He wrote on 24 August 1929 to Vissarion Zayanov: 'We are conducting a fight against any kind of narrow-mindedness and self-interest and the goal we set ourselves is cultural stimulus. The rising literary generation of *komsomoltsy* needs older allies' (MR, 176). But these brave phrases were directed towards strengthening an enterprise that was already on the point of collapse. The newspaper ceased publication at the end of the year.

Mandelstam was, of course, more concerned with the deeply wounding Ulenspiegel Affair than with the 'cultural stimulus' offered by the Komsomol newspaper. On 30 September 1929, he was expelled from the Leningrad section of the Writers' Union. In December 1929, after months of vain attempts to throw off the label of plagiarist and literary bungler, he gathered his strength for a massive settlement of accounts. He wrote a ten-page 'Open Letter to Soviet Writers'. It is a furious attempt to make a clean break, and a fiery proclamation of the dignity of a poet:

> I declare to the very face of the Federation of Soviet Writers that they have besmirched themselves by their infamous persecution of a writer, that they have used outrageous means to do this, and that they have had recourse to deception and distortion. They have suppressed facts, deliberately fabricated spurious documents, and made use of lying witnesses. With shameful cowardice they have shielded and continue to shield their apparatchiks. They have used their authority to cover up abuses in the system of publication and they have reacted to the first attempt by a writer in the USSR to intervene in publishing matters by mounting a scandalous criminal trial. (MR, 179–80)

In his letter of protest, Mandelstam dissociates himself from a writers' organisation 'which allows its organs to be perverted into a torture chamber where the work and honour of a writer is desecrated with impunity'. The functionaries of FOSP, he says, have introduced into the history of Soviet literature 'a chapter which gives off the smell of a corpse' (MR, 186). And the conclusion he draws as an individual is: 'I am leaving the Federation of Soviet Writers, and from now on I refuse to be a writer' (MR, 187).

Naturally, he means 'writer' in the official sense, because in December 1929, simultaneously with the 'Open Letter', Mandelstam opened a new phase in his prose-writing career with the polemical essay *Fourth Prose*, which turns into a general reckoning with Stalinism and its literary marionettes. According to Nadezhda Mandelstam, the strange title initially meant simply that it was his fourth foray into prose (after *The Noise of*

Time, *The Egyptian Stamp* and the collection of essays issued as *On Poetry*),[2] but it was also an allusion to the position of the 'Fourth Estate' in the nineteenth-century social structure of Russia. History has reserved the term for the 'proletariat', but Mandelstam uses it as a coded expression for the *raznochintsy*, a group with which he emphatically associated himself. These were the intellectuals of the nineteenth century, non-noble and 'propertyless', who emerged 'from below' and were often autodidacts. As he writes in *The Noise of Time*, 'The raznochinets needs no memory – it is enough for him to tell of the books he has read, and his biography is done' (RZ, 88; NT, 109–10).

The poem 'The First of January 1924' had already contained a 'vow' made by Mandelstam to this 'Fourth Estate' of Russian society:

> The frost is smelling of apples again
> Could I ever betray to gossip-mongers
> The great vow to the Fourth Estate
> And oaths solemn enough for tears?
> (TR, 167; CR, 51)

According to Mandelstam, the *raznochinets* is distinguished by his ethical approach, sense of honour and personal integrity. In a poem written in 1931, 'Midnight in Moscow', he would powerfully reaffirm his sense of belonging to this class of 'propertyless' intellectuals:

> Get away! Don't ask for anything!
> Don't complain!
> Is this why the intelligentsia
> Were downtrodden so that I could betray them now?
> We shall die like foot soldiers,
> But we won't glorify the looting, the hired labour, or the lies.
> (MM, 79; MN, 46)

Mandelstam's *Fourth Prose* is the status report of a *raznochinets* on the Soviet era. It is a grim balance sheet drawn up shortly before the end of the fourth decade of his life: 'And it was all as terrifying as in a child's

2 The themes that run through *Fourth Prose*: Afterword to O. Mandelstam, *Das Rauschen der Zeit*, 325–33. Nadezhda on *Fourth Prose*: N. Mandelstam, *Hope Against Hope*, 177–9 ('The Change of Values').

dream. *Nel mezzo del cammin di nostra vita* – midway on the path of life – I was stopped in the dense Soviet forest by bandits who called themselves my judges' (RZ, 267; NT, 187). This quotation from the opening lines of Dante's *Inferno* is how Mandelstam describes his entry into the hell of thirties Stalinism. His reply to the slanderous campaign against him was to affirm the commitment of a poet to going his own way, in an angry and self-justificatory pamphlet which declared his stubborn resistance to the attempt to crush him. Otherness was no longer a reason for self-accusation and silence, but for pride and steadfastness: 'My work, whatever form it may take, is seen as mischief, as lawlessness, as an accident. But that's how I like it, so I agree. I subscribe to it with both hands' (RZ, 271; NT, 189).

Otherness is also maintained in Mandelstam's unusual creative process, his rejection of 'writing' and the way his work as a poet finds expression 'from the voice': 'I have no manuscripts, no notebooks, no archives. I have no handwriting because I never write. I alone in Russia work from the voice while all around me the bitch pack writes' (RZ, 258; NT, 181). We should not be surprised that *Fourth Prose*, that manifesto of persistent outsider status, also contains a proud re-statement of Mandelstam's conscious Jewishness:

> Writerdom ... is incompatible with the honourable title of Jew, of which I am proud. My blood, burdened with its inheritance from sheep breeders, patriarchs and kings, rebels against the shifty gypsyishness of the writing tribe. (RZ, 265; NT, 186)

To express his scorn for 'the writing tribe' Mandelstam uses a defamatory cliché directed against the Roma. At another point, when searching for an image to express marginality and exclusion, he defines himself as belonging to the same group: 'The gypsy at least had his horse, but I am horse and gypsy in one person' (RZ, 270; NT, 188). But the pamphlet is also a public indictment of the 'murderers of Russian poets' and their accomplices, the official writers who have conformed:

> I divide all the works of world literature into those written with and without permission. The first are trash, the second – stolen air. (RZ, 257; NT, 181)

Mandelstam does not apply his condemnation of the 'writing tribe' to every Soviet writer. He excludes the satirist Mikhail Zoshchenko. He was 'the only man who ever showed us a worker', but he was 'trampled in the dirt'. Mandelstam therefore demands 'monuments to Zoshchenko in all the cities and provincial corners of the Soviet Union' (RZ, 271; NT, 189). He also quotes a verse by Sergei Yesenin ('I didn't shoot the wretches in the dungeons') and comments approvingly on it: 'There you have the symbol of faith, there you have the genuine canon of the true writer, the mortal enemy of literature' (RZ, 260; NT, 183).

His relationship with Yesenin, who committed suicide in December 1925 in the Leningrad hotel 'Angleterre', had always been problematic. During the seething era of the Imaginist revolt between 1919 and 1921, Yesenin insulted Mandelstam and vilified his poems – although he described them in private as 'magnificent'. Mandelstam at first regarded Yesenin as a self-intoxicated narcissist, with only one subject: 'I am a poet.' To the cultivated Acmeists, the peasant poet and rowdy Imaginist was an alien presence. But once, when Anna Akhmatova said something disparaging about Yesenin, Osip objected that he could forgive absolutely everything for the one line, 'I did not shoot the wretches in the dungeons.' It is this verse, from the 1922 poem 'I Shall Not Deceive Myself' (included in the 1924 volume *Tavern Moscow*), that is praised in *Fourth Prose*.

Mandelstam's essay takes aim at a whole range of targets, including Soviet journalism, the printing industry and conformist literary criticism. It is also a lament for 'the bloody Soviet earth', the misuse of young people, the crudeness and violence of the Stalin epoch, the lynch mentality, the arbitrary shootings and the lack of courage displayed by bystanders who failed to intercede. The main figure of the epoch is also unmasked in the text: 'at a time when their fathers have sold out to the pockmarked devil for three generations to come' (RZ, 257; NT, 181). The 'pockmarked devil' is only the first of many polemical characterisations Mandelstam would apply to the dictator Stalin in the years that followed. Stalin's face was in fact covered in pockmarks, which had to be airbrushed out of all the propaganda photographs.

There is no doubt that the writing of *Fourth Prose* had a therapeutic effect for Mandelstam. It was his personal exorcism, an act of liberation, and his later lyrical poetry would be unthinkable without it. The 'sick son of the age' (as referred to in the poem 'The First of January 1924') suddenly grasped that the age was sick, not he. Long after Mandelstam's death, *Fourth Prose* was still a clandestine document, preserved in ciphered form. Only Nadezhda Mandelstam, Anna Akhmatova and one or two other friends knew of its existence. Later, during the post-Stalin thaw and the Brezhnev period, and right up to the end of the Soviet era, the piece became a cult text for artists, human rights campaigners and dissidents. As Anna Akhmatova records in 'Pages from a Diary' (1957): 'This prose … is only now beginning to find its reader. Yet I constantly hear, mainly from young people, who are crazy about it, that there has never been prose like this in all of the twentieth century.'[3]

The 'Open Letter' and *Fourth Prose* are the documents of an angry rebellion; they are the work of a poet who is wiping the slate clean, who wants nothing more to do with official 'literature', but who already knows that he is heading towards a frost which will kill him:

> I tear off my literary fur coat and trample it underfoot. In nothing but my jacket and in a thirty-degree frost I shall run three times around the boulevard rings of Moscow … into a fatal chill, if only not to see the twelve lit Judas windows of that obscene building on Tverskoy Boulevard [[author's note: headquarters of the Federation of Organisations of Soviet Writers, FOSP]], if only not to hear the clinking of pieces of silver and the counting of the printer's sheets. (RZ, 267–8; NT, 187)

We should not allow the fury and virulence of Mandelstam's writing to blind us to his miserable state during this phase of his life. His defiant and vigorous rebelliousness was only one aspect of his mental condition. At the turn of the year 1929–1930, his everyday life was marked by frequent moments of dejection. The image the poet presents of himself in *Fourth Prose* is fluctuating and ambiguous. He describes himself as a proud Jew, as a 'furrier of precious furs' (RZ, 265, 267; NT, 187), but also as an 'ageing man', with a 'chewed off stump of a heart' and as the poorest of the gypsies (RZ, 270; NT, 188).

In the final section of *Fourth Prose*, the organ grinder from Schubert's *Winter Journey* song cycle appears, and Mandelstam repeats the phrase 'I am poor' in two languages, German and Russian (RZ, 272; NT, 189). His own 'winter journey' had begun. He was now living a split life. At home,

3 M.'s relations with Yesenin: O. S. Figurnova and M. V. Figurnova, *Osip i Nadezhda Mandel'shtamy*, 89–94 (N. Vol'pin). Akhmatova on *Fourth Prose*: A. Akhmatova, *My Half Century*, 100.

in his bleak room, *Fourth Prose* awaited, in its ciphered handwriting. The newspaper *Moskovskii Komsomolets* had ceased publication, but in January 1930 Mandelstam was taken on by the *Moscow Evening News*, though again this was only for a few weeks. There his job was to supervise the 'Circle of Worker-Correspondents' and on 23 February, he edited a 'gigantic display about the Red Army' (MR, 195). One can easily imagine what kind of 'literature' was involved here.

Summonses and interrogations by various prosecutors in the Ulenspiegel Affair came thick and fast. In a letter of 24 February 1930 to Nadezhda, who had travelled to Kyiv for her father's funeral, Mandelstam described it as his personal 'Dreyfus Affair' (MR, 195; CC, 542). Then, on 13 March 1930, he informed her that he had been summoned to a meeting with 'some university lecturer' who asked him detailed questions about his previous life. This was probably the secret police's concealed way of gaining information about him ('We must also know everything about you': MR, 199). The whole of Mandelstam's misery, the impossibility of washing away the 'lies' and the 'dirt' from his name, is plainly revealed in this letter:

> Dearest Nadenka!
>
> I'm at my wit's end. I'm miserable, Nadik. I should have stayed with you the whole time … As you walk around our room, darling, all that is precious and eternal is with you. You must cling, cling to this sweet immortal something till the very end. Don't give it away to anyone at any cost. I'm miserable, darling, I'm always miserable, but now I can't find the words to tell you. They've confused me and they are holding me here as if I were in prison; there's no light. I keep wanting to brush away this lie – and I can't. I keep wanting to wash away the dirt – and it's impossible.
>
> Should I tell you, what a delirium, what a frenzied, dreary nightmare everything is, absolutely everything …
>
> They've been tormenting me with the case. I've been summoned five times … But I know one thing: I'm out of work, I'm growing more uncivilised each day. I'm afraid of my newspaper office – there are no people there, only terrible fish … I must leave. I should have left long ago … It's too late … I must leave. And now. But where can I go? There's nothing but emptiness all around …

> I'm alone. I am poor. *Ich bin arm.* Everything is irreparable. The severance is a blessing. I must preserve it. I must not upset it.
> (MR, 197–200; CC, 543–5)

The phrase 'I am poor. The severance is a blessing' is uncompromisingly radical, just as was the answer Mandelstam gave to the newspaper questionnaire of November 1928, when he welcomed the end of intellectual dependence and the life of a cultural pensioner. In the 1930s, Mandelstam would have to pay for this 'blessing' with continuous poverty, homelessness and social isolation (not to mention exile and death in a labour camp). In a fragment of a letter sent in 1930 to an unknown addressee, he reports dispassionately:

> I never had a lasting material basis for my life, and I don't have one now. I am accustomed to working under constant pressure and in the most peculiar conditions … People in literature have long been used to my lack of material provisions and the fact that I am almost homeless, and I myself no longer find it surprising … My life has been difficult and laborious. (MR, 189–90)

The exhausting Ulenspiegel Affair of 1928–1929, together with the slanderous press campaign, and the calumnies, summonses and interrogations, were a low point in Mandelstam's difficult existence. But, strangely enough, the year 1930, which began in such adversity, had in store one of the happiest events in this poet's life.

17

One Additional Day

(Armenia 1930)

Mandelstam had a dream. He wanted to travel to the Caucasus, a region he had already got to know in the summer of 1921, when he passed through Kislovodsk, Baku and Tbilisi during his 'official trip' to Batumi with Lopatinsky. In the essay 'A Word or Two about Georgian Art' (1922) on Georgian eroticism in Russian poetry, Mandelstam declared that the classical Russian writers Pushkin and Lermontov saw the Caucasus as 'a mythological promised land', which was embodied in its finest form in Georgia (GP, 94; CC, 160). But it was of Armenia, which had not been on his itinerary in 1921, that he dreamed rather than Georgia. In his 1931–1932 notebook, he writes of his yearning to travel to Armenia, a land 'of which I have never ceased to dream' (AA, 67; CC, 382).

An opportunity almost arose during the dreadful year of 1929. The seventh section of *Fourth Prose* tells of an invitation from Askanaz Mravjan, People's Commissar for Education of the Armenian Soviet Socialist Republic, to give a seminar on poetry at the University of Yerevan. But Mravjan died that same year, and his successor saw no reason to bring Mandelstam to Armenia, as he was influenced by the slanderous stories spread about him in Moscow in connection with the 'Ulenspiegel Affair'. In *Fourth Prose* Mandelstam mourns his 'patron' in the 'Yerevan anthill' (RZ, 259). The dream of Armenia also fits into the playful gestures of liberation in *Fourth Prose*:

> If I had gone to Yerevan, I should have run for three days and three nights to the large buffets in the railway station, to eat buttered bread with black caviar. Helter-skelter! … And I should have got out at the railway station in Yerevan with my winter coat in one hand and my old man's walking stick – my Jewish staff – in the other. (RZ, 259–60; NT, 182)

But the dream of Armenia did not die. Thanks to Bukharin, it became a reality. The man who had made possible the publication of Mandelstam's last books had not yet been stripped of his power completely. He had, it is true, been thrown out of the Politburo in December 1929 for his opposition to Stalin's economic policy and deprived of his most important political functions. But he still had sufficient influence to send Mandelstam on an 'official mission' to the Caucasus. Soviet writers were being instructed at that time to visit construction sites and new industrial areas. They were expected to report with jubilation on the successes of the First Five Year Plan, which had started to operate in 1928, and to proclaim their enthusiasm for the construction of socialism in the Soviet republics. Mandelstam's complete lack of suitability for the task imposed upon him would not become clear until 1933, when the publication of his prose work *Journey to Armenia* gave rise to a big scandal.

In March 1930, a recurrence of Mandelstam's heart trouble forced him to visit a Moscow clinic. The cardiologist diagnosed myocarditis (an inflammation of the heart muscle) and referred him to a psychiatrist, who prescribed a stay in a sanatorium because he was in a condition of 'acute psychasthenia' (MR, 201). But Mandelstam wanted to go to the Caucasus, not a sanatorium. Bukharin mediated, and at the end of March 1930 Mandelstam finally got his way. Accompanied by his wife, he initially travelled to the Abkhazian capital Sukhumi on the south-eastern coast of the Black Sea, and he spent six weeks there sightseeing and making excursions. He visited the Olive Sovkhoz at New Athos, the coalmines at Tkvarcheli and other relevant 'construction sites'.

Mandelstam was accommodated, along with the other writers on the 'official trip', in the Ordzhonikidze House, a government dacha on Cherniavsky Hill. One of the guests staying there at the same time was Nikolai Yezhov, the man who later ran Stalin's purges. As had happened in 1923, when the Mandelstams shared a railway compartment with Vyshinsky, the later prosecutor in the show trials of the 1930s, on the journey to Gaspra, the paths of the executioners and their victims crossed prematurely in seemingly harmless places.[1]

While he was in Sukhumi, Mandelstam heard about Vladimir Mayakovsky's suicide in Moscow on 14 April 1930: the battle-weary 'drummer of the revolution' had fired a bullet into his heart. He received the news from the proletarian poet Alexander Bezymensky, who was a functionary of the same Russian Association of Proletarian Writers (RAPP) which had caused severe distress to Mayakovsky through its unrestrained attacks. In his last poem, 'At the Top of my Voice' (1930), he proclaimed that he himself had 'stepped on the throat of my own song', while in his goodbye letter 'To Everyone' he wrote that the 'boat of love' had been 'wrecked on the everyday'. But, in saying this, he was not just referring to his unrequited love for Lilia Brik or his last, tormented affair with the actress Veronika Polonskaya. His disagreements with the proletarian dogmatists, increasingly violent since 1929, had worn out his powers of resistance.

For many intellectuals, Mayakovsky's death was a symbolic event. It signified the end of an epoch and was a bad omen, indicating how precarious poetry's future was likely to be in the Soviet state. Mandelstam wrote in his notebook:

> It was in Sukhumi, in April, that I received the news of Mayakovsky's death, which overwhelmed me like a great ocean. It felt as if a mountain of water was lashing my spine. It took my breath away and left a salty taste in my mouth. (AA, 70; CC, 385)

In his 1922 and 1923 essays Mandelstam had criticised Mayakovsky for his didacticism, but he had no doubt that the loss of Mayakovsky meant the disappearance of yet another great poet of his generation, after the passing of Blok, Gumilyov, Khlebnikov and Yesenin. Sarcastic comments directed against Bezymensky both in his notebook and in the later text *Journey to Armenia* show the depth of Mandelstam's dismay at the failure of the officials and writers present in Sukhumi to react appropriately to the tragedy: 'The society which gathered in Sukhumi accepted the news of our unique poet's death with disgraceful equanimity … That very evening they danced Cossack dances and crowded around the piano,

1 Yezhov in Sukhumi: N. Mandelstam, *Hope Against Hope*, 322–5 ('A Scene from Life').

singing rowdy student songs' (AA, 71–2; CC, 385–6). The notebook goes on to mention his amazement and gratitude when he observed an ancestral, genuine act of mourning, the funerary ritual of the indigenous Abkhazian population: 'In Sukhumi I was transfixed by the ancient rite of the funeral lament' (AA, 73; CC, 386–7).

After waiting in sorrow and irritation for the official papers he needed for the next stage of the journey, Mandelstam set off 'for Erevan in May of 1930, to a foreign country, prepared to visually probe its cities and graves, to collect the sounds of its speech, and to inhale its most noble and intransigent historical spirit' (AA, 64; CC, 380). This was hardly an appropriate programme for a 'normal' writer making an official journey through a Soviet republic engaged in socialist construction. Mandelstam's notebook places the two requirements, his 'task' of praising socialist achievements and his personal poetic programme, in sharp antagonism to one another:

> I encountered the firm will and hand of the Bolshevik Party absolutely everywhere I went. Socialist construction was becoming something of a second nature to Armenia.
>
> But my eye, used to falling for anything out of the ordinary, for anything fleeting or ephemeral, picked up in my journey only the shimmering tremor of chance, the vegetal ornament of reality …
>
> Can I really compare myself to some spoiled child turning a pocket mirror in his hands to guide the sunbeams, urging them to follow wherever he goes? (AA, 64; CC, 380–1)

Mandelstam was looking for Armenia's 'first nature', its historical essence, its innate core. The biblical land, so to speak. He had already written in *Fourth Prose* of the land of Armenia as the 'younger sister of the Land of Judah' (RZ, 259; NT, 182). For the Jewish poet Mandelstam, Armenia becomes a piece of 'promised land'. No wonder it appears in biblical guise in a verse fragment composed in 1931:

> But before then I saw
> Rich Ararat with its biblical tablecloth
> And spent two hundred days in the Sabbath land
> Which is called Armenia.
> (AA, 135; MN, 48)

According to the first book of Moses (Genesis 8:4), Noah's ark landed on Mount Ararat. There his dove brought him an olive leaf, which promised a fresh start. The Armenians proudly maintain that they were the first humans to emerge after the Flood, and old Persian legends support their claim, describing Ararat as the cradle of humanity. Mandelstam would refer to this idea in one of the poems of the 'Armenia cycle' he produced after his return: 'The hollow book of the beautiful earth / From which the first men learned' (AA, 113; OM, 107).

The sacred mountain of the Armenians, Ararat, repeatedly flashes forth in Mandelstam's travel writing as well as his poems. He writes of 'furnace Ararat', 'tent Ararat' and 'father Ararat'. Soon, this non-Armenian poet developed a 'sixth sense, an "Ararat" sense', 'the sense of attraction to the mountain' (AA, 48; NT, 220). Here – and not just here – Mandelstam is no doubt looking back to his great predecessor Alexander Pushkin, who had set out for the Caucasus around a hundred years earlier, in 1829, and produced the pioneering travelogue *Journey to Arzrum* (published in 1836). Pushkin too stood in wonder before Ararat, and succumbed to its magnetism:

> 'What mountain is that?' I asked, stretching, and heard the answer: 'It's Ararat'. How strong is the effect of sounds! I gazed greedily at the biblical mountain, saw the ark, moored to its top in hopes of renewal and life.[2]

Mandelstam's journey led to one of the primeval cradles of civilisation, to a land with a tremendously rich cultural past which was also the first Christian country in history. For him, Armenia was a piece of Europe 'at the edge of the world' (the phrase is used in the fourth poem of the Armenia cycle); it was the eastern advance post of Jewish-Christian, European-Western culture. In 301 Trdat (Tiridates) III of Armenia had declared Christianity the country's state religion. The Armenian churches were archaic, though they also indicated the way Romanesque architecture would develop. Mandelstam would celebrate their fascinating qualities in the following passage from his Armenian travelogue, about the Church of Karmravor in Ashtarak, which was built in the seventh century:

---

2 A. Pushkin, 'Journey to Arzrum', 381.

> The door is quieter than water, lower than grass. I stood on tiptoe and glanced inside: but there was a cupola in there, a cupola!
>
> A real one! Like the one in St Peter's in Rome, above the thronged thousands, the palms, the sea of candles, and the Pope's sedan chair …
>
> Whose idea was it to imprison space inside this wretched cellar, this beggars' dungeon – in order to render it there a homage worthy of the psalmist? (AA, 48; SE, 215)

He arrived at Yerevan in May 1930 and spent the month of June there, using it as a starting point for excursions to places of symbolic significance. He visited the town of Etchmiadzin, twenty kilometres west of Yerevan, which was the headquarters of the Armenian church and the seat of its Catholicos. Not far from there, he saw the ruins of Zvartnots, a round church consecrated to the celestial angels, built by the 'builder Catholicos' Nerses III (642–652 C.E.), to which the seventh poem in the Armenia cycle is dedicated (AA, 105). In the ruins, he observed a sundial 'in the form of a zodiac or of a rose inscribed in stone' (AA, 14; SE, 187). This played a not unimportant part in moulding the new concept of time which was one of the benefits of his Armenian adventure. The first poem of the cycle, with its 'peasant bull churches' ('You breathe with the octahedral shoulders / Of peasant bull churches': AA, 93; OM, 99), suggests that Mandelstam also visited the monastery of Geghard, forty kilometres south-east of Yerevan. Above the portal of the church, which was built in 1215, there are carvings representing two fighting bulls.

These references to Mandelstam's visits to churches come from his poems, but no poems were composed during the trip itself. Mandelstam's Armenia cycle was created from memory, and it was written down in Tbilisi, Georgia, just after he had left Armenia on 16 October 1930. He did not do any writing during the journey. Instead, he looked around, keeping his senses open to new impressions. His Armenia project was a journey to find the source of civilisation, to explore it – and to explore himself – using all his senses. It was not just a pilgrimage by a cultural enthusiast to the site of an early civilisation. Mandelstam's aim was to track down in Armenia that 'first nature', that anti-utilitarian element, which Stalin's First Five Year Plan would never be able to harness.[3]

3 The Armenia project: Afterword to O. Mandelstam, *Armenien, Armenien!*, 205–21, and selected bibliography in the same volume, 201; R. Dutli, 'Sabbatland, Wildheit. Ossip Mandelstam und Armenien'; C. Sippl, *Reisetexte der russischen Moderne*.

For Mandelstam, one of the fundamental qualities of Armenia was its 'wildness'. The fifth poem in the Armenia cycle celebrates the 'wild' rose bush as an allegory of Armenia. The first poem praises Armenia's 'wild mob of children', and it is the 'wild children' of Armenia, resistant to any kind of training, who 'clamber like wild little beasts over the monks' graves' in the first section of *Journey to Armenia* (AA, 8; SE, 182). They are a contrast to the 'new Soviet man', half-dead and living a sham life, whose prototype he had already been horrified to encounter in Moscow. He also praises the 'wildcat' Armenian language as an antidote to the wooden political jargon of party functionaries:

The Armenian language is a wild cat.
It is the barbed speech of the Ararat gorge,
The predatory language of clay-baked cities,
The speech of hungering mudbricks.
(AA, 119; MN, 31)

As he rides on horseback over the nomads' pastures on Mount Aragats (Alagös), he ponders on this 'stubborn people', more ancient than the Romans (AA, 54). And we can be certain that he includes himself as well as the Armenians in this description. He wanted to inhale 'the immensely difficult and noble atmosphere' of Armenia's history, and he saw the country as the symbol of a desperate and persistent struggle for cultural self-preservation. In 1930, he was already being persecuted, and he had a feeling of solidarity with the Armenians, who had always been an endangered people. Their long history of oppression, dispossession and frightful decimation had sadly reached its height in 1915 with the massacres carried out as part of a Turkish policy of extermination – one and a half million were done to death. Bearing in mind this series of catastrophes, Mandelstam sets forth his confession of faith:

How I love this people living taut under strain,
Sleeping, screaming, giving birth,
This people nailed to the earth,
Who think each year is a century.
(AA, 121; MN, 31)

Mandelstam was seeking to discover an age-old Armenia with a continuous and elementally sensuous presence. But his writings by no means depict an Armenian idyll. It is always clear that in the present-day situation dominated by Stalin this much-tried country still lives a dangerous life: someone's 'death-mask' is removed in the fourth poem of the Armenia cycle (AA, 99). The unruliness and almost jubilant vitality radiated by Mandelstam's Armenian texts, in verse as in prose, should not mislead us: the Armenians were engaged in a ceaseless struggle against the powers of death.

Mandelstam had brought along Goethe's *Italian Journey* as travel reading (AA, 89; CC, 396). His Armenia project would turn into a meeting of the Orient and the Occident, a *West-Eastern Divan* on Goethean lines but of his own creation. The name of the poet Hafez (1320–1389), who was venerated by Goethe, is mentioned in the first poem of the Armenia cycle. Mandelstam also read the poet Ferdowsi (939–1020), author of the *Shahnameh* (Book of Kings), in a French translation. He was able to do this in Yerevan, in the office of the director of the Armenian National Library, Mamikon Gevorkian, a pleasure he equated with a fabulous oriental banquet: 'The books that are put on that satrap's table take on a taste of pink pheasant meat, bitter quails, musky venison, and roguish hare' (AA, 44; NT, 218).

The month of July 1930 was spent by Mandelstam in 'Armenia's first trade union rest home', which lay beside Lake Sevan, the largest mountain lake in the Caucasus, 1,900 metres above sea level. He devoted some of this time to contemplation on the island of Sevan, which is now a peninsula owing to a fall in the water level. 'On every island – be it Malta, Saint Helena or Madeira – life flows past in a sort of noble expectation … The ear lobe is more finely moulded and takes on a new twist' (AA, 10; NT, 195). The revitalisation of Mandelstam's senses brought with it a new feeling for time, and a new awareness of the value of life and the risks that threaten it: 'Life is a precious gift, inalienable' (AA, 43; NT, 17). He recounts an incident that occurred during his time there: the elderly chemist Gambarian was trying to swim round the island, having entered into a competition with a *komsomolets*. For several hours, it seemed as if he had drowned. When he re-emerged, he was greeted with applause. And Mandelstam remarked: 'That was the most splendid hand-clapping I have ever heard in my life: a man was being congratulated on the fact that he was not yet a corpse' (AA, 12; NT, 197). The passage clearly implies that

Mandelstam momentarily related the applause to himself: he was still alive!

This period of stillness and reflection allowed the images that would imbue his later work to ripen. One of the finest of these occurred to him on the banks of Lake Sevan. It was an image of the mutual interpenetration of culture and nature, of history – the biblical period, the Gutenberg epoch – and the present.

> The magnificent freshwater wind would tear into the lungs with a whistle. The clouds moved with a velocity that kept increasing by the minute and the incunabular surf would hasten to publish by hand in the space of half an hour a plump Gutenberg bible under the gravely glowering sky. (AA, 7; NT, 193)

The first chapter of what would later become *Journey to Armenia* is devoted to his sojourn beside Lake Sevan. On a spit of land called Tsamakaberd, Mandelstam came upon an archaeological site containing some remains dating back to the Urartu civilisation. Mount Ararat owes its name to the Kingdom of Urartu (ninth to sixth century B.C.E.), which was eventually conquered by the Assyrians. Having found at the site 'the porous, calcified little crust of someone's cranium', the traveller 'respectfully wrapped it up' in his handkerchief (AA, 10; NT, 195). He felt that he had arrived at the origin of mankind.

Mandelstam did not remain wrapped up in his own private mythical world. On the contrary, he made contact with local Armenian scientists and scholars, including the archaeologist Khachaturian, the regional studies specialist Sagatelian and the chemist Gambarian (the elderly swimmer who was applauded for his achievement!), and he describes all three in his travelogue. But he avoided the society of the usual 'official travellers' and their literature, about which his notebooks are invariably sarcastic. He writes of the 'great books of our made-in-Moscow literature' and the 'wooden rubbish of our well-intentioned bowling-alley literature': 'Give us some inkling that life is not lived in a bowling alley!' (AA, 63–4) The wooden and dogmatic proletarian bluster of RAPP was never more fiercely derided than in these phrases from Mandelstam's notebooks.

After his stay beside Lake Sevan, Mandelstam returned once more to Yerevan, and from there he travelled on horseback over the nomads' grazing lands to Mount Aragats and the village of Ashtarak perched on its southern slope, thirty kilometres north-west of the capital. The last two chapters of his Armenian travelogue are devoted to these excursions, which were more than merely the escapades of a tourist. 'It was a spacious day that fell to my lot! Even now, when I think back on it, my heart throbs. I got tangled up in it as in a long shirt pulled out of one of the trunks of my forefather Jacob' (AA, 52; NT, 222). Biblical Armenia once again! Joseph-Osip, the son of the patriarch Jacob, opens the biblical trunks in his memory.

But his last excursion from Yerevan led back into the all-Soviet nightmare. This was a journey to Nagornyi Karabakh. Nadezhda describes it in detail because it was the occasion for his political poem 'The Horse-cart Driver' (June 1931).[4] At dawn the couple set off by bus from Ganja to Shusha. The town began 'with an endless cemetery', the visible sign of a massacre which the Azerbaijanis, in alliance with the Turks, had committed against the Armenians in March 1920: there were 35,000 victims. Shusha is a town of death in the poem ('Dead windows, forty thousand': AA, 131). Mandelstam regarded the remaining Muslim population of the town as the murderers, and thought that in Shusha things were 'exactly as they were with us'. When the pair started their return journey, they came upon a driver who wore a leather mask to cover his disfigured face. The parallel was perfect with the 'devil's hired hand' and the 'Minister of the Black Death' Stalin, the 'pockmarked devil' of *Fourth Prose*.

From nowhere appeared a horse-cart driver,
Whose face was burned and wrinkled as a currant,
He was monosyllabic and sullen
Like the devil's hired hand
...
Hiding his terrible features
Behind a leather mask,
He whipped his horses,
Off to somewhere, until their last gasp.
...
I came to with a jolt. 'Hey, friend, stop!'
Damn it, now I remember:
He is the Minister of the Black Death,
With his horses gone astray.

4 The political poem 'The Horse-cart Driver': N. Mandel'shtam, *Kniga Tret'ia*, 162–4.

His disfigured destiny
Drives us to the delight of his soul,
So that the bitter-sweet earth
Could whirl endlessly like a merry-go-round.
(MM, 93–5; AA, 129–31; MN, 50)

A historical massacre and the Stalinist present merged into one single feeling of horror in Mandelstam's mind. He was so disturbed by his short stay in Shusha that he had to 'exorcise' it a year later, in this poem of June 1931.

By mid-October 1930, the Mandelstams were again in the Georgian capital of Tiflis (Tbilisi). Armenia already lay in the past. But then the miracle occurred: Mandelstam had written no poetry since the spring of 1925 (except children's verses), but now his painful awareness that the trip to Armenia was at an end caused him to recover his lyrical voicc. Between 16 October and 5 November 1930, he created the twelve-part Armenia cycle, drawing on his memories of the country. His time in Armenia had been a period of sharpened sensibility and heightened perception. The third poem of the cycle bemoans departure from the country as a loss of the senses of sight and hearing: 'O I see nothing, and my poor ear has grown deaf. / Of all those colours remain to me minium and raucous ochre alone' (AA, 97; OM, 101).

The eleventh poem states emphatically that he will never be able to return, even though the dream of Armenia would continue to accompany him well into the 1930s:

I will never see you again,
Near-sighted Armenian sky,
And will never look with screwed-up eyes
At the wayside shrine of Ararat,
And will never open
In the library of earthenware authors
The hollow book of the beautiful earth
From which the first men learned.
(AA, 113; OM, 107)

But the Armenia cycle is not dominated by nostalgia and grief. It rather celebrates the resurrection of the senses in verse – after they have first been lost. Mandelstam's poetry acquires a new harshness and intensity. Indeed, the poems on the periphery of the cycle contain vehement outbursts of fury. Mandelstam's stay in Georgia was initially protected by the local party secretary, Lominadze. But then the latter was suddenly summoned to Moscow, dismissed from his post and expelled from the Central Committee. As a result, Mandelstam's freedom of movement was curtailed, and an agent was assigned to shadow him.[5] His confrontation with this spy and 'official' (whose face was as 'terrifying as a gun') in a poem written in November 1930 turns into a vision of the disenchanting Soviet present and even for a moment dulls his enthusiasm for the Armenian language, which he usually celebrates unreservedly:

> The Armenian language is a wild cat,
> That tortures me and scratches my ear.
> If only I could lie on a broken-backed bed,
> Consumed by fever and the evil plague.
> …
> The official's face is terrifying as a gun –
> There is no one more pitiful, more ridiculous –
> Despatched on a mission, shunted off
> With no money or papers into the Armenian wasteland.
> …
> We were individuals and became the faceless mass,
> What is our fate to be? – who gave the orders? –
> It is the fatal thudding in our chests,
> And a bunch of Erzurum grapes.
> (AA, 125; MN, 33)

Soviet reality had recovered its grip on him. His heart problems also reemerged, along with his anxiety. Even so, when Nadezhda celebrated her thirty-first birthday on 31 October 1930 in Tbilisi, they were able to get hold of a nut tart. Mandelstam composed a little birthday poem for his wife, but fear, the constant theme of the poems of the first half of the 1920s, immediately returned to the surface.

---

5 The fall of Lominadze and the agent assigned to spy on the Mandelstams: Mandelstam, *Hope Against Hope*, 179–80 ('The Change of Values').

This life is terrifying for the two of us,
My comrade, with the generous mouth.
Our black market tobacco is crumbly,
And you sit cracking nuts, my simple little friend.
One could whistle through life like a starling,
Or eat it like your nut cake.
But – both of us know it's impossible.
(MM, 7; MN, 25)

It is a poem of disenchantment and clarity. But the biggest gain of the trip to the Caucasus was undeniable: Mandelstam had recovered the precious gift of poetic composition.

The Armenian episode brought other gifts too. One of them was a lasting friendship. In May 1930, Mandelstam had met the Moscow zoologist Boris Kuzin in a tearoom of the Yerevan mosque. Kuzin recorded the meeting in his colourful memoirs (AA, 144). He had been sent to Armenia by Moscow University to investigate the life-cycle of the cochineal insect, from which carmine dye is produced. He was a zoologist with an original mind, a well-read contemporary who loved the poetry of Pasternak and Mandelstam and venerated German cultural figures such as Goethe and Bach. Mandelstam's friendship with Kuzin at the beginning of the 1930s would provide the main incentive for his engagement with biology and the theory of evolution, but also with the German language. Some sections of *Journey to Armenia* are devoted to Boris Kuzin, as is the poem 'To the German Language', written in August 1932. After his 1930 break with the 'writers', the hated 'scribbling fraternity', Mandelstam would discover new acquaintances among the Moscow zoologists through his friend Kuzin. Armenia's gifts were manifold: the acquisition of a solid friendship was not the least of them.

It is impossible to overestimate the significance of the journey to Armenia for Mandelstam. He had gained 'one additional day, full of hearing, taste and smell', as he points out at the end of *Journey to Armenia* while re-telling an old legend, which came from the fifth-century *History of the Armenians* by Faustus of Byzantium. Mandelstam's transformation of this legend into a coded representation of the present was the main reason for the scandal that developed around this piece of writing in 1933. It was the story of the defeated Armenian king Arshak II, who had been imprisoned by the cruel Sassanid ruler Shapur II (310–379 C.E.) in the dungeons of Anush ('the fortress of oblivion'). Shapur owed an obligation to an Armenian courtier by the name of Drastamat, who decided to do his former master a favour. So Drastamat said to Shapur: 'Give me a pass to the fortress of Anush. I want Arshak to spend one additional day full of hearing, taste and smell, as it was before, when he amused himself with hunting and saw to the planting of trees' (AA, 56; NT, 225).

The story was a reflection of Mandelstam's own political situation. Shapur stood for Stalin, Drastamat ('the kindest and most well educated of the eunuchs') for Bukharin, and the defeated king Arshak II for Mandelstam himself. It is characteristic of Mandelstam that he made the cruel ruler Shapur alias Stalin into an 'Assyrian': 'The Assyrian has hold of my heart.' Mandelstam had already associated the coming of totalitarianism with Assyria in his earlier essay 'Humanism and Modern Life'.

Mandelstam's journey to Armenia was exactly the 'one additional day' he refers to here: it was a last chance to catch his breath before he passed into the nightmare of the 1930s under Stalin. This 'one additional day' would be followed by many black ones.

18

I Too Am a Man of My Time

(Leningrad and Moscow 1931)

After the fall of Lominadze, there was no longer any prospect of finding accommodation or work in Tbilisi, as Mandelstam had hoped. He returned to Moscow in November 1930, and in December he travelled on to Leningrad in search of somewhere to live. He renewed his acquaintance with the city of his childhood, which, since the shooting of Gumilyov in 1921, was also the city of his dead. He was shattered by the changes of recent times. In the December 1930 poem 'Leningrad', he oscillates between the old name of Petersburg and the new political label, between the city of childhood and the city of the dead:

> I've returned to my city of childhood illnesses and tears,
> The city that I know like the veins on the back of my hand.
> You've returned to it. Open wide, swallow quickly,
> The cod liver oil of the street lamps on Leningrad's embankment.
>
> I do not want to die yet, Petersburg! You still have
> All my friends' telephone numbers.
> Petersburg! I still have the addresses
> From which I can find the voices of the dead.
> (MM, 45; MN, 34)

The poem is overshadowed by presentiments of death, which are supposed to be magically banished by being voiced aloud. But the concluding verses of the poem were politically explosive:

> I live up a back flight of stairs, and when they tear at the bell pull
> The ringing hits me in the head.
> I wait until dawn for the dear guests to arrive,
> And each rattle of the slender door chain is like the clank of shackles.
> (MM, 45; MN, 34)

What Mandelstam meant by 'a back flight of stairs' was the place where his brother Yevgeny lived, on Vasilevsky Island, at number 31, Street Line 8. Who the nocturnal 'guests' were and why they were directly associated with a convict's shackles would immediately have been obvious to any contemporary reader. They were the arrest squads of the secret police, the OGPU, who usually appeared on the scene in threes, and always at night, when people were sleeping (or attempting to sleep despite their anxiety). The poem appeared on 23 November 1932 in *Literaturnaia Gazeta*, hidden in a collection of verses, and presumably only printed because of a mistake by the censorship. It is one of Mandelstam's most trenchant political utterances: it cries out against the arrests, and the deaths, of the time. In 1991, during the period of *glasnost'*, the first verse of the poem was engraved on a plaque affixed to the house on Vasilevsky Island where it was created.

A three-liner jotted down in January 1931, which remained unpublished during Mandelstam's lifetime, directly describes the city as 'a coffin' (MM, 51). Then, in the poem 'I Was a Child in the World of the Powerful', which was printed in April 1931 in the Leningrad journal *Zvezda* (no. 4), he definitively says farewell to the city of his childhood. The poem contains the dangerous verse 'Sensing future executions'; abusive remarks about Lenin's city, the 'cradle of the October Revolution', are also inserted:

> Fires and frost have made it even more brazen,
> Arrogant, cursed, empty and youthful.
> (MM, 47; MN, 35)

It really was time to leave Petersburg/Leningrad. In January 1931, the housing commission of the Leningrad Writers' Committee, chaired by the semi-official Soviet poet Nikolai Tikhonov, decided not to allow Mandelstam to settle there. They literally drove the poet out. Once again, he had neither work nor a place to stay, and there were other worries too. Nadezhda was sick: she was suffering from feverish attacks caused by her tuberculosis, which had still not been cured completely. Life in the same apartment as his younger brother Yevgeny was marked by severe tensions, because he got on far worse with Yevgeny than he did with Alexander, who was only one year his junior. The tensions are evident from a letter to his father (MR, 202).

The new departure for Moscow was a leap into the unknown. It was the starting point of the nomadic life the Mandelstams would lead during the thirties. It also coincided with Osip's fortieth birthday, on 14 January 1931. He wrote in a notebook: 'My fortieth birthday tolled in January … Constant search for a place of refuge. The hunger of thought is unappeased' (AA, 66). No other text could express this homelessness, this existence which swung between kitchen bivouacs (taking shelter among a few friends and relatives) and fresh departures, more succinctly than the kitchen poem that emerged in January 1931:

> Let's sit in the kitchen together,
> Smelling the sweet kerosene.
>
> There is a sharp knife and a loaf of bread –
> You could pump up the fuel stove,
>
> Or find some bits of string
> To tie up the bundle before dawn,
>
> So that we can go to the station
> Where no one can find us.
> (MM, 49; MN, 36)

Despite all its simplicity, this is a poem full of uneasiness, precisely because the reasons for their departure and their fear of discovery ('Where no one can find us') remain unexpressed. Homelessness pervades the poem, but not loneliness: the 'we' of the pair is evident throughout, as is the presence of Nadezhda, who would go on to share with Osip the Stalinist nightmare of the thirties. There is no 'I' in this poem.

By mid-January 1931, the pair were back in Moscow, but there they were both together and apart. In order to lighten the burden on their relatives, Mandelstam lived alone at first, with his brother Alexander and his wife, the painter Eleonora Gurvich. Their home was a single room of seventeen square metres in a communal dwelling at 10 Starosadsky Lane. Nadezhda lived on Strastnoi Boulevard with her brother Yevgeny. Mandelstam claims in a verse fragment that he was 'forcibly' brought to Moscow, and he attaches an epithet to the unloved city which is in this case extremely negative: 'Buddha-like Moscow' (MM, 85; MN, 48). For Mandelstam, who saw himself as the 'last Hellenic-Jewish-Christian poet', the adjective 'Buddhist' or 'Buddha-like' signified withdrawal from the world and the denial of life, rejection of individual existence and the blunting of perception, striving for nothingness and the emptiness of nirvana, and in political terms it meant 'Asiatic' and 'despotic'. He had taken that view since his essays 'Pushkin and Scriabin' (1916) and 'The Nineteenth Century' (1922). Despite saying farewell to Petersburg, he remained a Petersburg poet and a European. He had always mistrusted the new metropolis, continuing to regard it as 'the capital of filth' (TR, 183).

He described the poems he created in March and April 1931 as 'new poems' – they were produced after the Armenian miracle, the re-emergence of the lyrical gift – and they were unusually harsh and virulent in tone. The capital appears as a 'great mess'. It is 'Moscow the whore' (MM, 65; MN, 41). The 'six-fingered lie' is ever present, and even the poet cannot escape it (MM, 67). In Russian fairy tales, the possession of six fingers was an attribute of the witch Baba-Yaga, also known as Nepravda (Untruth). According to Nadezhda, there was a Moscow rumour that one of Stalin's hands had six fingers.[1]

The grim month of March 1931 was full of forebodings. In the famous poem about the 'wolfhound century', to which the agents of the NKVD (People's Commissariat of Internal Affairs) paid particular attention during Mandelstam's first arrest, which happened in May 1934, the poet's ego sharply differentiates itself from the wolf blood of its epoch. Transportation to Siberia is also prophesied:

1 Stalin alleged to have six fingers: N. Mandel'shtam, *Kniga Tret'ia*, 154.

> The wolfhound century leaps at my throat,
> But it's not wolf's blood that flows through my veins,
> You'd do better to shove me, like a cap, up the sleeve
> Up the hot fur coat of Siberia's plains.
> (FP, 71)
> …
> Lead me off into the night where the Yenisei flows,
> Where the pines reach up to the stars,
> Because I am not a wolf by blood
> And only my equal will take my life.
> (MM, 57; PO, 20)

Mandelstam would not produce a definitive conclusion to this poem until the end of 1935, when he wrote the last stanza during his Voronezh exile. It is a gigantic provocation. Stalin and his myrmidons no longer even have the right to be regarded as opponents of equal rank ('And only my equal will take my life'). Despite suffering from heart disease and fighting against shortness of breath, the poet takes on the greatness of an epic hero. These are tragic prophecies: the poet's voice can no longer be swept aside, though the human being will have to die in Siberia.[2]

One poem in the so-called 'Wolf cycle' refers directly to a convict in Siberia and to oppressive nightmares: 'Someone wonderful hurries me to forget something, / I feel I'm being smothered yet I want to live to the point of dying' (MM, 63; MN, 40). A poem dated 3 May 1931 is equally nightmarish. It portrays the Self as a rejected and 'unacknowledged' brother who has to look for an axe in the forest – for an old-fashioned beheading (MM, 73; MN, 44).

Even so, we can find an enchanting poem during this creative phase of dismal premonitions, a poem imbued with melancholy humour and dedicated to the Jewish musician Alexander Gertsovich, who always seems to be practising the same Schubert sonata.[3] The Mandelstams did in fact have a neighbour who practised the piano in an adjoining room in the communal dwelling on Starosadsky Lane. Solace is offered to the musician. The poet also attempts to comfort himself:

---

2 The poem about the 'wolfhound century': R. Dutli, *Ossip Mandelstam*, 257–72.

3 The Gertsovich poem and 10 Starosadsky Lane: L. Vidgof, *Moskva Mandel'shtama*, 137–44.

Isn't it dark outside
Alexander Herzowitz?
Give it up Alexander Scherzowitz,
What's the use?

Let the Italian girl
Fly after Schubert
On a narrow sledge
Across the crunching snow.

We're not afraid to die
With the dove music,
And then to hang like a black
Coat on the hook.

Alexander Heartsowitz,
It's all been played before.
Give it up Alexander Scherzowitz,
What's the use?
(MM, 61; MN, 40)

The 'Cherry Brandy' poem from the same month of March 1931 ('It's only maddening cherry brandy, / Angel mine!' MM, 55) was composed in the zoological museum on Bolshaia Nikitskaia Street, during a small party. Here Mandelstam was lubricated with Caucasian wine given to him by the circle of Moscow zoologists whom he had got to know through Boris Kuzin, the friend he had found in Armenia. He suddenly stood up and started to walk up and down, murmuring the words of the new poem.[4] Nadezhda thought it was addressed to her ('Mary, angel, drink your cocktail'). But the appearance of the name 'Mary' would immediately remind the Russian reader of a character from Alexander Pushkin's short tragedy *The Feast during the Plague* (1830). There is no need to think very hard about the plague Mandelstam had in mind: the poem is about the plague of the Stalin era. It contains motifs such as shame, salty foam on the lips, emptiness and poverty, which strongly urge the reader not to be misled

4 The 'Cherry Brandy' poem: Dutli, *Ossip Mandelstam*, 94–7; R. Dutli, *Europas zarte Hände*, 114–15.

by the merriness of the drinking song into ignoring the wretchedness of the actual situation.

A provocative and sarcastic tone has entered the poems, which can best be heard in another drinking song, the 'Asti Spumante' poem of April 1931, in which the narrator drinks to everything he has been accused of.

I drink to military asters, to all that I'm censured about,
To the Aristo's fur coat, to asthma, to the jaundiced Petersburg day,
To the music of pines in Savoie, petrol on the Champs-Elysées
To roses in a Rolls-Royce saloon, to Parisian pictures' oil paint,
I drink to the surf of Biscay, to a jug of cream from the Alps,
To English girls' red-headed hauteur, and distant colonial quinine;
I drink but still have to choose between wines:
Sparkling Asti Spumante or Châteauneuf-du-Pape …
(MM, 69; FP, 74)

The poem has a bitter overtone when one bears in mind that the poet who is drinking to his magnificent fur coat and his Rolls-Royce was already finding it difficult to procure the most basic food supplies each day. The supposedly 'aristocratic' or 'bourgeois' fur coat attributed to him was the moth-eaten second-hand raccoon coat he had acquired in Rostov on Don! The 'military asters', the flowery images and epaulettes on military uniforms, refer to the allegation that the poet was cheering on the 'militarist and imperialist West'; this was a particularly absurd accusation to direct at a poet who in 1916 had created 'Menagerie', an ode to peace. He was also censured for his lack of engagement with socialist construction and his excessive interest in Europe. No wonder the drinking song turned into an ironic little hymn to Europe, with its range of diverse countries. The two kinds of wine with which the poem ends are playful images of Italian and French culture, indeed of the culture of Europe in general. Mandelstam's deliberate 'rudeness' and impudence were not restricted to his explicitly political poems.[5]

It was encouraging that his Armenia cycle of poems was printed in March 1931 in the journal *Novyi Mir* (no. 3). His former fellow Acmeist Mikhail Zenkevich was a member of the editorial board. But even Zenkevich had not been able to get the politically explosive poems of

5 The 'Asti Spumante' poem: Dutli, *Ein Fest mit Mandelstam*, 53–7.

March and April 1931 (the Wolf cycle) past his editorial colleagues, not to mention the censorship. Mandelstam now presented ten more poems. But when only one of them was accepted for printing, he wrote on 3 July 1931 to the chief editor of *Novyi Mir*, Vyacheslav Polonsky, that he could not allow this poem to be printed in isolation. It would 'give the reader, from whom I am alienated enough as it is, a completely inadequate idea of the most recent stages of my poetry' (MR, 208).

Mandelstam wrote to his father in the middle of May 1931 telling him of the 'literary drudgery' he was forced to undergo, his lack of money and his stubborn determination to continue writing:

> We only have enough money for tomorrow's lunch … A big poetry cycle I finished a little while ago, after Armenia, hasn't brought in a single kopek. I can't get anything printed. The journals moan and groan and can't make up their minds … I am completely resigned to the situation, I've not put anything forward, and I've asked for nothing … The most important thing, dear Papa, is to produce works of literature, but where they find a home is a matter of Indifference … Everyday trifles like this have not caused me to lay down my pen, I am working happily and well. (MR, 206)

The letter also refers to reproaches addressed by Mandelstam's father, who had just composed some amateurish verses in praise of the Five Year Plan, to his refractory son, who had become an outsider and an 'apostate'. Mandelstam's reply contains a candid political confession of faith:

> You speak of the repellent selfishness and egoism of your sons. That is no doubt true, but we are no better than the whole of our generation. You are younger than we are: you write verses on the Five Year Plan, and I cannot. It is a source of great happiness to me that at least for my father words like collectivism, revolution and so on are not merely empty sounds …
>
> Could I ever have imagined that I might one day hear a Bolshevik sermon from you? Coming out of your mouth, it resonates more strongly for me than if it came from anyone else. You have made the most important point: he who does not live in harmony with his epoch, he who hides from it, will never be able to give anything to humanity and will never be at peace with himself. What is old no longer exists, and

> you have grasped that so late, and so well. There is no longer a yesterday, there is only the remote past and the future. (MR, 204)

But where is the present? Mandelstam's restrained rejoinder is that under Stalinism it is suppressed, to be replaced by the promise of a 'bright future'. Despite his father's remonstrances, they do not become estranged. On the contrary, Mandelstam's closeness to his father – after he had previously distanced himself in *The Noise of Time* (1925) – continues to grow.

The letter also reports how his dreams, as a homeless nomad, of a 'tiny little house', his vague prospects and shy hopes, have all come to grief owing to the opposition of an obstinate department head who points to the '2,000 Red Army men waiting for accommodation'. Mandelstam goes on to say that he then turned to 'authoritative comrades' (from Bukharin's circle?) who were of the opinion that 'I too was mobilised, in my way, and I too was standing in a queue' (MR, 205). The mobilised poet's dreams of accommodation were dashed to the ground, but in May 1931 a small miracle occurred, although not on the housing front.

After the poems of March and April, full of presentiments of violence, deportation and execution, after his rebellion against 'Moscow the whore' and the 'six-fingered lie', after all his bitter exorcisms, the poet now promises to confront his epoch in a freer and more open way. He does not barricade himself in Starosadsky Lane to write against a dishonest epoch, but walks through Moscow for hour after hour in order to absorb the new reality. Several poems contain commands, direct exhortations, springlike outbursts of vitality. The 7 June 1931 poem, for instance, which begins with the words: 'That's enough sulking! Shove the papers in the desk drawer!'

> I'll bet that I'm not dead yet
> And like a jockey, I'll stake my neck
> That I can still play tricks
> On the racetrack
>
> I am conscious that the beautiful year
> Thirty-one is blooming in cherry blossom,
> That the rain-moist earthworms are plumper,
> And all of Moscow is going sailing.
> (MM, 83; MN, 47)

In the poem 'Midnight in Moscow' (May/4 June 1931) he issues a threefold command: 'Get away! Don't ask for anything! Don't complain!' (MM, 79; MN, 46) In free verses and snapshots of reality the poetic rambler celebrates the 'sumptuously Buddhist summer', the night-time tram repairs, the parks, the museums and the crowds of 'chloroformed' people streaming out of the cinema 'in urgent need of oxygen' (what dreary propaganda films were they forced to view?). Mandelstam's enigmatic wit and trenchant vision allow him to get a fresh grip on his era. He is even able, significantly, to retract the statement in the poem of January 1924 denying his own contemporaneity ('No, Never Was I Anyone's Contemporary'). Now he offers a different kind of provocation:

> It's about time you knew, I too am a man of my time.
> I live in the age of the Moscow Clothes Co-op.
> Look how badly my jacket fits;
> How I walk and talk.
> If you tried to tear me from the age,
> I swear you'd break your neck.
> (MM, 79; MN, 46)

Mandelstam now prescribes a rejuvenation cure for himself. Many of his contemporaries confirmed that though only forty years old, he had aged terribly early. His teeth were decayed, he had heart trouble, he had breathing difficulties and he walked with a stick. But, in the summer of 1931, he invokes the impatience of the living. This happens in the poem 'After Having Dipped One's Little Finger', which ends with a hymn to the shining dark backs of young Tatar street workers and calls on the reader to take pleasure in restlessness:

> Every day I find it more difficult to breathe,
> But meanwhile I cannot gamble for time.
> Only the heart of man and horse
> Are born to enjoy the race.
> (MM, 101; MN, 52)

It was as if he wanted to defend himself with special energy against premature ageing. 'Still far from patriarch or sage': that is how a ten-stanza poem written in the same summer of 1931 begins. The poem evokes day-to-day urban existence in vivid poetic detail. There are street photographers, telephone conversations, hawkers, second-hand books, a Chinese laundry, squealing tramcars, asphalt and scaffolding ('When Leninist houses first rise'). The conclusion he reaches: 'I do not live, yet seem to live.' But the final stanza demonstrates his isolation, and the painful absence of a genuine conversation partner:

> But how I'd love to speak my mind
> To play the fool, to spit out truth,
> Send spleen to the dogs, to the devil, to hell,
> Take someone's arm and say: 'Be so kind,
> I think your way lies the same as mine.'
> (MM, 105; FP, 76)

This handful of poems, which reflect a markedly free and open interaction with the present day, does not, however, show us a poet who is reconciled with his epoch and is willing to conform and adapt to it. Pointed remarks about the age and his contemporaries repeatedly come to the surface. He forces himself to declare a renewed love for 'the Moscow laws', but he has no illusions about the violence that controls the present: 'In Moscow there's the laurel cherry and the telephones / And the days are distinguished by executions' (MM, 85; AA, 135; MN, 48). Even so, these are the poems of a person who wanted to go through Moscow with his eyes open, driven by the 'hunger to see' awakened in Armenia, and invoked in another fragment, dated 6 June 1931:

> Don't focus, just click, dear Kodak,
> The eye is a lens in a bird at a banquet
> And not a piece of glass. More light and shade,
> More! More!
> The retina is hungry …
> (MM, 87; AA, 137; MN, 48)

In June, the Mandelstams moved for a few months into a room on Bolshaia Polianka Street in the Zamoskvorechie district, the old merchants' quarter which lay opposite the Kremlin 'on the other side of the Moskva'. The room they rented until autumn was in the house of a lawyer who was often away, and it offered peace and quiet, something Mandelstam was much in need of, as he was working intensively on his prose essay, *Journey to Armenia.*

But the neighbours were surly, and they communicated a depressing picture of the new working class: 'Grim, Philistine families lived beside me. God had failed to provide these people with the gift of friendliness, which does after all brighten life up' (AA, 18). They all check up on one another, he added in his notebook, and they insist doggedly on the strict maintenance of the rules of communal living (AA, 67). When an old lime tree is felled in the courtyard, Mandelstam identifies himself with it ('He despised his attackers and the pike's teeth of the saw') and he mocks 'the incompetent executors of a shameful verdict' (AA, 19). These wretched surroundings inevitably made a strong contrast to the freshly awakened memory of Armenia's animated life: 'In no other time or place have I felt the watermelon emptiness of Russia more strongly' (AA, 19; NT, 201). The contrast between Russian emptiness and Armenian fullness would be one of the critical threads running through the emerging travelogue.

Journey to Armenia also became a book about a way of seeing that was unjaded and fresh. It celebrates the travelling, plunging, greedy eye: 'Calmly, without excitement – as the Tatar children in Alushta bathe their horses – you should plunge your eyes into a new material environment. And remember, the eye is a noble, but wilful, animal' (AA, 36; NT, 212). The chapter 'The French', which highlights Cézanne ('Greetings, Cézanne! Good old grandfather!'), Matisse ('the Persian whimsies of a Paris master!'), Van Gogh ('cheap vegetable pigments ... barking colours'), Renoir ('blisters on the palm'), Signac ('a sun made of maize') and others, presents to us what this liberated, sovereign eye can achieve.

Here, the eye is a universal organ which 'is possessed of hearing' (AA, 37), a fundamental organ which unites and inspires all the other senses. The whole of the chapter on the French impressionists and pointillists is a bold hymn to the possibility of dynamically viewing a picture independently of all preconceived ideas. It is peppered with impertinent comments, and it is an invitation to risk the adventure of seeing. This was not just a matter of aesthetics. It also implied a free vision unappropriated by any ideology. *Journey to Armenia* rejects any attempt to view reality through ready-made patterns.

But where could Mandelstam have seen those French pictures? It was in the 'State Museum of New Western Art' on the old Moscow Prechistenka (later 21 Kropotkin Street), in the former 'Palais Morozov'. The museum had been established in 1928 to house the paintings previously owned by two renowned pre-revolutionary private collectors, Sergei Shchukin and Ivan Morozov, which Lenin had nationalised. Mandelstam visited this museum frequently and enthusiastically. He called it the 'painting embassy'. *Journey to Armenia* also reports how he discovered a book by Paul Signac in a house on Bolshaia Iakimanka Street (where Boris Kuzin lived). The book was entitled *From Eugène Delacroix to Neo-Impressionism* (1899, Russian translation 1913), and Mandelstam experienced a kind of epiphany when he read it:

> Signac was trumpeting on his chivalric horn the final, ripe gathering of the Impressionists. Into the bright camps he summoned Zouaves, burnooses, and the red skirts of Algerian women.
>
> At the very first sounds of this theory, which inspires one and strengthens the nerves, I felt the shiver of novelty; it was as if someone had called me by name …
>
> It seemed to me as though I had exchanged my hooflike dusty city shoes for light Muslim slippers.
>
> In all my life I have seen no more than a silkworm. (AA, 17; NT, 200)

This led to a further extension of the Armenia project. Now his journey took him not just to the source of civilisation and sense perception, but to the origins of modern painting, indeed of modernity as such. It was impossible for him to mention Russian avant-garde painting, which had already been condemned as 'formalist', but he wanted to lay bare its roots in French modernism. Here too his Armenian watchword applied: back to the source!

The adventure of seeing enriched Mandelstam's perceptions in more than one way in 1931. It led him to penetrate more deeply into history. The mysterious poem 'Canzone', dated 26 May 1931, dreams the dream of Armenia once again, but it superimposes the 'promised land', Palestine, on the Armenian landscape. Mandelstam praises the sharp vision of Zeus, the father of the Gods, who can overcome space and time thanks to the 'Zeiss binoculars' he has received from King David, the psalmist, as a present ('King David's precious gift'). In 'Canzone' Mandelstam combines the three cultural streams that created the atmosphere he bathed in. The poem is a manifesto demonstrating his conviction that he is 'the last Hellenic-Jewish-Christian poet'. It also marks the zenith of his new awareness of Jewishness:

> Thus I'll quit these Hyperborean parts
> To steep in vision destiny's finale
> And say Selah to the Chief of the Jews
> For his crimson caress.[6]

'Selah' is a Hebrew formula of greeting, praise and thankfulness used in the Psalms, and it is an expression directed at the nameless God, meaning 'So be it, forever'. The 'protector of the Jews' is for Mandelstam not Moses, who led the exodus from Egypt and proclaimed the Ten Commandments, but King David, the psalmist and poet, who is mentioned twice. This is implied by the emblematic formula 'Selah'.

In the second volume of her memoirs, in the chapter headed 'The Chief of the Jews', Nadezhda Mandelstam explains the origin of the mysterious expression 'crimson caress'. She points to Rembrandt's painting of around 1666, *The Return of the Prodigal Son*, which had impressed Mandelstam deeply on his many visits to the Hermitage Museum in Petersburg. The father, dressed in a red shoulder cape, places his hands on the shoulders of the son who has returned and is kneeling before him, in a gesture of forgiveness. A warm, reddish tone spreads out from the figure of the father. According to Nadezhda, Mandelstam commented: 'Look how kind hands can be.' The language of forgiving hands became the 'crimson caress' in the poem.[7]

The poem is a final statement of commitment to Jewishness by Mandelstam, the 'prodigal son'. In it, after his rejection of the 'Jewish chaos' experienced in his childhood and youth, and depicted in *The Noise of Time* (1925), the gradual road to reconciliation reaches its endpoint. After the prose sketch 'Kiev' (1926), with its concentration on the Jewish quarter of the city, after the portrait of the actor Mikhoels (also written in 1926), which showed his fascination for the 'Jewish Dionysius', and finally after *Fourth Prose* (1929–1930), with its proud commitment to 'blood, burdened

6 MM, 75; AA, 127; M. Hayward, 'Translation of the Poem *Canzone*', 603.

7 The 'crimson caress': N. Mandelstam, *Hope Abandoned*, 613. An important chapter of this book, 'The Chief of the Jews', is missing from the German translation *Generation ohne Tränen* (1975) [but it is included in the English translation (Mandelstam, *Hope Abandoned*, 613–23)].

with its inheritance from sheep breeders, patriarchs and kings', Mandelstam approaches the 'chief of the Jews' in the poem 'Canzone' and greets him gratefully with the psalmist's formula 'Selah'.

Of course, Mandelstam's return to the 'house of his father' did not involve a return to the Orthodox *shtetl* Judaism of his paternal grandparents. It was impossible to reverse his assimilation into Russian culture. It is worth considering Nadezhda Mandelstam's comment that her husband feared the 'awesome, totalitarian power' of the God of the Old Testament. For him, the doctrine of the Trinity introduced by Christianity had overcome the undivided power of the Jewish God. His return to Jewishness was therefore not religiously motivated. Nor, as Nadezhda points out, was it a response to the 'call of the blood'. Mandelstam, she said, had returned to Jewishness 'through European thought and culture', bearing in mind the 'European world in which he lived'.[8] The 'tremendous artistic power' he had discovered for himself in the 'Mikhoels' portrait of 1926 bound him to Jewishness. From then on, Mandelstam the European no longer wanted to abandon the Jewish element in his 'Hellenic-Jewish-Christian' poetic synthesis. To exclude any one of these three elements would be to lose sight of the whole Mandelstam. With his 'crimson caress', Rembrandt pointed the way back to the chief of the Jews, whom he regarded as an artist and a poet. King David's gift was now more precious than it had ever been.

8 M. fears the might of the Old Testament God but believes the Christian doctrine of the Trinity has overcome it: N. Mandelstam, *Hope Against Hope*, 221 ('The Bessarabian Carriage'); his return to Jewishness 'through European thought and culture': N. Mandel'shtam, *Kniga Tret'ia*, 161.

19

Power Is Repulsive, Like the Barber's Fingers

(Moscow and the Crimea 1932–1933)

In autumn 1931, Nadezhda had to enter the Botkin clinic in Moscow. Mandelstam had already told his father in a letter sent in May that she was suffering from intestinal spasms, nausea and weight loss (MR, 207). As in 1929, when Nadezhda had her operation in Kyiv, Mandelstam worried about his 'little sun', and sent her 'cream and stewed fruit' to make her stronger (MR, 210). He did not leave her side, staying in the hospital overnight. Nadezhda wrote later that his sense of smell improved during this period. While his journey to Armenia and his involvement with the French painters had renewed his eyesight, the Botkin hospital had renewed his sense of smell.[1] A poem looking back on his life ('No, It's Not a Migraine': WH, 55) concludes with two sharply perceived sense impressions: the sound of a piece of gauze being torn and the smell of carbolic acid. Nadezhda thought they originated from the days he spent with her there.

In January 1932, the pair moved into a tiny room in the Writers' House at 25 Tverskoy Boulevard, where, ten years earlier, Mandelstam had first

1 M.'s sense of smell improves when he visits Nadezhda in the Botkin hospital: N. Mandelstam, *Hope Abandoned*, 442.

come into conflict with the All-Russian Union of Writers, and from which he had departed in fury. It was a sad return, but it put a roof over his head. Now, he lived in the right-hand wing, in a damp room of ten square metres. It was a kind of broom cupboard in the House of Soviet Writers, in which 'the drinking-water tap is located in a decaying lavatory, the walls are covered in mould, the dividing walls are just wooden boards, the floor is icy cold, and so on', as he complained in a letter to the responsible party official, Ivan Gronsky (MR, 212). And even this 'privilege' could only be acquired because Bukharin intervened yet again, providing him in addition with a miserable pension of 200 roubles because of his 'contribution to Russian literature in the past', although he was now generally 'useless' to Soviet literature. The decision is dated 23 February 1932. After he was exiled, he would lose this income again.[2]

Mandelstam was now a poverty-stricken early pensioner, declared useless to the state at a time when, according to Stalin, 'engineers of human souls' were needed. On 23 April 1932, the momentous party decree was announced, liquidating all existing writers' organisations, including the RAPP, and calling for the creation of one single Union of Soviet Writers. It meant the definitive enforcement of conformity in literature, which had already had to say goodbye in 1929 to its experimental phase. Now began the period of preparation for the doctrine of socialist realism, which was laid down as compulsory in 1934 in the statutes of the newly formed Writers' Union.

In the spring, Mandelstam's living situation improved, to the extent that he was allowed, after a certain amount of vacillation by the 'Housing Administration Troika', to move out of the damp broom cupboard in the House of Soviet Writers into a lighter, drier room next door. The year 1932 brought for Mandelstam a wide range of intellectual adventures, which somewhat compensated for his marginality. He was able to think more deeply about biology and the theory of evolution, thanks to his friend Boris Kuzin and his colleagues at the Zoological Museum on Nikitskaia Street. The naturalists Lamarck, Buffon and Linnaeus had made his 'mature years more colourful', but the whale's jawbone in the vestibule of the museum had 'awakened a child-like admiration for science', he wrote in his notebook (AA, 79).

2 The pension arranged for M. by Bukharin: L. Vidgof, *Moskva Mandel'shtama*, 98.

An entire chapter of his *Journey to Armenia* is devoted to his involvement with these naturalists. In addition, on 21 April 1932, the fiftieth anniversary of Charles Darwin's death, the journal *For Communist Education*, which was the organ of the People's Commissariat of Enlightenment, published an essay by Mandelstam on Darwin's 'literary style'. Here is a poet showing appreciation of the great zoologist as a writer. Darwin's attitude to nature, he writes, was that of a war reporter, an interviewer, a daring reporter. He notes 'how immensely well trained are his powers of visual analysis', and he praises the 'tremendous freshness' of his descriptions of nature, and the way he avoids rhetorical flourishes (GD, 93–110).

The essay on Darwin was published thanks to Alexander Morgulis, who worked for the journal and also arranged for Nadezhda to work there for a short time. Mandelstam had formed a friendship with Morgulis in 1927, when he was living in Detskoe Selo. Morgulis's wife, the pianist Isa Khantsyn, often played for Mandelstam, who was an enraptured listener. One peculiar piece of evidence for Mandelstam's special relationship with Morgulis is a series of what he called 'Margulettes'. These were short comic poems, which always started with the words 'Old man Margulis' (Morgulis was born in 1898, and was therefore seven years younger than Mandelstam: his life would end in a labour camp in 1938, in the same year as Mandelstam's ended). One example: 'The eyes of old man Margulis / Pursue me and rob me of sleep, / In them I read with horror: / "For the communist educational system!"' (BT, 143).

At the start of the 1930s, then, Mandelstam rediscovered his old gaiety, which had often been absent during the 'silent period' of the second half of the 1920s. Now, he again enjoyed improvising amusing poems, which often popped out when he was with groups of friends in pleasant conversation, over tea, or a bottle of wine, as Nadezhda recalls (BT, 168). He also continued his series of ironical self-portraits: 'Hat, bought at least ten years ago / In the Universal State Department Store, / Under you, I inevitably find, / I look as old as a bishop' (BT, 145).

He also created comic portraits of the group of zoologists around his friend Kuzin. One is devoted to the zoologist Yuly Vermel, who was an enthusiast for the philosopher Immanuel Kant and continually quoted him, a practice Mandelstam alluded to in a comic poem playing on the Russian expression 'sobaku s'yel' ('he has eaten the dog', or as one might say, 'he's completely mad about him'):

Vermel was well versed in Kant,
No, more than that, he burned for him
Completely canted you might say,
Just like his aunt he kenned old Kant.
The philosopher ran in his black frock coat
So rapid was his walk!
Vermel ate the dog of Kant
And Kant, the dog, consumed him whole!
(BT, 147)

Meetings with the zoologists were not just occasions of sociability and friendship; they also involved a serious confrontation with biological themes – and with the age they were living in. In a poem written in May 1932 about the French naturalist Jean Baptiste de Lamarck (1744–1829) – Boris Kuzin was a neo-Lamarckian – Mandelstam imagines himself dropping down Lamarck's scale of living beings, making a depressing descent from one stage of development to a lower one, a 'descent into hell', which resulted in a loss of sense perceptions and a cooling of the blood.

We went past the orders of the insects
That have shot glasses for eyes
He said all of nature is in fractures,
Vision ends – you see for the last time

He said: sonority is over
No more Mozart – you loved him in vain
Now begins the silence of cobwebs,
An abyss beyond our strength.
(MM, 113; PO, 24)

When one bears in mind that, in his Armenia texts, Mandelstam celebrated the human senses, including both sight and hearing, this descent into blindness and deafness is felt even more painfully. In the Lamarck poem, he cries out against the 'cobwebbed silence' of the Stalin era, and against determinism, the blind belief in progress and the notion of the 'new man'.

For Mandelstam, the year 1932 was also dominated by a fascination with the sound of languages. He enthusiastically started to learn Italian, so as to be able to read medieval and Renaissance poets such as Petrarch, Ariosto and Tasso. The poem 'Novellino' (22 May 1932) (MM, 123; MN, 61–2) picks up an episode from Dante's *Divina Commedia*, the work to which, a year later, he would devote his most important essay the 'Conversation about Dante'. The Dante essay includes a comment on his sensuous enjoyment of the Italian language, which has now begun to reveal its treasures to him:

> When I began to study Italian ... I suddenly understood that the centre of gravity of the speech movements had been shifted closer to the lips, to the external mouth. The tip of the tongue suddenly acquired a place of honour. The sound rushed towards the canal lock of the teeth. Another observation that struck me was the infantile quality of Italian phonetics, its beautiful childlike quality, its closeness to infant babbling, a sort of immemorial Dadaism. (GD, 116; SE, 28)

Increasingly alienated as he was from the contemporary Soviet reader, Mandelstam turned his attention to the Russian poets of the past. In May 1932, he wrote a poem in which he left a jokingly ironic legacy to Tyutchev, Baratynsky and Lermontov ('Guess why you've given / Tyutchev a dragon-fly': MM, 127; MN, 63). On 18 June, there followed a poem dedicated to the 'tender' classicist Konstantin Batyushkov (1781–1855), who was an equally great admirer of Italian poetry and wove phrases from Petrarch and Torquato Tasso into his Russian verses (MM, 129). In a cycle of 'Verses on Russian Poetry', Mandelstam addresses Gavril Derzhavin, the great eighteenth-century writer of odes, as if they were old friends, and asks him to join the group: 'Sit down, Derzhavin, make yourself comfortable' (MM, 131; MN, 64). Distance is gaily abolished, and all chronological obstacles are surmounted. Osip's salutations fall somewhere between the waggish and the disrespectful, but they also express the pain felt by a poet whose access to his contemporaries has been barred.

In August 1932, Mandelstam wrote 'To the German Language', dedicated to his friend Boris Kuzin, who was an enthusiastic admirer of German culture. The poem is a spiritual journey which leads him back to eighteenth-century Germany. In it, Mandelstam asserts his solidarity with Ewald Christian von Kleist (1715–1759), the poet and friend of Gotthold Ephraim Lessing, who was killed at the battle of Kunersdorf during the

Seven Years' War, fighting against the Russians as a Prussian officer. Poetry can form a bridge over epochs and languages; it breaks through into the unknown, scorning all personal danger:

> To my own ruin, to my own contradiction,
> Like a moth flying toward a midnight flame,
> I want to make an exit from our speech.
> For all that I will owe to it forever
>
> There is between us praise without flattery,
> And friendship to the hilt, without dissembling,
> So let us learn some seriousness and honour.
> In the West, from a foreign family.
> (MM, 139; PO, 26)

The poem takes us into the Valhalla of poets and to Frankfurt, a city in whose Jewish ghetto Mandelstam's forefathers perhaps once lived. It conjures up a meeting between Jewish mysticism and the eighteenth-century German Enlightenment, a marriage between the Kabbala and Reason. And it is also a hidden homage to both his mother and his father: it recalls Emil Mandelstam's enthusiasm for the German poets as well as the Haskala Judaism of his mother's family.

It is also, not least, a greeting to Heinrich Heine, who had also made his way out of the element of his own language into the company of foreigners. Mandelstam twice calls upon the 'nightingale God' in the poem, quoting Heine's poem 'In the Beginning Was the Nightingale'.[3] Poetry thus combines Kleist, Heine and Mandelstam into one single poetic figure. The 'nightingale's fever' (TR, 57), first invoked in 1918, was still acutely felt. In August 1932 – the year before Hitler came to power! – Mandelstam foresaw the coming of 'new plagues' and 'seven-year massacres', but despite this he proclaimed his confidence in the German language and in the primeval book of poetry he imagines:

> A foreign language will be my sanctuary;
> As long before I dared to be born,
> I was a letter, I was a line in a vineyard,

3 The 'nightingale God' as a quotation from Heine: O. Ronen, 'Osip Mandel'shtam', 17; R. Dutli, 'Das bin ich. Das ist der Rhein', 79–81.

I was a book you dreamed
…
God of the Nightingale, they still recruit me
For new plagues, for seven-year massacres.
The sound has narrowed, the words hiss and mutiny,
But you are alive, and with you I'm at peace.
(MM, 141; MN, 67)

All these fantasies about Russian poetry date from the summer of 1932, as does the dream of the primeval book. A new conflict, heavy with consequences, quickly pulled Mandelstam back to Soviet reality: the Sargidzhan affair. The young Soviet writer Sergei Borodin (who used the pseudonym Amir Sargidzhan) was Mandelstam's 'neighbour' and had presumably been instructed to spy on him in the Writers' House. After an argument, he forced his way into Mandelstam's room and struck his wife. The dispute had started over a debt Sargidzhan owed. Mandelstam had lent him either forty or seventy-five roubles and he could not, or would not, pay the money back to the poet, who was himself constantly short of money.

On 13 September 1932, a court of arbitration set up by the Writers' Union sat to decide on the issue, under the chairmanship of the 'Red Count', the officially approved Soviet novelist Alexei Tolstoy. This 'court of honour' condemned both parties: the violent debtor Sargidzhan, and the arrogant Mandelstam, who did not conceal his contempt for Sargidzhan. But Tolstoy is said to have spoken disdainfully to Mandelstam. According to one witness, Semyon Lipkin, the majority of those present sided with Sargidzhan. They were Soviet writers who had conformed, just as he had. Mandelstam, on the other hand, was treated as a 'former poet' and a troublesome contemporary, who was quite likely to cause a scandal. Another witness reports how furious Mandelstam was about the attitude of the court that was judging him: he jumped on a table, shook his small fist and shouted out in indignation.[4]

As in August 1923, when he resigned from the All-Russian Writers' Union, as in December 1929 when he wrote the 'Open Letter to Soviet Writers', Mandelstam felt humiliated and deprived of his rights, and he replied with a written protest to the Moscow Writers' Committee: 'An act

4 The Sargidzhan affair: Vidgof, *Moskva Mandel'shtama*, 106–8.

of violence worthy of a pimp or a police henchman' had been presented 'as a matter of honour', while Sargidzhan had been made his 'legal hangman' (MR, 213–14). It was clear to Mandelstam that the beating administered to his wife was actually meant for him. This was by no means the end of the affair: in May 1934, in Leningrad, Mandelstam publicly slapped Alexei Tolstoy in the face. He was arrested a week later.

Mandelstam the outsider was not on good terms with many of his colleagues in the Writers' House. He had a liking and affection for the peasant poet Sergei Klychkov (who was shot in 1937) and this was reciprocated. Lev Bruni and his wife often came to visit the Mandelstams: Bruni was the man who painted the renowned 'blue portrait' of him in 1916. He continued to have good relations with Viktor Shklovsky. But the writers of the inner circle in the 'Herzen House' were hostile. Their hostility was reciprocated. Mandelstam felt that he was completely misunderstood by his epoch. His verdict on his contemporaries, according to Nadezhda Volpin was this: 'They don't know who I am.'[5]

If he had needed official confirmation that he had been brushed aside by the literary authorities, he had simply to open volume six of the *Encyclopaedia of Soviet Literature*, which had just been published. There one could read that Mandelstam's work was 'the artistic expression of the consciousness of the big bourgeoisie', and that it was characterised by 'extreme fatalism', 'the coldness of an inner indifference to all current happenings' and an 'extreme bourgeois individualism'. The author of the article, Anatoly Tarasenkov, denounced his work as the 'coded ideological perpetuation of capitalism and its culture'. Ilya Ehrenburg would still express his indignation as late as 1961 over this dismissal of Mandelstam's work: 'It would be difficult to say anything more absurd about Mandelstam's poetry. Of all poets he was the one who least expressed the consciousness of the bourgeoisie, whether big, middle, or petty!' In conclusion, he made a devastating point which laid bare the mendacity and hypocrisy of the literati of the time: 'The article was written by a young critic, who came running to see me many times, enthusiastically showed me unpublished poems by Mandelstam, copied Mandelstam's works, had them bound, and gave them to his friends.'[6]

Two months after the deplorable verdict of the court of arbitration,

5 Nadezhda Volpin's memoirs: O. S. Figurnova and M. V. Figurnova, *Osip i Nadezhda Mandel'shtamy*, 91.

6 Ehrenburg's indignation over the entry on M. in the 1932 *Encyclopaedia of Soviet Literature*: I. Ehrenburg, *Men, Years – Life*, 107–8.

Mandelstam was able to take the offensive against the prejudice that he was an 'old poet' who had nothing more to say to his contemporaries. On 10 November 1932, he gave a reading in the editorial offices of *Literaturnaia Gazeta*, which were also located in the 'Herzen House'. This was the journal which had contributed decisively to the 1929 campaign against him. One witness, the avant-garde specialist Nikolai Khardzhiev, remembers a 'magnificent spectacle'. For two and a half hours, Mandelstam, a 'grey-bearded patriarch', enthralled his audience like a shaman, reciting all his new poems to them from memory. His 'incantations' were so 'terrifying' that many of those present took fright. Even Boris Pasternak was shocked. After the reading he whispered to Mandelstam: 'I envy your freedom. For me you are a new Khlebnikov. And just as strange. But I need constraint.'[7]

At the end of 1932, Mandelstam spent some time in the writers' village of Peredelkino, near Moscow, and he wrote to his father from there. He told him that the Writers' Union had had to allow him to give two readings, 'so as to put a stop to unwelcome rumours'. 'The readings were carefully screened from the broader public, but they passed off splendidly and vigorously, which was something the organisers had not foreseen. The result: not a word about them in the press' (MR, 215). Every step he took, he wrote, had always met with obstacles, and the unnatural isolation continued as before. *Literaturnaia Gazeta* had at least printed a handful of his poems: 'Midnight in Moscow', 'To the German Language' and – this was certainly a mistake by the censor – the 'Leningrad' poem of December 1930. In the first months of 1933, Mandelstam gave four more relatively 'public' readings, two in Leningrad and two in Moscow. The Writers' Union had the power to regulate such events by restricting the number of tickets issued or by inviting politically 'reliable' listeners. Nevertheless, these last public performances by Mandelstam were unexpectedly successful. He had a beard at that time, and he resembled a biblical prophet. As a shaman, who presented all his poems from memory and with unconcealed emotion, he was in his element. On 22 February 1933, he gave a reading in Leningrad, leaning arrogantly on the back of a chair, without even looking at his audience. According to Anastasia Tsvetaeva, his attitude delivered the message: I don't need you.[8]

---

7 Khardzhiev on the 1932 poetry reading: B. Eikhenbaum, *O Literature*, 532; the commentary section in the Russian edition of Mandelstam's works, Mandel'shtam, *Sochineniia v Dvukh Tomakh*, vol. 1, 502.

8 Anastasia Tsvetaeva's memoirs: Figurnova and Figurnova, *Osip i Nadezhda Mandel'shtamy*, 160. Anastasia was Marina Tsvetaeva's younger sister.

On 14 March 1933, Mandelstam gave a reading in the Moscow Polytechnic Museum, where Mayakovsky had once thundered out his verses to the public. When he stepped onto the stage, he was applauded vigorously and at length, something he himself found astounding. More admirers of his poetry had turned up than the organisers would have liked to see, and the evening turned into a triumph. The literary critic Boris Eikhenbaum introduced the occasion and gave an appreciation of Mandelstam's work. When Mandelstam thought he had heard someone make a critical remark about Mayakovsky, he jumped up and called out loudly that Mayakovsky was the 'whetstone of all recent poetry'. These complimentary remarks are Mandelstam's last reference to his fellow poet, after the critical comments in the essays of 1922–1923 and his expression of shock in April 1930 after hearing the 'overwhelming news' that Mayakovsky had committed suicide (AA, 70). On this occasion, Mandelstam also read some of his earlier poems from the *Stone* period; the applause continued for so long that he had to give several encores.

At the second Leningrad reading, given on 2 March 1933 in the House of the Press, he was provocatively asked whether he was still 'the same Mandelstam, the Acmeist'. After a short pause for reflection, he gave this reply: 'I am the same Mandelstam, who was the friend of his friends, the comrade of his comrades, and was, is and will remain the contemporary of Akhmatova.' That was also an unspoken – and dangerous – endorsement of his 'comrade-in-arms' Nikolai Gumilyov, shot in 1921. This was at a time when statements of solidarity were inadvisable. Disappearances were taking place without attracting much attention. The first arrest of the polymath Pavel Florensky, in May 1928, had shaken Mandelstam considerably at the time. He was re-arrested on 26 February 1933 and condemned to ten years in a labour camp. He would be shot in Solovki in December 1937.

On 3 April 1933, Mandelstam's friend Boris Kuzin was arrested for the first time on account of some incautious remarks he had made. Kuzin had independent political and scientific opinions, for which he was highly esteemed by Mandelstam. His views repeatedly brought him into difficulties with the authorities. Now Mandelstam made a desperate attempt to intervene in his favour. On 5 April, he wrote a letter to the Soviet writer Marietta Shaginian, stalwart author of 'production novels', and a party member with access to those in power. Mandelstam had met her in Armenia, when she was on an 'official mission' to celebrate the First

Five Year Plan. Now Mandelstam sent her his new prose work, *Journey to Armenia*, and a detailed plea for Kuzin's release, parts of which were bound to be discordant to official ears. Shaginian had already remonstrated with her ideologically unreliable colleague in Armenia. 'You always upbraided me for failing to hear the music of materialism, or dialectics – or whatever it's called, it's all one to me', he wrote. With Kuzin, he added, he had 'dissected the systems of idealism into their tiniest material filaments and laughed over the naïve and crudely idealist air bubbles of a vulgar materialism'. The letter also testified to Kuzin's significance for him personally: 'He and he alone is to be thanked for bringing the period of the "mature Mandelstam" into literature ... My conversation partner, my second self, has been snatched from me' (MR, 217–18).

Kuzin was freed after spending a week in the Lubyanka. Osip and Nadezhda Mandelstam were on the point of travelling to the Crimea, and they spontaneously decided to take him along as well. On 18 April 1933, the three arrived in Stary Krym, a town founded by Tatar khans in the south-east of the peninsula. There they were accommodated by Nina Grin, the widow of the writer Alexander Grin. Renewed acquaintance with the Crimea was a shock to Mandelstam. The effects of the forced collectivisation of agriculture (in the framework of the First Five Year Plan) were visible everywhere. On 1 February 1930, Stalin had ordered the 'liquidation of the kulaks as a class', thereby bringing unimaginable misery to the peasants of Ukraine, and the Don and Kuban regions of Russia. The expropriation of the kulaks did not just affect the large farmers, who were either immediately shot as 'counter-revolutionaries' or driven out of their confiscated farms and deported to Siberia. The wave of liquidation also hit the moderately well-off middle peasants, and even some small peasants, because the 'numbers in the official plan' had to be made up. The intention was to use the 'weapon of hunger' to force the peasants who remained behind into the collective farms. It was 'the greatest human catastrophe a people has ever suffered at the hands of its own government in peacetime', writes the historian Günther Stökl. It was implemented by the GPU, reinforced by liquidation detachments and 'workers' brigades', the armed mobs of the cities; chaos was unleashed systematically. Stalin headed his notorious *Pravda* article of 2 March 1930 'Dizzy with Success'. Agriculture had been ruined. The massacre caused food supply problems in the Soviet Union which lasted for decades.

Starving peasants were also wandering around in Stary Krym, begging for a piece of bread or breaking into houses to find something edible. The Mandelstams had to bring their meagre supply of bread for a whole month from Moscow, because there was no bread in the Crimea. Mandelstam, devastated by the hunger in the Crimea, wrote one of his most caustic political poems in May 1933:

> It's a cold spring.
> The Crimea is starving and fearful
> And as guilty as it was under Wrangel
>
> Nature can't recognise her own face:
> The refugees from the Kuban and the Ukraine are nightmare shadows.
> (MM, 143; MN, 68)

The poem found its way into the dossier of the investigating judge when Mandelstam was cross-examined in May 1934 in the Lubyanka. He had used the expression 'as it was under Wrangel', in other words 'as it was in the civil war' (between Reds and Whites). This was a sharp condemnation of Stalin's perfidious use of the 'weapon of hunger' against the peasants.

The paradoxes of a poet's life: in Stary Krym, Mandelstam's attention was focused not only on the excesses of Stalin's murderous collectivisation policy, but also at the same time on the Italian poets of the Renaissance, Ariosto and Tasso. The poetic and the political cannot always be clearly separated, however. In 'Ariosto', a poem on the author of *Orlando furioso* ('Raging Roland', 1505–1521), Mandelstam also castigates the contemporary Fascist Italy of Mussolini: 'Europe is cold. And Italy is dark. / Power is repulsive, like the barber's fingers' (MM, 145; PO, 30). The expression 'power is repulsive' was not meant to apply just to Mussolini.

Mandelstam's interest in foreign languages and Renaissance poets was not merely a hobby; it was a desperate attempt to break out into world poetry. He was tormented by feelings of guilt over this fascination for what was foreign. He had lost access to the contemporary reader, he was socially isolated, and so he tried to converse with the poets of the Middle Ages and the Renaissance. In a grim vision also produced in May 1933 ('Don't tempt yourself with foreign languages'), he sees a 'punishment for arrogance', a 'sponge soaked in vinegar', standing ready to be applied to the 'treacherous lips' of a man with impermissible enthusiasms (MM,

153; MN, 71). This allusion to the scene of the crucifixion is another of Mandelstam's prophecies of how his life will end.

There seems to be no salvation in sight for the 'friend of sound'. In the poem, his 'incorrigibility' is prophesied as insistently as his unavoidable execution. His devotion to the sounds of the foreign tongue, to European and world culture, was too strongly embedded in the foundations of his work to be jettisoned with ease. The concluding stanza of the poem 'Ariosto' demonstrates that he still felt himself to be a European. Confronted with the present 'coldness of Europe', he dreams of a utopian Europe of fraternal understanding, a Europe of the poets, in which the Italian Renaissance poet Ariosto and the modern Russian poet Mandelstam can each participate, in a unified area covering the Mediterranean and the Black Sea:

> Dear Ariosto, maybe a century shall pass –
> And we shall pour your azure and our black together
> Into one fraternal, vast, blue-black sea.
> We were there too. We too drank mead.
> (MM, 147; EW, 79)

The chasm between his poetry and Soviet literature had long since become unbridgeable. How deep it was already could be seen in May 1933, when Mandelstam's travelogue *Journey to Armenia* was printed in the Leningrad literary journal *Zvezda*. It would be the last publication of his work during his lifetime. The editor responsible for printing it, Tsezar Volpe, immediately lost his job. Volpe had defied the instructions of the censorship by including Mandelstam's re-telling of the old Armenian legend, in which coded references were made to the poet's own politically determined situation, with Stalin as the 'Assyrian', Bukharin as the 'educated eunuch' and Mandelstam himself as the vanquished poet-king.[9]

The scandal around Mandelstam's work now became all-embracing. He was subjected to destructive attacks in *Literaturnaia Gazeta* on 17 June 1933 and *Pravda* on 30 August 1933. It was asserted that instead of celebrating 'socialist achievements' such as mechanisation and collectivisation, he had sought out an immemorial Armenia, everlastingly true to

---

9 The scandal over the old Armenian legend, Volpe's dismissal: N. Mandelstam, *Hope Against Hope*, 315 ('Poetry Lovers').

itself. He was obviously not interested in an Armenia engaged in 'socialist construction' but rather in an Armenia which was biblical, eternal and yet continuously present. It was a complete provocation.

Hence, while Mandelstam was continuing his sojourn in hungry Crimea, black clouds were already gathering over him in the Soviet capital. On 28 May 1933, he moved from Stary Krym to Koktebel to live in the artists' refuge once owned by Maximilian Voloshin, already known to him because he had stayed there in the years 1915 and 1916. It had been converted after Voloshin's death in 1932 into a state-run rest home for writers. All his quarrels with Voloshin – such as the affair of the Dante edition which went missing during the civil war upheavals of 1920 – were now forgotten. Mandelstam climbed to Voloshin's grave high over the Gulf of Koktebel, and he wrote in his notebook a valedictory panegyric to the poet, who had been 'an honorary guardian of the wonderful accident of geology we call Koktebel', and had accomplished the 'outstanding Dantesque work of merging himself with the landscape' (GD, 193).

It is not an accident that the name of Dante comes to the surface here. While staying in Stary Krym, Mandelstam had already started to write an essay which would be one of his most important statements about the art of poetry: 'Conversation about Dante'. In long walks beside the Black Sea, along the gravelly shores of Koktebel, he had the idea of a 'conversation', for which he would find an unexpected interlocutor. The former Symbolist Andrei Bely was also staying at Koktebel in June and July 1933, while writing his book *Gogol's Artistry*. A group photograph exists, in which Mandelstam and Bely are sitting amid other summer visitors on the front steps of Voloshin's house in Koktebel. They are both looking at the photographer, but their thoughts are elsewhere – one with Gogol, the other with Dante. In this case as well, it was important for Mandelstam to draw a line under past conflicts.

No other poet of the Symbolist generation had been dealt with in Mandelstam's essays of 1922 and 1923 in such a polemical manner as Bely. He was the most devoted Russian pupil of the anthroposophist Rudolf Steiner, and Mandelstam had described him derisively as 'a lady who sprays out the unbearable glitter of worldwide charlatanism – Theosophy' (GP, 100) and as a 'painful and negative phenomenon in the life of the Russian language' (GP, 116; SE, 86). Mandelstam's polemics against Eastern doctrines of salvation, against 'Buddhism' and 'Theosophy', were imbued with his Hellenic-Jewish-Christian view of the world, and in

Bely he found his best target. Throughout his life, Bely had always had an extremely inquiring nature. He was highly receptive to the occult and the irrational, to the secrets of the East and to the intellectual atmosphere of Hinduism and Buddhism. In Mandelstam's extremely negative review of Bely's *Notes of an Eccentric* (1923), which was a sweeping polemical onslaught, he nevertheless refuses to treat Bely himself in a scornful way, as he was the author of the epoch-making novel *Petersburg* (1916): 'We have no desire to laugh at Bely, because he wrote *Petersburg*. No Russian writer has expressed the unrest and profound confusion that preceded the revolution as powerfully as Bely' (GP, 206).[10]

A different epoch had now dawned. Since the Central Committee resolution of 23 April 1932 and the enforcement of conformity on Soviet literature, these two important Russian poets no longer had any petty lines of demarcation to defend. What was now at stake was the life of the spirit and the freedom to discuss poetry, culture and Europe. Bely was one of the last exponents of the 'Silver Age' of Russian poetry, the representative of a culturally rich epoch which had gone down in ruins and was now prohibited. For Mandelstam, he was a worthwhile interlocutor in these spiritually dead times, ruled over by Stalin 'the Assyrian'.

Nadezhda Mandelstam recalls that the two poets, who sat side by side at the dining table of the writers' rest home, got on well with one another. Bely's wife Ksenia Bugaeva was opposed to this late reconciliation, but even so, Bely became the first person with whom Mandelstam discussed the 'Conversation about Dante', which was written in summer 1933. The 'Conversation' is a highly original attempt to come to grips with Dante, looking at the linguistic workshop of a poet of the thirteenth and fourteenth centuries, and it is, at the same time, an investigation into the dynamic essence of poetry, which Mandelstam approaches using increasingly bold and innovative metaphors.

But his text also had a political dimension. While Soviet literature was being pushed into a state of paralysis and enforced stagnation by the party's 23 April 1932 decree, Mandelstam was experimenting with motion and itineracy, walking and thinking: 'In Dante philosophy and poetry are

10 Meeting with Bely in Koktebel: ibid., 155–7 ('Two Voices'). For Mandelstam's polemic against theosophy and Buddhism, see the section 'The Anti-Buddhist' in the afterword to O. Mandelstam, *Gespräch über Dante*, 290–3. On the relationship between Mandelstam and Bely: R. Dutli, *Europas zarte Hände*, 61–80 ('Two Brothers Lately Reconciled').

forever on the move, forever on their feet' (GD, 118; SE, 29). As early as 1923, Mandelstam had remarked, in his article on Auguste Barbier, that the *Divina Commedia* had been 'the greatest political lampoon of its day' (GP, 216; CC, 186). He introduced the first verse of Dante's *Inferno* ('Nel mezzo del cammin di nostra vita') into his own anti-Stalinist pamphlet, the *Fourth Prose* (1929–1930), which was a way of highlighting his entry into the hell of the 1930s under Stalin.

When, in section seven of the 'Conversation about Dante', Mandelstam makes a point of discussing Ugolino's account (in Canto 33 of the *Inferno*) of how he and his sons were starved to death in a prison tower by Ruggieri, the Archbishop of Pisa, it is obvious that he is also referring to the overflowing prisons of the present, to Stalin's 'apparatus of intimidation' and to the 'astonishing insouciance' with which people were being thrown into jail (GD, 156). The impulse behind Mandelstam's involvement with Dante was his search for a deeper understanding of his poetry; but he was also engrossed in the fate of an exile. Less than a year after he had written the 'Conversation', he too was arrested and sent into exile – driven from the city, just as Dante had been driven out of Florence in 1302.

Mandelstam's 'Conversation about Dante' remained unpublished during his lifetime (it first appeared in 1966 in an American edition, then in 1967 in Moscow). When he returned from the Crimea to Moscow, he was confronted with *Pravda*'s scathing criticism of his Armenian travelogue, which appeared on 30 August 1933. The review in *Literaturnaia Gazeta* on 17 June had already been *extremely* negative, but now *Pravda* really let rip: 'poverty of thought', 'anaemic declamation' and 'old-fashioned, rotten chauvinism' dominate this work, which only praises Armenia's exoticism and its 'past enslavement'. Mandelstam, the review continued, had 'passed over with indifference the Armenia which is growing at breakneck speed and joyfully building socialism'. *Pravda* also took offence at his sarcastic comments about the proletarian writers. The RAPP functionary Bezymensky is portrayed in the *Journey to Armenia* as a 'strongman who lifts cardboard weights' and ridiculed as a 'dealer in birds': 'And he doesn't even sell birds but the air balloons of the proletarian writers' association' (AA, 33; NT, 210). What unheard-of impudence, directed against the sublime literature of the proletariat!

After these two press attacks, the publication of the *Journey to Armenia* in book form, which the Leningrad 'Writers' Publishing House' had planned, and the proofs of which Mandelstam had already read in July, became politically impossible. The version published in the journal *Zvezda* in May 1933 remained the last publication of his work during his lifetime. The GIKhL (State Publishing House for Artistic Literature) had agreed to publish a two-volume selection of his works, thanks to the influence of Bukharin, but the editor of the selection threateningly insisted that the *Journey to Armenia* must be left out. Mandelstam refused to abandon it, so this project also collapsed. The Armenia travelogue was a core element of his work, and Mandelstam was not one for artistic compromise. He preferred to let this final editorial project come to nothing, although he had already received advances on it.

He did, admittedly, hand in the 'Conversation about Dante' to the journal *Zvezda* and to the 'Writers' Publishing House', but he certainly had no hope of success. In a short letter sent on 3 September 1933, four days after the attack in *Pravda*, he asks the publisher to return the rejected manuscript (MR, 226). But the essay itself was more important to him than any other one: he was not prepared to let it moulder away in a drawer. He had already read it aloud to Andrei Bely and Anatoly Mariengof in Koktebel, and in autumn in Leningrad he read it out to the literary scholars Viktor Zhirmunsky and Yury Tynyanov, and the poets Benedict Livshits and Anna Akhmatova. Finally, in Moscow, he read it out to Boris Pasternak and the painter Vladimir Tatlin. Mandelstam's 'Conversation' yearned insistently to converse with other artists.

Anna Akhmatova was a particularly valuable conversation partner for Mandelstam, and they read Dante together. The *Divine Comedy* was an extremely important text for Akhmatova, and this was reflected in her poems ('The Muse', 1924; 'Dante', 1936). The creator of the *Inferno* evidently had more to say to the Acmeists who were suffering in their own infernal epoch than all their contemporaries put together. Shortly before her death, Akhmatova was asked what there was in common between herself, Gumilyov and Mandelstam. She replied: 'A love of Dante.' In 'Pages from a Diary' she recalled meeting Mandelstam in 1933, when 'Osip was all afire with Dante … and was reading *The Divine Comedy* day and night'. Mandelstam and Akhmatova could recite whole passages of the work from memory in Italian. Akhmatova recalls that on one occasion, he burst into tears while she was reciting. She became alarmed. But Mandelstam replied: 'No, nothing. To hear those words and in your voice.'[11]

11 Akhmatova on the 'love for Dante' which the three Acmeists had in common: A. Akhmatova, 'Dante', 9. M.'s reaction to Akhmatova's Dante recitation: Akhmatova, *My*

Political broadsides fired off by the Soviet press had thus destroyed three of Mandelstam's publishing projects almost simultaneously: *Journey to Armenia*, the two-volume selected works and 'Conversation about Dante'. The vinegar-soaked sponge for 'traitorous lips' was applied in stages, by a roundabout route. But Mandelstam had long since become accustomed to not getting into print. He sharply dismissed a young poet's complaint that he was not being published with the words: 'Did they publish André Chénier? Or Sappho? Or Jesus Christ?'

Half Century, 99. Comments on Chénier, Sappho and Jesus Christ: ibid., 106; R. Dutli: 'Dantes Gesänge – Gerät zum Einfangen der Zukunft. Ossip Mandelstams "Gespräch über Dante"', 2017.

20

Accursed Dwelling

(Moscow and Cherdyn 1933–1934)

At least there seemed to be a prospect of solving Mandelstam's housing problem, so that he could end his nomadic existence bivouacking in people's kitchens. In autumn 1933, he was finally able, after months of delay, to move into a house administered by a writers' cooperative, located in the Arbat district of Moscow, at 5 Nashchokinsky Lane. It had recently been renamed Furmanov Street, in honour of the writer Dmitry Furmanov, who died in 1926 and had served during the civil war as a political commissar under the legendary partisan leader Chapaev, whom the writer had subsequently immortalised in a novel. Three extra floors had been added to the house, and apartment number 26 on the fifth floor was assigned to Mandelstam, again thanks to Bukharin's discreet intervention.[1] To obtain the apartment, the poet had had to spend all the advances he received for the two-volume selection of his works (which was not in fact published) and to scratch around for money from other sources as well. Numerous party-line writers lived there, and they eyed him mistrustfully, as they doubted whether there was any justification for the privilege he had received. But another dubious contemporary also resided in the house, in apartment number 44. This was Mikhail Bulgakov, who continued to write his epoch-making novel *The Master*

1 Bukharin helps with M.'s housing problem: L. Vidgof, *Moskva Mandel'shtama*, 237–8.

and Margarita there until his death in 1940. It is an open secret that Bulgakov's 'Master' was a self-portrait, but he also found inspiration in the fate of his fellow resident Mandelstam when he created the figure of the tormented 'Master', who is referred to in the novel by the letter 'M'.

In a letter sent to his father in April 1933, Mandelstam had enthused about his 'delightful, elegant and sunny little two-room apartment' with gas stove and bath (MR, 223–4). But the splendid dwelling turned out to have been worked on by bodgers. It was in need of repair even before it had been completed (the house itself was demolished in 1976). The walls were thin and poorly sound-proofed, and the doors were insulated with felt, which was soon eaten by the moths which were constantly flying around the apartment. After finally moving in, Mandelstam began to worry that he might be expected to make artistic concessions in return for this act of 'generosity' by the authorities. To Anastasia Tsvetaeva, he described the apartment as a 'coffin', adding: 'There is only one way out of here: it leads to Vagankovo.' Vagankovo was a Moscow cemetery. When Boris Pasternak came on a visit, he congratulated him on the new apartment and remarked that now he had a place where he could write poetry. Mandelstam was furious; he exclaimed that he did not need a place to live to do that.[2] The episode indicates the difference between Pasternak, who although he had certainly not conformed, did have a tendency to 'reconcile himself with reality', and his irreconcilable, quarrelsome polar opposite Mandelstam. Mandelstam's response to the situation was the poem 'The Apartment: Silent like Paper', a fierce tirade against his new dwelling:

> And the cursed walls are thin,
> And there's nowhere left to run,
> And I'm forced to entertain someone,
> Like a fool playing a comb.
> …
> Some realist writer,
> Comber of the collective farm's flax,
> Someone with blood in his ink
> Deserves such a hell.
> (MM, 159; MN, 72)

---

2 Anastasia Tsvetaeva recalls M.'s detestation of his 'coffin-like dwelling': L. Vidgof, *Moskva Mandel'shtama*, 248. Pasternak's visit to the apartment, and M.'s fury: N. Mandelstam, *Hope Against Hope*, 150 ('The Antipodes').

This ten-stanza execration of his apartment is one of Mandelstam's most caustic political poems, and it also lays bare the violence that dominated the current scene, the 'executioners' asking him to 'put his head on the block', and the 'gush of age-old terror'.

In the same month as he wrote this poem, November 1933, Mandelstam also gave vent to his anger against Stalin, the supreme leader and dictator whom he regarded as responsible for all the misery in the country. He recalled the victims of dekulakisation, the starving peasants whom he had seen in the Crimea. In response, first of all he wrote a sarcastic cradle song for a 'kulak child', in which he lashed out at the 'rockabye despots of the collective farm' (MM, 163; MN, 73). 'I cannot be silent', he told his wife.[3] This was when he produced the fatal 'Epigram against Stalin', which eventually cost him his life. Or, more precisely: he created it in his head and recited it to a small circle of seemingly close 'friends' as well as to more distant acquaintances, a group which would increase dangerously in the next few months. Only later would he put it down in writing, in the Lubyanka, in the presence of the investigating judge.

> We live, deaf to the land beneath us
> Ten steps away no-one hears our speeches
> All we hear is the Kremlin mountaineer,
> The soul-corrupter and peasant-slayer
> His fingers are fat as grubs
> And the words, final as lead weights, fall from his lips,
> His cockroach whiskers leer
> And his boot tops gleam.
> Around him a rabble of thin-necked leaders –
> Fawning half-men for him to play with.
> The whining, purr or whine
> As he prates and points a finger,
> One by one forging his laws, to be flung
> Like horseshoes at the head, to the eye or the groin.
> And every killing is a treat
> For the broad-chested Ossete.
> (MM, 165; John Simkin, online translation)

3 'I cannot be silent': ibid., 158 ('The Path to Destruction').

Mandelstam told Anna Akhmatova that one must now write civic, political poems. But he could not go against his own nature: he was, above all, a lyrical poet. Almost at the same time as he wrote these satirical and political poems, he ventured forth on a new poetic enterprise. Between November 1933 and January 1934, he produced a cycle of eight-liners, the 'Octaves'. These were image-rich explorations of the nature and origin of poetry and the connection between writing poetry and breathing. Right from the start, the cycle presents the theme of the shortness of breath which afflicted him – not just caused by his heart disease – and he combines it with the liberating stream of fresh air produced by poetry:

I love how the cloth appears,
When after two or three, or
Maybe even four gasps of air
An expansive sigh comes,

And space, drawing green forms
With the sweeping arcs of racing sailing boats
Plays, half-asleep,
Like a child that never knew the cradle.
(MM, 167; MN, 74–5)

Poetry as a universal force and an instrument of understanding – in opposition to the rigidity of causal explanation – is celebrated in this eleven-part cycle. It evokes a knowledge of the 'infinity' which is contained in poetry, which is a universe with childlike features: 'The big universe sleeps in the cradle / Rocked by the small eternity' (MM, 185; MN, 77).

It is a beautiful paradox: poetic theory and pure lyricism stand alongside trenchant political invective. The free and unconventional adaptation of four sonnets from the *Canzoniere* of Francesco Petrarca (Petrarch) (1304–1374), written by Mandelstam in December 1933 and early January 1934 (MM, 188–97), continues his involvement with the Italian poets of the Middle Ages and the Renaissance, but it is also a reflection on the association between lyric poetry, love and death. This fascination for Petrarch and his adored Laura was not entirely unconnected with Mandelstam's brief – and unrequited – infatuation with the twenty-five-year-old poetess and translator Maria Petrovykh, who was introduced to him by Anna

Akhmatova. She lived with her sister in Granatny Lane, near the Nikita Gate, and Mandelstam often came to visit. Akhmatova, whose judgements were generally severe, valued her poetry and her natural, open character. Maria Petrovykh was a dainty woman with a girlish charm, but a strong personality. She was not a dazzling beauty like Olga Arbenina, who had aroused Mandelstam's enthusiasm in autumn 1920, or Olga Vaksel, who in 1925 had unleashed the worst marital crisis the Mandelstams ever suffered, but a range of contemporaries have described the warm, tender glances of this woman and the charm she radiated. In any case, it was for Maria Petrovykh that Mandelstam wrote on 13 February 1934 the poem Anna Akhmatova characterised as 'the most beautiful love poem of the twentieth century':[4]

> The expert mistress of guilty glances
> Who has such slender shoulders,
> Subdues the male's dangerous obstinacy,
> And drowns his words.
>
> The fish are fluttering their fins as they swim,
> Puffing out their gills. Take them,
> Mouthing their soundless 'O's',
>
> Feed them the half bread of flesh.
> …
> Don't be angry with me, dear Turkish woman,
> I'll sew myself up in a sack with you,
> Swallowing your dark words,
> Drinking the crooked water for you.
> (MM, 217; MN, 86)

The poem speaks of drowning with the beloved, and no one knows where the erotic scene is being played out: in a bed or in an aquarium? The concrete details of feminine beauty are tenderly evoked – glances, shoulders, a warm body, shining eyes, eyebrows, lips – but death lies in wait everywhere. And the dream of falling asleep, of dying together by drowning, ends with three commands:

4 M. writes 'civic poetry' as well as 'the best love poem of the twentieth century': A. Akhmatova, *My Half Century*, 101 and 90.

You, Maria, are the help of those who are perishing.
One must anticipate death, and fall asleep.
I'm standing at your harsh threshold,
Go away. Please go now. Please stay.
(MM, 217; MN, 86)

Maria Petrovykh was a frequent guest at 5 Nashchokinsky Lane. After their unstable nomadic existence, the Mandelstams enjoyed entertaining friends and acquaintances from their sparse resources. It soon became clear that some of the visitors were informers. Contemporaries have described the remarkable emptiness of the two-room apartment, with its obligatory mattress on the floor, its simple table bearing a telephone, scruffy suitcases and a couple of baskets. Thus, the new accommodation, though expensive, also expressed Mandelstam's lifelong indifference towards any kind of possession.

Even so, Mandelstam was now able to acquire a few books from second-hand booksellers, whereas during the 'kitchen bivouac' period, all his possessions had had to be stored in a wicker basket.[5] His adored medieval and Renaissance Italians could be lined up on a bookshelf, along with Old French epics, books in Latin and German and the Russian poets of the nineteenth century, as well as the literature of Old Russia. Mandelstam was particularly fond of the *Tale of Igor's Men*, which dated from the end of the twelfth century. Even while in exile in Voronezh, he would continue to derive strength from it: 'My string is taut as in the song of Igor, / After asphyxiation, / You hear in my voice the dry dampness / Of the black earth acres – my last weapon' (WH, 33; VN, 41). And he also set great store by the life story of the martyred Old Believer Avvakum (1621–1682), who died at the stake for his beliefs. For Mandelstam, he was the exemplar of recalcitrance and inflexibility. These were the modest *possessions* of a poet-nomad, who remained a homeless man even in his new accommodation, and who could never show off with a big library. In any case, the pair were only able to stay there for a few months, and according to Anna Akhmatova a 'shadow of calamity and doom' burdened this dwelling right from the start.

Akhmatova visited the Mandelstams almost immediately, in November 1933, and her twenty-two-year-old son Lev Gumilyov spent weeks with

5 M.'s library in the 1930s: N. Mandelstam, *Hope Against Hope*, 241 ('The Bookcase').

them as a guest. He, like Mandelstam, paid court to Maria Petrovykh, something which inspired Mandelstam to write a playful sonnet with a 'biblical' tinge ('I thought of an old apocrypha': BT, 151), which while poking mischievous fun at her also gives some indication of her erotic charm: 'Maria, by the way, is as soft as velvet / And her love, my God, is the stuff of dreams / Even her desert has so little sand, / That amber shines deep in her red hair / And her skin – which is smoother than linen', and so on. For Mandelstam, the love for her he shared with Lev (in both cases unrequited!) brought up haunting memories of autumn 1920 in Petrograd, a time when he and Lev's father Nikolai Gumilyov – a few months before he was shot – were both wooing the beautiful actress Olga Arbenina. For the prematurely ageing Mandelstam, who styled himself as a comic patriarch in the sonnet, the fragile girlish charm of Maria Petrovykh also represented a dream of youth gone by. It was hardly a serious threat to his love for Nadezhda, even if it led to a resurgence of 'treacherous verses'. As a pair, they were solidly established, and there was no suggestion of a marital crisis like the one in 1925. But as in the case of Olga Vaksel, this was a 'stunning' poem that just had to be written. And, for this, a poet was prepared to risk a moment of unfaithfulness – in thought alone.

Vladimir Piast, a poet who was homeless, having just returned from exile, found food and shelter for the night with the Mandelstams, and was also garlanded with comic verses. These were weeks of sociability, and the Mandelstams made many contacts, but their lives were also overshadowed with thoughts about death. Andrei Bely, the last surviving representative of the 'Silver Age' of Russian poetry, died on 8 January 1934. It was precisely for this Symbolist poet, whom he had treated so harshly in his essays of 1922 and 1923, and whom he first got to know better in summer 1933 in the Crimea, that Mandelstam wrote a long seven-part requiem in a highly individual tone, which lay somewhere between the seemingly disrespectful and the reverential:

> You had blue eyes and a feverish brow.
> The invigorating malice of the world attracted you.
> …
> They crowned you, but it was with the cap of the holy fool,
> Turquoise teacher, torturer, tyrant, jester.
> …

Skater and first of an age that hurled you out by the scruff
Of the neck onto the frosty dust of word spinning.
…
An icy bond is forming between you and this country,
So lie there and grow young, stretching into eternity

And let the young generations of the future never ask:
How do you feel there, you orphan, in your clean void?
(MM, 199; MN, 81)

Mandelstam told his wife: this is also *my* requiem. Was he identifying himself lately with Bely? Nadezhda found an explanation:

> It was only then that M. became fully aware that this theme of 'sharing' another's death, of 'feeling with' it, was preparation for his own end. When I said to him: 'Why are you holding your own funeral?' he replied that he must hold it while there was still time – who knew what was now in store for us?[6]

As if he had *already* known that *he* would not be given either a grave or a requiem, that his body would be covered with earth in some anonymous place, in a mass grave in the Far East, close to Vladivostok, as far away from his beloved Mediterranean region as if it had been on another planet.

When he met Anna Akhmatova in February 1934, Mandelstam said to her: 'I'm ready for death.' The epigram against Stalin was being passed around, although it had not yet been written down. Mandelstam certainly had an inkling that he had signed his own death warrant by producing it. At the end of March 1934, he met Boris Pasternak on Tverskoy Boulevard and recited the poem to him. Pasternak was terrified. According to the memoirs of Olga Ivinskaia, Pasternak's last partner, he replied:

> I heard nothing, you recited nothing. You know, strange and terrible things are happening now, people are disappearing; I fear the walls have ears, and perhaps even the paving-stones can hear and speak. Let us be clear: I heard nothing.

---

6 'This is also *my* requiem.' The cycle on the death of Bely: N. Mandelstam, *Hope Abandoned*, 444.

When asked what had led him to write the poem, Mandelstam declared that there was nothing he hated so much as fascism, whatever form it took.[7]

There were now only a few weeks left before his arrest. In the spring of 1934, he again came into conflict with the official representatives of Soviet literature. The background was as follows. Vladimir Bonch-Bruevich, an Old Bolshevik and friend of Lenin, who was the director of the Central Museum for Artistic Literature (later called the State Literature Museum), which had been founded in 1933, approached various writers, requesting them to sell their literary archives to the museum – and therefore to the state. Mandelstam, who was constantly in financial difficulties, also contemplated taking this step. He was living on loans, charitable gifts and chance sales of his possessions, which were meagre in any case.

According to its minutes for 16 March 1934, the Experts' Committee of the Literature Museum offered to buy Mandelstam's archive at the humiliating knockdown price of 500 roubles. This should be compared with the 25,000 roubles the Late Symbolist Mikhail Kuzmin received for his archive in December 1933. Mandelstam felt himself obliged to withdraw his papers from sale, and, on 21 March, after a furious telephone conversation, he composed an angry letter to Bonch-Bruevich:

> For some reason you have regarded it as necessary to present to me an exhaustive list of reasons why you have a low opinion of my work. In this way you have made the purchase of a writer's archive into a caricature of a posthumous evaluation … For me as a writer it is naturally disagreeable when errors of this kind undermine the authority of the Literature Museum of the People's Commissariat for Enlightenment, but your action in compelling a person who was invited by you yourself to listen to completely unnecessary speculations and candid remarks provokes my just indignation. (MR, 227–8)

There he is again, the poet who reacts in a completely un-Soviet way by insisting on his dignity as a human being, an artist and a contemporary, as he had done before in his letter of August 1923 to the All-Russian Writers' Union and in December 1929 in his 'Open Letter to Soviet Writers'. He also wrote a poem satirising the people he called 'archivanes' (BT, 155),

7 'I'm ready for death': A. Akhmatova, *My Half Century*, 99. M. recites his anti-Stalin poem to Pasternak: O. Ivinskaia, *A Captive of Time*, 86.

who sold writers' archives rather than buying them. In an alternative version of the poem, he implied that the authorities obtained the writers' archives through the museum to do whatever they liked with them, even to destroy them, and that the museum therefore only functioned as a rapacious and corrupt intermediary ('Its shabby trade is this: / To sell archives to those in power').[8]

Mandelstam's suspicions were not without foundation, when one bears in mind how many works were actually destroyed by the Soviet authorities in the twentieth century. There were cases where the archives of the NKVD or the KGB served as repositories of writers' works. One example was Mikhail Bulgakov's diary, which surfaced in the KGB archives in 1990, although the author had himself burned it in 1929. Unfortunately, this was the exception rather than the rule. The optimistic thesis 'Manuscripts do not burn', which the demonic Woland puts forward in Bulgakov's novel *The Master and Margarita*, is delightful but not always correct. The ovens of the Lubyanka consumed a lot of paper, including forty-eight manuscript pages of poems confiscated during Mandelstam's arrest. Of course, the secret police had not reckoned on Nadezhda Mandelstam's retentive memory. So Bulgakov turned out to be right after all, if indirectly.[9]

In mid-April 1934, Osip and Nadezhda travelled to Leningrad. On roughly 6 May, in the House of the Press, there occurred the incident Mandelstam's widow later regarded as so fateful that she placed it at the beginning of her memoirs: 'After slapping Alexei Tolstoy in the face, M. immediately returned to Moscow.'[10] Tolstoy had presided over the court of arbitration in the Sargidzhan affair on 13 September 1932, which had condemned both Sargidzhan and Mandelstam. The poet had been on the lookout for an opportunity to pay back the 'Red Count', who was an officially recognised Soviet writer. He confronted Tolstoy after a meeting in Leningrad, publicly slapped his face, and called out: 'I am punishing the hangman who gave the order to hit my wife.' Tolstoy seized Mandelstam's hand and hissed: 'Don't you understand that I can destroy you?' Snorting with rage, he went to see Gorky, who is alleged to have said: 'We will teach him what happens when someone strikes a Russian writer!'[11]

---

8 Dispute with the Literature Museum over M.'s papers: L. Vidgof, *Moskva Mandel'shtama*, 242–4.

9 Bulgakov's diary resurfaces: V. Shentalinsky, *Arrested Voices*, 74–81.

10 Mandelstam, *Hope Abandoned*, 3.

11 Alexei Tolstoy threatens M.: F. Vol'kenstein, 'Tovarishcheskii sud', 57. The reaction

This was probably one of the straws that broke the camel's back, but it was certainly not the only reason for Mandelstam's arrest. Reports about Mandelstam's 'counter-revolutionary' poems had already reached the OGPU long ago, through informers. Mandelstam could not or would not keep the anti-Stalin poem about the 'soul-corrupter' and 'peasant-slayer' as secret as caution would have recommended. He was not a cunning conspirator but a poet who wanted to be heard. People who were close to him, like Shklovsky's wife Vasilisa, uttered vain warnings: 'I said to him: "But what are you doing? And why? You are pulling the noose around your neck yourself." He replied "I can do no other." And there were some people who immediately denounced him.' Mandelstam could no longer restrain himself, not just from talking to individuals but from reciting the poem to several people at once. The terror this inspired in his listeners is still felt decades later in the memoirs written in October 1970 by his friend Boris Kuzin:

> I entreated Mandelstam, in the truest sense of the word, to promise me that his wife and myself would remain the only people who knew of the poem. He replied with happy and contented laughter. Nevertheless, he promised me that he would not recite these verses to anyone else ... No, he would not be able to keep his promise ... Literally two or three days afterwards he declared to me with a smile as sweet as sugar: 'I have read the poem (it was clear which poem) to Boris Leonidovich.' My heart stood still. Naturally Boris Pasternak was above all suspicion (as were Akhmatova and Klychkov) but there were always people buzzing around him, as they were around Mandelstam, people whom I had always avoided like the plague. And what was most important – it became clear to me during these few days Mandelstam had managed to recite these terrible verses to numerous acquaintances. The end of the story was entirely predictable.[12]

In the night of 16 to 17 May 1934, at about one o'clock, an arrest detachment of three OGPU agents knocked on Mandelstam's door. The house

---

of Gorky and Tolstoy to M.'s slap in the face: Shentalinsky, *Arrested Voices*, 169. Vasilisa Shklovskaia recalls her reaction to M.'s anti-Stalin poem: O. S. Figurnova and M. V. Figurnova, *Osip i Nadezhda Mandel'shtamy*, 109.

12 Boris Kuzin's memoirs: B. Kuzin, *Vospominaniia*, 176–7 (translated German extracts from these memoirs are included in the volume O. Mandelstam, *Armenien, Armenien!*, 154–5).

search they conducted went on until the next morning.[13] They were looking for quite specific 'seditious' texts, including the anti-Stalin poem (which was not preserved in written form), the poem about the 'wolf-hound century', the poem 'A Cold Spring' about the starving victims of forced collectivisation, the poem 'The Apartment' and other poems of a political character. All the nooks and crannies of the apartment were inspected, all the drawers were ransacked, every book was examined, even the bindings of the books were cut open. Suspicious manuscripts were piled on a chair, and the rest were thrown to the ground, where they were trampled on. The officials' suspicions were aroused even by the bitter satirical poem 'Sebastian and Bach' (BT, 155), which portrays a violent house manager destroying a harmonium in a coded attack on the state-sanctioned destruction of culture. Nadezhda Mandelstam describes the distressing details of that fateful night in two chapters of her memoirs *Hope Against Hope*: 'May Night' and 'Confiscation'. She recalls the sound of Semyon Kirsanov's Hawaiian guitar, which continuously resounded from the neighbouring apartment, and the young OGPU agent who contemplated the books regretfully and kept offering his victims hard candy from a little tin ... A creepy attempt to sweeten a brutal intervention into a poet's life.

These events had a distinguished witness. Anna Akhmatova had just arrived from Leningrad to visit them. Mandelstam had urgently begged her to come, shortly after he had slapped Alexei Tolstoy. She too remembered the ghastly scenario. At seven in the morning, Mandelstam was taken to the Lubyanka, the headquarters of the OGPU, and the suspicious manuscripts were confiscated. Nadezhda packed a suitcase with clothes and books, including Dante's *Inferno* (although no books were permitted in the cell). The arrest warrant was not signed by Yagoda, the head of the secret police, as Nadezhda believed, but by his representative Yakov Agranov, whose signature was similar. The next day, the OGPU agents returned to the house in Nashchokinsky Lane to rummage through the papers a second time, because the previous day's booty had not included the anti-Stalin poem.

Mandelstam was imprisoned in the so-called 'internal prison' in the courtyard of the Lubyanka. On 18 May 1934 he was brought before

13 The date of the house search is given by Nadezhda Mandelstam as 13–14 May 1934; Shentalinsky (*Arrested Voices*, 168) gives a date of 16–17 May 1934 on the basis of NKVD documents which surfaced in 1990.

investigating judge Shivarov for the first time: Nadezhda refers to him by his patronymic 'Christophorovich' in her memoirs. The interrogation lasted the whole of the night. The minutes came to light in 1991, under Gorbachev, when the archives of the KGB, with its documents on writers, were opened for a short time, and Vitaly Shentalinsky was able to inspect and publish Investigation Dossier No. 4108, on Mandelstam.

On Shivarov's instructions, Mandelstam recited the poems that might have led, in the poet's own opinion, to his arrest. He declaimed two stanzas from the 'Wolfhound Century' and a stanza from 'The Apartment'. Shivarov made notes, but then he played his trump card by pulling out of a folder the anti-Stalin poem in its original, sharpest version: including the verse about the 'soul-corrupter' and 'peasant-slayer'. The informer in Mandelstam's circle of acquaintances, whose name is unknown even today, had done a good job! Mandelstam did not dispute his authorship. He was then obliged to write the poem in his own hand and sign it. Nadezhda later wrote:

> I was angry because he had not denied he wrote it, which a conspirator was fully entitled to do. But it was completely impossible to imagine O.M. in the role of a conspirator – he was an entirely open person, incapable of being sly, and there wasn't the slightest trace of cunning in his make-up.

The interrogator described the poem as a 'counter-revolutionary document without precedent'. Unprecedented it certainly was … According to Shentalinsky it was 'more than a poem'; it was a 'desperately audacious act of civic bravery', unparalleled in the history of literature. There exists no other anti-Stalin poem with such an annihilating impact. To this day, we do not know whether Stalin himself knew the text of the poem: who among his subordinates would have dared to lay what the director of the investigation described as a 'terrorist document' before the vindictive ruler of the country?

Shivarov listed the names of the people who had visited Mandelstam at 5 Nashchokinsky Lane, as reported by his informer. The interrogator endeavoured to mislead Mandelstam into thinking that some of them had already been arrested and had made statements. Mandelstam had to give the names of the people to whom he had recited the poem. At first, he listed eight people, among them Anna Akhmatova and her son Lev, but not those who had heard the poem outside the apartment (Pasternak!). Since he believed that the copy Shivarov had in his hands had been written in Maria Petrovykh's handwriting, the next morning, on 19 May, he added her name to the list. She had been the only person at the apartment who had written down the poem – having promised to destroy the copy later. But no suspicion fell on this woman, who enjoyed Anna Akhmatova's confidence to the end of her life, and we do not intend to voice any suspicion here.[14]

In her memoirs, Yekaterina Petrovykh expresses the conviction that Mandelstam particularly wanted to incriminate her sister Maria in the eyes of the investigating officer because the rejected lover hoped in his delirium that they would be sent into exile together. There is nothing in the extracts of the minutes published by Shentalinsky and Polianovsky that might lead us to give credence to this supposition. It also appears outlandish, because Mandelstam could not have assumed he would be exiled; he had rather to fear the death penalty. The rumours around Mandelstam's confused behaviour in the Lubyanka evidently produced a strange kind of delirium among some of his contemporaries as well.[15]

Mandelstam's behaviour when in the clutches of the OGPU was not exactly heroic. He found imprisonment hard to deal with. One may recall an earlier episode in the Crimea, in August 1920, during the civil war, when he was arrested by General Wrangel's counter-espionage agency. He banged on the door of his cell and cried: 'You must let me out! I am not cut out to be in prison!' To imagine that Mandelstam could have shrouded himself in heroic silence during his interrogations would be to fail to recognise the full horror of the Lubyanka environment. The fear of torture, for which the OGPU had a trained and notorious staff of officers, was undoubtedly immense. Although systematic torture did not begin in the Lubyanka until 1937, the secret police already had well-calibrated methods of crushing a prisoner's spirit. Mandelstam was tormented with nightly interrogations, deprived of sleep through glaring lights and offered highly salted food without water. He was also placed in a straitjacket at one point: this was an item of clothing he had never seen

14 Shivarov and the 'counter-revolutionary document without precedent': Mandelstam, *Hope Abandoned*, 31–2 ('Interview'). V. Shentalinsky first published extracts from the file on Mandelstam found in the archives of the KGB in the Moscow journal *Ogonyok*, no. 1, 1991. They appeared in book form in 1993 in French, in 1995 in Russian and in 1996 in German and English. A word-for-word record of part of the minutes of M.'s interrogation has been published by E. Polianovsky (*Gibel' Osipa Mandel'shtama*, 74–92).

15 The memoirs of Yekaterina Petrovykh: Figurnova and Figurnova, *Osip i Nadezhda Mandel'shtamy*, 162–7.

before. While in prison, he suffered from a traumatic psychosis, including hallucinations. According to Nadezhda he heard voices and the sound of a woman weeping through the walls of his cell. He assumed that his wife had been arrested as well and was being physically mistreated. Or were the voices tape recordings fed into the cell as an instrument of psychological torture?

While he was in the Lubyanka, he attempted to commit suicide by cutting his wrists. He did this with a razorblade he had concealed much earlier in the heel of a shoe for this exact purpose, as he expected to be tortured. He summons up a telling image of this instrument of death in his *Fourth Prose* (1929–1930):

> The blade of the Gillette razor, with its faintly serrated bevelled edge, has always seemed to me one of the noblest products of the steel industry … The blade of the Gillette razor is the product of a dead trust, the shareholders of which are packs of American and Swedish wolves. (RZ, 258; NT, 18)

The suicide attempt failed. The guards arrived unexpectedly. He still had moments of clarity in prison, despite all his psychological confusion. This is shown by the questions he asked his 'fellow inmate' in the cell, who worked for the OGPU and had been put there to intimidate and manipulate him: 'Why do you have clean fingernails? Why do you smell of onions when you come back from interrogation?' Typical Mandelstam questions. His cellmate had to be transferred. From then on, Mandelstam had the cell to himself.

Another episode demonstrates the perverse collaboration between certain writers and the secret police. Piotr Pavlenko, party-line author of socialist realist works and a diligent apologist for Stalin, went around Moscow spreading trivial details intended to show how pathetically Mandelstam had behaved under interrogation: he had talked nonsense, and his trousers had kept slipping down. How could Pavlenko have known that? His assignment was presumably to strip Mandelstam of the aura of a tragic victim by spreading stories about his ridiculous behaviour. He had been invited by his friend Shivarov to hide behind the door or in a cupboard while the interrogation was being conducted. Mandelstam was convinced that he had seen Pavlenko in the Lubyanka. He told Emma Gerstein:

> I was being taken somewhere in the inner lift. Several people were standing around. I fell to the floor. I was thrashing about when suddenly, above me, I heard a voice: 'Mandelstam, Mandelstam, aren't you ashamed of yourself?' I raised my head. It was Pavlenko.

In March 1938, this literary henchman of the secret police would again play a grim role in the poet's life.[16]

During the interrogation on 25 May – seven nights had now passed – Mandelstam had to compose his political biography. For 1917: 'Extremely negative reaction to the October seizure of power.' From the end of 1918: 'Political depression, caused by the harsh methods used to put into effect the dictatorship of the proletariat.' For 1927: 'Superficial, but strong sympathy for Trotskyism.' For 1930: 'In political consciousness, deep depression, caused by the liquidation of the kulaks.' Then Shivarov came back to Mandelstam's chief crime: 'the counter-revolutionary pamphlet against the leader of the Communist Party and the Soviet state'. Mandelstam had to report the reactions of the people to whom he had recited the 'slanderous poem'. And he confessed that its 'striking expressiveness' made it 'broadly applicable as an instrument in the counter-revolutionary struggle'. There was enough material here to justify ten executions!

In the meantime, Mandelstam's friends and relatives had not been inactive. Nadezhda asked for Bukharin's help. He had already helped Mandelstam on many occasions, by promoting the publication of his books, facilitating the Armenia trip and using his influence over matters of accommodation. He was cautious at first ('He hasn't written something imprudent, has he?'), but then, for the last time, he intervened on his behalf. Nadezhda told a white lie by concealing the existence of the anti-Stalin poem from him – and thanks to this, she was able to prolong Mandelstam's life for four more years. Anna Akhmatova visited Pasternak immediately after the arrest, and the latter also asked Bukharin to do all he could for Mandelstam. Akhmatova herself then went to see Avel Yenukidze, a Georgian party official and member of the Central Committee who was close to Stalin. These joint endeavours to intercede were to some extent successful.[17]

---

16 M. in the Lubyanka prison: N. Mandelstam, *Hope Abandoned*, 74 ('Inside'); ibid., 79 ('Christophorovich'). Pavlenko, the accomplice of the interrogator Shivarov: ibid., 84–5 ('Christophorovich'); E. Gerstein, *Moscow Memoirs*, 78.

17 Intercession of Nadezhda and M.'s fellow poets Akhmatova and Pasternak in

The sentence was pronounced on 28 May 1934: three years' exile in Cherdyn, in the Perm district of the Urals, following the instruction handed down 'from above': 'Isolate, but preserve.' In view of the seriousness of the offence, this was an extraordinarily mild sentence, an act of particular clemency. Mandelstam could easily have been shot on the spot for his unprecedented 'terrorist document'. He himself expected that this would be the outcome. Or he might have been sent to build the White Sea–Baltic Canal, which was being constructed rapidly at that time by an army of enslaved convicts, who were being worked to death. There was an even greater concession, a double miracle: Nadezhda was allowed to accompany her husband into exile, because of his mental instability. She was summoned to the Lubyanka on 27 May, and there she saw her husband for the first time since his arrest – with bandaged wrists. She learned that the final question he had been asked was 'What is your attitude to Soviet power?' and that he had replied: 'I am ready to cooperate with all Soviet authorities, except the Cheka.' He had said this to a representative of precisely that institution.

This outcome was marked by several unusual circumstances. It was not without reason that Nadezhda employed the word 'miracle'. None of the persons named by Mandelstam during the interrogation was arrested or, still worse, shot. The absence of further arrests is evidence that Stalin was not informed of the poem by his subordinates. The 'broad-chested Ossete' with the 'cockroach whiskers' and the 'fat fingers', surrounded by 'a rabble of thin-necked half-men', would certainly have taken vengeance on those who had heard the verses as well as the poet himself. Maria Petrovykh continued to be convinced throughout her life that Stalin did not know the poem. Admittedly, Lev Gumilyov, who was one of Mandelstam's hearers, was arrested for the first time on 27 October 1935, but that was part of the wave of mass arrests after the murder of Kirov. As the son of the executed 'counter-revolutionary' Nikolai Gumilyov, and as a representative of his mother Anna Akhmatova, he was repeatedly detained, and eventually sent to a prison camp.

One can only speculate about the reasons for the mildness – which was, of course, only temporary – of the 1934 verdict. Mandelstam's arrest and imprisonment coincided with the preparations for the first Congress of Soviet Writers, which was expected to run from 17 August to 1

---

favour of M.: N.Mandelstam, *Hope Abandoned*, 21–2 ('Integral Moves'); ibid., 25 ('Public Opinion').

September 1934, and to function as a propagandistic manifestation of the unity of the party and the intelligentsia. In view of the book-burnings in Nazi Germany, the Soviet Union wanted to present itself to the world as a refuge for culture and humanity. This was the aim of the anti-fascist International Congress of Writers for the Defence of Culture, which was to be held in Paris a year later, between 21 and 25 June 1935. The shooting of Mandelstam for writing a political poem would not have been in keeping with this propaganda image. Another suicide – after Yesenin and Mayakovsky had taken their own lives in spectacular fashion in 1925 and 1930 respectively – would have been detrimental to a regime which was still striving to be recognised as legitimate. It was therefore only a miracle in appearance, and the holders of power themselves profited from it. It was a miracle at the time, but it was merely a postponement of Mandelstam's fate.

On 29 May 1934, the Mandelstams said goodbye at the Kazan station to their relatives and friends. Nadezhda's brother Yevgeny was there, and Mandelstam's brother Alexander. Anna Akhmatova had collected money for the exiles from people they knew at Nashchokinsky Lane. Elena Bulgakova, the wife of the author of *The Master and Margarita* (and the model for Margarita in the novel) tearfully turned out her pockets. The exiles were escorted by three armed and uniformed OGPU officials. The journey into exile lasted five days, from 29 May until 3 June 1934. The first leg was by railway to Sverdlovsk (which is now once again Ekaterinburg), followed by a narrow-gauge railway to Solikamsk, then by steamer up the Kama river to the small town of Cherdyn in the Urals, a miserable hole in the Perm district. For the whole of the journey, Mandelstam was in a psychotic state, suffering from hallucinations and a fear of being shot. One of the soldiers escorting them said to Nadezhda: 'Can't you calm him down? It's only in bourgeois countries that people are shot because of poems.'

In quieter moments, Nadezhda read Pushkin to him from a small volume she had brought with her on the journey. Pushkin's 1825 poem 'The Gypsies' (which includes the old gypsy's memory of the banished Ovid!) resounded through the carriage – the men of the escort listened as well. Mandelstam produced one small poem on the journey into exile, on 1 June 1934, while they waited for hours at the crowded station of Sverdlovsk for the connection to Solikamsk. It is a bitter, seemingly naïve poem about a tailor:

A tailor, glory to him!
He had a good head
He was condemned to the supreme measure, listen!
And what happened? Like a true tailor
He took his own measurements –
And so he is still alive.
(BT, 229)

The legal term 'the supreme measure' meant the death penalty and was part of the dismal daily routine in the Stalinist thirties. But the poem is an attempt to exorcise the danger of the 'supreme measure' through the magic of language: 'And so he is still alive.'

It was a moment of clarity during this traumatic five-day journey, the nightmare images of which would only spread into his poetry a year later when he composed the poems in the *Voronezh Notebooks*. It was the journey up the Kama river by steamer that stuck in his mind most of all. Here is the poetic diptych 'Kama', written in May 1935:

Thus I sailed down the river with drawn curtains at the window,
With curtains drawn at the window and a blazing head.

My wife stayed awake with me for five nights,
Stayed awake for five nights as she coped with the three guards.
(WH, 25; VN, 38)

The exile did not have the right to look at the view through the window. The curtains in the train carriages and the ship's compartments had to be kept closed. Despite this, some details of the journey shine out in the 'Kama' poem: a fir tree ablaze on the river bank corresponds with the fire in the tormented poet's head. But the most remarkable echo of the sleepless journey into exile reverberates in the long-drawn-out anapaests of a poem composed between April and June 1935 in Voronezh. With a mixture of fascination and horror, the poet experiences a hallucinatory vision of the endless forest and the immense expanse of the Russian space, 'risen with dough':

The day was five-headed. For five consecutive days
I shrank, proud of space because it rose on yeast,
Dreaming was greater than hearing, hearing was older than dreaming, blended
together, sensitised …
And the high roads chased us with coach horses.

The day was five-headed, and driven mad from the dance,
The horsemen rode and the unmounted walked, a mass of black
As the white nights dilated the aorta of power, the knife blades
Turned the eye into coniferous flesh.

Oh for an inch of blue sea, for just enough to go through the eye of a needle,
So that the pair of us escorted by time could be carried well under sail …
(WH, 35; VN, 42)

Since Alexander Pushkin's poem 'To the Sea' (1824), which addressed it as the 'free element', the sea has been a symbol of liberty. The condemned and deported poet Mandelstam saw an amount of freedom no larger than the eye of a needle as a fulfilment of his dreams; this indicates how little freedom he presently enjoyed.

Mandelstam was not shipped off to the sea he yearned for, but into a cold environment consisting of empty spaces, forest and marsh. Cherdyn was an unprepossessing town in the Urals, covered with snow and ice for most of the year and popular with swarms of mosquitoes during the marshy summer. It was a remote location in a distant corner of Russia, with muddy roads and without a trace of culture, and it was unchanged from how Chekhov might have described it in the nineteenth century. Mandelstam had only just arrived when he was admitted to the county hospital, after first being registered with the local OGPU headquarters. There he did not meet a sympathetic physician, as Ivan Gromov had done in Chekhov's famous story 'Ward No. 6'. In Cherdyn, there was only a district doctor, who followed her instructions to the letter.

Mandelstam's traumatic psychosis continued: he thought he could hear crude and intimidating male voices rebuking him for his transgressions. And he imagined that his fellow poet Anna Akhmatova had been shot and he had to look for her corpse in a ravine. He was also under the delusion that he himself would be shot 'at about six in the evening'. Nadezhda kept moving the hour hand of the clock on the wall back to deceive her husband about the time. He finally saw only one way out: suicide. During the night of 3 to 4 June 1934, he made another attempt. He jumped from a window on the third floor of the county hospital, fell into a dug garden, dislocated his right shoulder and broke a shoulder bone.[18] But this leap into space ended his delirium. His renewed clarity of vision is evoked in the third of the stanzas written at Voronezh in May or June 1935:

> Made quite numb by rowdies and slanderers
> I roll around in confusion, seven thumbs high,
> I'm like a cockerel in the bright summer night –
> There is food and spit, and swindling too
> I reject the woodpecker. I leap, and my mind is whole.
> (WH, 31; VN, 40)

In view of his threatened transfer to the Perm psychiatric clinic, which could have meant the end, Nadezhda acted immediately. She mobilised his fellow poets Anna Akhmatova and Boris Pasternak, and she spent the rest of her money on telegrams, to Bukharin and even to the Central Committee of the Communist Party. Bukharin wrote his famous letter to Stalin, which includes this weighty aphorism: 'The poets are always in the right, because history is on their side.' And he added: 'Pasternak is also worried.'

The authorities did not want to be saddled with the suicide of yet another poet, only a few weeks before the first International Writers' Congress. These were still, to use Anna Akhmatova's phrase, 'vegetarian times': Stalin's furious thirst for destruction did not find expression until the purges of 1936. On 12 June 1934, Mandelstam's sentence was changed, on instructions 'from above'. The next day, Stalin made his notorious telephone call to Pasternak, whom he wanted to sound out about Mandelstam's significance as a poet: 'He is a master of his craft, isn't that true?' Pasternak avoided giving an answer; he replied that he would prefer to discuss 'life and death'. Stalin rang off. His sudden attack of hypocritical leniency after Mandelstam's first arrest in 1934 also bears witness to his awareness that

18 M.'s attempted suicide in Cherdyn: ibid., 59 ('The Leap'); ibid., 60 ('Cherdyn').

his future fame would essentially depend on the poets. Would it not be possible to extract an ode in praise of the Soviet ruler from the allegedly brilliant poet Mandelstam? But Stalin's phone call to Pasternak is also an indication that the great leader was unaware of the devastating content of Mandelstam's epigram. Perhaps his subordinates had given him to understand that the refractory Mandelstam had been arrested for slapping Alexei Tolstoy? After all, the dictator himself would not have forgiven anyone for a slap in the face.[19]

The official telegram confirming the revision of the sentence arrived in Cherdyn on 14 June. Mandelstam could now choose his own place of exile, according to the 'minus twelve' formula: he could not go to Moscow, or Leningrad, or any of ten other important Soviet cities. On 15 June, in the presence of the local OGPU commandant, he chose the town of Voronezh in the central-Russian 'black earth' region, 600 kilometres south of Moscow. An acquaintance, the botanist Nikolai Leonov, whose father worked in Voronezh as a prison doctor, had once recommended the town in a conversation with Mandelstam. It offered better prospects for medical care and even – unlike the Uralian wasteland of Cherdyn – cultural life of a provincial type. And, as Mandelstam said to his wife, 'Who knows, perhaps I might turn out to need a prison doctor?'

On 16 June 1934, the Mandelstams travelled back to Moscow, via Perm and Kazan. They again experienced a 'five-headed day', but, this time, with the temporary prospect of improvement. In February 1937 Mandelstam would still remember this return to normal life, along with the giant portraits of Stalin displayed all over the place. He wrote a poem presenting an ambivalent image of the 'benefactor' to whom he owed the postponement of his ultimate punishment:

> The Komi-Perm language was spoken,
> Passengers were fighting,
> And the reproving stare of those eyes on the portrait on the wall
> Looked at me fondly – and drilled into me.
> (WH, 145; VN, 74)

When they arrived in Moscow, Nadezhda tried to speak to Bukharin again, but he was no longer willing to receive her. Yagoda, the head of

19 Bukharin's letter to Stalin: Shentalinsky, *Arrested Voices*, 183. Stalin's 13 June 1934 telephone call to Pasternak: Ivinskaia, *A Captive of Time*, 85–92.

'You shall fall in love with a Jew.' Photograph of Nadezhda Mandelstam-Khazina shortly after her marriage with Osip Mandelstam in March 1922.

'Here terror writes.' Photograph of Osip Mandelstam in 1923, at the time of 'The Finder of a Horseshoe' and the 'Slate Ode'.

'My desire is not to speak about myself but to track down the age, the noise and the germination of time.' Reproduction of the jacket of *The Noise of Time*, published by Vremia, Leningrad 1925.

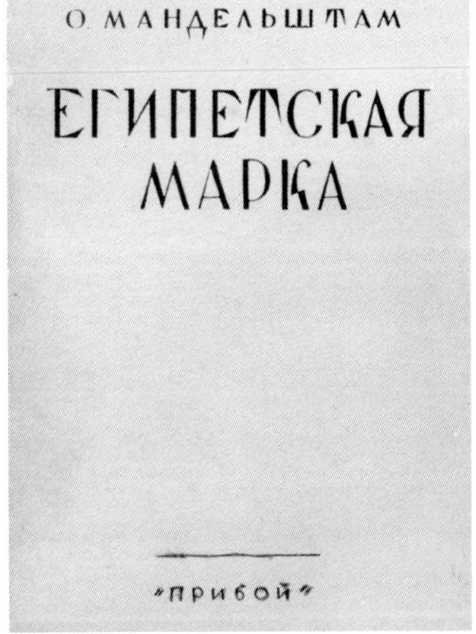

'Terror takes me by the hand and leads me.' The prose volume *The Egyptian Stamp*, 'Priboi' publishing house, Leningrad 1928.

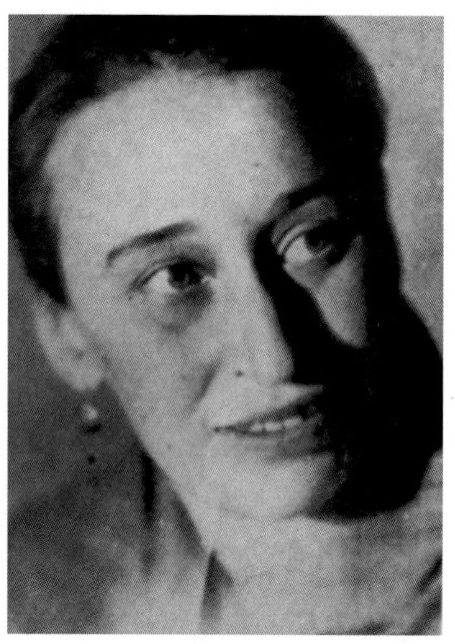

'It is as if we had never gone away': Nadezhda during the time at Detskoe Selo, 1927–1928.

О. МАНДЕЛЬШТАМ

СТИХОТВОРЕНИЯ

ГОСУДАРСТВЕННОЕ ИЗДАТЕЛЬСТВО
МОСКВА 1928 ЛЕНИНГРАД

'Every line of this book contradicts what you are intending to do': the volume *Poems*, the last book of poetry issued by Mandelstam in his lifetime, which the State Publishing House issued in 1928 thanks to Bukharin's intervention.

'Isn't it dark outside, / Alexander Herzowitz?' Eleonora Gurvich, the wife of Mandelstam's brother Alexander, with Osip and Nadezhda Mandelstam (from left to right), Moscow 1931.

'They don't know who I am': Osip Mandelstam in 1932, excluded on account of his 'general uselessness to Soviet literature'.

'The wonderful accident of geology we call Koktebel': the front steps of Voloshin's house in Koktebel, Crimea, in summer 1933. Andrei Bely is sitting between the first and second rows, wearing a cap; Mandelstam is on the far right of the second row.

'And the cursed walls are thin / And there's nowhere left to run': Alexander Mandelstam, Maria Petrovykh, Emil Mandelstam, Nadezhda and Osip Mandelstam and Anna Akhmatova (from left to right), 1933, in the apartment at 5 Nashchokinsky Lane. Here, in November, Mandelstam composed the anti-Stalin poem and other political texts that sealed his fate. Mikhail Bulgakov, author of *The Master and Margarita*, also lived in this house.

'The expert mistress of guilty glances': Maria Petrovykh, at the beginning of the 1930s.

'I'll sew myself up in a sack with you': autograph of the 'most beautiful love-poem of the twentieth century' (Anna Akhmatova), which Mandelstam wrote in 1934 for Maria Petrovykh.

'But it's not wolf's blood that flows through my veins': Mandelstam in the Lubyanka, after his first arrest in May 1934.

'Is it possible to praise a dead woman?' Olga Vaksel, with whom Mandelstam had a passionate affair in 1925, and who committed suicide in Oslo in 1932.

'A winter paradise . . . a penal battalion': Mandelstam in the Tambov hospital for nervous disorders at the end of 1935.

'Oaths remain imprinted on our lips': departure from Voronezh. Left, Osip and Nadezhda Mandelstam; above right, Natasha Shtempel; below right, one of her friends.

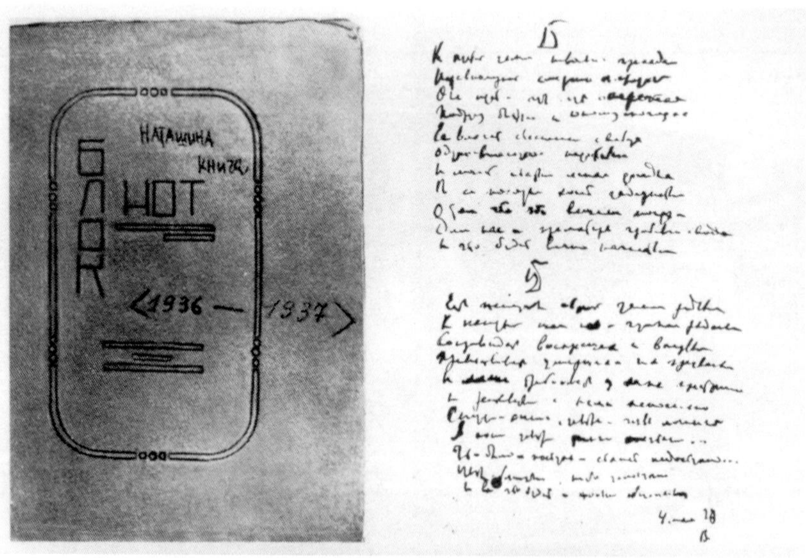

'And what will be is no more than a promise': *Natasha's Book*, which the Mandelstams gave to Natasha Shtempel in May 1937 on their departure from Voronezh; manuscript of the poem 'Levelling Herself upon the Hollow Ground'.

'They are all somehow . . . *desecrated*': Osip Mandelstam in the year of terror, 1937, before his expulsion from the hundred-verst zone surrounding Moscow.

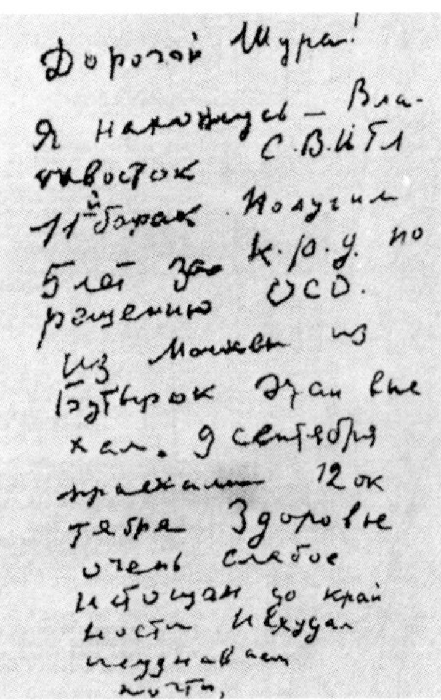

Дорогой Шура!
Я нахожусь — Вла-
дивосток С.В.ИТЛ
11й барак. Получил
5 лет за к.р.д. по
решению ОСО.
Из Москвы из
Бутырок этап вые-
хал. 9 сентября
приехали 12 ок-
тября. Здоровье
очень слабое
истощен до край-
ности исхудал
неузнаваем
почти,

'I am freezing without proper clothes': Mandelstam's last letter sent from the camp, November 1938.

'Oh for an inch of blue sea, for just enough to go through the eye of a needle': the last photograph from the Moscow Lubyanka – Osip Mandelstam in the 'internal prison' of the NKVD, May 1938.

'Seeing Oska Again': Nadezhda Mandelstam in the last year of her life, 1979.

the secret police, had, in the meantime, triumphantly confronted him with the anti-Stalin poem, whereupon a shocked Bukharin was obliged to dissociate himself from the poet.[20] Politically, he could no longer afford to have any dealings with Mandelstam. After a short stay of two to three days in the capital, the Mandelstams again boarded the train, but this time the journey went in the direction most desired by the poet – southwards. They arrived in Voronezh on around 25 June 1934. It was the beginning of what Nadezhda Mandelstam would describe decades later in her memoirs as a 'miracle'.

20 Yagoda recites M.'s anti-Stalin poem to Bukharin: Mandelstam, *Hope Abandoned*, 23 ('Integral Moves').

21

The Miracle of Voronezh

(Voronezh 1934–1936)

The town of Voronezh was situated on the banks of the river of the same name, a short distance above its confluence with the Don. Since 1585, the date of its official foundation, its role had been to secure Russia's southern borders against nomadic Turkic tribes. Peter the Great had ordered shipyards to be built there and he had pushed the power of the Russian state down the River Don and into the Sea of Azov. In the eighteenth century, when the boundary of the Russian Empire reached the shores of the Black Sea, Voronezh lost its strategic significance and sank into the typical condition of a Russian provincial capital, dominated by the trade in cereals, wool and leather. Its only claim to national fame was the Mitrofan monastery, the cells of which were used after 1917 by the Cheka for imprisoning and interrogating suspects. It was seriously damaged during the Second World War and eventually demolished. In fact, the whole of Old Voronezh suffered severely during the war. Between July 1942 and January 1943, the Soviet–German battlefront ran right through the town, and it was the scene of artillery duels between the Wehrmacht and the Red Army.

Since the nineteenth century, the town had taken pride in two of its sons who were literary luminaries: Ivan Nikitin and Alexei Koltsov. They were both people's poets, and even today, streets, parks and libraries are decorated with their names. But Voronezh is also the birthplace of Ivan Bunin, the first Russian to be awarded the Nobel Prize for Literature, in 1933, and Andrei Platonov, the author of *Chevengur* and *The Foundation Pit*. Now, Voronezh has acquired worldwide poetic fame, thanks to Osip Mandelstam. He would create his last poems there during his three years of exile: the *Voronezh Notebooks*. They are a high point not just of Russian but of world poetry in the twentieth century. They are poetic testaments of immeasurable tragedy. They provide evidence of misery and anxiety, but also of valiant efforts at recovery; they are messages to posterity which are imbued with a vigorous tenacity.

The poems did not emerge straight away. The first months were taken up in searching for accommodation and work, recovering from the Lubyanka-induced psychosis and getting used to life as an exile. There were many political exiles in Voronezh in the 1930s. Mandelstam had to report twice a week to the local offices of the NKVD, which by then had been reorganised. By the Central Executive Committee's decree of 17 July 1934, the OGPU, the previously separate secret police force, had been integrated into the NKVD under the name 'Main State Security Administration' (GUGB).

It was not easy to find accommodation. Landlords were not keen to house political exiles, who had been driven from the capital cities and were still objects of suspicion; they bore an indelible stigma. The Mandelstams first found accommodation in the Central Hotel on Revolution Prospekt. Then, during the summer months, they rented lodgings from a retired cook, close to the railway station, on Uritsky Street. This was not even a room but rather a small veranda. They had no actual roof over their head, but they were not on the street. At the end of June, Mandelstam was examined by a psychiatrist, whose diagnosis was that his traumatic psychosis had become less severe. Nadezhda, however, had caught typhus on the journey from Moscow, and she had to enter the infectious disease clinic on Friedrich Engels Street. Later, at the end of August, she had to return there on account of dysentery. On 31 October 1934, still in a weakened state, she wrote a desperate letter to the Soviet writer Marietta Shaginian:

> Isolation, outlawry and rightlessness – that is the background of Mandelstam's poems. It is this situation which led to the irresponsible verses, or, to put it better, the desperate lunge, for which he was exiled ... With Mandelstam poems are a way of discharging the burden of misfortune, the impermissible, the fear of death. They came out of a

> premonition of catastrophe and they called up a catastrophe … Mandelstam could not be fitted into any formula. He was a disturbing presence … Apart from that, there is the general chaos of our life: this conveyor belt of sickness and misfortune … I have always been astounded by Mandelstam's ability to survive, but now I no longer have this feeling. I think it is time to make an end. I believe this is the end. Perhaps this is a result of my typhus and dysentery, but I no longer have any strength, and I don't think we shall be able to last out.[1]

But, in fact, the end had not yet arrived. The first half of the Voronezh exile was a relatively mild experience. In September 1934, Mandelstam approached the Voronezh section of the Writers' Union with a request for employment, and in October he was allowed to join a group of journalists from the newspaper *Commune* to cover the opening of a village theatre in the Vorobyovka district. Pasternak had once again used his influence in favour of his fellow poet. He wrote in August to the head of the Central Committee's department for 'Culture and Propaganda', asking him to make it possible for Mandelstam to engage in literary activity in Voronezh, and, on 20 November 1934, a leading official of that department wrote to Comrade Genkin of the Communist Party's Voronezh District Committee instructing him to allow Mandelstam to work.[2]

Until the first Moscow show trial, in August 1936, which radically worsened his situation, Mandelstam was able to find various small opportunities for gainful employment, which when supplemented with donations from relatives and friends in Moscow were just enough to allow him to survive. He was occasionally employed as a consultant by the journal *Pod'yom* (Upsurge), he wrote reviews of a couple of ephemeral pieces of Soviet poetry and he planned to write a book with the title *The Old and the New Voronezh*.

He liked Voronezh. He liked its history as a frontier town under Peter the Great, and its proximity to Ukraine and the south. It had a theatre, a museum and a symphony orchestra and it enjoyed a modest cultural life. There was no comparison with Cherdyn. But he could not forget for an instant that he was a prisoner there. In a four-liner, he uses the magic

1 Letter from Nadezhda Mandelstam to Marietta Shaginian, in the collective volume O. G. Lasunskii et al., *Zhizn' i Tvorchestvo O. E. Mandel'shtama*, 75–7.

2 Letter of 20 November 1934 from the department for 'Culture and Propaganda' to Genkin: P. Nerler, 'On nichemu ne nauchilsia …', 92.

of words to invoke the name of Voronezh, the town of his banishment, reading into it the Russian words for 'raven' (*voron*) – the harbinger of death in Russian folklore – and 'knife' (*nozh*), the symbol of violence. The translation attempts to re-create the play on words in the original (nest, net, pest):

> Let me be free, Voronezh, hand me back –
> Let me go or better still lose me,
> You let me fall, you nest of ravens,
> Voronezh – net, Voronezh – pest!
> (WH, 159)

By the middle of October, it was no longer advisable to sleep on verandas. The Mandelstams again set out in search of rooms. Their first known address in Voronezh (from autumn 1934 to April 1935) was slightly to one side of the northern end of Revolution Prospekt. It was 'No. 4, Second Line (*Vtoraia Lineinaia*) Street'. The name referred to the nearby railway line. The house still exists (its present address is 4b Ulitsa Shveinikov). It is situated in a hollow, and on an incline.[3] Mandelstam played a self-deprecatory but also sarcastic game with the word 'line' in the street name and the low position of the house 'in the hollow' in a poem written in April 1935:

> What street is this?
> Mandelstam Street.
> What a devil of a name!
> However you turn it
> It sounds crooked, not straight.
>
> There was little of the straight line in him,
> His morals were not lily-white
> And so this street,
> Or rather this pit,
> Is named after
> This Mandelstam.
> (WH, 21; VN, 36)

3 The Mandelstams' addresses in Voronezh: N. Shtempel', *Mandel'shtam v Voronezhe*, 71–5; R. Dutli, 'Tote Luft getrunken', in *Frankfurter Allgemeine Zeitung*, no. 146, 27 June 1994, 25.

This was the dwelling place behind whose walls a landlord in Cossack boots, an agronomist by the name of Vdovin, strode up and down and hammered into the poet's mind a sense of his otherness. This is how he expressed it in a poem of the time: 'Behind the wall the crotchety landlord stamps / Around in his Russian boots.' Sleeplessness is the fate of the exile: 'I sleep badly in strangers' homes, / And my own life is not near me.' (WH, 11; VN, 33)

It was here, shortly before they moved out, that he wrote the first poems of the *Voronezh Notebooks*. They were written down in small and inexpensive school exercise books – hence the name. The first verses of the poem 'The Violinist' emerged on 5 April 1935 after a concert by the violinist Galina Barinova, whose hairstyle and way of moving reminded Mandelstam of Marina Tsvetaeva and the love affair of 1916. The playing of the violinist offered him consolation, and stimulated the unleashing of his life force: 'Play then till my aorta bursts, / Play with a cat's head in your mouth. / There were three devils, now you're the fourth, / The final wonderful devil in full flower' (WH, 47; VN, 47). It was the vitality of music which helped the poems to break through. The pianist Maria Yudina had already starred in Voronezh, on 12 and 13 November 1934. She had deliberately arranged her concert tour so that she could play before the exiled Mandelstam. She visited him and played for him in the empty hall of the House of the Red Army. But the time was not yet ripe for poems.

Not until the spring of 1935 did Mandelstam's vital energies re-awaken, after the traumatic experiences he had undergone. His discovery of Russia's 'black earth', the ploughed fields around Voronezh, played some role in this. Mandelstam, the poet of culture, now opened his mind to the nature that surrounded him, although 'black earth' was an image he had already long associated with poetry. In the essay 'The Word and Culture' (1921), he had called poetry a 'plough', which turns up the soil of time so that its 'black earth' comes to the surface (GP, 84; CC, 113). 'Black earth', the phrase that describes a particularly fertile type of land and is the geographical name for a wide area of Central Russia, is poetically enriched in Mandelstam's *Voronezh Notebooks*, until the word becomes an all-embracing metaphor, an image of the world and of life. The 'Black Earth' poem of April 1935 associates *speaking* with ploughing, poetry with ploughed-up earth ('A realm of heaps: speech, furrowed and rugged'), and invokes creative power and freedom:

Too weighty, too black, all that's piled up,
All that's heaped, shrinks, what's well-aired,
All of it crumbles, all shaping a chorus –
Moist light clods, my earth of freedom!
...
How pleasing the rich layers to the blade,
How silent the steppe, in April's ploughing.
Well: live long, black earth: be firm, clear-eyed –
Here there's a black-voiced silence working.
(WH, 9; FF, 40)

There is also a political allusion hidden in the phrase 'earth of freedom'. A congress of 'Land and Freedom' (*Zemlya i Volya*), a radical faction of the populist movement, took place in Voronezh in 1879, attended by prominent revolutionaries such as Georgi Plekhanov, Sofia Perovskaya, Vera Figner and Andrei Zhelyabov. This reference made to an event in revolutionary history by a man exiled by the Soviet regime lends the poem an ambiguous but also a provocative overtone. Mandelstam converted the revolutionary slogan of freedom into a personal manifesto of creative vitality. Complicity with the black earth liberated him, and in another poem, he directly called on himself to start living again: 'I must live, although I have died twice over' (WH, 13; VN, 33). As Anna Akhmatova recorded in 'Pages from a Diary': 'It's striking that space, breadth and a deep breathing appeared in Mandelstam's verse precisely in Voronezh, when he was not free at all.'[4]

But traumatic experiences and sombre visions had not been entirely overcome. In a nightmarish poem written early in his stay in Voronezh, he envisages the mistreatment a woman he loves will have to undergo:

Your thin shoulders whips will redden,
Whips will redden, and make ice leaden

Your childish arms will heave rail-tracks
Heave rail-tracks and sew string for sacks

4 Akhmatova on space, breadth and deep breathing in the *Voronezh Notebooks*: A. Akhmatova, *My Half Century*, 104.

Your tender feet will tread naked on glass,
Tread naked on glass and blood-wet sand pass

And for I am here, to burn – a black flare,
To burn – a black flare, frightened of prayer.
(WH, 7; TF, 27)

'Thin shoulders' are among Maria Petrovykh's attributes mentioned in the 1934 poem 'Expert Mistress of Guilty Glances' (MM, 217; MN, 86). But the word 'string' refers back to the 'bits of string' in the 1931 poem 'Let's Sit in the Kitchen Together' (MM, 49; MN, 36), which was dedicated to Nadezhda, and in her view the Voronezh poem expressed Mandelstam's anxiety about her in the summer of 1934, when she lay ill with typhus and dysentery. On the other hand, Emma Gerstein, in her memoirs, ascribes the impulse behind the poem to Mandelstam's remorse at having incriminated Maria Petrovykh during his Lubyanka interrogation. But, like an actual dream, this nightmarish poem undoubtedly blended the features of both women into a single person, who had to endure mistreatment on his account. A Self tortured with guilt-feelings fears for this person, and knows that her life is endangered because she is close to him. The black candlelight is a belated recollection of the 1916 motif of the black sun, in the poem on the death of his mother. It was Mandelstam's metaphor for guilt.[5]

The poems were now emerging like intense outbreaks of fever. The poems of the first Voronezh notebook arrived in rapid bursts between 17 April 1935 and July 1935. At the beginning of April, Mandelstam made the acquaintance of the young literary scholar Sergei Rudakov, who had been banished from Leningrad to the town, and he witnessed the re-awakening of Mandelstam's creative powers. On 20 April, he wrote to his wife:

> Mandelstam has been furiously at work. I've never seen anything like it. It's a rare sight … I stand before a working mechanism (perhaps an organism, it's the same thing) of poetry … He is no longer a human being but a Michelangelo. He sees and understands nothing. He walks up and

5 Uncertainty over the dedicatee of the poem 'Your Thin Shoulders': N. Mandel'shtam, *Kniga Tret'ia*, 198–200; seen as an expression of M.'s 'remorse' over Maria Petrovykh: E. Gerstein, *Moscow Memoirs*, 401–3.

> down, and mutters ... To get four lines he pronounces four hundred. I mean that quite literally.[6]

Rudakov had lively arguments and disputes with Mandelstam, he made notes for future commentaries, and he promised to prepare an edition of his poetry. Nadezhda Mandelstam severely takes him to task in a chapter of her memoirs entitled 'Archive and Voice'. According to her, he took Mandelstam's archive to Leningrad, including many original manuscripts, and there – after his death in the Second World War – his widow either destroyed it or flogged it off to the highest bidder. Nevertheless, Rudakov was a ray of light, a sign of hope, to Mandelstam, because he was always searching for a good 'interlocutor'. In December 1935 he wrote to him: 'You are the most magnificent fellow in the world' (MR, 236–7).

The exiled poet clung to every possible scrap of culture he could find. In addition to going to concerts, he enjoyed visiting the cinema on Revolution Prospekt, and he liked to watch Charlie Chaplin films such as *City Lights* and *Modern Times*. In April 1935, he went to see the first Soviet sound movie, *Chapayev* (1934), made by Sergei and Georgy Vasilyev, and he found it impressive. He had already amused himself at the expense of the early silent films in the 1913 poem 'Film', but now he was so taken by the 'talkie' about the legendary civil war hero Chapayev that he introduced the partisan into two of his poems, and even identified himself with the character:

> Our train was bound for the Urals. A talking Chapayev
> From a post-silent movie leaped into our wide-open mouths;
> Behind a timber fence, on a sheet of film,
> To die and leap back onto his horse.
> (WH, 35; FP, 87)

The attempt to overcome death in a new outburst of vitality and creative energy ran side by side with the wish to find a route into Soviet life, despite all the obstacles. Mandelstam decided to confront reality again. It was not the first time. His sense of himself as 'an apostate in the family of the people' (MM, 73), which he had expressed in a poem in May 1931, was a heavy burden. As a Russian intellectual, who had been close to the

6 Rudakov's letter of 20 April 1935: Gerstein, *Moscow Memoirs*, 124–5.

SRs in his youth, he did not find it easy to be separated from the people. In the 1918 poem 'The Twilight of Freedom', he had described the people as 'the sun' and 'the judge'. To be labelled an 'enemy of the people' caused him suffering, and indeed he occasionally dreamed that he might be able to belong. In the Voronezh stanzas (May–June 1935) he imagined his entry into the new world, along with 'good people':

> I do not want to squander
> The last penny of my soul among youths bred in a hothouse,
> Rather to go into the world as a landowning peasant
> Enters the collective farm – and the people are good.
> …
> A damned stitch, a ridiculous enterprise
> Separated us. And now understand this,
> I must live, breathing, growing big and Bolshevik,
> And before death I must become better-looking
> And still be around to play with people a little.
> (WH, 29; VN, 40)

Mandelstam's astonishing new motto, 'live, breathe, and grow Bolshevik', derives from the re-awakening in the spring of 1935 of his will to live. But the attempt to 'grow Bolshevik' did not last very long. Mandelstam would repeatedly be confronted with the spiritual narrowness of his surroundings in Voronezh. It was not easy for him to negate either his affinities with Europe or his rootedness in world culture. In February 1935, the cultivated city dweller had stood in front of an assembly of Voronezh writers and proletarian and peasant representatives. He was supposed to inform them about his literary past and his colleagues the Acmeists. It was expected that he would 'unmask' his Petersburg fellow poets, but, instead, he declared his unbreakable solidarity with them. After all, he had described himself in 1933 as 'Akhmatova's contemporary': 'I dissociate myself neither from the living nor from the dead.' He meant the living Anna Akhmatova and the dead Nikolai Gumilyov, shot in 1921. And his reply to the provocative question 'What is Acmeism?' was this famous proclamation: 'A nostalgia for world culture.'[7]

7 Acmeism as 'nostalgia for world culture': N. Mandelstam, *Hope Abandoned*, 246 ('Italy').

These answers must have seemed immensely provocative. In April 1936, Stoichov, the head of the Voronezh branch of the Writers' Union, complained to a party meeting that the statements Mandelstam had made in February 1935 had shown 'that he has learned nothing, that he has remained the same as he always was'. Stoichov would repeat his verdict after the first Moscow show trial, in a report on 'unmasking the class enemy on the literary front' for the attention of Vladimir Stavsky, the general secretary of the Soviet Writers' Union.[8] Mandelstam recalled his February 1935 appearance before the Voronezh writers in an April 1937 letter, describing it as 'moral torture' (MR, 270). He had been gripped in the vice of ideology, and, in the eyes of writers who conformed to the party line, he had failed the test.

It was elsewhere that Mandelstam looked for his allies and for signs of continuity. The poem 'I Must Live, although I Have Died Twice Over' (April 1935) invokes, along with the fertile black earth of Central Russia, the art of the Renaissance (the rebirth!). He imagined that he could perceive the sculptures of Michelangelo in the cloud formations hanging over Voronezh, no doubt associating them in his mind with the 'prisoners' in the Florentine Galleria dell'Accademia: 'The sky, the sky, is – your Buonarroti!' (WH, 13) In the spring of 1935, he had another opportunity to demonstrate indirectly his 'nostalgia for world culture', to indicate that European culture was his real homeland. He was asked to write radio essays for the Voronezh District Radio Committee on Goethe's youth and on his favourite opera, Gluck's *Orpheus and Eurydice*. The second essay has not survived, but fragments of the manuscript for the Goethe programme still exist. They bear witness to the activities of the period between May and July 1935, when the exiled Mandelstam, together with Nadezhda, pored over Goethe's works, reading his essay 'Poetry and Truth' and fascinatedly piecing together the earlier stages in the life of a more fortunate poet. Curious paradox: the pariah is writing about the man whose luck never ran out. A sympathetic portrait emerged from this, but he did not glorify Goethe, the favourite of fortune:

8 Stoichov's complaints about M.: in the collective volume *Slovo i Sud'ba. O. Mandel'shtam*, Moscow, 1991, 48; the correspondence section of the four-volume Mandelstam edition published in Moscow in 1997, 410, commentary on letter no. 223; P. Nerler, 'On nichemu ne nauchilsia ...', 91–4.

> The coachbuilders of Strasbourg are unhurriedly putting together a prison on wheels, a varnished coffin resting on shock-absorbers, in which they will transport Germany's greatest poet into a dwarf state, the Duchy of Weimar, where he will be made a minister under a better ruler and it will be possible to wheel him out before guests as an exotic little animal. (GD, 222)

Mandelstam's radio presentation of Goethe also reflected his youthful dreams. When observing the portraits of Goethe's women, he found that they all resembled Olga Vaksel. The high-spirited violinist Barinova had stirred up his memories of Marina Tsvetaeva, and now Goethe brought back to mind his most passionate affair, that of 1925 ('In that beyond-the-eyelid life / You will surely be my wife'). While still in Moscow, Mandelstam had accidentally learned from an acquaintance he met in the street that Olga Vaksel had committed suicide, shooting herself in 1932 in Oslo. Now he composed a belated threnody for her: 'Is It Possible to Praise a Dead Woman?'

> The rigid swallows of her curved brows
> Flew to me from the grave.
> To say they had laid down to rest
> In their cold Stockholm bed.
> …
> I cherish your unhappy memory,
> Wilding, bear cub, Mignon.
> But the wheels of the windmills hibernate in the snow,
> And the postman's horn is frozen.
> (WH, 41; VN, 44)

The image of the wounded swallow in Hans Christian Andersen's fairy tale 'Thumbelina' is combined with Goethe's figure of Mignon and Schubert's *Winter Journey* to express Mandelstam's sorrow and grief. Olga becomes a Mignon, and a symbol of the nostalgia for the south which can also be heard in Goethe's 'Song of Mignon' in *Wilhelm Meister's Apprenticeship* (Book 3, 1): 'Know you the land where the lemon trees bloom? / Where the golden orange glows amid the darkness of the leaves.'

For the exiled Mandelstam, however, this nostalgia is frozen by the snow. He is not in his beloved south, but on a personal *Winterreise*! The second poem dedicated to the dead Olga Vaksel, composed in June 1935, when summer was just beginning, is also full of memories of frosty weather in wintertime Petersburg: 'On lifeless eyelashes Isaac froze' (WH, 43).

The first Voronezh notebook was completed in July 1935. Its concluding poem is a retrospect on his life, permeated with sense impressions: he sees, he touches, he smells, he hears. It is also a list of losses, a catalogue of disappearances, which ends in clinical coldness and death:[9]

> No, it's not a migraine but pass the menthol stick anyway –
> Neither the languishing of art, nor the beauties of joyful space
> …
> No, it's not a migraine but the cold of genderless space,
> The whistle of ripped gauze and the noise of a carbolic guitar.
> (WH, 55; VN, 50)

Even so, the first notebook is not a journey through a realm of ghosts. The vital force that counteracts his depression is unmistakably there as well. The cycle celebrates the here and now; the little word 'still' conjures up the fullness that is endangered, as in the 24 May 1935 poem 'Children at the Barber's': 'We are still filled with life to a supreme degree' (WH, 23). Here, one again sees the Soviet law term 'supreme' as in 'the supreme penalty', namely the death penalty, which was part of the harsh daily experience of the Stalin epoch. Mandelstam takes this terrifying, ever-present legal expression and inflects it into an assertion of stoic vitality.

Nor is political virulence absent. Despite his expressed desire to 'grow Bolshevik', the first Voronezh notebook contains verses which demonstrate that Mandelstam's political acumen has not abandoned him. A poem dating from June or July 1935 is a parable, draping contemporary political events in orientalising décor, with slaves, paranoid sultans and cold-blooded eunuchs: 'Wave after wave runs on, breaking the wave's back / Throwing itself at the moon with a prisoner's longing' (WH, 49; VN, 48). What was it that unleashed this poem?

---

9 According to Nadezhda Mandelstam's memoirs, 'No, Not a Migraine' was the last poem in the first Voronezh notebook, but several editors of Mandelstam's works in Russian consider that it had already been written in 1931.

The sentence of banishment applied to Mandelstam alone, not to Nadezhda. She travelled repeatedly to Moscow to offer the new poems to the journals – always without success. No editor would have dared to print verses by the outlawed poet. The chasm between the exiled Mandelstam and contemporary Soviet poetry had long been unbridgeable. Thus, the *Voronezh Notebooks* remained messages for posterity. When Nadezhda returned from Moscow on 18 June 1935 after a second fruitless journey, she told Mandelstam that rumours were spreading about the hidden background to the murder of Kirov. The Leningrad party secretary had been assassinated on 1 December 1934. It was being speculated that Stalin himself had ordered the murder of a politician who had become too popular, so as to justify the use of mass terror to liquidate the 'murderers of Kirov'. After receiving this news Mandelstam entered a state of 'complete disillusionment'.[10] This was what produced the July 1935 poem about waves that break the backs of other waves. It is an astonishingly precise image for the waves of 'purge terror' that would blanket the country with innumerable horrors between 1936 and 1938.

Mandelstam had long since grasped his own situation clearly in his poetry. A four-liner from May 1935 indicates his stubborn defiance. He calls to mind his awareness that he is a prisoner, cut off from everything, but he also praises the irreplaceable instrument which is his 'last weapon' (WH, 33): the poet's lips, the organ of poetry that has remained intact.

> Having deprived me of seas, of running and flying away,
> And allowing me only to walk upon the violent earth,
> What have you achieved? A splendid result:
> You could not stop my lips from moving.
> (WH, 39; VN, 43)

The 'Voronezh miracle' consisted not just in the postponement of Mandelstam's elimination, but in the intensity of his poetic oeuvre, the unbroken movement of his lips. However, the poems of the three Voronezh notebooks did not emerge continuously, as a leisurely lyrical diary, but in three powerful creative thrusts: the first from April to July 1935, the second from December 1936 to February 1937 and the third from March

10 M.'s 'state of complete disillusionment' after hearing the rumours about Kirov's murder: N. Mandel'shtam, *Kniga Tret'ia*, 212.

to May 1937. Between the first and the second, there yawned a period of silence, marked by long months of depression and apathy, misery and sickness. By the end of July 1935, the first vigorous outpouring had run its course.

On 21 April 1935, the Mandelstams continued their Voronezh odyssey by moving into a new apartment. It was located in a house on the corner, where Street of the 25 October (house number 45) joins Revolution Prospekt. Mandelstam groped his way from one meagre source of income to the next: a translation of the short story 'Yvette' by Guy de Maupassant, the above-mentioned radio broadcast on Goethe and so on. One of the reviews for the journal *Pod'yom* concerned a collection of poems on the building of the Moscow metro. The first line of the Moscow underground railway was opened on 15 May 1935 and was greeted with a degree of propagandistic ballyhoo rarely equalled by Stalin's other building projects. And Mandelstam, whose preferred interlocutors were Ovid and Dante, had to discuss the clumsy celebratory doggerel of Soviet poets of dubious talent. At least it brought in a few copecks. And, for the moment, he was not complaining. He wrote to his father in the middle of July 1935: 'For the first time for many years, I don't feel like an apostate, *I am living socially*, and things are going very well' (MR, 235).

He was even awarded an 'official trip' to the Vorobyovka district, which lasted from 22 to 31 July 1935. He was commissioned by the newspaper *Kommuna* to visit a State Farm with a delegation and write an enthusiastic account of what he saw. But he was a completely unsuitable person to perform such a typically Soviet task. The newspaper rejected his scrawl. Only fragments of his failed attempt are still extant.[11] But a memory of this 'official trip' would suddenly surface in a poem written in December 1936:

> I circled round the fields of the State Farms,
> My mouth was full of air,
> The menacing suns of sunflowers
> Rotated right into the eyes.
> (WH, 83; VN, 58)

11 M. visits a sovkhoz and sleeps in a hay barn, according to O. Kretova, in the collective work O. G. Lasunskii et al., *Zhizn' i Tvorchestvo O. E. Mandel'shtama*, 37. M.'s rejected report on the sovkhoz is printed in O. Mandel'shtam, 'Ia predlagaiu dat' dokumental'noiu knigu o derevne', *Literaturnoe Obozrenie* 1, 1991, 21–8.

In one of the Sovkhoz villages, the alien urbanite's odd behaviour attracted notice: accommodated in a hay barn, he stayed awake during the night listening anxiously to the unusual noises, and he used his stick to drive off bats and grasshoppers. As a poet, he evidently had a greater affinity with heaven than with a Sovkhoz haystack. Nevertheless, in 1922, he had written a cosmically inspired poem in which he gazes from a dishevelled hayloft into the heavens:

> Up a little ladder I climbed
> To a hayloft in utter disarray –
> I inhaled the clutter of space,
> The detritus of milky stars
> …
> A hay wagon, enormous, unyoked,
> Athwart the universe stands.
> The ancient chaos of the hayloft
> Will tickle, prickle a man.
> (TR, 135; PO, 12)

On 10 October 1935, with the approval of the local branch of the Writers' Union, Mandelstam took up the modest position of literary adviser to the 'Great Soviet Theatre' of Voronezh, located on Karl Marx Street. Its usual repertoire consisted of ephemera of a progressive character, but it also performed Gorky's *Enemies*, Goldoni's *Servant of Two Masters* and Chekhov's *Cherry Orchard*, the last of which induced Mandelstam to write a malicious little essay on the renowned dramatist: 'Give the characters railway tickets, for example the "three sisters", and the piece has come to an end' (GD, 224). His tone had been different in October 1929, when he was working for the newspaper *Moskovskii Komsomolets*: 'Chekhov portrays the doctor, the engineer and the *personality* of the peasant in the same way: fearlessly, calmly and carefully' (GD, 277).

Mandelstam was not a man of the theatre but a poet, and his work there soon ended in failure, like all his previous employments. He was on superficially friendly terms with some of the actors, though they found him mysterious, and he never recited his poetry to them. He was not capable of becoming part of a 'collective', and his old symptoms of overstrain quickly resurfaced. On 19 November 1935, a Voronezh psychiatrist certified that he was suffering from severe exhaustion of the nervous system.

In mid-December Nadezhda again made the journey to Moscow, in search of work and publication outlets for Mandelstam's latest poems. Two days later, Mandelstam collapsed in the street (he describes it in a letter as his 'old tetanus'). He finally received a document admitting him to the Tambov rest home for nervous disorders, situated on the River Tsna, two hundred kilometres north-east of Voronezh. On 18 December, he travelled there via Michurinsk, arriving late at night in the town, which was covered in deep snow. It was a magical moment, which would blaze forth as an image in a poem composed a year later:

> I entered at night into the gauntleted
> Tambov, splendid with snow.
> I saw the Tsna – an ordinary river –
> White, white, it was covered in white.
> (WH, 83; VN, 58)

In a series of letters full of yearning for Nadezhda, he describes the 'winter paradise, the indescribable beauty' of Tambov. On 26 December 1935, he writes: 'We live on a steep bank of the Tsna River. It is a wide river, or seems to be wide, like the Volga. It flows into ink-blue forests. The gentleness and harmony of the Russian winter bring me great joy' (MR, 238–9; CC, 550). Every day, he was bathed and given electro-therapy ('electric massage of the spine') according to the customary procedures for healing people with psychiatric problems.

But his enthusiasm for the Russian winter did not last very long. He found life in the Tambov clinic tedious. On 1 January 1936, he wrote: 'These days have been like a bad dream! Some sort of penal battalion' (MR, 246; CC, 554). Oscillating between lethargy and nervous excitement, he managed to hold out for a few more days. But then, on 5 January, worn down by bad food, noise, boredom and a longing for Nadezhda, he returned to Voronezh. He would always remain a difficult patient in Stalin's mental hospital.

Even so, he now began to hope that his status as an exile might be changed. Shortly before his journey to Tambov, he had drafted out an appeal to the 'Minsk Plenum of Soviet Writers', which was due to meet in February 1936. He submitted it to the Voronezh section of the Writers' Union. When she went to Moscow, Nadezhda also intended to present copies of Mandelstam's appeal to Shcherbakov and Marchenko, officials of the Writers' Union and the writers' branch of the party organisation. The document has not yet been discovered, but its content can be deduced from Mandelstam's letter of 3 January 1936 to Nadezhda (MR, 248–9; CC, 556–7). It was a declaration of loyalty towards the Communist Party and the Writers' Union, or at least a sort of agreement to suspend hostilities. Mandelstam offered never to return to Moscow, and to settle instead in the Crimea, in the town of Staryi Krym. It can be assumed that this also involved an end to the writing of 'hostile' political texts, but he did want to have a guarantee of freedom of movement 'throughout the entire region' ('It would be terrible without that freedom'). It would be a 'tacit' exile in the south, at his favourite spot on the planet: the Crimea. When he told Nadezhda that, after writing the appeal, he was 'already free', this was a piece of wishful thinking, completely at odds with reality. The time for mild sentences and special conditions had passed by with appalling rapidity.

We do not know whether Mandelstam ever received an official reply. Having returned to Voronezh, he was again confronted with all the material and social problems of everyday existence. His life as an exile was pleasantly interrupted between 5 and 11 February 1936 by a visit from Anna Akhmatova. They spent their time in long discussions and poetry recitations. For one short week, Mandelstam enjoyed recovering at least a trace of the atmosphere of Petersburg culture and a bygone life. He had enticed his fellow poet to come to Voronezh with a telegram in which he suggested that he was close to death. She had hardly arrived when his liveliness returned. He said to her during this visit: 'Poetry is a power, because people are killed for it.'[12] After her return, Akhmatova wrote her famous poem 'Voronezh' (4 March 1936), which ended with the words: 'While in the room of the exiled poet / Fear and the Muse stand duty in turn / And the night is endless / And knows no dawn' (VN, 13).

After quarrelling with the landlord, who wanted to get rid of the suspect exile, the Mandelstams moved on 13 March 1936 into a new apartment. The address was 13 Friedrich Engels Street, apartment number 39 (in 1991 a plaque in memory of Mandelstam was affixed to the building). No new poems would emerge at this stage, but the couple were able to complete their written collection of Osip's current poetry, using the cover name 'Codex Vaticanus'. In addition to the poems in the first Voronezh notebook, the archive also included Moscow poems confiscated at the time of Mandelstam's arrest in May 1934 and now reconstructed from memory.

12 'Poetry is a power': N. Mandelstam, *Hope Against Hope*, 170 ('The Change of Values').

Both of them were suffering from health problems. At the beginning of April 1936, Nadezhda had a painful attack of hepatitis. In a begging letter to her brother, Yevgeny Khazin, Mandelstam described their desperate situation:

> We are completely alone … We are constantly anxious and uneasy and have a terrible sense of hopelessness. A few days ago it was proclaimed from the tribune of the District Plenum of the Writers' Union that I was a 'complete nonentity' that I wrote 'boudoir verselets' (bou-doir-verse-lets) and that they had 'had quite enough to do with me' … We are in such hell that we cannot stand it any longer, and there is no one here we can say a word to. Help us, because things will get very bad for us … We are at the end of our tether. (MR, 250–1)

To add to their misfortunes, on 13 April, Mandelstam suffered another heart attack, while walking along the street. He wrote on 28 April 1936 to Boris Pasternak:

> I am really very sick, and there is hardly anything that could help me now: since December I have become continuously weaker, and at present it is already difficult for me even to leave the room.
>
> The fact that my 'second life' is still continuing is due entirely to my only and inestimable friend – my wife. (MR, 250–1)

On 7 May, Mandelstam again suffered from acute heart pains while attending a performance of Beethoven's Ninth Symphony given by an orchestra which included the violinist David Oistrakh. He left the concert early, and put himself in the hands of the Voronezh polyclinic. There, he was declared too ill to work, and in the middle of June he was informed by the Voronezh theatre that he had been dismissed.

Boris Pasternak and Anna Akhmatova remained his most faithful allies. At the end of February 1936 they had approached the state prosecutor Katanyan, asking him to ease Mandelstam's situation, and they sent a thousand roubles to Voronezh after making a collection among their friends. With this money, the Mandelstams were able to rent a room from a peasant family in Zadonsk, a town ninety kilometres north of Voronezh on the steep banks of the River Don, for a few weeks of summer. The address was 10 Karl Marx Street. They set off on 20 June 1936, and they remained there until the beginning of September. It would be the last relaxing summer holiday they ever spent. Nadezhda painted watercolours, reverting to her time in Kyiv as an art student. In a poem composed months afterwards, in December 1936, Mandelstam wistfully recalled this 'last' summer:

> And the river Don is still a half-breed beauty,
> Silvery, shallow and awkward.
> Drawing half buckets of water
> She would get confused, like my soul,
>
> When the burden of the evenings
> Lay on hard beds,
> And the trees caroused and rustled
> Coming out from the banks.
> (WH, 81; VN, 57)

The poem begins with the verses: 'It's easy to take off the stubble of hibernation / With the thin blade of the razor. / Let's remember together / The half-Ukrainian summer.' The razor blade, the instrument of his first attempted suicide in May 1934 in the Lubyanka, now becomes a means of liberating him from the 'stubble of hibernation'. And perhaps also a way of banishing thoughts of suicide. In the future, Mandelstam would hardly be able to write such light-hearted verses, touched as they are with the breath of summer's profusion.

On 19 August 1936, Osip and Nadezhda heard on the radio that the first Moscow show trial had started. Silently, they went into the street: 'There was nothing to say about this – everything was clear.' This was the 'Trial of the Sixteen' against Zinoviev, Kamenev and other Old Bolsheviks and high party officials. In the jargon of the time, it was a trial directed against the 'Trotskyist-Zinovievist Terrorist Centre'. Reports of the trial were shot through with hate-filled tirades against the 'murderers of Kirov'. Its proceedings were transmitted to the population through street loudspeakers. The screaming voice of the state prosecutor, Vyshinsky, echoed through the air. And it was announced that further trials would be held. It was the beginning of the notorious *chistka*, Stalin's series of terror purges which lasted from 1936 to 1938, and which would destroy the lives of hundreds of thousands of people.[13]

13 While in Zadonsk, the Mandelstams hear radio reports on the first show trial: N. Mandelstam, *Hope Against Hope*, 195 ('The Last Winter in Voronezh').

22

I Am a Shadow

(Voronezh 1936–1937)

When the Mandelstams returned from Zadonsk to Voronezh at the beginning of September 1936, they found that their situation had worsened radically. After the first show trial, Moscow ordered 'heightened vigilance' in relation to 'class enemies and saboteurs'. Mandelstam lost all his sources of paid work, whether for the newspapers, the radio or the theatre. From that time on, he was a beggar and an invalid with heart problems, who was dependent on the charity of relatives and acquaintances.

The ideological climate steadily became worse.[1] A meeting of Voronezh writers on 11 September 1936 discussed the 'struggle against class enemies on the literary front'. Mandelstam's name came up. On 16 September, the newspaper *Kommuna* printed a polemic against 'manifestly alien people' who were alleged to have spread 'confused and harmful theories'. Mandelstam's name was again mentioned. On 28 September, the chair of the Voronezh section of the Soviet Writers' Union, Stoichov, sent a report to the general secretary of the union, Stavsky, who had inquired in a telegram about the progress he had made in 'exposing the class enemy'. Stoichov repeated what he had said six months earlier at a meeting of the party branch of the Writers' Union about Mandelstam's replies at the February

1 The ideological climate in Voronezh in September 1936: P. Nerler, 'On nichemu ne nauchilsia ...', 93.

1935 meeting: 'he has learned nothing, and he has remained the same as he always was'. One could hardly imagine a better way of denouncing the exiled poet.

The continuing deterioration of the ideological atmosphere was accompanied by a further growth in the personality cult around Stalin. On 27 August 1936, *Literaturnaia Gazeta* printed a resolution passed on 21 August by the writers of Moscow, under the heading 'Stalin's Life Is Our Life': 'Stalin has the qualities of genius appropriate to our country, and he mirrors our character: he is *immortal*. The life of Stalin is our magnificent present and future.' In this atmosphere of increasing agitation against 'class enemies' and glorification of the great leader, Mandelstam lost his accommodation as well as any chance of further employment, because even greater suspicion now fell on him as an exile. In October 1936, the couple had to change their place of residence yet again. An ordinary woman, a theatrical dressmaker, was prepared to let them one room in her small house. This would be Mandelstam's last Voronezh address: 50 Street of the 27 February. Various acquaintances now started to avoid him ostentatiously in the street. They no longer returned his greeting, and they pretended not to know him.

But, that autumn, there was one ray of light: the Mandelstams got to know a young teacher, Natasha Shtempel, who would play a special role in the preservation of Mandelstam's poems. Natasha knew of the Mandelstams through Sergei Rudakov, who had returned to Leningrad from exile in July 1936. Out of jealousy, Rudakov had extracted a promise from her that she would never visit them. But she decided to break this promise. She simply rang their doorbell one Sunday in September 1936. The pair had developed special antennae for spies over the years; indeed, they had even devised different categories for the spies they detected. For instance, they were quick to see through the spies who always brought with them the same statue of the Buddha to attest to their cultural expertise (thereby bringing the Buddha to the confirmed 'anti-Buddhist' Mandelstam, who called himself 'the last Hellenic-Jewish-Christian poet'!). Natasha Shtempel was not a spy. She became a true friend and a welcome visitor. She was almost the only person in Voronezh who still dared to maintain contact with the suspect pair and to stand by them.[2]

Moreover, Natasha came from an intellectual family with origins in

2 Different kinds of spy: N. Mandelstam, *Hope Against Hope*, 33–8 ('Theory and Practice'), 204–10 ('Golden Rules'). Natasha Shtempel's first meeting with the Mandelstams:

the impoverished aristocracy and with distant German ancestors, so she herself was 'socially suspect' in many respects. Even her mother warned her at first against visiting the Mandelstams: 'You know very well what consequences that can have.' The great arrest waves had started by then. Natasha and her mother listened at night to find out where the heavy, black limousines of the NKVD were stopping. In spite of this, she did not want to break off her visits, so the hungry Mandelstams were often invited into the Shtempel home at 40 Kaliaev Street, where they were hospitably entertained. The fact that the two women had the mettle to do this was an example of civic courage, a rare and mysterious phenomenon in a totalitarian system. There was no thought of heroism: what was involved here was personal integrity and simple humanity.

In better times, at the beginning of their exile, the Mandelstams had themselves still been able to help people. Another exile, Pavel Kaletsky, recalled that the Mandelstams were the only people in Voronezh who had reacted to the sickness and death of his wife by offering him 'great kindness and human sympathy'. He characterised Mandelstam as a very intelligent but highly irascible interlocutor who was extremely clumsy in dealing with practical matters. He could 'explode like a bomb at the slightest disagreement'. He was a 'very difficult and bewitching human being'.

But there was another ray of hope, too, at the end of the year. The month of December 1936 was one of Mandelstam's most intensive periods of poetic creation. The poems in the second Voronezh notebook emerged from this time of feverish intoxication. Mandelstam walked with a stick, had heart trouble, suffered from asthma, was officially ostracised as a 'class enemy' and had been abandoned by (almost) everyone else. Where he derived the strength for this outburst of creativity is a mystery. And he knew what he was doing. In a letter of 12 December 1936 to his father, he writes:

> Even now I cannot hold myself back: first and foremost, I am writing poems. With great determination. Powerful and energetic. I know their value, I don't need to ask anyone about this. Secondly, I have learned to read Spanish … Our situation is – simply appalling. The state of my health is such that at the age of 45 I have become acquainted with the delights of life as an 85 year old. (MR, 253)

N. Shtempel, *Mandel'shtam v Voronezhe*, 27–9. On Pavel Kaletsky: P. Nerler, 'On nichemu ne nauchilsia …', 95.

The main impulse for his Spanish studies was a book by his old friend Valentin Parnakh (one of the models for the figure of 'Parnok' in *The Egyptian Stamp*!). The title was *Spanish and Portuguese Poets as Victims of the Inquisition*, and it appeared in 1934 under the imprint of the Leningrad publishing house 'Academia'. As a victim of Stalin's inquisition, Mandelstam no doubt sought consolation from the book. He was particularly fascinated by one poet, a Spanish Jew, who composed a sonnet in his head throughout his stay in the dungeons of the Inquisition, and who remembered these fruits of imprisonment until he was released and could write them down.[3]

If it was music and black earth that helped the poems of the first Voronezh notebook to emerge, the same function was now fulfilled by small-scale everyday experiences: the smile of a little child, or the sight of an imprisoned bird, the goldfinch. The poem begun on 8 December 1936, 'The Birth of a Smile' (WH, 61), is a miniature cosmogony. Mandelstam's accidental glimpse of a baby's first smile is associated with the beginning of the world, and the child's discovery of objects is appreciated as perception at its origin.

> The instant when a child begins to smile,
> Partly in bitterness, partly in sweetness
> The end points of its smile – all jokes aside
> Become submerged in oceanic chaos.
>
> The baby feels unconquerably good,
> With the corners of its lips it plays in glory,
> And a rainbow-seam is already being stitched
> For the endless recognition of reality.
> (WH, 61; PO, 43)

It was a tragic coincidence that the child celebrated in this poem belonged to the writer Olga Kretova, who showered Mandelstam with ideological criticisms, and would in April 1937 write a vicious article for a Voronezh newspaper attacking 'Trotskyists and other class enemies', including the poet himself.

Mandelstam's self-association with a primeval life principle in these

3 On the Spanish Jew, who was a poet and a victim of the Inquisition: N. Mandelstam, *Hope Abandoned*, 563–4.

poems also had a political dimension: it should be read as an act of resistance against an epoch that was soaked in violent death. In a quatrain which accompanied 'The Birth of a Smile', the act of smiling is praised as 'incorruptible' and 'disobedient' (WH, 63), in other words as a refusal to come to terms with the hostility to life and contempt for human beings characteristic of an epoch distorted by Stalin's totalitarianism.

A child's smile was one ally; another was celebrated in Mandelstam's 'Goldfinch cycle'. Was he alluding here to Christian iconography, in which the goldfinch is presented as a symbol of the Passion of Christ? In any case, a poem of 4 February 1937 refers to a crucifixion scene painted by Rembrandt (WH, 131): a Golgotha picture hung in the Voronezh Museum, which had taken over the holdings of the old Dorpat Museum. A cultural and religious dimension cannot be excluded, but, as was often the case with Mandelstam, the impulse for the poem came from everyday life. Vadik, the small son of the new landlady, set traps for birds and carried on a trade with the birds he had trapped. Mandelstam identified himself with these caged fellow prisoners, in a poetic, shamanistic ritual: 'Goldfinch, I'll throw back my head, / Let's look at the world together' (WH, 65; VN, 53). Another poem mirrors his existence as a prisoner to an even greater extent:

> The plank and the perch are slandering
> The cage with a hundred knitting spikes is slandering
> And everything in the world is turned inside out,
> And there is a forest Salamanca
> For clever disobedient birds!
> (WH, 67; AT, 48)

The Spanish Civil War had begun in July 1936. Mandelstam found the events disturbing. In view of his new-found interest in Spanish poetry, he would naturally have heard of the murder of Federico García Lorca in the village of Víznar, near Granada, on 19 August 1936. On 4 January 1937, he read in *Pravda* about the death on 31 December 1936 of the poet Miguel Unamuno, who had been seized by Franco's henchmen in Salamanca. Mandelstam described Voronezh as 'a forest Salamanca', thereby equating the intellectual victims of Stalinism with those of fascism. He had already combined the two 'gardeners and killers' Stalin and Hitler into a single person in the stanzas of May–June 1935: 'I remember everything, the necks of German brothers, / And that man who was both gardener and executioner who filled / His leisure time with the lilac comb of the Lorelei' (WH, 33; VN, 41). Stalin was praised by his propagandists as 'the wise gardener'. It will be recalled that Mandelstam told Pasternak in spring 1934 that the justification for writing his anti-Stalin poem was his hatred of fascism, in whatever form it appeared.[4]

Stalin was still occupying Mandelstam's imagination in the same month of December 1936, when, having written 'The Birth of a Smile' and the goldfinch poems, Mandelstam wrote a weird poem about an idol:

> In idleness inside a mountain an idol dwells
> In protective, boundless, idyllic chambers,
> While necklaces fall from his neck like drops of fat,
> Protecting the ebb and flow of his slumber
> …
> Somnolent bone has been tied in a knot
> Hands, knees, and shoulders have been made human.
> He smiles with his extremely quiet mouth
> He thinks it in his bones, and feels it in his head,
> And struggles to recall his human figure.
> (WH, 75; PO, 45)

The lazy idol in the poem displays some attributes of the tyrant who was described in Mandelstam's epigram of November 1933 as 'the Kremlin mountaineer' – Stalin came originally from the Georgian town of Gori in the Caucasus and he had 'fat fingers' ('His fingers fat and grey as grubs': MM, 165). The increasing 'ossification' of a ruler and his transformation into an 'idol': could there be a more precise picture of the ever-increasing proliferation of the personality cult around Stalin?

Mandelstam often employs characters from myth and folklore as masks for political events. A poem about Natasha Shtempel's cat is followed by one about 'Koshchey's cat'. The figure of Koshchey appears in Russian fairy tales as an evil sorcerer who guards treasures. He is 'bones without flesh, a body without a soul', and is well known to music lovers through Rimsky-Korsakov's opera *Koshchey the Immortal* (1902) and Igor Stravinsky's ballet *The Firebird* (1910). Mandelstam composed an artful political fairy tale on

4 M. equates the victims of Stalinism with the victims of Hitler's fascism: I. Mess-Beier, 'Ezopov iazyk v poezii Mandel'shtama', 272–3 and 277. M.'s 'hatred of fascism': O. Ivinskaia, *A Captive of Time*, 86.

the subject, in which Koshchey – a mask for Stalin – treats himself to 'fiery cabbage soup', draws out pincers and operates with golden nails (WH, 91).

It was exactly this poem about the evil sorcerer that Mandelstam sent on 31 December 1936 to the Soviet poet Nikolai Tikhonov, in an attempt to obtain material support from officialdom ('Spare me from having to live openly as a beggar'). And he added: 'Eventually my little poem will be printed along with others, and it will belong to the Soviet people, to whom I have an immense debt' (MR, 254–5). But to his wife, he said: 'That is a golden nugget ... and I, a beggar, am sending him a piece of gold.'[5]

By January 1937, Mandelstam the beggar had reached his lowest point so far. He writes, in a letter to an unknown addressee:

> I am severely and incurably ill, and I have been robbed of any possibility of obtaining treatment. I have nothing to eat. I live in poverty ... Everything I have described is so incompatible both with the laws of the Soviet Union and with common sense that it seems to me like nonsense or a bad dream. I do not understand why my administrative exile has grown at the end of its third and final year into a sentence to endure hunger and homelessness ... In a well-ordered Soviet city ... and before the eyes of a multiplicity of passive witnesses I have been eliminated from every social network ... I am a human phantom, whose destruction is sanctioned by everyone's passivity. (MR, 260–1)

In this situation, 'with the noose around his neck', as his wife formulated it, Mandelstam decided on 12 January 1937 to risk a last attempt to change his fate. He decided to compose an 'Ode to Stalin', to save his own life and that of his wife. In a chapter of her memoirs entitled 'The Ode', Nadezhda describes how Mandelstam changed his writing habits for this purpose. Until then, he had always spoken his poetry aloud, muttering the words as he walked back and forth. Now he sat down at a table, and got paper and pencils ready in order to accomplish his laborious task.

But he could not manage to produce a hymn of praise to the ruler, something hundreds of subservient Soviet poets had already achieved. The result of his work was an extremely ambiguous ode, which oscillated

5 The Koshchey poem: N. Mandel'shtam, *Kniga Tret'ia*, 233. I. Chinnov, analysing the poem in *Novyi Zhurnal* (New York) 88, 1967, 127–8, identifies Stalin as Koshchey, the terror as 'fire soup', Stalin's colleagues, such as Molotov, as 'speaking stones', their gilded uniform buttons as 'golden nails' and the head of the secret police, Yezhov, as 'the cat'.

between exaggerated praise with elements of parody, and camouflaged abuse. The first of seven long stanzas already reveals what a torture this task was for Mandelstam. It starts with a phrase in the conditional mood, followed by a hypothetical subjunctive, and it shows the poet engaged in an 'unreal' activity, as an artist drawing with charcoal:

> If I were to employ charcoal for the highest praise –
> For the unalloyed gladness of a picture –
> I'd cut up the thin air with the most subtle rays,
> Feeling of care and alarm a mixture.
> So that the features might reflect the Real,
> In art that would be bordering on daring,
> I'd speak of him who shifted the world's axis,
> While for the customs of a hundred peoples caring.
> I'd raise the eyebrow's corner up a bit,
> And raise it once again, and keep on trying
> Look how Prometheus has got his charcoal lit –
> Look, Aeschylus, at how I'm drawing and crying.
> (WH, 231–2; PO, 52)

Calling for the protection of Prometheus, who stole fire for humanity, he paints a portrait of the ruler which is the opposite of flattering, thereby following in the footsteps of the Greek tragedian Aeschylus (whose *Prometheus Bound* dates from around 470 B.C.E.). The expressions that find their way into the text were dictated to him by either his imprudent unconscious or a roguish cypher-wizard. Joseph Brodsky has described the ode as a 'brilliant poem'. Mandelstam set out to create a gigantic ode, couched in coded, 'Aesopian language', in which Stalin was implicitly denounced under cover of grotesquely formulated eulogies.[6]

'I'd speak of him who shifted the world's axis' (line 7): anyone who does this is not a benefactor but a destroyer, because a sphere with a shifted axis will stagger into chaos. This is one example of the hyperbolic mock praise put together by Mandelstam. His January 1937 ode, supposedly a

6 Joseph Brodsky's view of the 'Ode to Stalin' (he calls it a 'brilliant' and 'splendid' poem): S. Volkov, *Dialogi s Iosifom Brodskim*, 32–3 and 249. In German in the journal *Kontinent* 1, 1989, 76–89. The 'Aesopian' language of the ode deciphered: Mess-Beier, 'Ezopov iazyk', 286–336. The historian G. Koenen (*Die grossen Gesänge*, 144) interprets the ode as a case of 'extreme blasphemy' containing 'a flood of distorted metaphors' reminiscent of Goya's *Caprichos*.

panegyric to the Soviet dictator, was a coded continuation of the November 1933 epigram aimed at unmasking him. Here is another example:

> And I would like to thank the very hills
> Which bred his hand and bone and gave them feeling:
> Born in the mountains, he too knew the prison's ills.
> I want to call him – no, not Stalin – Dzhugashvili!
> (WH, 231; PO, 53)

The bone and cartilage motif also points us to the 'Idol' poem of December 1936. The emphasis laid here on his origin 'in the mountains' insistently recalls the phrase about the 'Kremlin mountaineer' from the devastating November 1933 epigram. Moreover, Mandelstam deliberately introduces the surname 'Dzhugashvili', mention of which was always forbidden by Stalin after he had adopted his 'steely' pseudonym. In Georgian, the name means 'Son of the Ossetian'. But the anti-Stalin epigram had ended with the words: 'And every killing is a treat / For the broad-chested Ossete' (MM, 165).

Even the unfree 'Ode to Stalin' contains four 'free' lines, which speak of the resurrection of the poet, and of his unshaken ability to distinguish the true sun from the false one (Stalin was glorified by propagandists as 'the sun'!):

> Into the distance stretch the mounds of people's heads
> I become small up there, where no one will espy me;
> But in kind-hearted books and children's games, instead,
> I'll rise again to say the sun is shining.
> (WH, 121/237; PO, 55)

Mandelstam said to his wife: 'Why do I only see heads before me – mounds of heads – when I think of him? What is he doing with all those heads?' There is plenty of evidence that Mandelstam was well aware of what was happening to the millions of people arrested and deported. But, even to his wife, he did not clarify all the coded expressions in his political poems. He feared that she would be arrested and interrogated. In that case, her fate might be made easier if she were genuinely astonished by the 'hidden meaning' of Mandelstam's texts. Then she would not appear as an accomplice, privy to his secrets.[7]

---

7 Mounds of heads: Mandelstam, *Hope Against Hope*, 203 ('The Ode'). M.'s coded statements and his conscious decision not to explain their hidden meaning to Nadezhda:

The view that the 'Ode to Stalin' is nothing but an enforced concoction aimed at preserving his own life is not shared by all those who have written on Mandelstam. Some people have expressed the opinion that this text, like a number of other 'pro-Soviet' or 'loyal' poems written by him during the Voronezh period, was a genuine attempt to become reconciled with the spirit or the demon of the epoch (in the sense of the verse from the stanzas: 'I must live, breathe, and grow Bolshevik'). A more convincing thesis, put forward by Sofia Margolina, is that in view of the erosion of European humanism and the upsurge of fascism and National Socialism in the 1930s, Mandelstam deliberately drew closer to the 'relative truth' of Stalinist socialism, before he laid aside this illusion in a final change of mind and began to write free poems in the expectation of approaching death.

It is clear that all his intellectual crises are also documented in the *Voronezh Notebooks*. The 'consciousness of being in the right', which Mandelstam claimed for poets in 1913 in his essay 'About the Interlocutor', was occasionally shattered during his period of exile. This also applies to the notions he had already developed before the revolution about the role of the autonomous personality in history and the 'unchangeable scale of values' (ST, 137; OS, 173). He was haunted more than once by a confused mixture of feelings of gratitude and guilt over the 'merciful' decision not to shoot him immediately for his anti-Stalin poem.

> And to him, into his heart's core
> With no permit I entered the Kremlin,
> Tearing through the canvas of distances
> Weighed down by my penitent head.[8]

From time to time, Mandelstam endeavoured to believe seriously in his epoch, but these attempts never lasted long. The memoirs of his friend Boris Kuzin shed some light on desperate impulses of this kind:

---

ibid., 171 ('The Change of Values'). G. Freidin (in *A Coat of Many Colours*) sees the 'Ode to Stalin' as a 'sincere' and 'loyal' work, and the summit of his creative activity, not a concoction aimed at preserving his own life. M. Gasparov (in *O. Mandel'shtam*) sees it as an essential component of his 'civic' poetry of 1937. For the thesis that he drew closer to the 'relative truth' of Stalinism but then became disillusioned and liberated himself from this attitude, see S. Margolina (*Mirovozzrenie Osipa Mandel'shtama*).

8 WH, 147; C. Brown, 'Into the Heart of Darkness', 595. This article will henceforth be referred to as IH.

> He was evidently under a particularly strong temptation to believe in our official ideology, to accept all the horrors hidden under its cloak, and to be one of those people who actively fought for great ideas and a glorious socialist future. By the way, he did not demonstrate a fanatical conviction that these crazy ideas were correct. Everyone who enjoyed close and friendly contact with him knew how uncompromising he was in everything that concerned art or morality … But when he reverted again to muttering orthodox views and I got seriously angry, he did not fly off the handle, he did not insist hot-headedly on his positions, but simply asked me for my understanding. 'Well, Boris Sergeievich, that is right, isn't it?' And then, after perhaps two days: 'Did I say that? Oh, what rubbish! What absolute nonsense!' (AA, 153)[9]

Nadezhda thought that the poet's desire to 'grow Bolshevik' in the Voronezh period was a result of the traumatic psychosis set off by his imprisonment in the Lubyanka, and a kind of hypnosis:

> The only thing that seemed to me an aftereffect of his illness was an occasional desire he now had to come to terms with reality and make excuses for it. This happened in sudden fits and was always accompanied by a nervous state, as though he were under hypnosis. At such moments he would say that he wanted to be with everybody else, and that he feared the Revolution might pass him by if, in his short-sightedness, he failed to notice all the great things happening before our eyes.[10]

Mandelstam's tragic state of ambivalence during his exile is evident from the way his wish to be reconciled with the epoch co-existed with the bitter comprehension that he would not be able to accept its lies or the man who was responsible for spreading them. But the split of consciousness had already been a theme of Mandelstam's poetry in 1923, as, for example, in the 'Slate Ode':

9 Boris Kuzin on M.'s 'pro-Soviet' moods: B. Kuzin, *Vospominaniia*, 166.

10 The after-effects of the Lubyanka psychosis. M.'s desire to come to terms with reality, expressed by him in a semi-hypnotic state: Mandelstam, *Hope Against Hope*, 126 ('Doctors and Illnesses').

Who am I? Not a real stone mason,
No shipwright I, I don't roof buildings,
I'm a double-dealer with a double soul
The friend of night, the day's assailant.
(TR, 159; FP, 61–2)

It must have been immensely difficult for an individual to resist universal Stalinist brainwashing, and to hold out against the question: What if I'm wrong, and everyone else is right? But, when Mandelstam, dismayed and deluded by the cult of Stalin that surrounded him, wanted to draw closer to the false saviour of mankind, his poetry, the voice of truth, pulled him in the opposite direction. Mandelstam the man occasionally wanted to become submerged in the epoch and to survive, but Mandelstam the poet had long ago spoken the decisive words (in February 1934, to Anna Akhmatova) – 'I'm ready for death' – and placed his confidence in the future impact of his poetry.

The 'Ode to Stalin' was a pragmatic undertaking by Mandelstam the man, the desperate expression of an endeavour to prolong his life. He sent it to several journals, but none of them dared to print this poem, which pullulated with extremely complex images. Nor would they print anything else by the exiled pariah and beggar. Mandelstam's complex, monstrous ode had nothing in common with the epoch's primitive hymns in praise of Stalin. And, ultimately, it failed to save him. In speaking to Anna Akhmatova, he described the ode as 'a result of sickness'. Natasha Shtempel was given copies of all his unpublished poems, but, when Mandelstam was about to leave Voronezh, he asked her to destroy the 'Ode'.[11]

However, the hybrid object Mandelstam had forced himself to create did have *one* fruitful effect. It disturbed him deeply and thereby set off a drive for self-purification through the writing of 'true' poems. The second Voronezh notebook contains a complete anti-Ode cycle full of sorrow and revolt against the obnoxious concoction. This new cycle is an attempt to come to terms with himself and his true poetic destiny.

11 The 'Ode to Stalin' a result of 'sickness': A. Akhmatova, *My Half Century*, 101. Natasha Shtempel is asked to destroy the Ode: N. Shtempel', *Mandel'shtam v Voronezhe*, 135.

In the beggar memory
First you'll sense the blind ruts,
Full of copper water –
And you'll follow in the tracks,
Unknown, unloving yourself,
Both the blind man and the guide.
(WH, 101; VN, 63)

But I'm depressed – my direct
Task gabbles perversely:
Something else passed through it,
Mocked me, and broke the axle.
(WH, 103; VN, 63)

His clarity of vision and freedom of judgement quickly returned. The hypnosis induced by Stalinist reality had no lasting impact. Only four days after the 'Ode to Stalin', on 16 January 1937, he wrote the poem 'What Is to Be Done with the Slaughtered Plains', in which the old, powerful verdicts surface alongside the bad dreams:

And the question grows and grows, where are they headed? From where?
And is there not slowly crawling over their surface
One of whom we shriek in our sleep –
The Judas of peoples to come.
(WH, 111; IH, 594)

The description of Stalin as the 'Judas of peoples to come' is one of a series of explicit denunciations which make Mandelstam's later work a tribunal of accusation. Anyone who has any doubts about the ambiguity of his praises of Stalin in the 'Ode to Stalin' should bear in mind the many unflattering expressions he applies to the dictator. Stalin is the 'pockmarked devil' (RZ, 257) in the *Fourth Prose* of 1929–1930. He is the 'six-fingered lie' (MM, 67) in a poem written in April 1931; he is the 'devil's coachman' and the 'plague-breath president' (MM, 93; AA, 129) in the June 1931 poem 'The Horse-cart Driver'. He is the cruel ruler Shapur (AA, 56), described as an 'Assyrian' in *Journey to Armenia* (1931–1932). He is the 'soul-corrupter', 'peasant-slayer' and 'broad-chested Ossete' (MM, 165) in the fatal anti-Stalin poem of November 1933. In the late

Voronezh Notebooks, he is the 'idol inside the mountain', the 'Judas of peoples to come' and, implicitly, the 'spider', in a poem dedicated to the fifteenth-century poet and vagabond François Villon (WH, 75, 111, 203).[12]

Mandelstam's late work of the 1930s is a confrontation with a terrible epoch, in which he desperately maintains his right to bear witness. But it is also a laborious struggle against the pollution and distortion of the language (and therefore of the truth as well) by totalitarian propaganda. The oath Mandelstam swore in 1931 in the poem 'Midnight in Moscow' remained valid to the end, despite all his crises and doubts, despite all his impulses of illusory gratitude and feelings of personal guilt: 'We shall die like foot soldiers, But we won't glorify the looting, the hired labour, or the lies' (MM, 79; MN, 46).

The degree to which his role as a witness threw him into depths of despair and loneliness is strongly evident from another poem written shortly after the completion of the 'Ode to Stalin': 'In This January Where Can I Go?'

> I slide into the warty dark of the pit,
> On my way up to the frozen over pump-house
> Where I trip and eat the dead air
> As the rooks scatter feverishly
>
> And I let out a sigh and shout
> At the frozen wooden tub:
> 'Oh for a reader, a counsellor, a doctor!
> Oh for a conversation on the barbed staircase!'
> (WH, 127; VN, 69)

In an atmosphere of bottomless distress, family ties also started to fray. Mandelstam gave free rein to his despair in letters sent in January 1937 to his brother Yevgeny, who was seven years younger. 'We have sunk into the blackest poverty', he wrote (MR, 257–8). Yevgeny said he was not in a position to send any money to the exile, and Mandelstam replied by forbidding him to describe himself as his brother in the future.

12 In a late poem dedicated to Villon, the narrator, identifying himself with Villon, 'spits' on 'the spider's laws', which represent the illegality and arbitrariness of Stalinism: R. Dutli, *Ossip Mandelstam*, 272–86.

Indigence did not prevent him from creating poems in which shortness of breath and intensity of perception join hands. Nadezhda appears as his natural ally and accomplice in his attempts to recover liberty and dignity after the alienating experience of writing the Stalin ode. The poem of 15–16 January 1937 is a declaration of commitment to his 'beggar-woman' and a sign that the Self is beginning to recover its equilibrium:

> I still haven't died, I'm still not alone,
> While – with a beggar-woman for companion –
> I'm delighted by the immense plains,
> And the haze, and hunger, and snow-storms.
>
> I live in miraculous poverty, opulent privation –
> Alone, at peace, consoled;
> These days and nights are hallowed,
> And honey-voiced this innocent labour.
> (WH, 105; EW, 85)

The period from 16 January until 10 February 1937 was one of extreme tension. Mandelstam said to his wife: 'Don't disturb me, I must hurry, otherwise I shan't manage it.' It was his reply to her attempts to persuade him that he should have a breather, lie down, step outside for a while ... If he did leave his room, breathing hard and walking with a stick, but with his head held back at an angle, as was his habit, he was noticed even by the local scallywags: 'Little boys would often ask him "Are you a priest or a general, mister?", to which O.M. always replied "A little bit of both."'[13]

Natasha Shtempel was his only audience apart from Nadezhda; she writes in her memoirs that Mandelstam 'the wizard' was able more than anyone else to leave his fate behind him and achieve 'spiritual freedom' when reciting his poems: 'This freedom of the spirit raised him above all the circumstances of his life. It was a feeling which also communicated itself to others.' The power of his poetic imagination and his 'bright nostalgia' carried him forth on imaginary journeys. A poem of 18 January 1937

13 The tense period between 16 January and 10 February 1937: N. Mandel'shtam, *Kniga Tret'ia*, 240. 'Are you a priest or a general?': Mandelstam, *Hope Against Hope*, 195 ('The Last Winter in Voronezh'). M. achieves 'spiritual freedom' through reciting his poems: Shtempel', *Mandel'shtam v Voronezhe*, 56.

took him to Tuscany, for example, to the 'land of nostalgia' in a dual sense, because the Russian word *toska* signifies both nostalgia and melancholy:

> I appealed to the air, my servant,
> Waiting for service or news,
> I prepared for a journey, swam along the arc
> Of voyages which would never start.
>
> I'm ready to wander where I shall have more sky.
> But that bright longing cannot release me now
> From the still-young hills of Voronezh
> To the bright, all-human ones of Tuscany.
> (WH, 113; EW, 87)

Many of his dreams are about Italy, and he repeatedly invites Nadezhda to come with him to Italy by a secret route, so that they can walk together inside the Florence Baptistery.[14] Other imaginary excursions lead to the Black Sea, to his beloved Crimea ('Breaks of the rounded bays': WH, 133; EW, 90), to Abkhazia, the ancient Colchis ('I sing when my throat is moist, my soul dry': WH, 135; VN, 71) and to 'pistachio green' Tiflis (WH, 141; VN, 73), where he had stayed in 1920, 1921 and 1930, enjoying the society and hospitality of the Georgians. Now, in the inhospitable and wintry Voronezh of the years of terror, he yearns nostalgically for the light of the south. The dreams of the traveller who is forbidden from travelling are mixed with melancholy.

> Why is a different sand laid under my head?
> All my rights are here, in this flat region,
> Or in the throaty Urals, or in the broad-shouldered area around the
> Volga,
> And I must still breathe them in deeply.
> (WH, 133; VN, 71)

Mandelstam's poems of the period shortly after he composed the simulated 'Ode to Stalin' continue to invoke the power of genuine poesy – and they are also attempts to shake off the crippling hypnosis of Stalinism:

14 Dreaming of Italy: Mandelstam, *Hope Against Hope*, 197 ('The Last Winter in Voronezh'); 246–52 ('Italy').

> The people need light, pale blue air,
> And they need bread and the snow of Mount Elbrus.
> ...
> The people need a poem that is both mysterious and familiar
> So that from it, they should wake up for eternity
> And bathe themselves in the flaxen-curled,
> Chestnut wave of its sound.
> (WH, 117; VN, 67)

In the months of February and March, he sent begging letters to Kornei Chukovsky and Nikolai Tikhonov (MR, 263–4). They are testimonies to his bitter poverty. But the stream of poetic creation did not dry up until the end of his exile. He evoked his own Golgotha when writing of a crucifixion scene painted by Rembrandt ('Like Rembrandt, martyr of light and dark / I've gone into the depths of time': WH, 131; EW, 89), but he himself did not fall silent, continuing instead to versify against the 'deafness of spiders' of the Stalin epoch. The second Voronezh notebook ended on 12 February, and the third was started at the beginning of March 1937.

In the second half of February, Mandelstam again attempted to create a supposedly 'loyal' and life-saving text. This is the ambiguous poem entitled 'If Our Enemies Capture Me' (WH, 157; VN, 78). Its closing verse praised the ruler with the words 'Stalin will awaken reason and life'. But Mandelstam also wrote a variant which turned the line into a curse, 'Stalin will destroy reason and life', by altering one letter: *budit'* became *gubit'*.[15] The second show trial had begun in Moscow on 23 January 1937. This was the 'Trial of the Seventeen Trotskyist Conspirators' (Radek, Pyatakov and others), whose condemnation was noisily anticipated by press reports that dripped with hatred. Here is *Pravda*'s headline for 29 January 1937: 'Shoot the rabid Trotskyist dogs!'

During the final months of his exile, in this atmosphere of persecution and violence, Mandelstam's poetry took on a prophetic quality. The new cycle was dominated by the 'Verses on the Unknown Soldier', which emerged in agonising bursts of creativity during February and March 1937. This was a complex 'oratorio' (Mandelstam's own description) dealing with the themes of war, death and the cosmos. It is Mandelstam's requiem for the nameless victims, the 'casually murdered millions' – he himself among

15 The poem 'If Our Enemies Should Capture Me', with its variant readings 'awaken' (*budit'*) and 'destroy' (*gubit'*): Mess-Beier, 'Ezopov iazyk', 279–85.

them. A poet lives through the slaughters of world history, recalling the scenes of madness and annihilation. Nuclear war, the apocalyptic stroke of destruction and the self-liquidation of mankind are foreshadowed in these visionary verses. But it is always the misery of the individual which pushes its way through the overarching metaphor of the 'unknown soldier':

> And the people, cold and feeble
> Will kill and starve and freeze,
> While inside his well-known monument
> The unknown soldier lies
>
> Teach me, you little swallow
> Who has forgotten how to fly
> How this airy grave is handled
> With neither wings nor rudder
>
> In the name of Mikhail Lermontov
> I'll give a strict report
> On how the grave sets right the crooked flesh
> And draws it to an airy pit.
> (WH, 167; PO, 62–3)

The 'Unknown Soldier cycle' signifies a revolt against war and annihilation. It is linked to Mandelstam's earlier anti-war poems such as 'Reims and Cologne' (1914), 'Menagerie' (1916) and 'The Heavens Are Pregnant with the Future' (1923). And, in the sixth poem of the cycle, he reflects on human creativity: 'Does the skull have to develop / From temple to temple, forehead-wide / So that through its cherished eye-sockets / Troops might be poured inside?' (PO, 66) Mandelstam sent these poems to the journals as well. Like the rest, they were never printed. But on one single occasion a reply came back, as Nadezhda tells us: 'The editorial board of *Znamia* informed him that there were just and unjust wars, and that pacifism as such could not be approved. But to us even this stilted bureaucratic reply was very welcome: at least someone had bothered to communicate with us.'[16]

---

16 For selected literature on the 'Unknown Soldier' poem, see O. Mandelstam, *Die Woronescher Hefte*, 330–1. The reply from *Znamia* criticising the pacifism of M.'s poem is in Mandelstam, *Hope Against Hope*, 183 ('Work').

Nadezhda frequently travelled to Moscow in the final months of their exile to sound out employment possibilities and get some idea of their future prospects. At the beginning of April 1937 Mandelstam wrote to Nadezhda's mother, Vera Khazina, asking her to come to Voronezh:

> *Breathing is always difficult*. When I'm with Nadia I breathe normally, but when she has to leave I literally begin to suffocate. Subjectively speaking, it is unendurable: I sense the end. Each minute seems like an eternity. When I'm alone I can't take a single step by myself … There's no one to stay with me. Only *my own* people can comfort me. (MR, 266; CC, 559–60)

Mandelstam's feeling of 'suffocation' was both physical and psychological. It derived from both his heart disease and his inability to remain by himself. In his letters to Nadezhda he often refers to the 'sickness of being without you' (MR, 272).

By April 1937, he had reached rock bottom. On 10 April, he wrote to Nadezhda's brother Yevgeny Khazin: 'We have enough money for two to three days … We are completely isolated in Voronezh. From the 13th we shall run out of provisions, i.e. tea, bread, porridge, eggs. There is no one from whom we can borrow' (MR, 268–9). Mandelstam had long resisted the idea of becoming a 'shadow'. The shadow metaphor exercised him greatly. In the poem of 15–16 January 1937, 'I Still Haven't Died, I'm Still Not Alone', which conjures up the plains, the snow, the hunger and his 'beggar-woman' Nadezhda, he strives to stay away from a life as a shadow.

> Unhappy any man whom, like his shadow,
> A dog's bark scares and the wind scythes down.
> And poor indeed one who, half-alive,
> Begs favour of a shadow.
> (WH, 105; EW, 85)

A letter of 21 January 1937 to Yury Tynyanov had also featured the shadow metaphor: 'Please do not regard me as a shadow. I am still casting off my shadow' (MR, 259; CC, 563). But now, in a letter to Kornei Chukovsky written shortly before 17 April, the shadow gains the upper hand:

> What is happening to me cannot go on any longer. Neither my wife nor I any longer have the strength left to prolong this nightmare. What is more, we are firmly resolved to put an end to it in any way possible …
>
> I have said those who judged me were right. I have found historical meaning in everything. Fine. I rushed headlong into my work. For this I was beaten, rebuffed and subjected to a moral trial. All the same, I worked. I denied myself my self-esteem. I considered it a miracle that I was allowed to work. I regarded our whole life as a miracle. After a year and a half I became an invalid. About that time, although I had done nothing else wrong, everything was taken away from me: my right to live, to work, and to treatment. I was put in the position of a dog, a cur …
>
> I am a shadow. I do not exist. I only have the right to die. My wife and I are being driven to suicide. (MR, 270; CC, 561–2)

And Mandelstam asks Chukovsky to turn to Stalin for assistance, although he does not mention him by name:

> There is only one person in the whole world to whom I can and must turn for help in this matter … If you want to save me from inevitable ruin – to save two people – help me, persuade others to write a letter.

A week after this letter, on 23 April 1937, an inflammatory article by Olga Kretova appeared in the Voronezh newspaper *Kommuna*, in which Mandelstam was included among the 'Trotskyists and other class enemies'.[17] In 1937, the year of the Great Terror, that was a fatal accusation. Kretova would later assert that she had been compelled by the general secretary of the Writers' Union, Stavsky, to write an article 'exposing Mandelstam', because her husband had been arrested as an 'enemy of the people'. Mandelstam complained about his treatment in a letter sent on 30 April 1937 to Stavsky himself. He stated that he regarded this procedure of exposure as 'absolutely impermissible' (MR, 280–2). He was not to know that he was complaining to one of his executioners, the man who would send him to the Gulag hell exactly a year later …

At this point, Nadezhda was again struggling to achieve something in Moscow. It was her longest period of absence from Mandelstam: between the middle of April and 10 May she was attempting to prepare their

17 Olga Kretova recalls her inflammatory article in the collective work O. G. Lasunskii et al., *Zhizn' i Tvorchestvo O. E. Mandel'shtama*, 39–40.

return to a 'normal' life, something which would never in fact take place. Meanwhile, Mandelstam wrote some of his most intimate and tender love letters to her. On 28 April 1937 he wrote:

> Nadik, my little one!
>
> What shall this letter say to you? Will it be delivered in the morning, or will you find it in the evening? Then 'good morning', my angel, and 'good night', and I kiss you whether you're sleepy and tired, or clean, fresh, efficient, and bustling with inspiration about your shrewd, clever, good deeds. I envy everyone that sees you. You're my Moscow, my Rome and my little David. I know you by heart and you are always new and I can always hear you, my joy. Ah! Nadenka!
>
> …
>
> In fact I'm uncommonly healthy now, and ready for life. We'll begin our life, whatever fate may cast us. Now I shall be stronger than the poems. Enough of their ordering us about. Let's mutiny! Then the poems will dance to our pipe and what do we care if no one dares to praise them. I kiss your bright, intelligent eyes, your darling old young brow. (MR, 276–7; CC, 566–7)

Uncommonly healthy, ready for life, life will start again … Mandelstam attempts once more to raise his hopes for the future, but other letters show that he no longer expects very much and has no illusions. This wavering between optimism and disillusionment is reflected in letter after letter. A joint suicide, the solution repeatedly proposed by Nadezhda, is no longer always rejected. On 22 April 1937, he writes: 'We are not weak people by any means. And during difficult times, we'll do what we must' (MR, 274; CC, 565). A little later, the idea of suicide is again brushed aside by Osip, who continues to enjoy life despite everything. On 4 May: 'Remember, it's shameful for us to despair. Who knows what lies ahead? … Anything could happen … We'll survive' (MR, 286; CC, 572). It is only his love for Nadezhda that provides certainty. He writes on 2 May 1937:

> It seems to me that we must stop *waiting*. Our ability to do that has run short … Anything you please but waiting. Nothing is frightening for you and me … We are together eternally, and that fact is growing to such a degree and growing so formidably, that there is nothing to fear. I kiss you, my bright eternal friend. (MR, 283–4; CC, 570)

Mandelstam had already begun to take his leave from life in the poems of the third Voronezh notebook. In Voronezh he allows himself to be directed for the last time by his 'nostalgia for world culture'; he communicates with the poets he loves (Aeschylus, Sophocles, Dante and Villon), along with the musicians and the artists. Certain artists have a special place of honour in the *Voronezh Notebooks*: Michelangelo, Ruisdael, Raphael, Rembrandt, Breughel. The poet who has been cut off from all the world's pictures closes his cycle about artists by evoking Leonardo da Vinci's *Last Supper* (WH, 185; VN, 86). He stands before it 'like a boy', with a cold back and aching eyes, and calls to mind the 'new wounds' of the old fresco.

He also takes his leave of the places that had granted him fulfilment, the centres of the 'world culture' for which he yearned. On 3 March 1937, he says goodbye to France, in a dazzling poem which offers a kaleidoscopic mixture, combining literary, musical, architectural, cinematographic and historical reminiscences with personal memories of his stay in Paris (1907–1908) (WH, 161).[18] There are images from Chaplin's *City Lights* and Bizet's *Carmen*, there are invocations of Notre Dame and Victor Hugo's Esmeralda, and of Tristan and Isolde …

On 16 March, in the poem 'Rome', he bids farewell to Italy. The image is, however, darkened and distorted by the fact that the 'eternal city' is in the grip of the fascism of Mussolini, a 'degenerate dictator'. Rome is frequented by the Blackshirts, 'hirelings of brown blood', 'the evil whelps of dead Caesars'. And what of Rome's artistic nimbus? 'Michelangelo, all your orphans / Are clothed in stone and shame' (WH, 163; VN, 81).

Mandelstam's parting message of 21 March 1937 to the world of antiquity, on the other hand, is bathed in the light of the Mediterranean Sea. The impulse for the poem came from the Greek vases held in the city's modest museum. In Mandelstam's hands, the leaping dolphins of Minoan culture are transformed into a command to enjoy life:

> Blue island, joyful Crete, famous for its potters,
> Whose talent has been baked
> Into the ringing earth. Do you hear the subterranean
> Beat of the dolphins' fins?
>
> …

18 The artists mentioned in the *Voronezh Notebooks*: Michelangelo, Ruisdael, Raphael, Rembrandt, Breughel, Leonardo da Vinci (WH, 13, 81, 95, 131, 155, 163, 185). The 'France' poem of 3 March 1937: Dutli, *Ossip Mandelstam*, 296–311.

Get well then, be radiant,
Star of the ox-eyed heaven,
And you, flying fish of chance,
And you, water saying 'Yes'.
(WH, 197; VN, 89–90)

The final poems in the *Voronezh Notebooks* deal with death and resurrection. They are affirmations of life, testimonies of a humble acceptance of death, vibrant swan songs, as in the poem 'I Am Lost in the Sky' (9–19 March):

You can't separate me from life – it dreams
Of killing and caressing at once,
So that the nostalgia of Florence fills
The ears, the eyes, the eye sockets.
…
And when I die, having served my time,
The friend for life of all living people,
Let the sky's response burst out
Louder and higher in my cold breast.
(WH, 187; VN, 87)

On 23 March 1937, Mandelstam created an actual Voronezh testament, a poem in which he entrusts his work, his poesy (metaphorically converted into 'whispering' and 'murmuring'), to a star, a beam of light, which will lead him to other times and other places. Nadezhda (the Russian word for 'hope'), whom he refers to as 'my child', as he does in many of his letters, is also entrusted to the beam of light:

Oh, how I wish
I could fly along a star beam,
Unknown to anyone,
Where I wouldn't exist at all.

And you, you must shine in a circle,
There is no other happiness,
And learn from a star
The meaning of light.

It is only a beam,
It is only light,
Because it has the power of a whisper
And the warmth of murmured words.

And I want to say to you
That I am whispering,
That I entrust you, my child,
To the starbeam with this whisper.
(WH, 193; VN, 88)

Mandelstam experienced one more spring in Voronezh, and, as had happened in April 1935, his vitality shone forth again – despite his awareness of the approach of death. He went for a walk with Natasha Shtempel in the Voronezh Botanical Gardens, now verdant and full of blossom. A poem of 30 April 1937 again reflects the conflict between intensity of perception and the threatening loss of sensation:

I raise this greenness to my lips,
This sticky promise of leaves,
This breach-of-promise earth:
Mother of maples, of oaks, of snowdrops.

See how I'm dazzled, exalted,
Obedient to the lowliest root.
And aren't my eyes miraculously
Blinded by the explosions of this park?
(WH, 211; EW, 95)

Natasha was due to marry her fiancé Boris Molchanov at the end of May, and Mandelstam gave her a poetic 'wedding present', as well as several humorous ditties. But death even creeps into one stanza of this bright and cheerful poem: 'Oaths remain imprinted on our lips / And eyes dash under horses' hooves to die' (WH, 209). Natasha was also the recipient of a strange love poem written on 4 May 1937, which Mandelstam considered the best he had ever written. It is the poem 'Levelling Herself upon the Hollow Ground', which invokes the cycle of life and death, mortality and a fresh start: 'For all will start again forever.' Even Natasha's lameness, the result of bone tuberculosis in her childhood, is mystically inflated: it is 'her vivifying imperfection'. The poem is a hymn to women and their strength as companions and protectors:

> There are women who belong to the damp earth,
> Whose every step is like resounding sobbing
> To escort the resurrected and to be the first
> To greet the dead is their calling
> To demand tenderness from them is a crime
> And to part with them is beyond our powers
> Today, an angel, tomorrow, a worm from the grave,
> And the day after – nothing but a shadow …
> That which was movement once shall be removed –
> Flowers are immortal, the sky is all-embracing,
> And what will be is no more than a promise
> (WH, 215; PO, 80–1)

In this, his last spring in Voronezh, Mandelstam was probably a little in love with Natasha, who was his only audience apart from Nadezhda. He is supposed to have confessed his love to her on one occasion. This was a confession mixed with dreams of flight and the tremulous expectation of a radical new beginning: 'We shall live together, wherever you want, in Moscow, or in the south.' But Natasha started to cry, saying: 'What a pity, everything was so beautiful and now it has been destroyed.' Mandelstam calmed her down, and promised that everything would still be as it was before. In Natasha's mind, Osip and Nadezhda were completely inseparable.

There is further proof of her loyalty to both the Mandelstams. When she was evacuated from the already burning city of Voronezh in July 1942, in the face of the approaching German army, she salvaged the poems Mandelstam had entrusted to her, and his letters to Nadezhda. But his letters to her she abandoned to the ruins. By rejecting Mandelstam in 1937, she saved him from an act of great stupidity: he would have created antagonism between the two women who would in the future contribute decisively to the preservation of his work – and hostility towards himself as well. Perhaps he had an inkling that this would happen. In any case, he never came back to the idea. The poem for Natasha ends with these words: 'And what will be is no more than a promise.'

The period of exile came to an end on 15 May 1937. The Mandelstams made copies of all the Voronezh poems (1935 to 1937), and the unpublished Moscow poems (1930 to 1934), entered them into three blue notebooks, wrote *Natasha's Book* on the covers of each, and gave them to her as a goodbye present. The handwriting is Nadezhda's. Mandelstam himself inserted the date of composition and a 'V' for 'Voronezh' under each poem. Natasha preserved the notebooks throughout the Second World War and returned them to Nadezhda when it had ended. *Natasha's Book* has continued to be one of the most important textual sources for Mandelstam's work. The Mandelstams had chosen their friend well. Mandelstam wanted Natasha to send the love poem of 4 May 1937 to Pushkin House after his death, as his legacy to Russian poetry. He also wanted her to destroy the 'Ode to Stalin'. She did neither. She made her own decision, which was to hand both poems back to Nadezhda after the war. And that was the right choice – for Mandelstam.

On 16 May 1937, the pair left Voronezh. Despite all the misery and anxiety they suffered there, exile in Voronezh had signified a postponement of Mandelstam's fate, an unexpected lengthening of his life, a 'second life' as he put it. Not least, it was the town in which it had been possible to compose at least a hundred significant poems. They could not know that through this, Voronezh would find a place on the map of world poetry. Later on, Nadezhda would write in her memoirs: 'Voronezh was a miracle, and only a miracle could have brought us there.'[19]

19 M. tells Natasha he loves her: Shtempel', *Mandel'shtam v Voronezhe*, 134. She preserves M.'s manuscripts: ibid., 63–4 and 88. 'Voronezh was a miracle': Mandelstam, *Hope Against Hope*, 144 ('Money').

23

Descent into the Hell of Gulag

(Savyolovo and Kalinin 1937, Samatikha and Vladivostok 1938)

On 17 May 1937, the Mandelstams returned to live in Moscow, at 5 Nashchokinsky Lane. Nadezhda's mother, Vera Khazina, occupied one room. An eager stool pigeon by the name of Kostariov had been personally installed in the other room during Mandelstam's absence by the general secretary of the Writers' Union, Stavsky. But, when the Mandelstams returned, he disappeared without trace. They took this as a good omen and cradled themselves in the illusion that they would now be left in peace.

They were able to meet Anna Akhmatova and other old friends and acquaintances. But they were scrutinised even more suspiciously than before by the inhabitants of the writers' cooperative, and they were certainly under observation by the NKVD. On 25 May, Mandelstam suffered another heart attack. But a new poem also emerged during the second half of the month. It is a homage to Charlie Chaplin, whose films *City Lights* and *Modern Times* had been enthusiastically watched by Mandelstam at the Voronezh Film Theatre on Revolution Prospekt. In the poem, he identifies Chaplin with himself. Charlie passes through the Stalinist Moscow of the terror year, 1937. What he sees is not amusing to anyone. He writes: 'We all live badly somehow – like aliens, aliens' and 'The alien remoteness stands absurdly naked' (WH, 239, 241). There is no talk of a 'bright future' of the kind proclaimed by state propaganda. Emma Gerstein recalls Mandelstam's mood at the time. Moscow disturbed him. There was something there that he could not recognise: 'And the people have changed … They are all somehow …' – he moved his lips, searching for a definition – 'they are all somehow, somehow … *desecrated*.'[1]

During this period, Anna Akhmatova and Mandelstam were both reading James Joyce's *Ulysses*. He read the German translation by Goyert; she read the book in its original language. They started to discuss the novel a couple of times, 'but by then we were no longer in the mood for books', as Akhmatova recalled bitterly. Even so, Mandelstam enjoyed his renewed contact with metropolitan culture. In Voronezh, he had said to his wife: 'If I were ever to return to Moscow, my first trip would be to the "French".' He meant the Impressionist paintings in the 'Museum for New Western Art' in the former Morozov Palace, at 21 Kropotkin Street. These offered the miracles of light and colour celebrated in the chapter 'The French' of *Journey to Armenia*. 'One must look at as much as possible, before something else happens', he added, as if he already suspected that he would not be able to spend much time in the capital city.[2]

In fact, the same Kostariov who had disappeared from the Mandelstams' Moscow dwelling was now organising the expulsion of Mandelstam from the city so as to regain possession of the apartment. As a 'convicted person', Mandelstam now lost his right to remain in the city. He even considered returning to his place of exile, and he telephoned his last landlady there, only to learn from the militia that in addition to losing the right to remain in twelve cities of the Soviet Union, as had been the situation after the revision of the first verdict against him (the 'minus twelve' formula), he was now excluded from more than seventy, among them Voronezh. He was also forbidden to stay within one hundred versts around Moscow.[3] This marked his exclusion from urban and cultural life of any kind.

On 25 June, a militiaman appeared at the Mandelstams' flat and ordered that they leave Moscow within twenty-four hours. Their nomadic life was

---

1 The Chaplin poem: C. Cavanagh, *Osip Mandelstam*, 296–303. M.'s mood on returning to Moscow ('They are all somehow, somehow … desecrated'): E. Gerstein, *Moscow Memoirs*, 79.

2 Reading James Joyce's *Ulysses*: A. Akhmatova, *My Half Century*, 108. M. dreams of meeting 'the French': N. Mandelstam, *Hope Against Hope*, 216 ('One Extra Day').

3 A Russian unit of distance, now obsolete, a verst was equivalent to 3,500 English feet, or slightly more than one kilometre.

about to be resumed. In desperation, Mandelstam thought he could compel the authorities to allow him to remain in Moscow by simulating a heart attack. Emma Gerstein was asked to help by screaming, after his pretended collapse close to the building's entrance, 'An atrocity! They are throwing a poet out of his home! They are expelling a sick poet from Moscow!' And Mandelstam is supposed to have mumbled some nonsense to the effect that 'simulation is the most well-tried method of political struggle'. But she refused to take part in these pitiful theatrics. The Mandelstams had got to know her in October 1928 in the TseKUBU sanatorium in Uskoye. She was often in contact with them in the 1930s, and, many years later, as a ninety-five-year-old woman, she published some very critical recollections about the couple on the basis of a closeness which was perhaps only imagined. Decades after the event, she continued to be resentful towards Osip and Nadezhda for 'abusing' her by treating her as a slave rather than a friend. Nevertheless, she also admitted that the poet had been 'severely traumatised'. She was probably unaware of the extent of his desperation.[4]

In any case, Mandelstam was mistaken about the historical moment they were passing through: by 1937, the year of terror, simulation and protest were pointless, because no one could now insist on special treatment. Since the second Moscow show trial of January–February 1937, the machinery of destruction had accelerated rapidly. Yezhov, the head of the NKVD, the executor of Stalin's 'purge' terror, enjoyed the encouragement and support of his boss. On 27 July 1937, he received the Order of Lenin from Stalin's hands, for the ardour he had displayed in destroying the enemies of the people. In the period between September and December 1937, he would order the preparation of thirty-five more show trials. Each trial would be accompanied by a massive wave of arrests and shootings.

At the end of June 1937, the Mandelstams started to search for a temporary place to live as close as possible to the edge of the hundred-verst zone around Moscow. They chose Savyolovo, to the north of the city, on the banks of the River Volga, opposite the town of Kimry. And they made the dangerous decision to ignore the prohibition on visiting Moscow. They repeatedly surfaced in the city, trying to get hold of money and work. Only a few people dared to make themselves criminally liable by providing shelter for the outlawed couple. Terrified littérateurs no longer even took the risk of greeting Mandelstam the revenant, the ghost, in the

4 M. asks Emma Gerstein to help him simulate a heart attack (June 1937): Gerstein, *Moscow Memoirs*, 82.

street. But the most important of their Moscow refuges was easy to reach from the Savyolovo station. It was located at 17 Lavrushensky Lane, and it was an apartment belonging to their trusted friends Vasilisa and Viktor Shklovsky. Nadezhda devotes a special chapter of her memoirs to them. 'The Shklovskys' flat was the only place where we felt like human beings again. This was a family that knew how to help lost souls like us.'[5]

Even their children, Varya and Nikita, had been taught how to act when the Mandelstams appeared: 'Children generally reflect their parents' standard of behaviour. They would take us into the kitchen, give us food and drink, and entertain us with their chatter.' Then, when Vasilisa Shklovskaia came home, she would prepare a bath, give the Mandelstams fresh laundry and cater for them as if this all went without saying. Viktor Shklovsky attempted to raise Mandelstam's spirits with jokes, recounted the most recent events and racked his brains to find some way of helping him. If the doorbell rang, they hid the Mandelstams in the kitchen or the children's room. If the lift was operated at night, they all rushed into the corridor to find out where it stopped. 'In the years of terror, there was no house in the whole country where people did not tremble when they heard a car go past or the sound of a lift.' The Mandelstams feared that they might bring the Shklovsky family to ruin, so they looked for other places to spend the night as well.

They sometimes slept in Maryina Roshcha, an outer suburb of Moscow, at 43 Alexandrovsky Lane, the home of Vasilisa Shklovskaia's sister Natalia. There was a tiny room in her apartment, usually occupied by the literary theorist Nikolai Khardzhiev, and he generously handed it over to the unfortunate guests. There was considerable risk involved: on one occasion, a spy followed the Mandelstams to the house, looked brazenly through the window of Khardzhiev's room on the ground floor, and was in no hurry to leave. The artists Lev Bruni and Alexander Osmyorkin, who made two pencil drawings of Mandelstam on 1 October 1937, as well as the architect Lev Nappelbaum (the son of the well-known photographer Moise Nappelbaum) and his wife Lyudmila were all brave enough to shelter the Mandelstams. Apart from them, there were Nyura and Ignaty Bernstein (who used the pseudonym Alexander Ivich), who also hid Mandelstam's archive in their house from 1946 onwards. These few courageous people alleviated the hardships of Mandelstam's existence as a beggar in the final

5 Staying with the Shklovskys: Mandelstam, *Hope Against Hope*, 346–9 ('The Shklovskys').

year of his life. They were not a group of cunning conspirators but a tiny cluster of people who behaved towards the outlawed poet with a degree of humanity.

Mandelstam's final poems were composed in Savyolovo. This was a cycle of ten or eleven texts, only four of which have survived. In mid-July 1937, Natasha Shtempel came from Voronezh to visit her friends. Mandelstam recited his new poems to her while they went for walks along the banks of the Volga. According to her memoirs, one of them was a poem against the death penalty, an outcry against the executions, which is no longer extant. But there was also a series of strange love poems, which Mandelstam did not dare to show to his wife.

They were dedicated to Yelikonida (Lilia) Popova, the ex-wife of the actor Yakhontov, about whom Mandelstam had written a prose sketch in 1927, when they were neighbours in Detskoe Selo. Yakhontov and Popova were people Mandelstam particularly enjoyed meeting after his return from exile. He fell in love with the beautiful Lilia, who had big black eyes. This was risky, not only as regards Nadezhda, but also because she was an ardent Stalinist. She gushed enthusiastically about the 'brilliant leader' and 'saviour of mankind', and she wanted to convert Mandelstam to the true faith. According to Nadezhda, she was a 'Stalinist of the sentimental kind' (there were such people). She wanted to persuade him to send a letter of apology to Stalin. To remind Stalin of the epigram Mandelstam had written against him at a moment when the terror was at its most intense would have been a catastrophic move. Popova also planned to write to Stalin herself, to tell him that Mandelstam 'must be helped' to find 'the correct path'.[6]

Mandelstam clung to this attempt to save his life, suggested by Lilia, like a drowning man to a straw. He had said to Anna Akhmatova in February 1934: 'I'm ready for death.' But the 'miracle of Voronezh' had restored his vitality. The voice of his poetry had long since chosen death, but after his period of exile, Mandelstam the human being wanted to keep living, with the same tragic hunger for life which he had already invoked in a poem written on 2 March 1931:

6 Natasha's memories of the Savyolovo poems, including the lost poem against the executions: N. Shtempel', *Mandel'shtam v Voronezhe*, 15. Lilia Popova's 'sentimental Stalinism' and her intention of writing to Stalin: Mandelstam, *Hope Against Hope*, 220–1 ('The Bessarabian Carriage').

Eyelashes sting with tears as a sob wells up in the chest.
I sense the storm is imminent but I am not afraid.
Someone wonderful hurries me to forget something,
I feel I'm being smothered yet I want to live to the point of dying.
(MM, 63; MN, 40)

In the Savyolovo poems, the erotic aura of Lilia Popova is combined with the image of a supposedly 'rejuvenated' Moscow, which the returned exile Mandelstam sets himself to love. Unsurprisingly, the poem contains not only Lilia's raven tresses, her Caucasian appearance and her other feminine charms, but also Stalin's 'thunderous name', which the adored Lilia whispers tenderly.

My glory, you with blackest brows,
Bind me with them, daring
Still to look death in the eye
You pronounce in tender whispers
Stalin's thunderous name
In a vow suffused with love and tenderness.
(WH, 243–4)

Once again, Mandelstam delegates the job of praising Stalin; he puts the words in the mouths of other people. In the 'Ode to Stalin' it was a charcoal sketch artist, in the Popova poem an enthusiastic admirer of the 'great leader'. And, on 4–5 July 1937, Mandelstam wrote another group of stanzas, similar to those with which he had tried to 'bolshevise' himself in Voronezh. They were, presumably, commissioned by Lilia Popova, and were intended to form part of a montage of texts created by the production team of Popova and Yakhontov to celebrate both Stalin and the twentieth anniversary of the October Revolution. But these late stanzas were also unsuccessful, and they had no impact. Now Mandelstam took to reciting the 'Ode to Stalin' with feeling in the streets of Moscow, hoping in this way to gain the attention of the literary authorities.[7] The slightest prospect of an extension of his life was precious to him. But it was a long time since anyone had been interested in Mandelstam's 'loyalty'. The exuberant metaphors of the Ode sank without trace in an epoch distorted by

7 The Savyolovo cycle: V. Shveitser, 'Mandel'shtam posle Voronezha'. M. recites the 'Ode to Stalin' in the streets of Moscow: Gerstein, *Moscow Memoirs*, 83.

sheer terror. When he returned to the capital in 1937, he had described his Moscow contemporaries as 'desecrated'; but the word can be applied to him too, even to the broken Self of the hybrid stanzas.

The final blasts of the poetic trumpet inspired by Popova are swan songs in a major key, their enthusiasm painfully sustained. But even here, Mandelstam's poetry is unable to be untrue to itself. The desire to believe in his epoch is evident, but also his deep-seated inability to hold onto this belief consistently, to merge himself into it. Despite his love for Lilia, he cannot override the horrors of the epoch. The stanzas contain motifs like 'abandonment' and 'pain' (WH, 251), which signal the split in his consciousness. The Savyolovo cycle of Mandelstam's poetry will remain a muddled wreck, barring the rediscovery of the vanished poem against executions, whose existence is attested to by Mandelstam's reliable friend Natasha Shtempel, although there is at least a hint of a protest against the death penalty in one of the four poems that have survived: 'The goose too dislikes a knife / Driven through its tender neck' (WH, 247).

Lilia was a passionate embodiment of this epoch of Stalinist delusion, and Mandelstam, who had been deeply traumatised by the years of exile followed by his expulsion from Moscow, wanted to let himself be deceived just for a short while. Despite his enthusiasm for the 'vigour of the epoch', Yakhontov did not entirely share his partner's blindness. He threw himself out of a window in 1945 in a panic, fearing that he would be arrested. When the Mandelstams left Moscow, Lilia wanted to give the poet some edifying Marxist literature, as he needed to be educated. Yakhontov, however, gave him his Bible. Presents that spoke volumes!

In autumn 1937, their paths diverged forever. The Yakhontov–Popova team were fully absorbed in preparing a gigantic montage to celebrate the twentieth anniversary of the October Revolution. The Mandelstams continued their indigent existence. On 17 November, they moved house from Savyolovo to Kalinin (which has now reverted to its previous name, Tver), where they rented a room on the edge of town, at 43 Nikitinskaia Street. Isaac Babel had told them: 'Travel to Kalinin, Erdman lives there.' Nikolai Erdman, who had also just completed a period of exile, in his case in Siberia (Yeniseisk and Tomsk), was the author of the banned satirical comedy *The Suicide* (1928).

Mandelstam now again met his fellow poet Anna Akhmatova for a short time, when the outlawed couple appeared in prohibited Leningrad for two days. They had travelled from Kalinin and were literally sitting in the street. Osip said to Nadezhda: 'One must be able to change professions. Now we are beggars', and 'Beggars always have an easier time of it in summer.' Akhmatova relates: 'It was an apocalyptic time. Misfortune was at all our heels. They had absolutely nowhere to live. Osip had great difficulty breathing and gasped at the air with his lips.'[8] The terror shredded all family ties. Every visit was a life-threatening undertaking. Contact with Mandelstam's younger brother Yevgeny had already been broken off in Voronezh. Akhmatova was there when Mandelstam was informed that his father had no warm clothing. He took off his pullover and asked for it to be handed over to him. The beggar no longer needed anything.

It is pointless to speculate over whether Mandelstam could potentially have survived if he had behaved less obtrusively, if he had not shown his face in Leningrad and Moscow, if he had not begged for money before the very eyes of the literary bureaucrats and if he had ceased to ask for anything. The terror was also raging in Kalinin. It was not restricted to the capital cities. The NKVD had its branches everywhere. At no time was Yezhov short of personnel. Nor was he short of innocent victims, including those who lived inconspicuously.

Mandelstam's journeys from Kalinin to the forbidden city of Moscow were desperate attempts to get hold of money, but fewer and fewer people were able to give him any. Fear was omnipresent. Nadezhda writes in her memoirs: 'That winter [of 1937 to 1938] I began shouting in my sleep at night. It was an awful, inhuman cry, as if an animal or a bird were having its neck wrung.' The terror was in full swing. Mandelstam had no illusions: 'They know what they are doing: the aim is to destroy not only people, but the intellect itself.'[9] On 8 October 1937, Sergei Klychkov was executed. He was a peasant poet and a good friend. On 16 October, Benedict Livshits, an old friend of both the Mandelstams, and their marriage witness, was arrested in Leningrad. He would be shot in 1938. Pavel Florensky, whose first arrest in 1928 had so dismayed Mandelstam, was shot in Solovki on 8 December 1937. This list could be continued indefinitely.

In January 1938, the State Meyerhold Theatre closed its doors, to the accompaniment of loud and slanderous propaganda in *Pravda*. The renowned avant-garde director Meyerhold would be arrested in 1939,

---

8 Prohibited visit to Leningrad in the autumn of 1937: Akhmatova, *My Half Century*, 108.

9 Nadezhda cries out in the night: Mandelstam, *Hope Against Hope*, 352 ('Maryina Roshcha'); 'They are destroying the intellect': ibid., 363 ('The First of May').

grievously tortured, and shot in February 1940. Mandelstam had once found shelter in his apartment. When he saw the unbridled smears in *Pravda*, he heaved a sigh of despair, exclaiming, 'We are already dead!' The news threw him into a deep depression, which is still evident from a letter of 26 February 1938 to Boris Kuzin: 'I am weary. I am constantly waiting for something … Forgive my silence. I am very tired' (MR, 290).

To Mandelstam's surprise, in the spring of 1938 the Writers' Union again started to show some interest in him. Before that, though, a reading of his poetry was first announced at short notice for 15 October 1937, then cancelled, and the poet, who was still looking for work, received a commission to translate the diary of the brothers Goncourt from French, only to have it withdrawn again. Finally, the director of the State Publishing House, Luppol, informed Mandelstam that there was no work for him (MR, 290). But, on 2 March 1938, he suddenly received permission to stay for two months in the remote rest home of 'Samatikha'. It lies thirty kilometres away from Cherusti, a station on the railway line to Murom and Kazan. This was supposedly intended to allow him to improve his severely damaged health. We now know that the Samatikha offer was a trap. The poet who had previously spent his time commuting between Kalinin and Moscow was now to be isolated in a remote place and cut off from all his contacts, so that he could be arrested without any complications at the appropriate time. And the 'appropriate time' was quick to arrive.

The third Moscow show trial took place between 2 and 13 March 1938. This was the 'Trial of the Twenty-one' against Bukharin, Rykov and others. The tribunal had already had plenty of practice. The presiding judge was the military lawyer Ulrikh; the prosecutor was the notorious state attorney Vyshinsky. In the background was Stalin himself, pulling the strings. Bukharin had already been arrested in February 1937. The NKVD chief Yezhov had proposed to a Central Committee Plenum held at that time that Bukharin and Rykov should be shot. The verdict had been given long before the trial started. But the show trial against the 'anti-Soviet bloc of Rights and Trotskyites' took thirteen months to prepare. That is the amount of time the NKVD needed to 'process' the accused. Bukharin, Lenin's former companion in arms, 'the darling of the whole party', according to his testament, and the author of the Bolshevik classic *The ABC of Communism*, put up a stubborn resistance at first, despite being subjected to torture. In August 1937, the Central Committee of the party prescribed the systematic use of 'methods of physical pressure' by the secret police.

This gave them *carte blanche* for the worst possible tortures, which Yezhov, the 'evil dwarf', made use of uninhibitedly. Bukharin finally surrendered when his wife and little son were also threatened, signing all the fanciful inventions of the NKVD thugs. In his final speech to the court, on 12 March 1938, he said: 'I bend my knee before the country, before the party.' And he described Stalin, the monster who stood behind the show trials, as 'the hope of the world – the creator'. The accused made confessions of unsurpassed absurdity: they had planned gigantic acts of sabotage, attempts to assassinate Stalin and so on. On 15 March 1938, barely a day after the trial ended, the 'self-confessed traitors' were murdered in the cellars of the Lubyanka.[10]

Mandelstam's future fate was closely connected with the third show trial. This was not just because its most important victim, Bukharin, had long been his actual 'protector', promoting the publication of his last books in 1928, bringing about his trip to the Caucasus in 1930 and enabling the revision of his sentence of exile in 1934. It was also because the poet was caught up in the massive wave of terror that followed the third show trial. There are various estimates of the number of victims. The historian Volkogonov says that 3.5 to 4.5 million people were arrested and deported in 1937–1938, and 600,000 to 800,000 were shot. Other authorities give still-higher estimates.

Mandelstam was arrested for the second time on 2 May 1938. We now know, thanks to a discovery made in the archives of the KGB by Vitaly Shentalinsky and published in 1991, that the trigger for this was a letter of denunciation sent on 16 March 1938 to Yezhov. It had been written by no less an authority than Vladimir Stavsky, the general secretary of the Soviet Writers' Union from 1936 to 1941! The date is striking: the letter was sent immediately after the third show trial, a day after Bukharin was shot. General Secretary Stavsky did not want to lose any time. He described to Yezhov in the letter, classified as 'strictly secret', how Mandelstam, who was prohibited from visiting Moscow, was defying this prohibition and begging for money from writers in the city, how they were making him into a 'martyr' and 'a writer of genius who was not being recognised by anyone'. Stavsky did not fail to remind Yezhov twice that Mandelstam had written a 'filthy, slanderous and insulting poem' against the leadership

10 Bukharin in the 'Trial of the Twenty-one': G. Koenen, *Die grossen Gesänge*, 130; D. Volkogonov, *Stalin: Triumph and Tragedy*, 300. The estimated number of people deported and executed in 1937–1938: ibid., 307.

of the party and the Soviet people (this was the 1933 epigram against Stalin), and he emphatically called on the head of the NKVD 'to solve the Mandelstam problem'. Yezhov had a solution available for such problems which had already been tried and tested hundreds of thousands of times, as the general secretary of the Writers' Union was naturally aware. Stavsky also attached a disparaging evaluation of Mandelstam as a writer by Piotr Pavlenko. This was the same literary stooge who had trumpeted forth stories of Mandelstam's 'ridiculous' behaviour during his Lubyanka interrogation in May 1934. Now, he sent in a report asserting the 'uselessness' of Mandelstam's new poems – and thereby Mandelstam's own 'uselessness'. He characterised the language of the poems as complex and obscure. Even in the 'Ode to Stalin' there was 'a lot of incomprehensible babbling, which is inappropriate when Stalin is the theme' (MR, 299).[11]

Hence Mandelstam was already ensnared in the trap of distant Samatikha when the head of the NKVD, in accordance with the request made by the general secretary of the Writers' Union, set to work 'to solve the problem' he presented. Meanwhile, the poet himself was under the impression that his problems were on the point of being finally solved. On 5 March, having received permission on 2 March to spend time in Samatikha, he was received by Stavsky. After that, he went once again with Nadezhda to Leningrad to ask for money from his friends. He also had a brief meeting with Anna Akhmatova. It would be his last. On 8 March 1938, the Mandelstams arrived in Samatikha. The journey to the rest home, thirty kilometres away from the railway station of Cherusti, could only be accomplished with a horse-drawn sleigh. While he was at Samatikha, Mandelstam repeatedly requested permission to travel once to Cherusti, but they always rejected his pleas, giving various excuses. The head doctor, the director of the rest home, Fomichev, evidently had orders not to allow the poet to leave the premises under any circumstances.

Nadezhda Mandelstam relates in her memoirs (in the chapter 'The Young Lady of Samatikha') that there was also a young woman there, whom she assumes had the job of spying on Mandelstam. The woman asked Mandelstam to tell her who was interested in his poetry, and where his poems were being kept. 'Alexei Tolstoy!' he replied angrily. The officially

11 Stavsky's 16 March 1938 letter of denunciation to Yezhov: first published in Russian in the journal *Ogonyok* 1, 1991, 20. In German in V. Shentalinsky, *Das auferstandene Wort*, 363–4 and in O. Mandelstam, *Du bist mein Moskau und mein Rom*, 297–9. In English in V. Shentalinsky, *Arrested Voices*, 186.

approved writer whom Mandelstam had publicly slapped in May 1934! What a bitter piece of sarcasm! The head doctor of the rest home received numerous telephone calls 'from the Writers' Union' asking whether Mandelstam was still alright. These were no doubt intended to make sure that the poet was still stuck in the trap.[12]

The Mandelstams were accommodated in a hut separate from the main building, away from the crowds. 'The main building was so noisy, there was such a din, and so much singing, stamping and dancing that we should not have been able to stand it' (MR, 293) wrote Mandelstam on 16 April 1938 to his father, and he expressed his pleasure at the 'great relaxation' he was enjoying. He had also brought books with him: Dante and Pushkin as usual, and also – the whole of Khlebnikov. This is a late testimony to the high esteem in which he continued to hold the Futurist writer, about whom he had written some of the best passages in his essays. Music could also be heard in Samatikha, Shostakovich's Fifth Symphony, for instance, composed in 1937, the year of terror. Mandelstam disliked it intensely: 'Here his Fifth Symphony is blaring out. What soul-destroying intimidation … I find it unacceptable. No thought. No mathematics. No goodness. It may be art, but for me it is unacceptable!' (MR, 292)

Mandelstam was at first very happy about the sudden change in his life brought about by the Writers' Union. The depression of the first months of the year 1938 now vanished. The previous year (in a letter of 7 May 1937 from Voronezh) he had written that he could no longer believe in 'anything good', but now he again believed in miracles, and he had hardly arrived in Samatikha when on 10 March 1938 he sent an enthusiastic, hopeful letter to his friend Boris Kuzin:

> Yesterday I fetched a tambourine from the equipment room of the rest home. I shook it and banged it, and I danced across our room: this is how the new situation has affected me … I still don't know what to do with myself. As if I were still very young … 'Social restoration of health' – that surely means that they expect something good from me, that they believe in me. I am ashamed and delighted. (MR, 291)

On 16 April, he wrote to his father: 'Now we have nowhere to live, and everything that follows will depend on the Writers' Union' (MR, 293).

---

12 M. in Samatikha: Mandelstam, *Hope Against Hope*, 356–9 ('The Young Lady of Samatikha'); ibid., 360–3 ('The First of May').

How true! General Secretary Stavsky's letter of denunciation had been with the NKVD for a month, and its bureaucratic mills were beginning to grind. Perhaps Yezhov wanted to discuss the matter first with the supreme leader himself. But now the 'Main State Security Administration' (GUGB) discovered evidence that would have been enough for *ten* arrests. The findings of the investigation give a clear picture of the nature of the accusations levelled against Mandelstam. Here is the report delivered on 27 April 1938 by State Security Lieutenant Viktor Yuryevich to his superior, Alexander Shurbenko, director of the Fourth GUGB Section of the NKVD:

> According to MANDELSTAM'S own admissions, his attitude to the Great Proletarian Revolution was negative in the extreme. He called the Soviet government a 'government of usurpers' and in his literary works of that period he slandered Soviet power …
>
> In the year 1927, as he himself confesses, MANDELSTAM was strongly sympathetic to Trotskyism. He had an extremely hostile attitude to the policy of the CPSU (B) as regards the liquidation of the kulaks as a class, and this is reflected in a series of his works in the years 1930–1933.
>
> In the year 1933, MANDELSTAM wrote a highly counter-revolutionary and insulting poem against comrade STALIN and he spread it among his acquaintances by word of mouth.
>
> In the year 1934 O. MANDELSTAM was sentenced to three years' exile in the city of Voronezh for anti-Soviet activity …
>
> After his sentence of exile had expired, MANDELSTAM surfaced in Moscow and attempted to influence public opinion in his favour by intentionally making an exhibition of his 'desperate situation' and his illness.
>
> Anti-Soviet elements among the writers are using MANDELSTAM for purposes of hostile agitation, they are presenting him as a 'martyr' and organising the collection of money for him among writers …
>
> According to the available evidence, MANDELSTAM has continued to hold anti-Soviet views up to the present.
>
> Owing to his psychological instability MANDELSTAM is capable of aggressive actions.
>
> I consider it necessary to arrest and isolate MANDELSTAM.[13]

13 The NKVD investigation report: P. Nerler *'S gur'boi i gurtom …'*, 86–7. In German in Mandelstam, *Du bist mein Moskau und mein Rom*, 300–1.

Mandelstam, who walks with a stick, has heart disease and suffers from severe breathing difficulties, is regarded here as a potential terrorist, a man 'capable of aggressive actions'. The investigation file reflects the paranoia of the society, its obsessive belief that it is surrounded by dangerous 'wreckers', 'saboteurs' and 'spies'. On 29 April 1938, the assistant chief of the NKVD, Frinovsky, decreed Mandelstam's arrest. The arrest order was formally issued the next day.

Early on the morning of 2 May 1938, two NKVD agents knocked on Mandelstam's window. Head doctor Fomichev was also present. The Mandelstams' possessions were tipped from their suitcase into a sack. The whole procedure took only a couple of minutes. Nadezhda was not even allowed to accompany her husband to the Cherusti railway station. Silently, she took her leave of him. She would never see her husband again. Their life together had lasted exactly nineteen years, from 1 May 1919 to 2 May 1938. Decades later, Nadezhda attempted to understand their helplessness and paralysis:

> Why did we never try to jump out of the window or give way to unreasoning fear and just run for it – to the forests, the provinces, or simply into a hail of bullets? Why did we stand there meekly as they went through our belongings? Why did O.M. obediently follow the two soldiers, and why didn't I throw myself on them like a wild animal? What had we to lose?[14]

Mandelstam was first transferred to the NKVD's 'internal prison' in the courtyard of the Lubyanka. The last photograph of him was taken at this time, on 3 May 1938: both in profile and facing the camera, as was the usual practice with criminals. But Mandelstam once more holds his head back at an angle, in the posture witnessed by many of his contemporaries. His bleak gaze indicates exhaustion, but also pride and tenacity, for one last time. Investigations were no longer conducted in the Lubyanka as they had been in May 1934. In the terror year of 1938, all such procedures were curtailed. The only recorded interrogation took place on 17 May. Mandelstam denied any guilt: 'I have not been engaged in any anti-Soviet activities.'[15] On 20 May, the NKVD ordered the house in Kalinin

14 'Why didn't I throw myself on them like a wild animal? What had we to lose?': Mandelstam, *Hope Against Hope*, 369 ('The Trap').

15 M.'s second incarceration in the Lubyanka. The interrogation on 17 May 1938,

to be searched, with the aim of seizing 'weapons, correspondence and other pieces of evidence'. The agents found nothing. Mandelstam's only 'weapons' had always been his poems, and Nadezhda had returned in great haste from Samatikha to Kalinin to collect them together and put them in a basket. She herself hid in Nikolai Khardzhiev's flat in Moscow for the first few days after the arrest.

The bill of indictment issued on 20 July 1938 only repeated the statements in the NKVD's file of investigation and at some points it was a word-for-word copy of Stavsky's letter of denunciation to Yezhov. It underlined Mandelstam's contacts with the 'enemies of the people' Stenich and Kibalchich (this was the pseudonym of Victor Serge, a 'known Trotskyist') and added a comment about the prisoner's state of mind, as certified on 24 June: 'The medical investigation showed that Mandelstam's personality has psychopathological elements and he has a tendency to obsessive delusions and the invention of fantasies' (MR, 302–3). But he was found to be 'sane in the legal sense'.

He was accused of 'anti-Soviet agitation and propaganda falling under Article 58-10'. On 2 August 1938 a three-member special tribunal of the NKVD pronounced judgement and imposed a sentence of five years in a labour camp for counter-revolutionary activities. Given Mandelstam's precarious state of health, the verdict clearly constituted a death sentence. Since 1929, the special courts of the OGPU (and subsequently the NKVD) no longer needed to prove the guilt of the accused. The reports of spies and secret service investigations were sufficient. The prisoner was no longer even questioned by the 'troika' tribunal. The procedure lasted a few minutes: enough time to stamp the document and collect signatures.

Mandelstam now entered the 'world outside the world' which Alexander Solzhenitsyn would reveal to the international public in 1973 in his monumental documentary study *The Gulag Archipelago*. The universe of the 'GULag' (the word is an acronym for 'Chief Administration of Corrective Labour Camps') has been presented in many documentary and semi-documentary works. To quote just a few of the classics: Yevgenia Ginzburg's *Into the Whirlwind*, Varlam Shalamov's *Kolyma Tales* (one of which, 'Cherry Brandy', is devoted to Mandelstam's death in the camp) and Gustav Herling's *A World Apart*.

---

transfer to Butyrki: P. Nerler, *'S gur'boi i gurtom …'*, 17–23; Shentalinsky, *Arrested Voices*, 189–91.

On 4 August 1938, he was transferred to Moscow's Butyrki prison to await transportation to a labour camp in the Kolyma region. More than 300 men were crammed together into a holding cell. A large tub stood in one corner, into which the prisoners had to relieve themselves in public. The stink was unimaginable, as was the lack of space. Mandelstam spent more than a month in Butyrki. In her book, Yevgenia Ginzburg tells of the unbearable sounds of torture heard during the ghastly 'Butyrki nights':

> Not one, but many groans and screams from people being tortured burst through the open window … Over the screams of the tortured we could hear the shouts and curses of the torturers. Added to the cacophony was the noise of chairs being flung about, fists thumping on tables, and something else elusive and spine-chilling.[16]

On 7 September 1938, the convicts were transported from the various NKVD prisons in Moscow and the Moscow district to the railway station of Krasnaya Presnya. There, a train thirty-four carriages long was waiting. According to documents that have only recently come to light, Convict Transfer No. 1152 comprised 1,770 prisoners and 110 guards. On 8 September 1938, the mass transport train left Moscow. No doctors accompanied the convoy, and the dead were simply unloaded at stations. The daily food ration consisted of 400 grams of bread, a bowl of thin soup with fish heads floating in it and a tin cup of boiled water. The journey was made in a *teplushka*, a sealed goods wagon provided with wooden pallets for approximately eighty people, and it took almost a month. It was impossible to get up and move around. In the middle of the floor of the wagon there was a gaping hole, which was used as a toilet. The clashing of the wagon buffers against each other, the continuous pitching and rolling of the wheels and the noise from the railway tracks penetrated the minds of the prisoners, who gradually became numb to their surroundings. If they looked through cracks in the walls when the train passed a station, they could see banners and posters bearing the ever-present image of Stalin, portraits of the 'great leader' and 'saviour of mankind', to whom they owed their present good fortune.

During the hours of daylight, the immensely long train usually remained stationary on railway sidings, while, at night, it continued its journey.

16 Nights of torture in Butyrki: Y. Ginzburg, *Into the Whirlwind*, 122.

The Siberian route passed through Sverdlovsk, Mariinsk, Krasnoyarsk and Urulch, and at Izvestkovaya sixteen wagons were detached, to bring their complement of 1,038 people into the local labour camps. The 700 prisoners (*zeks*) who were destined for the Kolyma labour camps continued on to Vladivostok, the seaport on the Sea of Japan. Mandelstam was among them. On 12 October, the train, with its human cargo of 'enemies of the people', finally reached Vtoraya Rechka (Second Rivulet) station near Vladivostok.[17] Mandelstam was accommodated in Barrack 11 (for 'counter-revolutionaries') of Transit Camp 3/10. Today, the town of Vladivostok has increased greatly in size, so that it includes the whole of what used to be the camp area.

According to various reports of conditions in the Gulag, the barrack leaders served as a link to the camp administration. They were mostly brutal criminals, appointed to intimidate and harass the 'intellectuals' and the 'politicals'. But in Vtoraya Rechka, there were separate camp zones for criminals and 'politicals'. Who was being protected from whom in this case? In the logic of the Gulag, the criminals, thieves and murderers were still distinguished by their 'social affinity' to the proletariat, whereas the political 'fifty-eighters' (named after the article under which they had been condemned for 'anti-Soviet agitation and propaganda') counted as particularly dangerous 'wreckers' whose ideas might infect others.

The official name of the camp was Vladivostok Dalstroy Transit Point, or 'Vladperpunkt' in the jargon of Soviet institutional abbreviations. Altogether, 12–14,000 prisoners were held in the two separate camp zones of the 'criminals' and the 'politicals', which were surrounded by high barbed-wire entanglements. Later, the convicts were placed in the holds of ships, where they were crammed together like sardines, and sent on an eight-day voyage across the Sea of Japan and the Sea of Okhotsk to the harbour of Nagayevo and then on to Magadan, after which they were taken to the labour camps on the Kolyma river. This was, in fact, a slave army for the state-run Dalstroy Trust, which was responsible for exploiting the reserves of gold, tin, tungsten, cobalt and coal in north-eastern Siberia. The hundreds of thousands of able-bodied *zeks* were human material which Dalstroy could make use of according to need, and they were worked to death, or died of cold and hunger. They were a crucial factor in the Soviet economy. Over the twenty years between 1932–1933

17 Details about Convict Transfer No. 1152 in September 1938: P. Nerler and N. Pobol', 'Delo Mandel'shtama', 169–70.

and 1953, the secret police (OGPU, then NKVD, then MGB) delivered roughly 100,000 prisoners a year to Dalstroy as replacement supplies. The death rate in the Kolyma camps was enormous. This was the Gulag's 'pole of cruelty', marked by extremely brutal conditions of imprisonment and higher mortality figures than anywhere else. Georgy Demidov has described Kolyma as an 'Auschwitz without ovens'.[18]

Owing to his obviously bad state of health, Mandelstam was spared from working in the mines. He was very quickly 'filtered out' and assigned to spend the winter in the transit camp. There were camps for invalids in Mariinsk. But the camp administration clearly preferred to save the cost of transferring him there. Only one letter sent by Mandelstam from the camp is known to exist. He addressed it to his brother Alexander, as he had to assume that Nadezhda had also been arrested and sentenced. On either 2 or 3 November 1938, the prisoners in the camp had received special permission, in view of the forthcoming holiday in honour of the revolution (7 November), to send a letter home on a scrap of wrapping paper. The letters then spent three or four weeks with the camp censorship before they were sent off. Mandelstam's letter was date-stamped Vladivostok 30 November 1938.

Dear Shura

I am in Vladivostok, North-Eastern Corrective Labour Camps, Barrack No.11. I was given five years for counter-revolutionary activity by a Special Tribunal. The transport left Butyrki on 9 September, and we got here on 12 October. My health is very bad, I'm extremely exhausted and thin, almost unrecognisable, but I don't know whether there's any sense in sending clothes, food and money. You can try all the same. I'm very cold without proper clothes.

My darling Nadia – are you alive my dear? Shura, write to me at once about Nadia. This is a transit point. I've not been picked for Kolyma and may have to spend the winter here.

I kiss you, my dear ones. OSIA.

Shura: one more thing. The last few days we've been going out to work. This has raised my spirits. This camp is a transit one and they send us on from here to regular ones. It looks as though I've been rejected, so

18 Statistical data about the 'Dalstroy' Trust and the Kolyma camps: P. Nerler and N. Pobol', 'Delo Mandel'shtama', 165–7. Kolyma as the 'pole of cruelty' and an 'Auschwitz without ovens' (G. Demidov); V. Shentalinsky, *Arrested Voices*, 134 and 135–8.

> I must prepare to spend the winter here. So please send me a telegram and cable me some money.[19]

Mandelstam's relatives received the letter on 15 December 1938. At that point, he had just two weeks to live. For decades afterwards, rumours and legends circulated about his period in the camp, brought back by ex-prisoners who had been released into so-called freedom. Ilya Ehrenburg was the first to publicise some of these stories told by returnees, in his memoirs, *Men, Years – Life*, which were published in 1961. One of them was the legendary account related by the biologist Vasily Merkulov, who claimed that the poet had recited sonnets by Petrarch to his fellow prisoners gathered round the fire. In reality, Mandelstam's life came to an end in a less poetic fashion. In the last two chapters of her memoirs, *Hope Against Hope*, Nadezhda Mandelstam endeavoured with great dignity to extract a tiny kernel of truth from the testimonies of those who returned from the camps. But it was very hard to separate truth from fantasy.

> It was a feature of almost all the former camp inmates I met immediately after their release – they had no memory for dates, or the passage of time, and it was difficult for them to distinguish between things they had actually experienced themselves and stories they had heard from others. Places, names, events and their sequence were all jumbled up in the minds of these broken people, and it was never possible to disentangle them.[20]

The physicist L. described a picturesque scene in which Mandelstam calmly recited poems in the barrack occupied by the criminal gang leader Arkhangelsky and his associates, and, an unheard-of luxury, was offered white bread and canned food. This legend celebrates once again the radiant power of poetry. It should be treated with caution.

If one compares the reports of those who returned, one or two elements stand out again and again: the rapid decline in Mandelstam's vital forces, his increasing misery and his mental confusion, which was considerable. 'He gradually became insane before our eyes', wrote another former fellow prisoner, David Zlotinsky, in a 1963 letter to Ilya Ehrenburg. At

19 MR, 294; Mandelstam, *Hope Against Hope*, 373.

20 Fact and fancy in the stories of camp survivors: Mandelstam, *Hope Against Hope*, 379 ('The Date of Death').

the beginning, Mandelstam walked around the camp zone restlessly. On many occasions, he approached the barbed-wire fencing that enclosed the prohibited area and was coarsely yelled at and threatened by the guards. The idiom he heard in the camp was *mat*, the crude language of Russian insult, separated by an astronomical distance from the sonnets of Petrarch. And, yet, poetry was not entirely absent from the universe of the Gulag. People attempted to overcome the horror of the camp regime mentally, with poetry. Mandelstam was once told by a fellow prisoner that in one of the death cells of the Lefortovo prison in Moscow, a line from one of his early poems had been scratched on the wall: 'Is it true, and am I real, / And will death really come?' (ST, 57) When he heard this, according to Nadezhda, he cheered up, and was made calmer for a few days. The phase of nervous restlessness was quickly followed by apathy, and he started to lie down on his bunk bed more often.[21]

Whether Mandelstam continued to compose poems in the camp is a question that emerges repeatedly. Here too, poetic legend conflicts with brutal reality. According to the testimony of Merkulov, the only thing Mandelstam was able to write was the line 'Black night, a suffocating barrack, fat lice.' He is simply stammering here, but even so, it is a precise statement of what he was experiencing. However, he did recite poems he had already written, including his requiem for Andrei Bely, whom he often mentioned: 'Bely, a wonderful poet'. So, even in delirium, he did not lose the poetic thread. In January 1934, after he had written the Bely requiem, he said to Nadezhda: 'This is also *my* requiem.' And the physicist L. reported what Mandelstam said when sitting on a pile of stones: 'My first book was *Stone*, and my last will be stone, too.'[22]

He had written in his last letter: 'I am freezing without proper clothes.' The old yellow coat, made of leather, which Ehrenburg had given him (it can be seen in the last Lubyanka photograph) had suddenly disappeared. The confused poet had exchanged it for two pieces of sugar, because he had heard that to survive the human organism needs sugar first and foremost. But the sugar was immediately stolen from him in the barracks. A recurrent theme of eyewitness reports was Mandelstam's suspicion

21 The Arkhangelsky story told by the physicist L.: Mandelstam, *Hope Against Hope*, 393–4 ('One Final Account'). David Zlotinsky's letter of 23 February 1963 to Ehrenburg: the commentary to Nadezhda Mandel'shtam, *Vospominaniia*, 522–3.

22 Further eyewitness reports from camp survivors: E. Polianovsky 'Smert' Osipa Mandel'shtama'; P. Nerler, *'S gur'boi i gurtom …'*, 27–58.

that the camp administration wanted to poison him. Most of the time, therefore, he did not touch the meagre food ration, thereby accelerating his decline. Instead, he laid hands on other prisoners' bread rations, for which they beat him. According to Merkulov, he also ate leftovers and licked out other people's bowls.

His fear that the camp authorities would murder him in the barracks with a night-time injection indicates the tormented poet's increasing paranoia. Perhaps Mandelstam's descent into madness was the only adequate answer to the madness of the surrounding world of the camps. It was the only possible reply to ten years of persecution, psychological demoralisation, life as a beggar, and anxiety. His paranoia was therefore a reaction to a paranoid system, which had lost its mental balance through the constant search for 'wreckers', 'spies' and 'saboteurs'. The madness was certainly not restricted to the inflamed brain of a single poet. In the Stalin epoch, it was an ever-present phenomenon. As Mandelstam had cried out in his cell in 1920 when he was arrested during the Russian Civil War, 'I am not cut out to be in prison!'

Nadezhda Mandelstam never obtained definite information about the circumstances of her husband's death. Not until ten years after her own death did a new batch of prisoners' recollections emerge. Articles about the poet started to appear in various magazines and newspapers in connection with the hundredth anniversary of his birth in January 1991. The most important addition to the reports of camp witnesses was the letter by Yury Moiseyenko printed in the 22 February 1991 issue of the newspaper *Izvestiia*: 'How Osip Mandelstam Died'. A five-part series of articles in the same newspaper, which had a print run of millions, between 25 and 29 May 1992, also aroused a great deal of interest. It was written by the journalist Edwin Polianovsky, who had been able to interview Moiseyenko in the meantime.

Yury Moiseyenko occupied the bunk next to Mandelstam's in Barrack 11 for 'counter-revolutionaries'. He had been arrested in 1935 as a twenty-one-year-old student. He arrived in Vtoraya Rechka on 14 October 1938, two days after Mandelstam. According to this witness, the poet was still scribbling on a scrap of paper at the beginning. He possessed a small pencil, although this was forbidden. 'He was occupied with his own thoughts', according to his former prison companion. In the camp, Mandelstam was just described as 'the poet'. He sometimes recited poems, even the anti-Stalin poem on one occasion, but it was drowned out by the noise in the barracks, while other poems were incomprehensible to his fellow prisoners. Even in this universe, this 'world outside the world', he was perceived as an eccentric and alien presence.

A few days after he had written his only letter from the camp (2–3 November), Mandelstam's energies declined noticeably. By the middle of November, he was only taking a little food each day. In addition to hunger and cold ('I am freezing without proper clothes'), he was visited by another torment: the presence of large numbers of lice. The lice infestation in the barracks was so intense that the prisoners were constantly scratching themselves. At the beginning of December, an epidemic of spotted typhus broke out – transmitted by the lice. Barrack 11 was placed under quarantine. Every day the corpses of the dead were carried out of the building. After 20 December, Mandelstam no longer got up from his bunk bed. It was almost impossible to get a reply from him. According to Moiseyenko, a certain Kovalyov, a beekeeper from Blagoveshchensk, took special care of Mandelstam, bringing his bowl of food to the bunk. When asked whether a doctor should be called, Mandelstam replied: 'Absolutely not.' Right to the end, he was terrified that he would be killed with injections in the infirmary barracks.

On the morning of 27 December 1938, the authorities decided to conduct a de-lousing procedure. All the inmates of the barracks were driven to a laundry, where their clothes were to be disinfected in hot sulphurated steam. Mandelstam staggered out apathetically, propped up by Kovalyov. The hygienic procedure required the prisoners to strip naked in the icy cold of a vestibule, and to pass their clothes into the heating chamber. They had to hold out for forty minutes in the vestibule, where the temperature was almost as low as it was outside. At the end of December, powerful snowstorms were raging along the Pacific coast. It was a scene that could have been taken from Dante's *Inferno*, the book Mandelstam regarded as his most important possession. It had accompanied him everywhere during the 1930s, only not into the camp. There the place of hell was occupied by the reality of the Gulag.

When the disinfection of the clothing had been completed, the door of the heating chamber was pulled open, Moiseyenko's account continues, and a pungent smell of sulphur blasted out. At that moment, Mandelstam took a few steps, threw his head back, clutched at his heart and collapsed. The doctor was called, and he certified that death had occurred. The naked body of Mandelstam was carried into the infirmary by two attendants.

The death certificate has been found in the Dalstroy Archive in Magadan. The cause of death is given as 'Heart paralysis and arteriosclerosis'. The documents also record that Mandelstam was delivered to the infirmary on 26 December. Moiseyenko assumes that the camp authorities wanted to conceal the tremendous mortality rate by presenting false data.

The body was disinfected with sublimate of mercury chloride. The attendants then attached a piece of wood to the deceased's big toe, bearing his inmate number. The wrestler Maturin, another witness, had to carry the body to the mortuary, which lay in the criminal zone of the camp. The criminals, or *urkas*, then extracted any gold teeth with pliers, in order to sell them. The clothes, or rags, Mandelstam was wearing at the end were sold rather than being burnt, which ought to have been the procedure with typhus.

The naked corpses were first piled up into a heap. Only later were they thrown into a mass grave. In Vtoraya Rechka, the ground was frozen solid in winter. If the graves that had been dug out before the onset of winter were full, the authorities had to wait until spring before the piled-up corpses could be buried hurriedly in mass graves. Osip Mandelstam died as one of hundreds of thousands of others in Stalin's icy Gulag jungle, and his body was thrown naked into a mass grave, with a small identification tag attached to his big toe. In March 1937, he had already anticipated the anonymity of his death in his 'Verses on the Unknown Soldier', in which he refers to his 'airy grave', which became a mass grave:

And the people, cold and feeble
Will kill and starve and freeze,
While inside his well-known monument
The unknown soldier lies

Teach me, you little swallow
Who has forgotten how to fly
How this airy grave is handled
With neither wings nor rudder
(WH, 167; PO, 62–3)

24

Nadezhda Makes Herself Invisible

(The Second Life 1938–1980)

After Mandelstam's arrest on 2 May 1938, Nadezhda had travelled back to Kalinin from Samatikha to collect together the manuscripts that remained there. A little later, some NKVD agents appeared with an arrest order, but she was no longer there. For the first few days, she hid in Moscow with Nikolai Khardzhiev, then she disappeared to the house of an acquaintance in Maloyaroslavets. After that, she settled in the town of Strunino (eighty kilometres north-east of Moscow). On 30 September 1938, she started work at the textile factory 'October', where she operated spooling machines. She repeatedly travelled to Moscow to try to find out more about Mandelstam's fate. At the NKVD counter near Kuznetsky Bridge, described in a chapter of her memoirs as 'the window on the Sophia embankment', she was informed that Mandelstam had been transferred on 4 August to Butyrki prison and condemned by a special tribunal to imprisonment in a labour camp. On 22 October 1938, she wrote her 'last letter' to her husband.

> Osia, my beloved, faraway sweetheart!
>
> I have no words, my darling, to write this letter that you may never read, perhaps. I am writing it into empty space. Perhaps you will come back, and not find me here. Then this will be all you have left to remember me by.

Osia, what happiness it was living together like children – all our squabbles and arguments, the games we played, and our love …

Remember the way we brought back provisions to make our poor feasts in all the places where we pitched our tent like nomads? Remember the good taste of bread when we got it by a miracle and ate it together? And our last winter in Voronezh. Our happy poverty and the poetry you wrote … And I have kept those days in my memory: I understand so clearly, and ache from the pain of it, that those winter days with all their troubles were the greatest and last happiness to be granted us in life.

My every thought is about you. My every tear and every smile is for you. I bless every day and every hour of our bitter life together, my sweetheart, my companion, my blind guide in life.

Like two blind puppies we were, nuzzling each other and feeling so good together. And how fevered your poor head was, and how madly we frittered away the days of our life. What happiness it was, and how we always knew what happiness it was.

Life can last so long. How hard and long for each of us to die alone. Can this fate be for us who are inseparable? Puppies and children, did we deserve this? Did you deserve this, my angel? Everything goes on. I know nothing. Yet I know everything – each day and each hour of your life are plain and clear to me as in a fever dream

You came to me every night in my sleep, and I kept asking what had happened, but you did not reply …

I do not know where you are. Will you hear me? Do you know how much I love you? I could never tell you how much I love you. I cannot tell you even now. I speak only to you, only to you. You are with me always, and I, who was such a wild and angry one and never learned to weep simple tears – now I weep and weep.

It's me: Nadia. Where are you?

Farewell.

Nadia.[1]

On 15 December 1938, she received Mandelstam's only letter from the camp, which revealed that he was being held close to Vladivostok. On 19 January 1939, she attempted to change Mandelstam's fate by writing another letter. The background to this was the fall of Yezhov, the man

1 'The last letter': N. Mandelstam, *Hope Abandoned*, 620–1. German in: O. Mandelstam, *Du bist mein Moskau und mein Rom*, 304–5.

who had put into effect the 'Great Terror'. On 7 December 1938, he had been dismissed from his position as head of the NKVD. The apparatus of terror had reached such a level of murderous efficiency that those in charge realised it was impossible to continue at that rate. The Soviet Empire was tearing itself to pieces. Yezhov's successor was Lavrenty Beria. The tempo of the killing machine was cut back. For a short while, there were fewer arrests and fewer executions. The population was permitted a moment to take breath. Nadezhda tried to take advantage of the change at the summit of power, and she called on Beria to review the verdict against Mandelstam. In her letter, she daringly pointed to its illegality, on the ground that she herself had not been brought into the investigation, either as a possible accomplice in Mandelstam's 'counter-revolutionary activity' or at least as a witness (MR, 306). The letter bears witness to her immense courage. But it was courage of a tragic and useless kind.[2]

When she wrote it, Mandelstam was already dead, a fact Nadezhda could not have known. Only on 5 February 1939 was a parcel she had sent to the camp returned to her marked 'Addressee Deceased'. A bitter coincidence: on the same day, *Literaturnaia Gazeta* had printed a long list of writers honoured with decorations and medals. There were two old acquaintances among the 166 names on the list: Stavsky, who had written a letter of denunciation to Yezhov asking him to 'solve the Mandelstam problem', received the 'medal of honour', and Pavlenko, who had denied Mandelstam's 'usefulness' in the expert's report attached to the denunciation, received the Order of Lenin. The system did not give out its decorations without a good reason: here two deserving hangmen were being honoured. During a party held to celebrate the award of decorations to writers honoured by the regime, Fadeyev, a top functionary of the Writers' Union, is said to have shed a drunken tear when the news of Mandelstam's death spread around the assembly, saying: 'What a poet we've destroyed!'[3]

Nadezhda informed her closest friends, and she sent Natasha Shtempel, who had immediately travelled from Voronezh, to visit Anna Akhmatova in Leningrad with the message 'Osia is dead.' After Mandelstam's death in the camp, Nadezhda's second life began. She now had a new life's work:

2 Nadezhda's letter of 19 January 1939 to Beria: P. Nerler, *'S gur'boi i gurtom ...'*, 61–2. German in: O. Mandelstam, *Du bist mein Moskau und mein Rom*, 306–7.

3 Honours for the executioners, and Fadeyev's tears: N. Mandelstam, *Hope Against Hope*, 377 ('The Date of Death'); V. Shentalinsky, *Arrested Voices*, 193.

> It was not in my power to alter O.M.'s fate, but some of his manuscripts had survived, and much more was preserved in my memory. Only I could save it all and that was why it was worth keeping up my strength.

The new task inexorably banished the ideas of suicide she had entertained so frequently in the past. She no longer had a right to die before her time. In preserving her husband's work, Nadezhda Mandelstam performed a task of inestimable value. For years, she learned his poetry by heart to preserve it from the clutches of Stalin's creatures. She set up hiding places for the documents and she handed copies of the texts to a small circle of friends in the hope that some of them would survive the Stalin era.

She herself survived, as if through a miracle, by making herself invisible in obscure provincial backwaters and distant Soviet republics. 'I too was saved from arrest by not having a home … So I was not caught in a trap, and because I was homeless they overlooked me. That is why I was able to survive and preserve M's poems.'[4] The two capital cities were dangerous places. Cynical though this may sound, she was also perhaps saved by the Second World War. It was easier to avoid the attention of the NKVD in wartime. In August 1941, on the eve of the occupation of the town by the German Wehrmacht, Nadezhda was evacuated from Kalinin. After spending a year in Dzhambul in Kazakhstan, she went to live in the Uzbek capital of Tashkent, near her friend Anna Akhmatova, who had also been evacuated. The two women became sworn allies.

The list of Nadezhda's wanderings between 1938 and 1964 indicates the stages in her all-Soviet odyssey: Maloyaroslavets and Strunino not far from Moscow, Kalinin (until 1941), Muynak on the shores of the Aral Sea, Dzhambul in Kazakhstan, the Uzbek capital Tashkent (until 1949), Ulyanovsk (until 1953), Chita in eastern Siberia (until 1955), the Chuvash town of Cheboksary halfway down the Volga (until 1958), Vereya, Tarusa on the River Oka (150 kilometres south of Moscow), and finally Pskov, close to the border with Estonia (until 1964). Decades of bitter loneliness and anxiety lie behind the magic of these exotic place names. It was this uneasy peregrination from refuge to refuge that Joseph Brodsky had in mind when, in an inversion of the roles of classical legend, he described Nadezhda as 'Eurydice', the widow of a modern Orpheus:

---

4 Nadezhda's new task in life: Mandelstam, *Hope Against Hope*, 15 ('Morning Thoughts'). 'I too was saved from arrest by not having a home': ibid., 136 ('The Disappointed Landlord').

> Sent to hell, he never returned, while his widow dodged across one sixth of the earth's surface, clutching the saucepan with his songs rolled up inside, memorizing them by night in the event they were found by Furies with a search warrant.[5]

Nadezhda did not see herself as Eurydice, but as a frustrated Antigone.[6] She writes that she envied Antigone, the figure immortalised by Sophocles, who demanded from the ruler Creon the right to bury her brother and sacrificed her life for this (she was punished by being immured in a vault of stone). The Soviet Union, however, was a country where millions of Antigones had to hide, and not only could they not bury their nearest and dearest; they were not even allowed to weep for them.

> Nobody will ever know where those near or dear to them are buried. The mass graves into which the bodies with tags on their legs were thrown are inaccessible … As a widow who was unable to bury her husband, I send the last gift of love to a body with a tag on its leg, remembering and mourning without tears, because we belong to a tearless generation.

The frustrated Antigone first obtained factory work, then painted children's toys working from home, cleaned turnips in Uzbekistan and finally worked as a teacher of English in provincial colleges. She was animated by her tremendous love for Mandelstam and driven by her dogged readiness to undergo any adversity to preserve his work. She was helped in this endeavour by a few true friends and accomplices. Even so, there were some losses. The part of the archive entrusted to Sergei Rudakov in Voronezh did not survive. In her memoirs, Nadezhda tells us of her suspicion that Rudakov's wife may have destroyed or hawked the papers. The losses included the autographs of almost all Mandelstam's poems of the 1910s and 1920s, which were marked by the peculiar imprint of heavy boots: traces of the house search of 1934, when the OGPU agents threw politically irrelevant texts onto the floor and walked around on them. Manuscripts covered by footprints: an appropriate image of the fate of poetry in the Soviet era.

---

5 LG, 134–5; J. Brodsky, 'The Child of Civilization', 144.

6 Nadezhda the frustrated Antigone: Mandelstam, *Hope Abandoned*, 169–70 ('First Quarrels').

Other manuscripts were preserved more securely. On 4 July 1942, their Voronezh friend Natasha Shtempel was evacuated from the already burning town just hours before the entry of German troops. She took with her, along with her few personal possessions, the poems and letters that had been entrusted to her. When she met Nadezhda again in 1947, in Voronezh, she returned everything: all the original letters from Mandelstam to Nadezhda which had been hidden in a tea case, including the final letters given to her after his death, and the three large blue notebooks containing the unpublished Moscow and Voronezh poems which had been handed to her in May 1937 as *Natasha's Book*.[7] Mandelstam had already foreseen in November 1920 that his work would be preserved by 'blessed women':

> In the black velvet of the Soviet night
> In the velvet of universal emptiness,
> The dear eyes of the blessed women sing on,
> Immortal flowers ever bloom.
> …
> We warm ourselves from boredom at the bonfire
> Maybe centuries will pass
> And the dear hands of blessed women
> Will gather our light ash.
> (TR, 97; TA, 298)

In 1942, when she was evacuated, Nadezhda herself brought Mandelstam's manuscripts to Tashkent. There, the undaunted Alisa Usova helped her to make handwritten copies and hide the texts. The codeword used for the poems was 'How are the goldfinches getting on?' a reference to the 'Goldfinch cycle' in the *Voronezh Notebooks*.[8] Towards the end of the Second World War, Nadezhda had a feeling that she was being spied on again, so she had to find a new hiding place for the archive. On 15 May 1944, Anna Akhmatova flew to Moscow with the manuscripts and handed them to Emma Gerstein. But in August 1946 Gerstein herself lost her nerve, because she feared that her house would be searched, and so she handed the archive back to Nadezhda. This was the period of the infamous smear campaign mounted by Politburo member Andrei

7 The preservation of M.'s manuscripts by Natasha Shtempel: N. Shtempel', *Mandel'shtam v Voronezhe*, 63–4 and 88.

8 'How are the goldfinches?': Mandelstam, *Hope Against Hope*, 366 ('Gugovna').

Zhdanov against Anna Akhmatova and the satirist Mikhail Zoshchenko. Akhmatova was defamed by Zhdanov, who called her 'half a nun, half a whore'. The atmosphere of repression against intellectuals and artists had worsened rapidly since the end of the war.

Nadezhda had to find new allies very quickly. From autumn 1946, the major part of the archive was kept safe in Moscow by Ignaty Bernstein (pseudonym: Alexander Ivich), the author of children's books who had already offered the persecuted couple a refuge in the capital city in 1937–1938. He was the brother of the well-known sound specialist Sergei Bernstein, who had recorded the voices of Russian poets on wax cylinders in the 1920s, including Blok, Yesenin, Mayakovsky – and Mandelstam. He too would contribute to preserving the Mandelstam archive without any hesitation when Ignaty sensed the approach of danger. After all, he was used to conserving the voices of poets! When Nadezhda gave him a cardboard folder he accepted it without comment. In 1948, the part of the archive that had been hidden with Nadezhda's brother Yevgeny Khazin also found its way to the Bernstein brothers. Khazin suspected that he was under police observation, and he thought it best to remove the valuable and dangerous manuscripts from his house. The works of Mandelstam, the 'enemy of the people', began their own odyssey from one hiding place to the next. Their custodians needed great courage.[9]

In 1949, a press campaign was mounted against 'Alexander Ivich' (Ignaty Bernstein in other words), defaming him as a 'cosmopolitan'. He was one of many victims of the state-directed anti-Semitism of Stalin's final years of paranoid decrepitude. In spite of the danger, Ignaty wanted to keep faith and continue preserving the Mandelstam archive. When the Bernsteins were staying during summer in dachas around Moscow, Nadezhda travelled from her provincial places of refuge to visit them, bringing texts that had just come to light and variant readings reconstructed from memory. A complete body of text was then established at the Bernstein family table. They were conducting what could be called the first act of 'conspiratorial' Mandelstamian philology.

Even after Stalin's death on 5 March 1953, Nadezhda did not believe that she would live long enough to witness the publication of her husband's works. On 9 August 1954, she designated the young daughter of the

9 The preservation of Mandelstam's archive by Ignaty Bernstein: O. S. Figurnova and M. V. Figurnova, *Osip i Nadezhda Mandel'shtamy*, 360–82.

Bernsteins, Sofia,[10] as her heiress, saying 'We shall not survive long enough, but perhaps she will.' On 28 February 1957, however, during the 'thaw' that followed the Twentieth Party Congress, held in 1956, a committee was set up to publish Mandelstam's works. It included Nadezhda's brother Yevgeny, Anna Akhmatova, Nikolai Khardzhiev and Ilya Ehrenburg. Nadezhda responded by abruptly decreeing that the valuable literary legacy should be handed over to the committee. She could be ruthless, harshly cancelling earlier decisions if they appeared to endanger the exclusive goal of her life.

But the publication committee had to fight hard for years against the bureaucrats and hard-line adherents of ageing Stalinism. In December 1966, Nadezhda abandoned any hope of publishing the work. She wrote *My Testament* and she bequeathed the literary inheritance to those who would contribute to the preservation and publication of Mandelstam's work.[11] It must never come into the possession of the Soviet state, which was only interested in suppressing it! In 1972, eight years before her death, she arranged for the whole of the archive to be smuggled to Paris. Then, in 1976, it was transferred to the United States, where it is still kept today, at Princeton University (New Jersey), in the manuscript department of the Firestone Library.

As well as preserving Mandelstam's writings, Nadezhda also tirelessly endeavoured to secure his rehabilitation. Her 1939 application in the letter to Beria for the verdict to be reviewed was answered with a rejection a full two years later in a woodenly bureaucratic letter from an NKVD official called Nikitochkin, who declared that Mandelstam's 'anti-Soviet activity' had been proved (MR, 308–9).[12] Long after Stalin's death, the 'evidential material' of the anti-Stalin poem continued to weigh too heavily. On 24 August 1955, with the coming of the 'thaw', Nadezhda sent an application for Mandelstam's rehabilitation to the USSR state prosecutor. But, even after the 1956 Party Congress – the scene of Khrushchev's secret speech about Stalin's crimes – full rehabilitation was not granted. On 31 July 1956, the USSR Supreme Court informed 'citizeness Nadezhda Mandelstam' that only the 1938 trial (based on his breaches of the prohibition on visiting Moscow) had been recognised as illegal, but not the 1934 trial (based on the anti-Stalin poem). Nadezhda did not live to see

10 Sof'ia Bernshtein-Bogatyrova.

11 N. Mandel'shtam, *Kniga Tret'ia*, 5–16.

12 Nikitochkin's 1941 refusal to revise the verdict on M.: P. Nerler *'S gur'boi i gurtom …'*, 80. In German in O. Mandelstam, *Du bist mein Moskau und mein Rom*, 308–9.

his definitive rehabilitation, which took place on 28 October 1987 in the context of Gorbachev's policy of *glasnost'*. By then, Mandelstam had long since been recognised all over the world as one of the most important poets of the twentieth century. Nadezhda's memoirs, which were published in New York in 1970, had also given a powerful boost to the poet's international recognition.

If the party's functionaries had suspected the impact these memoirs would have on the *samizdat* underground, on dissident circles and on Western countries, they would hardly have allowed Nadezhda to settle in Moscow again in 1964 after two and a half decades spent wandering restlessly through the Soviet Empire. She was given shelter in the city by the Shklovskys, then in 1965 she obtained a one-room dwelling in the 'Cheryomushki' (Bird Cherry Tree) district of the city. Her address was: Bolshaia Cheryomushkinskaia No. 14, Block 1, Dwelling 4. Mandelstam would have appreciated the address! Bird cherry trees have a special aura in his poetry, as for example in the 1918 poem 'That Tick-tock of Grasshoppers', the 'nomad' poem of 1925, the late Voronezh poem of 4 May 1937, and several others:

> Rain murmuring on the roof:
> That's black silk burning,
> But from the bottom of the sea
> The bird cherry hears forgiveness.
> (TR, 57; MT, 48)

> I will race through the dark street's bivouac
> Behind the bird cherry branch in a black sprung carriage
> (TR, 175; OM, 95)

> The pear tree and the cherry tree have taken aim at me –
> Their scattershot force strikes at me unfailingly.
> (WH, 213; PO, 79)

The poet's widow was finally a Moscow resident, but nothing and no one could placate her. As early as 1958, during the 'thaw', in Vereya, she had begun to write her memoirs in secret. They would be a relentless settlement of accounts not only with the Stalin regime but also with its assistants and accomplices among the intellectuals. Nadezhda depicts an artistic life under threat at the darkest moments of the Stalin epoch, and at the same time paints an unforgiving and clear-sighted picture of twentieth-century totalitarianism. Joseph Brodsky wrote in Nadezhda's obituary: 'Her memoirs are something more than a testimony to her times; they are a view of history in the light of conscience and culture.'[13] They are a record of the life of a 'widow to culture' (Brodsky) and memoirs of the century in the truest sense. The first volume was published in New York in Russian in 1970 (as *Vospominaniia*). It came out in English, also in 1970, as *Hope Against Hope*, and in German in 1971 under the title *Das Jahrhundert der Wölfe*. The memoirs matched Alexander Solzhenitsyn's *The Gulag Archipelago* (1973) in significance and explosiveness. Soviet dissidents and human rights campaigners finally had a vade mecum to refer to. Nadezhda's book can confidently be counted as one of the charges of intellectual dynamite that contributed to the collapse of an unjust regime. The nails in the Soviet Empire's coffin were many and various, but this was certainly one of them!

The explosive impact of the work was heightened by its high artistic quality. Nadezhda had an unmistakable style of writing. She had an instinct for succinctness and an ability to portray vivid details and pick out subtle associations. On returning home one day, she sees someone else's cigarette ends in the ashtray, left there deliberately by an agent who had gone through her drawers, to intimidate her. Then there is the OGPU agent who contemplates his victims' books regretfully and keeps offering them hard candy from a little tin. Nadezhda's memoirs were feverishly read and copied at night. They circulated in *samizdat*, robbing some readers of their sleep, because they were prepared to risk punishment for a taste of the freedom offered by their night-time reading.

When the second volume of her memoirs appeared in Paris in 1972 (it was issued in a considerably shorter German version in 1975 under the title *Generation ohne Tränen*), all hell broke loose in Moscow intellectual circles. The first volume had already attacked not just the violent Soviet regime but the complicity of the intelligentsia, which had spinelessly adapted itself to totalitarian rule or even offered its services to Stalin. The second volume directed numerous accusations and imputations against survivors of the Stalin epoch. Nadezhda Mandelstam had already put herself in the position of a judge; now she became an avenger. Some people

13 Brodsky's obituary of Nadezhda Mandelstam (her 'boundless devotion to justice'): J. Brodsky, 'Nadezhda Mandelstam', 145–56.

found that impossible to forgive. Others admired the combative old lady's inexorable and unbending character. Andrei Sinyavsky, who had lived in exile in Paris since 1973 and was now far away from the witches' kitchen of Moscow, was interviewed in a documentary film in which he suggested that Nadezhda was limited to a single perspective: she viewed everything through the black hole of the mass grave into which her husband had been thrown in 1938 in the Far East transit camp, unclothed and with a wooden identification tag attached to his toe. In his 1981 obituary, Joseph Brodsky wrote of her 'boundless devotion to justice'. But, for some, she had gone too far: 'They would rush to their dachas to tap out anti-memoirs.'

Nadezhda Mandelstam had achieved international fame in one stroke in 1970 with the publication of the first volume of her memoirs. In 1973, a Dutch television team managed to persuade her to give them an interview. Frank Diamand produced what would remain the only motion pictures of Nadezhda. She allowed the interview on the condition that the film would not be transmitted until she had died.[14] This was because of her continued fear of the KGB, which shadowed her with even greater persistence after her memoirs had appeared. Lying on a sofa, smoking *papirosy*, and speaking English in her distinctively Russian accent, the seventy-three-year-old described Mandelstam's loneliness and alienation during that frightful era: 'He was surrounded by enemies' and 'he was different from other people'.

She also recalled the active love life that had bound the two together: 'We were the start of the sexual revolution, we had nothing to lose.' They had often quarrelled during the day, but the nights of love had been good. Plain speaking of this kind was typical of Nadezhda, who once again had nothing to lose. Their happiness and success as a couple still animated her as an old lady. She had long since ceased to be the ordinary widow of a poet. For the dissidents of the 1960s and 1970s, she was a cult figure and a brazen saint who proclaimed painful verities. Her mental acuteness, her scorn and her refusal to compromise were admired – and also feared.

In her final years she became an Orthodox believer, and in her memoirs she sometimes presented Mandelstam as more of a Christian than he had been. She received spiritual support from Alexander Men, a charismatic priest and intellectual who was later murdered by the KGB. Under his influence, the woman who had been obsessed with taking vengeance turned into a generous lady with the wisdom of old age, who helped many

14 Filmed interview with Nadezhda Mandelstam (1973): Frank Diamand, Netherlands Television NOS; German version: WDR/WDF 1986.

people intellectually and materially.[15] Every visitor who was able to do so put some money into a little box in her flat. Thanks to this, parcels of provisions could be sent to imprisoned dissidents. She had many visitors, including writers from the West such as Arthur Miller and Bruce Chatwin. She received many letters and gifts, which she immediately passed on. Earlier, in the terrible years, she had dreamed of prosperity and money. Now her indifference towards material objects and physical comfort was as strongly developed as her openhandedness. Vladimir Nabokov sent her a practical present of bedsheets of synthetic fabric. These she kept, until they were riddled with holes made by her strong *papirosy* – of the 'Belomorkanal' brand. If any remuneration found its way to her, she celebrated with friends, buying gin, anchovies and artichokes.

She seemed to be protected by her international fame. But there are grounds to look more closely at the old lady's apparent fearlessness, which led young Russians to hang on to every word she spoke in her kitchen. For the whole of her life until then, she had feared arrest – and with good reason. Only a failure to recognise the horror of the Stalin epoch, and even the incompetent brutality of the epigones of the Brezhnev era, could lead one to doubt the demoralising effect of this continued anxiety. Under Brezhnev, the physical liquidation characteristic of the Stalin epoch was replaced by utterly perverse methods of repression such as the 'treatment' of dissidents in psychiatric clinics. The most prominent victim of the misuse of psychiatry was the former general Piotr Grigorenko, while the dissident Vladimir Bukovsky underwent twelve years of involuntary psychiatric treatment. Complaisant Soviet psychiatrists cured 'anti-Soviet tendencies' by inventing the diagnosis of 'atypical schizophrenia'. The Soviet regime was never harmless, and certainly not in Nadezhda Mandelstam's final years.

For years, she had been haunted by nightmares. One witness reports that, even in her Moscow apartment (after 1965), she often cried out in her sleep, uttering the 'animal-like screams' that had started back in the terror winter of 1937–1938. But during her years in Pskov (1962–1964), she 'overcame her fear' in a dream, and she remembered this dream ever afterwards. In it, a lorry was standing in a courtyard with the engine running. Mandelstam came in and woke her up with the words: 'Get up,

15 Nadezhda becomes increasingly 'charitable' as she grows older: Figurnova and Figurnova, *Osip i Nadezhda Mandel'shtamy*, 405 (L. Kostiuchuk), 422 (V. Gel'shtein), 452 and 454 (V. Shklovskaia-Kordi) and others.

they've come for you this time … I am no longer here.' And she replied, still in her dream: 'You are no longer here, so I do not care.' Then she turned over and went into a deep sleep without dreams. In other dreams, Osip called on her to join him. She was convinced that he was waiting for her. She believed that she would see him again, and she yearned for this to happen. Her later days revolved around 'Oska', as she tenderly named him. He was the meaning of her life; he was her second self. To outsiders it appeared as if she was still living with her husband, although in fact she was forced to survive for decades without him.[16]

Nadezhda spent only nineteen of the eighty-one years of her life by Mandelstam's side, and forty-two years as his widow. In the first few years after the publication of her memoirs, she seemed to enjoy the admiration. It was a belated recompense for the decades of loneliness. But, eventually, she became 'tired of adulation'; she 'no longer wanted to be liked', as Joseph Brodsky has written. All she wanted now was 'to die in her bed'. With the poems saved and preserved, the memoirs written, and the archive transported to America, the inflexible old lady regarded her life's work as complete, and calmly faced the prospect of death. Right at the end, she became very unwell after a heart attack, and was cared for round the clock by friends, following a plan organised by her doctor Yuri Freidin. In her final night, she complained of 'cats in my chest'. Then she uttered the words: 'Hunger in Russia' in the delirium of her death throes. Then she repeated 'Russia, Russia' twice. Her last words, which were spoken to her carer, were 'Just don't be scared.'

Nadezhda Mandelstam died on 29 December 1980 at 6 a.m. Her burial took place on 2 January 1981 at the old Troyekurovskoye cemetery in the Moscow suburb of Kuntsevo. It turned into a silent, defiant demonstration, predominantly by young Russians. But informers and KGB agents were also present. The state security organs had not allowed her to be interred at the central Vagankovo cemetery because they feared that her grave might become a place of pilgrimage. For those who attended Nadezhda's burial in Kuntsevo, it was also a ceremony of commemoration for her husband, the poet whose body had been tossed into a mass grave in Vladivostok. Dmitry Shakhovskoy had carved a massive wooden cross for Nadezhda,

16 Nadezhda is haunted by nightmares and dreams about Osip: Figurnova and Figurnova, *Osip i Nadezhda Mandel'shtamy*, 401–2 (L. Kostiuchuk), and 425 (V. Gel'shtein). She yearns to see 'Oska' again: 395–6 (T. Osmerkina). She dreams that she has overcome her fears: Mandelstam, *Hope Abandoned*, 691.

and soon there stood on the grave beside it, as if sheltering under one of its arms, a small, shining memorial stone, bearing the chiselled inscription: 'To the shining memory of Osip Mandelstam'.

When the funeral meal took place, Nadezhda's Voronezh friend Natasha Shtempel overcame her shyness and spoke a few quiet words about how fortunate she had been to meet the Mandelstams. This was followed by a very emotional moment. Without any invitation, the mourners stood up one by one to recite poems by Mandelstam from memory. As Natasha Shtempel comments in her memoirs:

> And the poet Osip Mandelstam arose in his full greatness before the agitated onlookers, who were astonished by this completely unexpected turn of events. There has probably never been such an inspired literary portrait as this one. It had the ring of a requiem. And the death and the sorrow disappeared. What overwhelming strength is possessed by poetry!

The KGB immediately sealed the flat in Cheryomushki. Nadezhda's doctor and friend Yuri Freidin had already prudently removed some of her things. For several years afterwards, he gave shelter to Mandelstam's modest book collection, along with photocopies and microfilms of the archive that had been sent in 1976 to Princeton University. Nadezhda's decision to send the archive abroad soon turned out to be well judged: in the summer of 1983, the KGB searched Freidin's apartment and confiscated all his papers, including Nadezhda's personal documents.[17] They were never returned. Even so, the secret police were unsuccessful in their endeavours. It was no longer possible to delay or prevent the emergence of the truth. Mandelstam the poet had long since begun his journey back from obscurity into the light of day.

---

17 Nadezhda's death, burial and funeral meal: Shtempel', *Mandel'shtam v Voronezhe*, 78–82. Description of her final night: Figurnova and Figurnova, *Osip i Nadezhda Mandel'shtamy*, 503–4 (V. Lashkova). Her flat sealed by the KGB; the confiscation of her papers: ibid., 456 (V. Shklovskaia-Kordi), 504–5 (V. Lashkova). House search by the KGB in 1983: Y. Freidin, 'Sud'ba arkhiva poeta', 13.

25

Return from the Underground

(The Verdict of Posterity, 1956 to the Present)

After 1956, with the coming of the 'thaw', Mandelstam's poems gradually began to circulate in the *samizdat* underground. For many nonconforming artists and intellectuals of the sixties and seventies, he became a symbol for the indomitable persistence of artistic creation under the most untoward political circumstances. Mandelstam, the 'modern Orpheus' (to use Joseph Brodsky's expression), became a clandestine revelation. Throughout the night, the texts of his poems were hammered out by typewriters through five sheets of carbon paper or copied by hand and passed on.

It continued to be impossible to mention his name officially, but the memoirs of Ilya Ehrenburg, *Men, Years – Life*, published in 1961, contained a significant defence of Mandelstam, as well as of other outlawed poets: 'I remember many of his verses, I repeat them again and again as incantations, I look back and feel happy that I lived alongside him … What harm could he possibly have done, this poet with an ailing frame, who filled our nights with the music of his poetry?' Ehrenburg was sharply criticised by Stalinists for 'overvaluing' the poetry of the outcast writers.[1]

On 13 May 1965, there took place the first ever memorial evening for Mandelstam. It was held at Moscow University, with Ehrenburg in the chair, in the presence of Nadezhda Mandelstam. Varlam Shalamov read

1 Ehrenburg's remarks in defence of M.: I. Ehrenburg, *Men, Years – Life*, 107–8.

his story about Mandelstam's death in the Gulag, 'Cherry Brandy'. But, by then, the long-yearned-for 'thaw' had already come to an end. Khrushchev had been removed (October 1964), and Brezhnev was in power. Joseph Brodsky, a young poet and an admirer of Mandelstam, had been exiled to the north of the country in March 1964 after an outrageous trial on charges of 'parasitism' and 'idleness'. In the frostier political atmosphere of 1965, the Mandelstam memorial evening had an almost conspiratorial character.

Anna Akhmatova gave a short personal address at a further meeting, held in Moscow in the Bolshoi Theatre on 19 October 1965 to commemorate the 700th anniversary of Dante's birth. It was her last public appearance. Her death on 5 March 1966 marked the departure from the scene of the last representative of the 'Silver Age' of Russian poetry, the poetic witness of a vanished culture. At the Moscow University meeting in May 1965, the audience had been students and confirmed admirers of poetry, whereas the Bolshoi Theatre meeting was attended by many officials and dignitaries of the Soviet regime. When Akhmatova mentioned the enthusiasm for Dante of her Acmeist colleagues Gumilyov and Mandelstam, it was felt that she had broken a taboo.[2] Two 'unmentionable' characters, one a 'counter-revolutionary' shot by the Cheka in 1921 and the other an 'enemy of the people' and the author of an 'unprecedentedly counter-revolutionary document' who ended his life in a forced labour camp, were being given an honourable public mention by their accomplice. This unprecedented occurrence took place at a ceremony to commemorate an exiled Italian poet who started his journey into the beyond in 1300 and who reported in the *Inferno* and the *Purgatorio* on his experiences before he arrived in paradise. But for the Acmeists, their period in purgatory and on the mountain of purification had by no means come to an end. Even so, Mandelstam's first prose work to appear since 1928, the 'Conversation About Dante', was published in 1967 in Moscow. This text, unpublished during his lifetime, had already surfaced the previous year in a Russian-language American edition.

It is impossible to estimate how many copies of his work were circulating underground among Soviet intellectuals and connoisseurs of poetry, but, in terms of formal publication, he long remained a poet in exile. In 1955, the Chekhov Press, run by Russian exiles in New York, published a

2 Anna Akhmatova's speech at the meeting held on 19 October 1965 to commemorate the 700th anniversary of Dante's birth: A. Akhmatova, *My Half Century*, 266–7. Commentaries on this: Akhmatova, *My Half Century*, 343–8 and 401–8.

one-volume edition, which included all the texts published while he was still alive. Then there were two further editions, also published in New York, one of two volumes between 1964 and 1966, and another of three volumes between 1967 and 1971. These were allegedly funded in part by the Central Intelligence Agency. Mandelstam as a secret weapon in the Cold War? This was the kind of absurdity retailed about his work by the pig-headed functionaries of Soviet literature. During house searches, copies of the American edition were confiscated as prohibited literature; a little later, the possession of a copy of Nadezhda Mandelstam's memoirs was another reason for punishing dissidents. Mandelstam's poetry was smuggled into the country, and it carried a subversive message.

Officially, therefore, Mandelstam continued to be ostracised for many decades after his labour camp death. The authorities' continued refusal to give him complete rehabilitation (this eventually took place on 28 October 1987 under Gorbachev) also caused the publication of his works to be delayed. It was not possible to wash away the label of 'counter-revolutionary' and 'enemy of the people'. For a long time, Mandelstam continued to be stigmatised as an outlaw and an alien presence in Soviet literature. The anti-Stalin poem outweighed everything else.

In 1922, Mandelstam had stressed the 'moral force' inherent in Acmeism (GP, 129), and, in 1923, he had described it in a letter as the 'conscience of poetry' (MR, 38). Both these features of Acmeism, morality and conscience, were inconvenient and dangerous to the holders of power. The commandment 'Thou Shalt Not Kill' surged forth with biblical power from *Fourth Prose* and other texts by Mandelstam. But his 'nostalgia for world culture' was as explosive as his explicitly political texts. In an isolated society enslaved by ideology, the yearning for civilisation, civil rights and freedom was as dangerous as the unmasking of Stalin as the 'corrupter of human souls'.[3]

Nadezhda Mandelstam had abandoned all hope that her husband's works would be published in Brezhnev's Soviet Union. Despite this, she lived long enough to experience this triumph, albeit in a distorted and

3 R. Lauer, *Geschichte der russischen Literatur*, 493, on the long-lasting marginalisation of the Acmeists in the Soviet Union: 'the Soviet government saw them as dangerous. One can in fact hardly imagine a contrast greater than that between the Soviet and the Acmeist models of culture. On the Soviet side you had doctrinal monism, class struggle, dictatorship and the total political instrumentalisation of all cultural spheres; the Acmeists favoured dialogue, openness, world civilisation, liberalism and cultural freedom.'

mutilated form. In 1973, sixteen years after the establishment of the publication committee during the 'thaw' period, thirty-five years after Mandelstam's death in the camp and forty-five years after the last time a collection of his poetry had been published in the Soviet Union, a severely censored selection of poems finally appeared as part of a series entitled 'Biblioteka Poeta'. No 'counter-revolutionary' or anti-Stalinist texts had been included. Only 15,000 copies were printed, which was a very small edition for Soviet conditions. A considerable number were sold abroad for dollars or displayed in the foreign-currency *Beryozka* shops, which were inaccessible to Soviet citizens. I was also informed by a reliable witness that the printers of the book had stolen many copies, because they knew the value of what they were printing. A copy was worth more on the black market than the monthly salary of an engineer. What was most painful was that the volume had been disfigured by a preface written by the veteran Stalinist Alexander Dymshits, which was full of suppressions and distortions. The censor had removed the proposed preface by Lidiya Ginzburg, who was a well-qualified literary scholar and a contemporary of Mandelstam. The party-line author who took over said nothing of Mandelstam's political persecution, the abject poverty of his years of exile in Voronezh or his humiliating death in a Siberian labour camp. This falsifier of the facts, who in 1962 had already assailed Ehrenburg's liberal memoirs, had been given the job of misinforming the reader and shrouding history in mist. He was able to achieve this by uttering drivel about Mandelstam's 'nervous sickness', 'contradictions' and 'complicated circumstances'.

The publication of Nadezhda's memoirs in New York in 1970 had perhaps hastened the appearance of this edition, which was intended to serve as an alibi for the authorities. But Brezhnev's literary functionaries were once again made ridiculous before world public opinion by their suppression of Mandelstam's work. The 'widow to culture' died on 29 December 1980 without having held in her hands any better Soviet edition of Mandelstam's poems than this one. Not until 1990, in the later stages of Gorbachev's *glasnost'* policy, did an uncensored Mandelstam edition in two volumes appear in Moscow, just in time for the hundredth anniversary of the poet's birth, which fell on 15 January 1991. This edition, printed in 200,000 copies, was sold out within days.

The authorities allowed an international symposium to take place in Moscow and Leningrad in January 1991 to commemorate the hundredth anniversary of Mandelstam's birth:[4] in the night of 12 to 13 January 1991, just before it was due to meet, Soviet special forces moved into Vilnius and fired shots at an unarmed crowd of people. The independence unilaterally declared by the Lithuanian government was endangered. The malevolent spirit that had suppressed Mandelstam's work was still very much alive. The putsch of August 1991 seemed to confirm people's worst fears, but then a rapid turn of the wheel of history brought the end of the Soviet Union. A little later, the city where Mandelstam had spent his childhood reverted to its original name.

Since 1991, there has been a memorial plaque on the wall of number 31, Street Line 8, Vasilyevsky Island, Petersburg, where Mandelstam several times took refuge in his brother's apartment. It is inscribed with the opening words of the famous 'Leningrad/Petersburg Poem' of December 1930: 'I've returned to my city of childhood illnesses and tears / The city that I know like the veins on the back of my hand' (MM, 45; MN, 34). Plaques have also been affixed to buildings in other places associated with Mandelstam: Paris and Heidelberg, where he studied, the Tverskoy Boulevard in Moscow, and Voronezh, the town to which he was exiled. The 'orphan of his epoch', who was 'homeless on an all-Union scale' (Joseph Brodsky), seemed to have come home to Russia exactly when the Soviet Union came to an end.

But had he really returned? A memorial to Mandelstam sculpted by Valery Nenazhivin in Vladivostok was destroyed by vandals in 1999, probably on 20 or 22 April. Was this on Hitler's birthday (the 20th), or Lenin's (the 22nd)? The police played down the suggestion: it was a pure coincidence, they said. There was no political background. But one policeman openly used the words the authorities wanted to avoid: 'No inch of Russian land for a slanderer.' In any case, it is doubtful whether Mandelstam even needs a physical memorial. He speaks in his poems, from his 'airy grave'. Even so, the incident did indicate the doubtful progress made by Russia in coming to terms with its past. Andrei Bitov, the chair of the Russian PEN Centre, sent an open letter along with other writers protesting to the regional governor and the mayor of Vladivostok about what had

4 Hundredth anniversary celebrations for Mandelstam in Moscow and Leningrad, 13–24 January 1991: R. Dutli, 'Eine Rückkehr und erneuter Frost?', *Neue Zürcher Zeitung*, no. 34, 11 February 1991, 17 (foreign edition: no. 33, 10/11 February 1991, 33).

happened. But a moulded metal reproduction of the memorial was also smeared and damaged.[5]

Hence the collapse of the Soviet Union did not bring the time of trial to an end. Mandelstam's advance to the position of poetic saint and protector of civil rights advocates had reached such mythical heights that the pendulum inevitably swung back the other way. The late *perestroika* epoch saw not just the final publication of Mandelstam editions but also attempts at political de-mythologisation. The artistically and morally uncompromising poet and clear-sighted dissident *avant la lettre* was now presented as an ambivalent writer, who was more severely infected by the evil spirit of Stalinism than the legend would have it. Benedikt Sarnov's 1990 book *Hostage of Eternity: The Mandelstam Case* puts forward the thesis that even such a remarkable poet as Mandelstam was unable to resist the general brainwashing during that frightful Stalinist epoch. The proof of this lay not so much in the enforced concoction of the January 1937 'Ode to Stalin' as in the poem 'In the Midst of People's Noise and Hurry' (February 1937), which was an 'honest', 'sincerely meant' attempt to excuse himself:

> And to him, into his heart's core
> With no permit I entered the Kremlin,
> Tearing through the canvas of distances
> Weighed down by my penitent head.
> (WH, 147; IH, 595)

This, Sarnov claims, is Mandelstam's confession of guilt and an attempt to apologise for the fatal epigram against Stalin, and it therefore confirms that he capitulated to the dictator. In reading this thesis, published in 1990 in the time of *glasnost'* but allegedly written twenty years earlier, an observer from the West cannot avoid suspecting that this is part of a process of self-justification and self-exculpation engaged in by Soviet intellectuals. Their acts of cowardice and conformity can more easily be excused if the 'Mandelstam case' is borne in mind. According to this comforting anti-legend, even an independent spirit like Mandelstam was no

5 Reports of the destruction by vandals of the Mandelstam memorial in Vladivostok: *Neue Zürcher Zeitung*, no. 125, 3 June 1999; *Frankfurter Allgemeine Zeitung*, no. 149, 1 July 1999; A. Bitov, 'Tekst kak povedenie (Vospominanie o Mandel'shtame)', 14–16.

hero, and he was by no means always immune to the seductive potential of the ruling ideology.

It is certainly true that Mandelstam was more deeply rooted in his own time than the legend of the unworldly saint might suggest. Paul Celan, in the afterword to his 1959 German translation of a selection of Mandelstam's poems, wrote of 'what was most intimately inscribed' in them, namely 'his deep and therefore tragic agreement with the epoch'. To view Mandelstam solely as an 'outlaw' and an absolute loner, completely uninvolved in his era, would be to miss the profundity of his tragedy. But the Mandelstam case was not a representative case shared by other writers or artists during the Stalin era: nowhere, in no other literary work than Mandelstam's, does there exist such a clear insight into the contempt for humanity and the sheer dishonesty of that era, nowhere else was there such an explicit condemnation of the 'corrupter of human souls'. Despite all the doubts, crises and feelings of guilt he underwent in that violent epoch, Mandelstam spoke with the voice of conscience, truthfulness and world culture. He was a representative of the moral quality of art in a time of state-organised repression of unparalleled severity.

Political de-mythologisation was finally followed by attempts to dissect his personality. The 'anti-memoirs' foreseen by Brodsky, in other words the reply to Nadezhda Mandelstam's memoirs of a century, took some time to emerge. But by 1998, the time was ripe. One of Mandelstam's former friends, Emma Gerstein, now ninety-five years old, published her memoirs in St Petersburg, for which she pocketed both the Russian Booker Prize and the Anti-Booker at the same time. The book evidently brought relief to the Russian public, portraying as it did the commonplace human behaviour of the former hero. It contains a large number of detailed and specific recollections of contemporaries, and it is a harsh settlement of accounts with the Mandelstams. Nadezhda is a malicious person with an unrestrained urge to provoke, the couple lack all consideration for other people and they are skilled at making a theatrical display of their sufferings. Nadezhda is presented as a 'bisexual exhibitionist' and a 'shameless female ape', Osip as a sadist and a satyr (although Gerstein never casts doubt on his poetic genius). On the eve of the hundredth anniversary of her birth, in 1999, Nadezhda Mandelstam was thus turned into an ambiguous, even a demonic, figure, an angel of death.

Until then, there was a single stereotype for the posthumous reputation of a Russian poet: oppressed while still living, transfigured after death.

Confrontation with these myths, as with any kind of illusion, can certainly be a healthy phenomenon. It is as reasonable for Russians to expect to be told the truth as it is for us. This is bound to cause pain. In Russia too, there is more than one truth today, but the 'new truth' of these memoirs should not be put in place of the old truth without careful consideration. The relatives of contemporaries presented by Gerstein in a distorted fashion raised considerable objections to some of her claims. The daughter of the poetess Maria Petrovykh said in an interview that Gerstein had deliberately held back from publishing her memoirs until no other witness to that epoch was still alive (Gerstein herself died in June 2002). Varvara Shklovskaia-Kordi, the daughter of Viktor and Vasilisa Shklovsky, objected that Gerstein had only understood the gossip of the period, and did not have the mental capacity to give an adequate account of the intellectual stature of people like Mandelstam and Shklovsky. She had been guided in everything by her desire to take revenge on Nadezhda: there is no word in Gerstein's memoirs about Nadezhda's clarity of vision, no word on the generosity with which she helped many people and no word on her courageous preservation of Mandelstam's work, against all obstacles.

It had long been impossible to quibble over Osip Mandelstam's stature as a poet. The brilliance of *Hope Against Hope*, those 'wonderful memoirs which several generations of educated Russians have grown up with' (Viktor Krivulin), stands there as an unshakeable literary fact. Hence, sexual calumny was the sole line of attack Mandelstam's opponents had left. Gerstein's memoirs betray the severe attitude of a prudish generation, whose sexual morality emerged under Stalin, towards the behaviour of the previous generation, which saw itself as standing at the beginning of the 'sexual revolution'. The considerable sexual energy which imbued the life of the Mandelstams as a couple and which Nadezhda continued to recall in her 1973 television interview must have seemed outlandish to a virtuous bystander. Or was it simply painful for Emma Gerstein, who lists her own disappointments in love in a 'catalogue of wrongs', to have to observe the 'unbelievable, inconceivable love' (according to Anna Akhmatova) of two human beings who stuck together desperately to the end, notwithstanding all their frivolous escapades?

More weighty is her claim that Nadezhda played with the idea of death, manoeuvring the fun-loving, joyful poet who clung to life into dangerous situations and then pressing him to kill himself. Nadezhda herself recalls in *Hope Against Hope*, in the chapter 'The Leap', that the couple repeatedly considered joint suicide. She also gives Mandelstam's reply to the suggestion: 'Why do you think you ought to be happy?'[6]

The late settling of private scores with people who have long been dead can help to gloss over a dark historical reality. This is very much in the interests of the former executioners. If Nadezhda Mandelstam is styled as an angel of death, this obscures the role of those who really caused his death. As we know, it was Stavsky's letter of denunciation sent to Yezhov on 16 March 1938 which led to Mandelstam's renewed arrest. In that letter, the general secretary of the Writers' Union asked Yezhov to 'solve the Mandelstam problem'.

The memoirs of Emma Gerstein, in which she accuses the Mandelstams of having base instincts and indulging in immoral and unethical behaviour, reveal an uncomprehending and very Soviet view of that unusual couple, whom she regarded as social aliens.[7] The unforgiving resentment displayed in the Gerstein memoirs is a clear indication that in personal relations, the poet could not always get on well with his contemporaries. But no one described Mandelstam's character as a 'difficult person' more accurately than his friend Boris Kuzin:

> Even before I got to know Mandelstam, I had heard that he was a very difficult person with a difficult character. How did people come to form this opinion? There was reason enough, I think. Mediocre people cannot tolerate in others the good qualities they themselves lack. They cannot believe that such qualities even exist, and they regard other people's perspicacity, decency, generosity, kindness etc. as deception and hypocrisy. But what is particularly unbearable for them is a sharp and witty tongue ... A sharp-tongued person is therefore always a potential danger.
>
> For me too, friendship with Mandelstam was difficult. But there was only one reason for this. It was terrible to watch him rushing almost intentionally towards his doom.[8]

---

6 'Why do you think you ought to be happy?': N. Mandelstam, *Hope Against Hope*, 56.

7 Gerstein's 'sexual' characterisation of the Mandelstam couple and her claim that Nadezhda 'played a game with death': E. Gerstein, *Moscow Memoirs*, 390–4, 406–11. Criticism of distortions in Gerstein's memoirs: O. S. Figurnova and M. V. Figurnova, *Osip i Nadezhda Mandel'shtamy*, 174–81 (A. Golovacheva), 294 (V. Shklovskaia-Kordi) and 386–7 (T. Osmerkina); M. Vorob'eva et al., *Smert' i Bessmertie Poeta*, 274 (Y. Tabak). Viktor Krivulin's comment on Nadezhda Mandelstam's memoirs: *Frankfurter Allgemeine Zeitung*, no. 208, 8 September 1999.

8 Boris Kuzin remembers M.'s 'difficult character': B. Kuzin, *Vospominaniia*, 175; AA, 154.

There is a remarkably consistent theme running through Mandelstam's letters to Nadezhda. In his very first letter, on 5 December 1919, he writes: 'With you nothing will be frightening' (MR, 27; CC, 484). And one of the last letters from Voronezh, on 2 May 1937, appears to contain an echo of this two decades later: 'Nothing is frightening for you and me' (MR, 283; CC, 570). And, in other letters, he calls her 'my fearless, shining one'.

Mandelstam had as few doubts about Nadezhda as he had about the future impact of his work. For the whole of his life, he was imbued with the calm confidence that the people who came after him would preserve it: 'And if they don't, that would mean no one needs it and it is of no value.'[9] But did he have any inkling of the immense efforts Nadezhda would have to make to fulfil his prophecy? Mandelstam's letters contain references to the meagre possessions that accompanied the couple through the years, one of them being the worn-out plaid blanket which assumes a special role in the May 1931 poem 'Midnight in Moscow'. This poem has the sound of a solemn testamentary oath:

> We shall die like foot soldiers,
> But we won't glorify the looting, the hired labour, or the lies.
> When I die you will cover me
> With our threadbare tartan blanket as if with a flag.
> Let's drink, little friend,
> To our sty-like sorrow.
> (MM, 79; MN, 46)

In 1938, when Mandelstam was hastily buried in a mass grave in the Soviet Far East, he had neither the old plaid blanket nor a last gesture of love. But, perhaps Nadezhda's feat of memory in preserving the poems and the composition of her memoirs were a worthwhile substitute for the Scottish plaid, as they made certain that Mandelstam would be remembered.

Mandelstam believed in his poetic return, because he believed in the cyclical nature of human experience. As early as 1918, in the poem 'Tristia', he had written these lines: 'All happened long ago, all will happen again, / Only recognition of the moment is sweet' (TR, 65; FP, 47). And he reaffirms his certainty on this point in the last poem of the *Voronezh Notebooks*: 'For all will start again forever' (WH, 215; PO, 80). He believed in his return, in the sense that his poetry would work a transformation. On 21 January 1937, he wrote from his Voronezh exile to Yury Tynyanov:

9 'People will preserve it': N. Mandel'shtam, *Kniga Tret'ia*, 7 ('My Testament').

> Please do not regard me as a shadow. I am still casting off my shadow. But recently I am becoming intelligible to virtually everyone. That's terrifying. It's already been a quarter of a century that I, confusing essentials with trifles, have been steadily encroaching on Russian poetry; but soon my poems will merge with it, thereby altering something of its structure and composition. (MR, 259; CC, 563)

Future generations have testified to this ability to change the future shape of poetry. Among the poets of the twentieth century, people of very divergent temperaments, but of outstanding quality, have expressed their admiration for the 'eccentric' Mandelstam: Anna Akhmatova, Marina Tsvetaeva, Vladimir Nabokov, Paul Celan, René Char, Philippe Jaccottet, Pier Paolo Pasolini, Adam Zagajewski, Durs Grünbein and many others. A selection from this chorus of poetic voices is appended to this book (see Appendix II, 'The Poets on Osip Mandelstam').

It is remarkable how emphatically the three great poets who were awarded Nobel prizes towards the end of the twentieth century – Joseph Brodsky, Derek Walcott and Seamus Heaney – have declared their allegiance to Mandelstam and his poetry. Brodsky, who lived in exile in America from 1972 onwards, had a great role in increasing the fame of Mandelstam. He saw himself as his 'heir', and he felt tremendously indebted to him. In his 1981 obituary for Nadezhda, he referred to Mandelstam as 'Russia's greatest poet in this century'. In his 1987 speech accepting the Nobel Prize, he mentioned Mandelstam first – followed by Marina Tsvetaeva, Robert Frost, Anna Akhmatova and W. H. Auden – as one of the five poets 'whose deeds and whose lot matter so much to me, if only because if it were not for them, I, as both a man and a writer, would amount to much less; in any case I wouldn't be standing here today'. He had already written in 1977, in the essay 'The Child of Civilization':

> The world has yet to hear this nervous, high, pure voice, shot through with love, terror, memory, culture, faith – a voice trembling, perhaps, like a match burning in a high wind, yet utterly inextinguishable. The voice that stays behind when its owner is gone.[10]

10 Quotations from Brodsky's obituary for Nadezhda Mandelstam, his Nobel Prize acceptance speech and his essay 'The Child of Civilization': J. Brodsky, 'Uncommon Visage', 45; J. Brodsky, 'Nadezhda Mandelstam', 145; J. Brodsky, 'The Child of Civilization', 144.

The Irish Nobel Prize winner Seamus Heaney has vigorously put the case for Mandelstam in his essays on poetry. In 'The Government of the Tongue' (1986) he made him his chief witness in dealing with Dante and with poetry in general. And Mandelstam's poetic energy has penetrated as far as the Caribbean: Derek Walcott, the Nobel Prize winner who came from the island of Saint Lucia in the Antilles, described Mandelstam in his poem 'The Forest of Europe' (1979) as the glowing fire that still warms the poetry of the present. Among the French poets, René Char associates him with the 'central fire of humanity' and Philippe Jaccottet with a raging torrent. The elements of fire and water seem to speak for Mandelstam's poetry.

Among writers in the German language, Paul Celan took on a pioneering role with his selection of translated poems published in 1959. These provided Mandelstam with 'the opportunity at least to exist', as he pointed out in a note appended to the work. But his initiative was far more significant than this: it allowed the German reader for the first time to gain an inkling of Mandelstam's poetic status. Celan presents his encounter with Mandelstam in terms of a Jewish community of fate and a sense of fraternity. In 'Brother Osip', an unfinished poem which dates from 1961, he writes: 'Pain plays with words / Passes on some names / Seeks the no man's land, / And there you wait. / You are the Russian Jew, / The Jewish Russian.' Celan was not wrong to emphasise Mandelstam's Jewishness in this way, as is shown by the attempts of Russian nationalists and anti-Semites to marginalise him. At the end of the 1960s, the shameful dictum that Mandelstam was 'a Jewish abscess on the pure body of Russian poetry' circulated among 'right-wing nationalist' critics. This saying also came to the attention of his widow.[11]

Paul Celan dedicated his 1963 volume of poetry, *Die Niemandsrose*, 'to the memory of Osip Mandelstam'. It contains the poem 'Afternoon with Circus and Citadel', in which the Russian poet appears as a poetical epiphany and a mystical revelation ('there I saw you, Mandelstam'). And in the poem 'Everything Is Changed', an exchange of limbs sets the seal on the gesture of identification:

11 'An abscess on the pure body of Russian poetry': N. Mandelstam, *Hope Abandoned*, 476 ('Completely Perverse Views').

The name of Osip approaches you, you tell him
What he already knows, he takes it, he takes from you, with hands,
You take his arm from the shoulder, the right one, the left one,
You raise yours to replace them, with hands, with fingers, with lines,
What has been torn off grows together again.

Paul Celan's 1960 radio essay 'The Poetry of Osip Mandelstam' was undoubtedly a first step on the way to his great speech about poetry, 'The Meridian'. The 'painfully silent vibrato' he perceived in Mandelstam's poems stood not only for the Jewish community of fate but also simply for poetic truthfulness. In a letter sent on 29 February 1960 to Gleb Struve, Celan wrote: 'Mandelstam: I have rarely had the feeling, as with his poetry, that I was following a path in the direction of the irrefutable and the true, and if I did it was *thanks to him*.'[12]

Mandelstam became a secret, cherished myth even in the German Democratic Republic, thanks to the 1975 selection of his poetry, published under the title *Hufeisenfinder*. Its editor, Fritz Mierau, is to be commended for bringing Mandelstam out of the shadows despite the censorship and other obstacles he faced. The book became a valuable under-the-counter commodity there, and it could also be imported into the Soviet Union, where it was a coveted gift because it was printed in both languages. West of the Iron Curtain, two volumes of selections were published in the Suhrkamp series – *Die Reise nach Armenien* in 1983 and *Schwarzerde* in 1984 – while between 1985 and 2000 the Ammann Press in Zürich brought out a complete edition of Mandelstam's works in ten volumes. The present book constitutes the final stage of that Zürich project.

Among contemporary German poets, it was Durs Grünbein, a recipient of the Georg Büchner Prize, who was particularly impressed by Mandelstam, as he demonstrated in two interviews recorded in 2001: 'Nonchalance in the midst of historical catastrophe, musicality bordering on madness, while the world spirit rages and the revolutionary phrase swallows everything: no one else has expressed this in such a complex fashion.' When an interviewer pointed out that Grünbein had previously

12 Paul Celan's relation to M.: C. Ivanović, *Das Gedicht im Geheimnis der Begegnung*, 77–107, 212–60 and 321–45. His unfinished poem 'Bruder Ossip' is printed in *Die Gedichte aus dem Nachlass*, Frankfurt 1997, 371. Celan's radio essay on Mandelstam was published in the author's book of readings, *Im Luftgrab* (Ammann Verlag 1988). It was a preliminary version of Celan's 'Meridian' speech: P. Celan, *The Meridian: Final Version*.

been regarded as 'a sheepdog of Gottfried Benn', he responded by distancing himself from Benn's disillusionment and his aesthetic of coolness, and by admitting: 'I hope the future belongs to Mandelstam and not to Benn.'[13]

All over the world, Mandelstam has found the friends and 'providential interlocutors' he dreamed of. He was convinced that this miracle of restoration would occur. He always had the calm certainty that his poems would have an impact, and that all the attempts of the authorities to muzzle a poet and obliterate his achievements would end in failure. A poem composed on 8 February 1937, during his time in exile in Voronezh, expresses both the hope *and* the certainty that it will have a meaning for his *friends*:

> A selfless song is its own praise,
> A comfort for friends, and for enemies – tar.
> (WH, 135; IH, 598)

Mandelstam's poetry speaks of the fragile dignity of the human being at a time when it was most endangered, and of the preservation of the individual self, persistently but without arrogance, during the age of its attempted obliteration. It is precisely because his poetry had to prove itself in an epoch of dictatorship and an atmosphere of unbounded and domineering faith in progress and the future, precisely because it had to survive through inconspicuous and secret messages in a time of mass culture, that it is topical and effective today.

Mandelstam invoked the vitality of his own poetry in a fragment written in 1931, in which the Self has left childhood and death behind in order to become the voice of poetry:

> I am a child no longer. You, grave,
> Do not presume to instruct a hunchback – silence!
> I speak with such strength for all,
> That the palate may become the sky, that lips
> May crack like pink clay.
> (MM, 87; OM, 129)

Palate and lips, the mouth as a whole, are seen here as the location of poetry, the promise of poetic universality. Poetry is thus defined as a

13 Durs Grünbein interviews: Grünbein, *Gespräch*, 14; Grünbein, 'Benn schmort in der Hölle', 79. See also: Grünbein, *Das erste Jahr*, 24–5 and 74.

continuing force, which transcends the poet's impermanence and mortality, and creates a macrocosm. Another poem asserts that the fundamental antithesis of being is not 'mortal body/immortal soul', but 'dying body' and 'thinking, immortal mouth' (MM, 153). A new world continuously emerges from the 'palate space' and the thinking mouth of the poet.

If one looks back at Mandelstam's work, one is astonished by two things: his strangeness and his freedom. He was aware that he was an outsider in his epoch. In the poem 'The First of January 1924', he writes:

O the pain of peeling back the raw eyelids
to look for a lost word, and with lime
slaking in the veins, to hunt
for night herbs for a tribe of strangers!
(TR, 163; CR, 51)

But he could also contemplate his own strangeness, his eternal otherness, with self-irony. Here is one of his humorous ditties, written in 1922:

THE SONG OF A FREE COSSACK

I am a Lesbian among men
Alien, alien, yes, an alien
Reared in Lesbos, nowhere else
O Lesbos, Lesbos, Lesbos![14]

Mandelstam was a Russian-Jewish Odysseus who took the liberty of striking up the 'song of a free Cossack' while at the same time proclaiming, with mischievous irony, his descent from the first lyricists of the Western world – Alcaeus and Sappho, the poets of Lesbos. The verse 'I am a Lesbian among men' also means 'I am a poet'. Hence the freedom of the outsider has a verse dedicated to it.

Mandelstam does not need to be portrayed as a legendary saint or a mythical hero. He was simply the voice of the world poetry to which he refers even in the humorous lines of 'The Song of a Free Cossack'. The desire for freedom, as always, is also perceptible in these verses. 'Silent freedom' is apostrophised in one of his earliest poems, written in 1908. His reading of Chaadaev's philosophical works led him to discover 'inner

14 BT, 123; Mandel'shtam, *Polnoe Sobranie Sochinenii*. Tom I, 333.

freedom' in 1914. Then there is the invocation of 'wondrous freedom' in a poem of 1915. Finally, in the period of exile in Voronezh, we hear the troubled, timid and attenuated voice of freedom in the voice of a poet who has been imprisoned in a system of compulsion. And the unwavering desire for liberty is still there, right to the end:

> Oh for an inch of blue sea, for just enough to go through the eye of a needle!
>
> (WH, 35; VN, 42)

Appendixes

I Chronology

1891 14 January. Osip Mandelstam is born in Warsaw to Jewish parents. He is the eldest son. His father, Emil-Khazkel Mandelstam, a leather merchant, came originally from the Courland *shtetl* of Shagory in Kovno *gubernia*. His mother, Flora Verblovskaia, came from Vilna. She is a piano teacher. Mandelstam spent his childhood first in the town of Pavlovsk, close to St Petersburg, and then, from 1897, in the city itself.

1900 He becomes a pupil in the progressive Tenishev School.

1907 He continues his education in Paris (until May 1908).

1908 Trips to Switzerland and Italy.

1909 He studies Romance Languages and the History of Art at the University of Heidelberg (until March 1910).

1910 His first published poems appear in issue number 9 of the Petersburg art journal *Apollon*. He spends time in Berlin.

1911 He has himself baptised as a Christian at Viborg in order to be able to study in Petersburg. He enrols in the Romance language department of the university. He takes part in the 'Poets' Guild' founded by Nikolai Gumilyov. He makes the acquaintance of Anna Akhmatova.

1912 The 'Poets' Guild' decides to start the 'Acmeist' movement with the aim of ending the domination of Russian Symbolism.

1913 Mandelstam's first volume of poems, *Stone*, is published in Petersburg. His earliest literary essays ('About the Interlocutor' and others) appear in the journal *Apollon*.

1914 The First World War begins. Mandelstam is exempted from military service on account of his heart trouble. He travels to Warsaw to volunteer as a hospital orderly dealing with the war-wounded. He visits the Warsaw ghetto.

1915 He stays in Koktebel on the Crimean Peninsula; his first Crimea poems.

1916 Second, expanded edition of the poetry volume *Stone*. Friendship with Marina Tsvetaeva, exchange of love poems. *26 July*: Mandelstam's mother dies.

1917 Breaks off his studies at the university. Negative poem about the Bolsheviks' October Revolution, condemning the 'yoke of violence and malice'.

1918 Writes 'Twilight of Freedom', a poem about the revolution, which is soaked in apocalyptic images. Briefly holds an appointment in Lunacharsky's People's Commissariat for Enlightenment.

1919 Hunger in Moscow. Terror. Shootings. *1 May*: in Kyiv, in the midst of the disorders of civil war, he meets his future wife, Nadezhda Khazina.

1920 Spends time in the Crimea, in the civil war–ridden town of Feodosiia. He is arrested by the 'Whites' as a 'Bolshevik spy', then released. He travels to the Georgian port of Batumi and is again arrested, this time by the Mensheviks. Returns to Moscow.

1921 Journey to the Caucasus in search of work and bread. He learns of the death of his friend and fellow poet Nikolai Gumilyov, who was shot in Petrograd as a 'counter-revolutionary'.

1922 Marriage with Nadezhda Khazina in Kyiv. Another volume of poems, *Tristia*, is published in Berlin.

1923 Third, and newly expanded, edition of the volume *Stone*. The second edition of *Tristia* is published in Moscow, under the title *The Second Book*.

1925 His love affair with Olga Vaksel brings about a crisis in his marriage. His autobiographical prose work *The Noise of Time* appears in Leningrad, as well as two small children's books, *The Primus Stove* and *The Two Trams*. First heart attack. Breathing difficulties. He enters a period of silence: for the next five years he will not write any more poems.

1926 Nadezhda Mandelstam goes to Yalta, in the Crimea, to cure her tuberculosis. From this year onwards Mandelstam undertakes numerous literary translations to earn money. He produces two more children's books: *Air Balloons* and *The Kitchen*.

1928 The last book-length publications during his lifetime, made possible by the influence of Nikolai Bukharin: *Poems (1908–1925)*, *The Egyptian Stamp* (prose) and *On Poetry* (essays). He replies to a newspaper questionnaire on the theme 'The Soviet writer and the October Revolution': 'I feel indebted to the revolution, but I offer it gifts for which it still has no need.' The beginning of the 'Ulenspiegel Affair', which develops into a campaign of slander and harassment against him, directed by official circles.

1929 He replies by writing the polemical anti-Stalinist text *Fourth Prose*, as well as an 'Open Letter to Soviet Writers', which marks a break with officially approved literature.

1930 Mandelstam is questioned by the judge investigating the 'Ulenspiegel Affair'. He writes in a letter: 'Nothing can be put back as it was before. The break is – wealth. I must keep hold of it. I mustn't squander it.' He is given the opportunity of travelling to the Caucasus, thanks to Bukharin's intervention, and he visits Abkhazia, Armenia and Georgia. While in Abkhazia he learns of the suicide of Vladimir Mayakovsky. After moving from Armenia to the Georgian capital, Tbilisi, he recovers his lyrical voice after five years of silence, and composes the Armenia cycle of poetry, followed by a series of *New Poems*.

1931 The organisations of official Soviet writers oppose his plan to take up residence in Leningrad. The move to Moscow. He begins *The Moscow Notebooks*, including the poem about the 'wolfhound century'.

1933 A Leningrad literary journal prints the essay *Journey to Armenia*. This is the last publication of Mandelstam's work while he was still alive. It is subjected to polemical attacks in the newspapers. He works in the Crimea on his essay 'Conversation about Dante'. After years of nomadic existence, he is assigned an apartment in Moscow. There he writes his fateful epigram against Stalin, unmasking him as a 'soul-corrupter and peasant-slayer'.

1934 Meets Boris Pasternak and recites the anti-Stalin poem to him (his justification for writing it: 'There is nothing I hate so much as fascism, in whatever form it appears'). He publicly slaps the face of the official Soviet writer Alexei Tolstoy. *16–17 May*: night-time house search and arrest, confiscation of manuscripts and interrogation in the Lubyanka prison in Moscow. *28 May*: sentenced to three years' exile and transported to the town of Cherdyn, in the Urals. Attempts suicide by jumping out of a window. The sentence is altered. New place of exile: Voronezh.

1935 His reply to provocative questions by Voronezh writers about the nature of Acmeism: 'nostalgia for world culture'. He writes the first poems which will be included in the *Voronezh Notebooks* (by May 1937 he has produced three notebooks of poems).

1936 The first Moscow show trial and the beginning of Stalin's terror purges. Mandelstam is deprived of any opportunity to work. Material hardship.

1937 Heart disease. Breathing difficulties. From an April letter: 'I am a shadow. I do not exist. I only have the right to die. My wife and I are being driven to suicide.' *23 April*: Mandelstam is included among 'Trotskyists and other class enemies' in a defamatory article in a Voronezh newspaper. *16 May*: the three-year sentence of exile comes to an end. Return to Moscow, where Mandelstam now loses the right to remain. The Mandelstams move to Savyolovo on the Volga river, then to Kalinin.

1938 *2 March*: given permission to stay in a rest home in Samatikha (it is a trap). *16 March*: letter of denunciation sent by Vladimir Stavsky, the general secretary of the Soviet Writers' Union, to Yezhov, the head of the NKVD, asking him to 'solve the Mandelstam problem'. *2 May*: Mandelstam is arrested in Samatikha and taken to the Butyrki prison in Moscow. *2 August*: a special court condemns him to five years in a labour camp for counter-revolutionary activities, under Article 58-10 ('Anti-Soviet Agitation and Propaganda'). *8 September*: transportation to Siberia. *12 October*: arrives at Transit Camp 3/10 'Vtoraya Rechka' near Vladivostok, and is placed in Barrack 11, for 'counter-revolutionaries'. From his last letter, written at the beginning of November: 'My health is very bad, I'm extremely exhausted and thin, almost unrecognisable, but I don't know whether there's any sense in sending clothes, food and money. You can try all the same. I'm very cold without proper clothes.' An epidemic of spotted typhus breaks out. *27 December*: Mandelstam dies in the camp during a disinfection procedure.

II The Poets on Osip Mandelstam

'Why I love Mandelstam with his confused, weak, chaotic thoughts, sometimes amounting to nonsense, and the never-changing *MAGIC* in every line. What is involved here is not "classicism" but *ENCHANTMENT*.'

Marina Tsvetaeva (letter to Alexander Bakhrakh, 5–6 September 1923)

'Osip Mandelstam grazed in the house like a sheep and wandered through the rooms like Homer. He's an extremely intelligent man in a conversation. The deceased Khlebnikov named him the "marble fly." Akhmatova said that he's one of our greatest poets. Mandelstam loved sweets to distraction. Living in extremely difficult circumstances – without boots, without heat – he contrived to be treated like a spoiled child. He was as disorganized as a woman and light-minded as a bird – and not entirely guileless in this. He had all the habits of the true artist. An artist will even lie to free himself for his all-important work. He's like the monkey, who, according to the Hindus, keeps quiet so that he won't be put to work.'

Viktor Shklovsky (*Sentimental Journey*, 1923)

'He is full to overflowing of rhythms, just as he overflows with ideas and wonderful words. When reciting his poems, he sways gently from side to side, moves his arms, and inhales pleasurably in time with his words – he looks like a dancing master, and one imagines his company prancing behind him. His way of walking makes you laugh, as his back is too rigid, and he almost goes on tiptoe. Mandelstam is viewed as a madman, and in fact he does appear to be a madman among people who are accustomed to hiding or falsifying their impulses. Anna Akhmatova says: "Osip is a wardrobe full of surprises." He swings his arms around, and his eyes express complete abstraction – from the furniture, from his interlocutor, and from the half-eaten sandwich on the plate. His manner of speaking is in line with his poems: stammering, sublime and brazen. Mandelstam is a theatrical spectacle that inspires optimism in his hearers.'

Lidiya Ginzburg ('From Old Diaries', 1933)

'He remembered once how a Chinese man from the basement laundry in the building in which he grew up had stopped him on the street. The man had chanced to take him by one hand, then seized the other. The man turned the palms upward and excitedly shouted something in Chinese. It turned out that he was declaring a child so marked to be unquestionably very lucky. The poet often recalled that sign of luck – especially when he published his first collection of verse. Now he remembered the man without anger or irony; he just did not care … He died towards evening. They "wrote him off" two days later. For two days his inventive neighbours managed to continue getting his bread ration. The dead man would raise his hand like a puppet. So he died before the recorded date of his death – a not insignificant detail for his future biographers.'

Varlam Shalamov ('Cherry Brandy', 1958, *Kolyma Tales*, 73–5)

'He also wrote very tenderly about the poets of the Pushkin pleiad, and about Blok and his contemporaries, about the Kama river, the steppe, dry, hot Armenia and his home town of Leningrad. I remember many of his verses, I repeat them again and again like incantations, I look back and feel happy that I lived alongside him. What harm could he possibly have done, this poet with an ailing frame, who filled our evenings with the music of his poetry? He was terrified of drinking a glass of un-boiled water, but real courage dwelt within him, and it sustained him throughout the whole of his life – right up to the Petrarch sonnets he recited in the camp to his fellow-prisoners sitting around the fire.'

Ilya Ehrenburg (*Men, Years – Life*, 1962)

'I once witnessed a meeting between Mayakovsky and Mandelstam. They saw each other at the same moment, reacted with a silent greeting, and for a certain length of time they stared at one another, Mayakovsky looking poisonously from Mandelstam's head to his feet, Mandelstam looking arrogantly from Mayakovsky's feet to his head. I realised that Mayakovsky was trying to think of a cutting remark, while Mandelstam was searching for a rebuff that would really hurt. But then they briefly shook hands and silently went their separate ways. Mayakovsky gazed for a fairly long time after Mandelstam, who was proudly leaving the scene, and then he suddenly stretched out his arms as if on a stage, and, throwing me a glance with flashing eyes, in a voice that was full of enthusiasm, indeed pride, so that the whole room could hear, he recited Mandelstam's verse "Russia, Lethe, Lorelei". Then he turned to me, as if he wanted to say: "Well? How was that verse? Magnificent!"'

Valentin Kataev (*The Grass of Oblivion*, 1963)

'One of the most optimistic masters of Russian poetry. An optimism acquired through suffering, which had passed through despair, tears and death. But let us bless all the momentary temptations and enchantments of life! For a long time the "silent joy of breathing and living" did not abandon him. It could also be seen in his sparkling, happy eyes and his purposeful, almost boyish, way of walking. Most of the time I met him at Anna Akhmatova's flat. She could tell who it was from the forceful way he rang the doorbell: "That's Osip." Soon the small room was filled with the sound of laughter. It seemed as if he had only come to see her to have a month's worth of amusement. "I have never laughed so well with anyone else" recalled Akhmatova.'

Kornei Chukovsky ('A Master', 1966)

'Mandelstam was not only one of Russia's best lyrical poets, he was also a subtle exponent of poetic theory. Major Russian poets such as Akhmatova and Pasternak, who have long since been recognised as classics, regarded him as an innovator who had propelled Russian poetry so far forward that his achievement could only be evaluated correctly many years later. He never did anything wrong against his contemporaries. He went to meet his epoch, and he needed nothing more than the chance to create freely. In our literature his poetry occupies a high rank, and his tragic death dismays and confuses us.'

Veniamin Kaverin ('The Unknown Friend. How I Did Not Become a Poet', 1966)

'One of the saddest cases is perhaps that of Osip Mandelstam – a wonderful poet, the greatest poet, among those trying to survive in Russia under the Soviets – whom that brutal and imbecile administration persecuted and finally drove to death in a remote concentration camp. The poems he heroically kept composing until madness eclipsed his limpid gifts are admirable specimens of a human mind at its deepest and highest.'

Vladimir Nabokov (in conversation with Robert Hughes, 1965)

'Mandelstam: I have rarely had the feeling, as with his poetry, that I was following a path in the direction of the irrefutable and the true, and if I did it was *thanks to him*.'

Paul Celan (letter to Gleb Struve, 29 February 1960)

'Nimble, clever, witty, elegant, one might even say dandyish, joyful, sensual, always in love, honest, clear-sighted, and happy even in the darkness of nervous breakdown and political terror, youthful, indeed almost boyish, weird and sophisticated, loyal and imaginative, smiling and patient, Mandelstam has bestowed on us some of the most felicitous poetry of the century.'

Pier Paolo Pasolini ('Osip Mandelstam', 1972)

'A voice which can still be heard even when its owner is no longer there. Mandelstam was … a modern Orpheus: sent to hell, he never returned, while his widow dodged across one sixth of the earth's surface, clutching the saucepan with his songs rolled up inside, memorizing them by night in the event that they were found by the Furies with a search warrant. These are our metamorphoses, our myths.'

Joseph Brodsky ('The Child of Civilization', 1977)

'Frightened and starved, with divine fever,
Osip Mandelstam shook, and every
Metaphor shuddered him with ague.
…
But now that fever is a fire whose glow
Warms our hands …'

Derek Walcott ('The Forest of Europe', 1979)

'It is this wild and indomitable power for which he was murdered – but murdered in vain, because his words now manifest themselves anew, like the water of a torrent when it strikes one's face like the lash of a whip.'

Philippe Jaccottet ('Notes on Mandelstam', 1981)

'The thought is too overwhelming. That little man, born in 1891 between centuries, people, history, towns, and letters, disappears reeling beneath a snowstorm, beyond the boundaries of this world. From you, poor fellow, we demand every movement of the tongue, every gurgle of the throat, to the very last drop.'

Birgitta Trotzig ('Mandelstam', 1982)

'They just have to smother my voice, and cut me out from the reader's memory like tearing a page out of an encyclopaedia. He who is heard by no one chokes on his own words. Now five deep breaths tell me that you have saved my manuscripts. No one writes after death, you say. But that is not true, Nadia! If I stopped, if my heart ceased to beat, Russia would remain a dismal notion.'

Kjell Espmark ('I'm Still Called Osip Mandelstam', *Den Hemliga Måltiden*, 1984)

'And then Mandelstam comes along. It is extraordinarily lively and convincing, a happy inspiration in this work of such a confusingly rich genius. It is the most magnificent song of praise to domination produced by the poetic imagination. Mandelstam brings Dante out of the pantheon and back to the roof of the mouth.'

Seamus Heaney ('The Government of the Tongue', 1986)

'Mandelstam had the eye that winnows the extremes and brings them closer, giving them a chance of fame. With him we penetrate into the tremors of the earth's crust, its manifold rituals. This is the privilege of the inspirational poets, who combine the central fire of humanity with the moisture of their diverse senses.'

René Char ('Praise of a Suspect', 1987)

'If Russia had been founded by Anna Akhmatova, if Mandelstam had been its law-giver, if Stalin had only been a marginal figure in a vanished

Georgian epic, if Russia had stripped off its shaggy bearskin, if it had been able to live by the word not by the fist, if Russia, if Russia …'

Adam Zagajewski ('Poems', 1989)

'Mandelstam's verses have the quality of intelligent cradle-songs. They console by inspiring one to think. Nonchalance in the midst of historical catastrophe, musicality bordering on madness, while the world spirit rages and the revolutionary phrase swallows everything: no one else has expressed this in such a complex fashion … He breathes life into everything and saturates it with soul and actuality. He has an intimate understanding of the world's sorrow. I hope the future will belong to Mandelstam.'

Durs Grünbein (conversations with Heinz-Norbert Jocks and Helmut Böttiger in 2001–2002)

References

The following abbreviations are used in text references to the ten volumes of the complete German edition of Mandelstam's works, translated and edited by Ralph Dutli, published between 1985 and 2000 by Ammann Verlag, Zürich:

AA *Armenien, Armenien!* [Armenia, Armenia!] (Prose, diary, poems, 1930–1933)

BT *Die Beiden Trams* [The Two Trams] (Children's poems and humorous verses, epigrams on contemporaries, 1911–1937)

GD *Gespräch über Dante* [Conversation about Dante] (Collected Essays II: 1925–1935)

GP *Über den Gesprächspartner* [About the Interlocutor] (Collected Essays I: 1913–1924)

MM *Mitternacht in Moskau* [Midnight in Moscow] (The Moscow Notebooks: Poems, 1930–1934)

MR *Du bist mein Moskau und mein Rom und mein kleiner David* [You Are My Moscow and My Rome and My Little David] (Collected letters, 1907–1938)

RZ *Das Rauschen der Zeit* [The Noise of Time] (Collected 'autobiographical' prose of the 1920s)

ST *Der Stein* [Stone] (Early poems, 1908–1915)

TR *Tristia* (Poems, 1916–1925)

WH *Die Woronescher Hefte* [The Voronezh Notebooks] (Last poems, 1935–1937)

In addition:

GW Marina Tsvetaeva and Osip Mandelstam: *Die Geschichte einer Widmung.* Gedichte und Prosa. Ammann Verlag, Zürich, 1994.

LG Osip Mandelstam: *Im Luftgrab*. Ein Lesebuch. Mit Beiträgen von Paul Celan, Pier Paolo Pasolini, Philippe Jaccottet, Joseph Brodsky. Ammann Verlag, Zürich, 1988.

Bibliography

Russian-language editions of Mandelstam's works:

Mandel'shtam, Osip, *Sobranie Sochinenii v Trekh Tomakh*. Edited by G. P. Struve and B. A. Filippova. I: Washington 1967; II: New York 1971; III: New York 1969; IV (N. A. Struve) (Supplementary Volume: Paris 1981).

Mandel'shtam, Osip, *Sochineniia v Dvukh Tomakh*. Edited by P. Nerler, with an introductory essay by S. S. Averintsev, Moscow 1990.

Mandel'shtam, Osip, *Sobranie Sochinenii v Chetyrekh Tomakh*. Edited by P. Nerler, A. Nikitaev, S. Vasilenko and Y. Freidin, Moscow 1993–1997.

Mandel'shtam, Osip, *Polnoe Sobranie Stikhotvorenii*. Edited by A. G. Mets, with introductory essays by M. Gasparov and A. G. Mets, St Petersburg 1995 (in the series *Novaia Biblioteka Poeta*).

Mandel'shtam, Osip, *Voronezhskie Tetradi*. Edited by V. Shveitser, Ann Arbor, MI, 1980.

Mandel'shtam, Osip, *Kamen'*. Edited by L. Ya. Ginzburg, A. G. Mets, S. V. Vasilenko and Y. Freidin, Leningrad 1990.

Mandel'shtam, Osip, *Shum Vremeni*. Preface by A. Bitov. Annotations by A. A. Morozov. Text prepared by S. V. Vasilenko and A. A. Morozov, Moscow 2002.

Mandel'shtam, Osip, *Polnoe Sobranie Sochinenii i Pisem v Trekh Tomakh, Tom I. Stikhotvoreniia*. Edited by A. G. Mets, Moscow 2009.

Texts in German:

Mandelstam, Osip, *Das Gesamtwerk in Zehn Bänden*. Aus dem Russischen übertragen und herausgegeben von Ralph Dutli. Ammann Verlag, Zürich 1985–2000.

Mandelstam, Osip, *Das Rauschen der Zeit. Gesammelte 'autobiographische' Prosa der 20er Jahre*, Zürich 1985.

Mandelstam, Osip, *Mitternacht in Moskau. Die Moskauer Hefte. Gedichte 1930–1934*, Zürich 1986.

Mandelstam, Osip, *Der Stein. Frühe Gedichte 1908–1913*, Zürich 1988.

Mandelstam, Osip, *Über den Gesprächspartner. Gesammelte Essays I: 1913–1924*, Zürich 1991.

Mandelstam, Osip, *Gespräch über Dante. Gesammelte Essays II: 1925–1935*, Zürich 1991.

Mandelstam, Osip, *Tristia. Gedichte 1916–1925*, Zürich 1993.

Mandelstam, Osip, *Armenien, Armenien! Prosa, Notizbuch, Gedichte 1930–1933*, Zürich 1994.

Mandelstam, Osip, *Die Woronescher Hefte. Letzte Gedichte 1935–1937*, Zürich 1996.

Mandelstam, Osip, *Du bist mein Moskau und mein Rom und mein kleiner David. Gesammelte Briefe 1907–1938*, Zürich 1999.

Mandelstam, Osip, *Die Beiden Trams. Kinder- und Scherzgedichte, Epigramme auf Zeitgenossen 1911–1937*, Zürich 2000.

In addition:

Mandelstam, Osip, *Im Luftgrab. Ein Lesebuch*. Mit Beiträgen von Paul Celan (Erstdruck), Pier Paolo Pasolini, Philippe Jaccottet und Joseph Brodsky. Herausgegeben von Ralph Dutli, Zürich 1988.

Translations of Mandelstam's works into English (used in this translation):

Bernstein, Ilya, *The Poems of Osip Mandelstam. Translated from Russian into English*, EPC Digital Edition, 2014. Abbreviated PO.

Brown, Clarence, 'Mandelstam's Acmeist Manifesto', *The Russian Review* 24: 1, January 1965, 46–51. Abbreviated AM.

Brown, Clarence, 'Into the Heart of Darkness: Mandelstam's Ode to Stalin', *Slavic Review* 26: 4, December 1967, 584–604. Abbreviated IH.

Brown, Clarence, *The Noise of Time. The Prose of Osip Mandelstam. Translated with Critical Essays by Clarence Brown*, San Francisco 1986. Abbreviated NT.

Brown, Clarence, and Merwin, W. S., 'Concert at the Railway Station', *The American Poetry Review* 2: 1, January/February 1973, 51. Abbreviated CR.

Glazova, Marina, 'The Artist as Transgressor', *Studies in Soviet Thought* 36: 1–2, July–August 1988, 1–61. Abbreviated AT.

Goldberg, Stuart, '"To Anaxagoras" in the Velvet Night: New Considerations on the Role of Blok in Mandelstam's "V Peterburge my soidemsia snova"', *The Russian Review* 69: 2, April 2010, 294–314. Abbreviated TA.

Hayward, Max, 'Translation of the Poem *Canzone*', in Nadezhda Mandelstam, *Hope Abandoned*, 602–3.

Hingley, Ronald, *Nightingale Fever. Russian Poets in Revolution*, London 1982. Abbreviated NF.

Kline, A. S., *Mandelshtam. Twenty-four Poems*, online edition, 2000. Abbreviated TF.

Kline, A. S., *Mandelshtam, Forty-Four More Poems*, online edition, 2005. Abbreviated FF.

Kneller, Andrey: online translation in *Russian Poetry in English: Osip Mandelstam.*

Mandelstam, Osip, *Complete Poetry of Osip Emilevich Mandelstam, translated by Burton Raffel and Alla Burago*, Albany, NY, 1973. Abbreviated CP.

Mandelstam, Osip, *Osip Mandelstam. Selected Poems, translated from the Russian by David McDuff*, New York 1975. Abbreviated OM.

Mandelstam, Osip, *Selected Poems. Osip Mandelstam, translated by Clarence Brown and W. S. Merwin*, Harmondsworth 1977 [1973]. Abbreviated SP.

Mandelstam, Osip, *Osip Mandelstam's Stone, translated and introduced by Robert Tracy*, Princeton, NJ, 1981. Abbreviated OS.

Mandelstam, Osip, *Osip Mandelstam. The Eyesight of Wasps. Poems translated by James Greene*, London 1989. Abbreviated EW.

Mandelstam, Osip, *Poems from Mandelstam, translated by R. H. Morrison*, London 1990. Abbreviated PM.

Mandelstam, Osip, *The Collected Critical Prose and Letters, edited by Jane Gary Harris* (translated from the Russian by Jane Gary Harris and Constance Link), London 1991. Abbreviated CC.

Mandelstam, Osip, *The Moscow Notebooks, translated by Richard and Elizabeth McKane*, Newcastle upon Tyne 1991. Abbreviated MN.

Mandelstam, Osip, *The Voronezh Notebooks, translated by Richard and Elizabeth McKane*, Newcastle upon Tyne 1996. Abbreviated VN.

Mandelstam, Osip, *Tristia, translated from the Russian by Kevin J. Kinsella*, Los Angeles, CA, 2007. Abbreviated MT.

Meares, Bernard, *50 Poems. Osip Mandelstam*, New York 1977. Abbreviated FP.

Monas, Sidney, *Osip Mandelstam's Selected Essays. Translated by Sidney Monas*, Austin, TX, 1977. Abbreviated SE.

Probstein, Ian, 'Armenia by Osip Mandelstam, Translated from the Russian by Ian Probstein', *The International Literary Quarterly: Interlitq* 13, November 2010.

Sarkisyants, Evgenia: online translation in *RuVerses: Osip Mandelshtam.*

Simkin, John: online translation in *RuVerses: Osip Mandelshtam.*

Spektor, Alexander, 'Family Romances in "The Noise of Time". Mandelstam's Autobiography as an Allegory for Literary Activity', *The Russian Review* 71: 1, January 2012, 79–99.

Terras, Victor, 'The Black Sun: Orphic Imagery in the Poetry of Mandelstam', *Slavic and East European Journal* 45: 1, Spring 2001, 45–60. Abbreviated BS.

A selection of literature relating to Mandelstam:

Akhmatova, Anna, *Poem ohne Held*. Edited by Fritz Mierau, Göttingen 1989, 296–320.

Akhmatova, Anna, *My Half Century. Selected Prose, edited by Ronald Meyer*, Ann Arbor, MI, 1992.

Akhmatova, Anna, 'Listki iz dnevnika: Mandel'stam' [Leaves from a Diary: Mandelstam], in Anna Akhmatova, *Sobranie Sochinenii v Shesti Tomakh*, vol. 5, Moscow 2001, 21–59 (commentaries on pp. 441–526).

Akhmatova, Anna, 'Dante', in Anna Akhmatova, *Sobranie Sochinenii v Shesti Tomakh*, vol. 6, Moscow 2002, 7–19 (commentaries on pp. 343–8 and 401–8).

Amelin, Grigorii, and Morderer, Valentin, *Miry i Stolknoveniia Osipa Man-del'shtama*, Moscow and St Petersburg 2000.

Baines, Jennifer, *Mandelstam. The Later Poetry*, Cambridge 1976.

Bek, Tat'iana (ed.), *Antologiia Akmeizma. Stikhi. Manifesty. Stat'i. Zametki. Memuary*, Moscow 1997.

Bitov, Andrei, 'Tekst kak povedenie (Vospominanie o Mandel'shtame)', in Osip Mandel'shtam, *Shum Vremeni*, Moscow 2002, 5–16.

Brodsky, Joseph, *Erinnerungen an Leningrad*. Translated from English by Sylvia List and Marianne Frisch, Munich 1987.

Brodsky, Joseph, 'S mirom derzhavym ia byl lish' rebiacheski sviazan', in *Mandelstam Centenary Conference, London 1991*. Edited by Robin Aizlewood and Diana Myers, Tenafly, NJ, 1994, 9–17.

Brodsky, Joseph, 'Uncommon Visage. The Nobel Lecture', in *On Grief and Reason. Essays*, London 1996, 44–58.

Brodsky, Joseph, *Bol'shaia Kniga Interv'iu. Sost. Valentina Poluchina*, Moscow 2000.

Brodsky, Joseph, 'Less than One', in *Less than One. Selected Essays*, London 2011, 3–31.

Brodsky, Joseph, 'Nadezhda Mandelstam (1899–1980). An Obituary', in *Less than One. Selected Essays*, London 2011, 145–56.

Brodsky, Joseph, 'The Child of Civilization', in *Less than One. Selected Essays*, London 2011, 123–44.

Brown, Clarence, *Mandelstam*, Cambridge 1973.

Broyde, Steven, *Osip Mandel'shtam and His Age. A Commentary on the Themes of War and Revolution in the Poetry 1913–1923*, Cambridge, MA, and London 1975.

Cavanagh, Clare, *Osip Mandelstam and the Modernist Creation of Tradition*, Princeton, NJ, 1995.

Char, René, *Éloge d'une soupçonnée*, Paris 1988.

Dutli, Ralph, 'Der Bau, das denkende Auge und die Bewegung der Lippen. Drei Zugänge zu Ossip Mandelstam (1891–1938)', *Akzente, Zeitschrift für Literatur* 2, 1982, 114–23.

Dutli, Ralph, *Ossip Mandelstam – 'Als riefe man mich bei meinem Namen'. Dialog mit Frankreich. Ein Essay über Dichtung und Kultur*, Zürich 1985.

Dutli, Ralph, 'Sabbatland, Wildheit. Ossip Mandelstam und Armenien', *die horen: Zeitschrift für Literatur, Kunst und Kritik*, vol. 160, 1990, 164–8.

Dutli, Ralph, *Ein Fest mit Mandelstam. Über Kaviar, Brot und Poesie. Ein Essay zum 100. Geburtstag*, Zürich 1991.

Dutli, Ralph, 'Uns bleibt als Einziges der Name. Marina Zwetajewa und Ossip Mandelstam', in Marina Tsvetaeva and Osip Mandelstam, *Die Geschichte einer Widmung. Gedichte und Prosa*, Zürich 1994, 117–37.

Dutli, Ralph, 'Tote Luft getrunken', *Frankfurter Allgemeine Zeitung*, no. 146, 27 June 1994, 25.

Dutli, Ralph, *Europas zarte Hände. Essays über Ossip Mandelstam*, Zürich 1995.

Dutli, Ralph, '"Das bin ich. Das ist der Rhein." Tierseele und Lorelei: Osip Mandel'shtams Jugendgedichte, der "Heidelberger Zyklus" 1909/1910 und deutsche Echos im Spätwerk der dreißiger Jahre (Ergänzungen zum Thema "Mandel'shtam und Deutschland")', in *Osip Mandel'shtam und Europa*. Edited by W. Potthoff, Heidelberg 1999, 61–82.

Dutli, Ralph, *'Meine Zeit, mein Tier'. Ossip Mandelstam. Eine Biographie*, Zürich 2003.

Dutli, Ralph, 'Mandelstams Stimme', in Ossip Mandelstam, *Bahnhofskonzert. Das Ossip-Mandelstam-Lesebuch*, Frankfurt am Main 2015, 373–81.

Dutli, Ralph, *Mandelstam, Heidelberg. Gedichte und Briefe 1909–1910. Mit einem Essay über deutsche Echos in Ossip Mandelstams Werk: 'Ich war das Buch, das euch im Traum erscheint'*, Göttingen 2016.

Dutli, Ralph, *Dantes Gesänge – Gerät zum Einfangen der Zukunft. Ossip Mandelstams 'Gespräch über Dante'*, Göttingen 2017.

Ehrenburg, Ilya, *Men, Years – Life. Volume II: First Years of Revolution 1918–1921*. Translated by Anna Bostock, London 1962.

Faivre Dupaigre, Anne, 'Bergsonovskoe chuvstvo vremeni u rannego Mandel'shtama', in *Mandel'shtamovskie Dni v Voronezhe. Materialy*, Voronezh 1994, 27–31.

Faivre Dupaigre, Anne, 'Mandelstam lecteur de Tchaadaïev à la veille de le première guerre mondiale', in *Osip Mandel'shtam und Europa*. Edited by W. Potthoff, Heidelberg 1999, 83–108.

Figurnova, O. S., and Figurnova, M. V., *Osip i Nadezhda Mandel'shtamy v Rasskazakh Sovremennikov*, Moscow 2002.

Freidin, Gregory, *A Coat of Many Colours. Osip Mandelstam and His Mythologies of Self-Presentation*, Berkeley, CA, and London 1987.

Freidin, Yuri, 'Sud'ba arkhiva poeta', *Literaturnaia Gazeta* 1: 5327, 9 January 1991, 13.

Gasparov, Mikhail, *O. Mandel'shtam. Grazhdanskaia Lirika 1937 Goda*, Moscow 1996.

Gerstein, Emma, *Moscow Memoirs*. Translated and edited by John Crowfoot, London 2004.

Ginzburg, Lidiia, *Zapisnye Knizhki; Vospominaniia; Esse*, St Petersburg 2002.

Gordin, Iakov (ed.), *Osip Mandel'shtam*, St Petersburg 1993 (in the series 'XX Vek. Gibel' Poetov').

Grishunin, A. L., 'Blok i Mandel'shtam', in *Slovo i Sud'ba. Osip Mandel'shtam. Issledovaniia i Materialy*, Moscow 1991, 152–60.

Heaney, Seamus, *The Government of the Tongue. Selected Prose 1978–1987*, London 1988.

Isenberg, Charles, 'Associative Chains in *Egipetskaia Marka*', *Russian Literature* 5: 3, 1977, 257–76.

Ivanov, Georgy, *Disintegration of the Atom. Petersburg Winters*, Brighton, MA, 2016.

Kablukov, Sergei, 'O. E. Mandel'shtam v zapisiakh dnevnika i perepiske S. P. Kablukova', in Osip Mandelstam, *Kamen'*, Leningrad 1990, 241–58.

Karpovich, Mikhail, 'Moe znakomstvo s Mandel'shtamom', *Novyi Zhurnal* 49, 1957, 258–61.

Kreid, Vadim, and Necheporuk, Evgenii, *Osip Mandel'shtam i Ego Vremia*, Moscow 1995 (recollections of Mandelstam by forty of his contemporaries).

Kupchenko, V. P., 'Osip Mandel'shtam v Kimmerii', *Voprosy Literatury* 7, 1987, 186–202.

Kupchenko, V. P., 'Ssora poetov. K istorii vzaimootnoshenii O. Mandel'shtama i M. Voloshina', in *Slovo i Sud'ba. Osip Mandel'shtam. Issledovaniia i Materialy*, Moscow 1991, 176–83.

Kuzin, Boris, *Vospominaniia. Proizvedeniia. Perepiska*, St Petersburg 1999.

Lanne, Jean-Claude, 'Mandel'shtam i futurizm. Vopros o zaumi v poeticheskoi sisteme Mandel'shtama', in *Mandelstam Centenary Conference, London 1991*. Edited by Robin Aizlewood and Diana Myers, Tenafly, NY, 1994, 216–27.

Lasunskii, O. G., et al., *Zhizn' i Tvorchestvo O. E. Mandel'shtama. Vospominaniia. Materialy k biografii. 'Novye Stikhi.' Kommentarii. Issledovaniia*, Voronezh 1990.

Lekmanov, Oleg, *Mandel'shtam i Antichnost'. Sbornik Statei*, Moscow 1995.

Lekmanov, Oleg, *Kniga ob Akmeizme i Drugie Raboty*, Tomsk 2000.

Leontiev, I., 'Chelovek, zastrelivshii imperatorskogo posla. K istorii vzaimootnoshenii Bliumkina i Mandel'shtama', *Sokhrani Moiu Rech'*, *Zapiski Mandel'shtamovskogo Obshchestva*, 3: 2, Moscow 2000, 126–44.

Lipkin, Semyon, 'Ugl', pylaiushchii ognem. Vstrechi i razgovory s Osipom Mandel'shtamom', *Literaturnoe Obozrenie* 12, 1987, 94–101.

Mandel'shtam, Evgenii, 'Vospominaniia', *Novyi Mir* 10, 1995, 119–78.

Mandel'shtam, Nadezhda, *Kniga Tret'ia*, Paris 1987.

Mandel'shtam, Nadezhda, '"V etoi zhizni menia uderzhala tol'ko vera v Vas i v Osiu ..." Pis'ma N. Ia. Mandel'shtam A. A. Akhmatovoi', *Literaturnoe Obozrenie* 1, 1991, 97–105.

Mandel'shtam, Nadezhda, *Vospominaniia* (Podgotovka teksta Iurii Freidin, primechaniia Aleksandr Morozov), Moscow 1999.

Mandel'shtam, Nadezhda, *Vtoraia Kniga* (Podgotovka teksta Sergei Vasilenko, predislovie i primechaniia Aleksandr Morozov), Moscow 1999.

Mandel'shtam, Nadezhda, '192 pis'ma k B. S. Kuzinu 1937–1947', in Boris Kuzin, *Vospominaniia. Proizvedeniia. Perepiska*, St Petersburg 1999, 513–752.

Mandelstam, Nadezhda, *Das Jahrhundert der Wölfe*. Translated from Russian by Elisabeth Mahler, Frankfurt am Main 1971.

Mandelstam, Nadezhda, *Generation ohne Tränen*. Translated from Russian by Godhard Schramm, Frankfurt am Main 1975.

Mandelstam, Nadezhda, *Hope Abandoned*, Harmondsworth 1976.

Mandelstam, Nadezhda, *Hope Against Hope. A Memoir*, New York 1983 [1975].

Margolina, Sof'ia, *Mirovozzrenie Osipa Mandel'shtama*, Marburg an der Lahn 1989.

Mess-Beier, Irina, 'Ezopov iazyk v poezii Mandel'shtama 30-kh godov', *Russian Literature* 29: 3, 1991, 243–393.

Mets, Aleksandr, 'O. Mandel'shtam. "Skriabin i Khristianstvo"', *Russkaia Literatura* 1, 1991, 64–78.

Mochul'skii, Konstantin, 'O. E. Mandel'shtam', *Vstrechi* 2, 1945, 30ff. Reprinted in *Mandel'shtam i Antichnost'*, edited by Oleg Lekmanov, Moscow 1995, 7–11.

Morderer, Valentin, *see* Amelin, Grigorii.

Morozov, Aleksandr, 'Mandel'shtam v zapisiakh dnevnika S. P. Kablukova', *Vestnik Russkogo Khristianskogo Dvizheniia* 129: 3, 1979, 131–55.

Nerler, Pavel, '"On nichemu ne nauchilsia ..." O. E. Mandel'shtam v Voronezhe: novye materialy', *Literaturnoe Obozrenie* 1, 1991, 91–5.

Nerler, Pavel, *Osip Mandel'shtam v Geidel'berge*, Moscow 1994 (Zapiski Mandel'shtamovskogo Obshchestva. Tom 3).

Nerler, Pavel, *'S gur'boi i gurtom ...' Khronika poslednogo goda zhizni O. E. Mandel'shtama*, Moscow 1994 (Zapiski Mandel'shtamovskogo Obshchestva. Tom 5).

Nerler, Pavel, 'Parizhskii semester Osipa Mandel'shtama', in *Osip Mandel'shtam und Europa*. Edited by W. Potthoff, Heidelberg 1999, 257–79.

Nerler, P., and Pobol', N., 'Delo Mandel'shtama', in *Smert' i Bessmertie Poeta. Materialy mezhdunarodnoi nauchnoi konferentsii, posviashchennoi 60-letiiu so dnia gibeli O. E. Mandel'shtama (Moskva 28–29 dekabria 1998 g.)*, Moscow 2001, 162–73 (Zapiski Mandel'shtamovskogo Obshchestva no. 11)

Nerler, Pavel, and Zubarev, D., '"Nekii evrei Mandel'shtam ..." Po dokumentam

Departamenta politsii', *Sokhrani Moiu Rech'* 3: 2, 2000, 105–25 (Zapiski Mandel'shtamovskogo Obshchestva).

Nikol'skaia, T., Timenchik, R., and Mets, A. (eds), *Kofeinia razbitykh Serdets. Kollektivnaia shutochnaia p'esa v stikhakh pri uchastii O. E. Mandel'shtama*, Stanford 1997.

Nilsson, Nils Åge, 'Insomnia. Homer', in *Osip Mandel'shtam. Five Poems*, Stockholm 1974, 35–46.

Nilsson, Nils Åge, 'Sumerki svobody', in *Osip Mandel'shtam. Five Poems*, Stockholm 1974, 47–68.

Nilsson, Nils Åge, 'Mandel'shtam and the Revolution', in *Art, Society, Revolution in Russia 1917–1921*. Edited by N. Å. Nilsson, Stockholm 1979, 165–78.

Nilsson, Nils Åge, '"To Cassandra". A Poem by Osip Mandel'shtam from December 1917', in *Poetica Slavica. Studies in Honour of Zbigniew Folejewski*. Edited by J. Douglas Clayton and Gunter Schaarschmidt, Ottawa 1981, 105–13.

Nilsson, Nils Åge, 'Mandel'shtam's *Sumerki* Poems', *Russian Literature* 30: 4, 1991, 467–80.

Parnis, Aleksandr, 'Shtrikhi k futuristicheskomu portretu O. E. Mandel'shtama', in *Slovo i Sud'ba. Osip Mandel'shtam. Issledovaniia i Materialy*, Moscow 1991, 183–204.

Pasolini, Pier Paolo, 'Osip Mandel'shtam', in *Descrizioni di descrizioni*, Turin, 1979, 8–12.

Pasternak, E. V. and E. B., 'Koordinaty liricheskogo prostranstva', *Literaturnoe Obozrenie* 2, 1990, 48–50.

Polianovsky, Edwin, 'Smert' Osipa Mandel'shtama', *Izvestiia* nos 121–5, 25–9 May 1992.

Polianovsky, Edwin, *Gibel' Osipa Mandel'shtama*, St Petersburg and Paris 1993.

Pushkin, Alexander, 'Journey to Arzrum' in *Novels, Tales, Journeys. The Complete Prose of Alexander Pushkin*, London 2016, 359–401.

Ronen, Omry, *An Approach to Mandel'shtam*, Jerusalem 1983.

Ronen, Omry, 'Osip Mandel'shtam', *Literaturnoe Obozrenie* 1, 1991, 3–18.

Rothe, Hans, 'Mandel'shtam – Argonaute und Odysseus', *Richerche Slavistiche* 42, 1995, 347–95.

Sarnov, Benedikt, *Zalozhnik Vechnosti. Sluchai Mandel'shtama*, Moscow 1990.

Sedakova, Olga, 'Poeziia i antropologiia', *Russkaia Mysl' (La Pensée russe)* 4239, October 1999, 12 (in German in: *Wespennest* 120, September 2000, 76).

Segal, Dmitrii, *Osip Mandel'shtam. Istoriia i Poetika* (Chast' I, Kniga 1 & 2), Jerusalem and Berkeley 1998 (*Slavica Hierosolymitana* 8 and 9).

Semenko, Irina, *Poetika Pozdnego Mandel'shtama*, Rome 1986.

Shalamov, Varlam, *Kolyma Tales*, London 1994.

Shentalinsky, Vitaly, *Raby Svobody. V Literaturnykh Arkhivakh KGB*, Moscow 1995.

Shentalinsky, Vitaly, *Arrested Voices. Resurrecting the Disappeared Writers of the Soviet Regime*, New York 1996.

Shentalinsky, Vitaly, *Das Auferstandene Wort* (Verfolgte russische Schriftsteller in ihren letzten Briefen, Gedichten und Aufzeichungen. Aus den Archiven sowjetischer Geheimdienste. Aus dem Russischen von Bernd Rullkötter), Bergisch Gladbach 1996.

Shtempel', Natal'ia, *Mandel'shtam v Voronezhe. Vospominania*, Moscow 1992.

Shveitser, Viktoriia, 'Mandel'shtam posle Voronezha', *Voprosy Literatury* 4, 1990, 235–53.

Sippl, Carmen, *Reisetexte der Russischen Moderne. Andrei Belyj und Osip Mandel'shtam im Kaukasus*, Munich 1997.

Smol'evskii, Arsenii, 'Ol'ga Vaksel' – adresat chetyrekh stikhotvorenii Osipa Mandel'shtama', *Literaturnaia Ucheba* 1, 1991, 163–9.

Struve, Nikita, *Ossip Mandelstam*, Paris 1982.

Struve, Nikita, 'Mandel'shtam v Parizhe', *Vestnik Russkogo Khristianskogo Dvizheniia* 160: 3, 1990, 255–7.

Surat, Irina, '"Smert" poeta. Mandel'shtam i Pushkin', *Novyi Mir* 3, 2003.

Taranovsky, Kiril, *Essays on Mandel'shtam*, Cambridge, MA, and London 1976 (Harvard Slavic Studies, vol. VI).

Toddes, E. A., 'Stat'ia "Pshenitsa Chelovecheskaia" v tvorchestve Mandel'shtama nachala 20-kh godov', *Tynianovskii Sbornik* 3, 1988, 184–217.

Tsvetaeva, Marina, *Milestones. A Bilingual Edition*. Translated with an introduction and notes by Robin Kemball, Evanston, IL, 2003. Abbreviated as MI.

Tsvetaeva, Marina, *Selected Poems*. Translated and introduced by Elaine Feinstein, fifth edition, Manchester 1999.

Tsvetaeva, Marina, and Mandelstam, Osip, *Die Geschichte einer Widmung*. (Gedichte und Prosa. Aus dem Russischen übertragen, herausgegeben und mit einem Nachwort-Essay von Ralph Dutli), Zürich 1994.

Vidgof, Leonid, *Moskva Mandel'shtama. Kniga-ekskursiia*, Moscow 1998.

Vol'kenstein, Fedor, 'Tovarishcheskii sud po isku Osipa Mandel'shtama', in *Sokhrani Moiu Rech'. Mandel'shtamovskii Sbornik*, Moscow 1991, 53–757.

Volkov, Solomon, *Dialogi s Iosifom Brodskim*, Moscow 1998.

Vorob'eva, M. Z., et al., *Smert' i Bessmertie Poeta*. Materialy mezhdunarodnoi nauchnoi konferentsii, posviashchennoi 60-letiiu so dnia gibeli O. E. Mandel'shtama (Moskva 28–9 dekabria 1998 g.), Moscow 2001 (Zapiski Mandel'shtamovskogo Obshchestva no. 11).

West, Daphne M., *Mandelstam: The Egyptian Stamp*, Birmingham 1980.

Zavadskaia, Elena, 'Tramvainoe teplo', *Detskaia Literatura* 11, 1988, 54–6.

Zhirmunskii, Viktor, 'Na putiakh k klassitsizmu – O. Mandel'shtam "Tristia"', *Teoriia Literatury, Poetika, Stilistika*, Leningrad 1977, 138–41.

Zhirmunskii, Viktor, 'Preodolevshie simvolizm' *Teoriia Literatury. Poetika. Stilistika*, Leningrad 1977, 106–33.

Further Literature:

Babel, Isaac, *Collected Stories, translated by David McDuff*, London 1994.

Babel, Isaac, *1920 Diary, edited by Carol J. Avins, translated by H. J. Willetts*, New Haven, CT, 1995.

Babel, Isaac, *Red Cavalry, translated by Boris Dralyuk*, London 2014.

Birkenmaier, Willy, *Das Russische Heidelberg. Zur Geschichte der Deutsch-Russischen Beziehungen im 19. Jahrhundert*, Heidelberg 1995.

Celan, Paul, *The Meridian: Final Version – Drafts – Materials, edited by Bernhard Böschenstein and Heino Schmull, translated by Pierre Joris*, Stanford, CA, 2011.

Espmark, Kjell, *Den Hemliga Måltiden*, Stockholm 1984.

Ginzburg, Yevgenia, *Into the Whirlwind*, London 1989 [1967].

Gippius, Zinaida, *Dnevniki. 1 & 2*, Moscow 1999.

Grünbein, Durs, 'Benn schmort in der Hölle. Ein Gespräch mit Helmut Böttiger über dialogische und monologische Lyrik', *Text + Kritik* 153, January 2002, 72–84.

Grünbein, Durs, *Das Erste Jahr: Berliner Aufzeichungen*, Frankfurt am Main 2001.

Grünbein, Durs, *Gespräch mit Heinz-Norbert Jocks*, Cologne 2001.

Haumann, Heiko, *A History of the East European Jews*, Budapest 2002.

Herling, Gustav, *A World Apart, translated by Joseph Marek*, Oxford 1987 [1951].

Ingold, Felix Philipp, *Der Grosse Bruch. Rußland im Epochenjahr 1913. Kultur, Gesellschaft, Politik*, Munich 2000.

Ivanović, Christine, *Das Gedicht im Geheimnis der Begegnung. Dichtung und Poetik Celans im Kontext seiner Russischen Lektüren*, Tübingen 1996.

Ivinskaia, Olga, *A Captive of Time: My Years with Pasternak, the Memoirs of Olga Ivinskaya*, translated by Max Hayward, London 1978.

Jakobson, Roman, *Meine Futuristischen Jahre. Herausgegeben von Bengt Jangfeldt. Aus dem Russischen von Brigitte van Kann*, Berlin 1999.

Khlebnikov, Velimir, *Werke 1 (Poesie) & 2 (Prosa)* (Herausgegeben von Peter Urban), Reinbek 1972.

Khodasevich, Vladislav, *Necropolis, translated by Sarah Vitali*, New York 2019.

Koenen, Gerd, *Die Grossen Gesänge. Lenin, Stalin, Mao Tse-tung. Führerkulte und Heldenmythen des 20. Jahrhunderts*, Frankfurt am Main 1991.

Kusmina, Jelena, *Anna Akhmatova. Ein Leben im Unbehausten* (Aus dem Russischen von Swetlana Geier), Berlin 1993.

Lauer, Reinhard, *Geschichte der Russischen Literatur von 1700 bis zur Gegenwart*, Munich 2000.

Livshits, Benedict, *The One and a Half-Eyed Archer, translated by John E. Bowlt*, Newtonville, MA, 1977.

Lustiger, Arno, *Stalin and the Jews: The Red Book: The Tragedy of the Jewish Anti-Fascist Committee and the Soviet Jews*, New York 2003.

Majakowski, Wladimir, *Werke in zehn Bänden, Zweites Buch, Gedichte*, Frankfurt am Main 1980.

Mariengof, Anatoly, *A Novel Without Lies*, translated by Jose Alaniz, Moscow 2000.

Miłosz, Czesław, *Beginning with My Streets. Baltic Reflections*, translated by Madeline G. Levine, London 1992.

Nabokov, Vladimir, *Speak, Memory. An Autobiography Revisited*, London 1999 [1967].

Olschner, Leonard Moore, *Der feste Buchstab. Erläuterungen zu Paul Celans Gedichtübertragungen*, Göttingen and Zürich 1985.

Pilnyak, Boris, *The Naked Year, translated by Alexander Tulloch*, Ann Arbor, MI, 1975.

Pushkin, Alexander, 'Journey to Arzrum', *Novels, Tales, Journeys. The Complete Prose of Alexander Pushkin*, translated by Richard Pevear and Larissa Volokhonsky, London, 2016, 359-401.

Rougle, Charles, 'The Intelligentsia Debate in Russia 1917–1918', in *Art, Society, Revolution in Russia 1917-1921*. Edited by N. Å. Nilsson, Stockholm 1979, 54–105.

Schlögel, Karl, *Petersburg. Das Laboratorium der Moderne 1909–1921*, Munich 2002.

Shalamov, Varlam, *Kolyma Tales* (translated from the Russian by John Glad), London 1994.

Shklovsky, Viktor, *Kindheit und Jugend* (Aus dem Russischen von Alexander Kaempfe), Frankfurt am Main 1968.

Shklovsky, Viktor, *A Sentimental Journey: Memoirs, 1917–1922*, Ithaca, NY, 1970.

Shklovsky, Viktor, *Third Factory*, Chicago 2002 [1977].

Solzhenitsyn, Alexander, *The Gulag Archipelago 1918–1956*, London 1974.

Stökl, Günther, *Russische Geschichte* (Dritte, erweiterte Auflage), Stuttgart 1973.

Tsvetaeva, Marina, *Art in the Light of Conscience. Eight Essays on Poetry, translated by Angela Livingstone*, Tarset 2010 [1992]. Abbreviated as AL.

Tsvetaeva, Marina, *A Captive Spirit. Selected Prose, translated by J. Marin King*, London 1983.

Tsvetaeva, Marina, *Liebesgedichte*, Zürich 1997.

Volkogonov, Dmitry, *Stalin: Triumph and Tragedy. Edited and translated by Harold Shukman*, London 1991.

Index of Names

Acknowledgements

I am deeply grateful to the dedicated and enthusiastic Swiss publisher of my ten-volume Mandelstam Complete Edition, Egon Ammann in Zürich (1941–2017), who also published my four books on Mandelstam. I am equally grateful to his wife and co-publisher Marie-Luise Flammersfeld, Berlin. I thank my friends for wise counsel and various kinds of support: Professor Urs Heftrich, University of Heidelberg, and my French publisher Antoine Jaccottet (Éditions Le Bruit du Temps, Paris), who was also helpful in sharing the illustrations in this book. Thanks to my sister Jacqueline for much help, and for maintaining my website: ralph-dutli.de. Many thanks to my wife Catherine and my sons Boris and Olivier for all their love, humour and patience.

I dedicate this biography to all of Mandelstam's friends who carry on his poetry.